LANGUAGES
IN THE
INTERNATIONAL PERSPECTIVE

Delaware Symposia on Language Studies

Series Editor

Robert J. Di Pietro

LANGUAGES IN THE INTERNATIONAL PERSPECTIVE

Nancy Schweda-Nicholson, Editor

Delaware Symposium 5

Proceedings of the 5th Delaware Symposium on Language Studies
October 1983
The University of Delaware

ABLEX PUBLISHING CORPORATION
NORWOOD, NEW JERSEY

Copyright © 1986 by Ablex Publishing Corporation

Printed in the United States of America

Library of Congress Cataloging in Publication Data

Main entry under title:

Languages in the international perspective.

(Delaware symposia on language studies ; 5)
Selected papers from the proceedings of the
Fifth Delaware Symposium on Language Studies,
"Languages in national policies and international
relations."
Bibliography: p.
Includes index.
1. Language policy—Congresses. 2. Language
planning—Congresses. I. Schweda-Nicholson,
Nancy. II. Delaware Symposium on Language Studies
ISBN 0-89391-268-9

Ablex Publishing Corporation
355 Chestnut Street
Norwood, New Jersey 07648

Table of Contents

DEDICATION
For my parents,
June and Leon Schweda,
whose unwavering love and support
have always sustained and motivated me

Preface to Delaware Symposium Series on Language Studies

Robert J. Di Pietro
Series Editor

The volumes in this series are intended to bring to larger audiences select papers from the annual symposia on language studies held at the University of Delaware. These symposia are sponsored by the Program in Linguistics at the University. Each year a general theme is chosen in the application of linguistics and a call is sent out for papers dealing with that theme in some way. The abstracts received as a result of this call are evaluated anonymously by a committee of linguists. The program for each symposium is made up of the papers chosen through this evaluation process. In addition to the refereed papers, several plenary lectures are arranged and invitations to present them are sent out to leading scholars in the field. A second evaluation takes place after each symposium and results in the papers published here.

The present volume, edited by Nancy Schweda-Nicholson, is the second of the series. It comprises the proceedings of the fifth symposium, held in October 1983. The first symposium took place in the fall of 1979 and dealt with linguistic studies of language contact, second-language acquisition, and bilingualism. Papers from that symposium have been published by the University of Delaware Press under the editorship of Robert J. Di Pietro, William Frawley, and Alfred Wedel. The second symposium addressed the application of linguistics to law, medicine, business, and governmental bureaucracy. The proceedings of the second symposium were edited by Robert J. Di Pietro under the title *Linguistics and the Professions* and are available as volume VIII in the Ablex series, *Advances in Discourse Processes*. The papers of the third symposium were edited by William Frawley and were published by the Plenum Company under the title *Linguistics and Literacy*. Stephanie Williams is the editor of *Humans and Machines: The Interface through Language,* the fourth symposium and the first proceedings volume to be published in this series. Thanks to a close collaboration between Ablex and the Program in Linguistics at the University of Delaware, a broad range of significant and timely papers is being made available to a general readership in language and related areas.

Preface to Volume 5

Nancy Schweda-Nicholson, *editor*

The Fifth Delaware Symposium on Language Studies, "Languages in National Policies and International Relations," was held October 13–15, 1983 at the University of Delaware in Newark. Nationally- and internationally-known authorities from academic institutions, government organizations, private industry, research institutes, and interpretation and translation associations participated in the symposium.

The current volume is divided into six parts. Part I is composed of the two invited papers.

James E. Alatis ("Language Policy and Global Interdependence") highlights the diversity of world cultures and the way economic interdependence forces different populations together. He emphasizes the serious deficiencies in cross-cultural awareness in the United States. Alatis suggests that a solution to this problem would be to require more foreign language and cultural understanding programs in our American educational system. Such programs, demonstrating a consistent, coherent language policy, would facilitate the breakdown of the linguistic barriers among nations.

Kenneth L. Pike ("On the Value of Local Languages") observes how one's language affects world view which, in turn, affects life and society. He states that self-image in adult life is closely related to the mother tongue. It is often important, however, for diverse ethnic groups to learn the official, national language in order to become integrated into the larger, dominant society. Pike stresses that, in language planning and educational development, it is imperative to put "person above thing" and "personal dignity above program."

Part II is entitled "Official and Indigenous Languages in National Policy Making." In her paper ("Introduction of New Writing Systems: The Turkish Case"), Erika Gilson traces various stages of development in the programs to eradicate illiteracy in Turkey. She discusses not only writing changes themselves, but also the cultural, religious, and political implications of such measures with respect to Turkish society. The real force behind the movement to conquer illiteracy was Mustafa Kemal. He drew up Bill 1353, the Alphabet Reform Law, which was passed by the Third Grand National Assembly on November 1, 1928. This bill adopted a Turkish alphabet based on Latin graphs, and Arabic was abandoned.

Fanny Argüello describes the effort (almost 40 years old) to educate all Ecuadorians in her paper "Adult Literacy Campaigns in a Multilingual Country: Official vs. Indigenous Languages." Spanish is the only official language in Ecuador, but there are many Quechua speakers. It is hoped that the goal of "functional bilingualism" will one day be achieved through this national bilingual/bicultural educational effort, thereby reducing the current 70% illiteracy rate of the rural Indian population.

Mohammed Sawaie ("Arabic Language Academies as Language Planners") discusses the academies' roles in terminology development for science and high technology. He refers to such processes as "Arabization" and "analogical derivation" (which is favored). Sawaie stresses that there are numerous complications which inhibit the work of the language academies. For example, coordination of activities is often difficult because of the intense political upheaval in the Arab countries. Moreover, there is a lack of coordination among the academies themselves as well as between the academies and government agencies and professional groups.

Part III focuses on "Language Planning: The Interface with Minority Groups." Roger Gannon ("English for Immigrants: An Analysis of Governmental and Private Attitudes toward, and Support for, ESL in Canada") states that, from 1967 to the present, there has been a huge increase in ESL (English as a Second Language) programs in Canada. However, many problems were evident in the 1980–81 federally-sponsored courses, such as (a) the lack of coherent standards from one institution to another; (b) isolation of country/rural residents from the programs; and (c) discrimination against women (only "breadwinners" were eligible to take the job-oriented courses). Gannon writes that many recommendations for improvement of these programs have been made, but few changes have been implemented. It is clear that much remains to be done in ESL immigrant education in Canada.

Many problems are encountered when, within one country, there is a dominant, official language as well as numerous other languages spoken by multicultural minorities. D. P. Pattanayak ("Communication: Perspectives from the Developing World") highlights these problems, and also refers to communication boundaries between developed and developing countries. In this connection, he draws attention to the very real threat that our world may be evolving toward "communication for a few" and "deprivation for many."

The linguistic reality in Catalonia is discussed by Kathryn Woolard in her paper, "The Politics of Language Status Planning: 'Normalization' in Catalonia." She describes the Law of Linguistic Normalization, approved in April, 1983 by the Catalan parliament, but currently being challenged on constitutional grounds by the Spanish government. What is at issue are the future official status and role of Catalan and Castilian in Catalonia. At the present time, the overriding opinion there is that Catalan should be the single "normal language of relations in society" and Castilian should be a "second language."

Part IV concentrates on "Language as a Cultural, Political, and Social Marker." Klaus Obermeier ("Human Rights: An International Linguistic Hyperbole") states that there are numerous meanings and interpretations of the term "human rights."

In this connection, he discusses both metaphysical and metaethical considerations. Obermeier stresses that one's values and ethics are closely connected to the kind of society in which one lives. Throughout his paper, he looks at uses of the term "human rights" in different cultural, political, and ideological contexts.

Language strategists (writers, singers, poets, translators, and others) use new linguistic forms in their creative work in an effort to effect political and/or social change. Brian Weinstein ("Language Strategists in India") describes in detail both the Tamil and Bengali movements in India, and discusses the work and influence of the strategists (Bharati, Tagore, and others) associated with these movements. He consistently illustrates the very close connection between language and political change.

E. Luther Johnson ("Foreign Languages as a Means of Attaining Political Ends") looks at foreign languages and how their use and familiarity are promoted by centers of power in interactions with other nations. In this connection, he examines broadcasting networks (where particular languages are broadcast and which countries broadcast in which languages). Johnson also reviews broadcasting done by nongovernmental (religious, business) organizations. It is interesting to see how and where nations project their image and messages abroad.

Japanese and American negotiation strategies are discussed in detail by Don McCreary and Robert Blanchfield in their paper, "The Art of Japanese Negotiation." They examine three crucial constructs: *amae, haragei,* and the pragmatics of negotiating. McCreary and Blanchfield emphasize that American negotiators must never assume that the Japanese use words such as "yes" and "no" in the same way they do. In conclusion, suggestions are offered for effective training of future negotiators.

"Bridging the Language Gap: Interpretation and Translation" is the title of Part V. The linguistic, social, and political situations in present-day Brazil are described by Leland McCleary in "Translation Policy in Brazil." He notes that, recently, the interpreting and translating professions have grown extensively, both in Brazil and worldwide. According to McCleary, Brazil's situation with respect to translation and interpretation is similar to that found in most other countries of the world: the professions are virtually unrecognized as such, and there is very little regulation of translators' and interpreters' work. He hypothesizes that the most effective pressure to establish official interpretation and translation policies will probably come from multinational corporations.

Kyoko Inoue ("The Constitution of Japan and its English Translation") compares the English and Japanese versions of Chapter III of the Constitution, "The Rights and Duties of the People," citing differences in sentence patterns, verb phrases, and semantics. The rights expressed in this chapter are very similar to those found in the American Bill of Rights and the Declaration of Independence. These rights have greatly influenced Japanese social change in the last 35 years. Inoue notes that the Constitution is written in colloquial Japanese. Its use set a precedent, and all government documents have been drafted in colloquial Japanese since that time.

The deaf constitute a linguistic and cultural minority in America. In the course of his paper ("Sign Language Interpretation and Public Policy in the United States"), Robert Ingram discusses three major laws and their implications for our deaf population: The Rehabilitation Act of 1973 (PL 93–112), The Education for All Handicapped Children Act (PL 94–142), and the Court Interpreters Act (PL 95–539). Ingram also emphasizes the need for our government to recognize American Sign Language (ASL) as a language.

The paper presented by Bettina Cothran and Anne Harland ("Foreign Language Use in International Trade and Commerce: Trends in the Southeastern United States") is divided into two parts. First, Anne Harland speaks about "International Business in the Southeastern United States and Its Foreign Language Needs". She highlights a number of reasons for increasing foreign investment interest in the Southeast, such as (a) the desire to expand markets; (b) labor cost; and (c) the domestic tax situation. In a study which examines each Southeastern state individually, Harland finds that Germany and Japan are the primary investors. She stresses that foreign language skills are required in trade offices, Chambers of Commerce, law, banking, and real estate, to name only a few. Bettina Cothran follows with "The Universities' Response" to the growing language needs. In a survey of programs/courses offered at 76 Southeastern educational institutions, she discovered a "new crop" of courses which deal with commercial, medical, and legal contexts as well as with interpretation and translation. Cothran states that it is imperative for educational institutions to shift their priorities and establish more interdepartmental cooperation. She also stresses that there is a critical need for Japanese, yet very few schools have to date responded with pertinent training to fill this linguistic gap.

Cothran's presentation appropriately completes the section on Interpretation and Translation and introduces Part VI: "Language Planning in Education." As an introduction to her paper, Georganne Weller ("Guerrero: A Pilot Study for the Decision-Making Process on Language Policy in Mexico") describes various educational programs implemented by the ex-President López Portillo and the current President, Miguel de la Madrid. Her study examines three specific phases of evaluation in the Montaña de Guerrero program. Weller stresses the importance of obtaining basic information about teachers' and students' skills in Indian languages and Spanish in order to effectively design and implement bilingual/bicultural education programs. After emphasizing that socioeconomic and attitudinal factors must be examined along with linguistic data, she closes by suggesting that the research methods outlined in her paper may very well be applicable to Third World nations that face similar language planning and policy problems.

Robert Crane ("Re-training of French Teachers in the United States in French as a Business Language: An Example of Franco-American Cooperation") traces the recent developments in Business French courses at American universities. Moreover, he stresses the involvement of the Chambre de Commerce et d'Industrie de Paris (CCIP) (Paris Chamber of Commerce and Industry) which offers four seminars in Business French for French teachers abroad. Crane also describes two new training seminars in Lyon and Vichy which were held for the first time in July 1983. All of these courses are helping to fill the existing gap in the area of business training for French teachers who have literary backgrounds.

To complete the volume, John Hutchison ("Language Policy for Education in Niger") states that post-independence African nations must attain social, economic, and linguistic independence in order to solidify political autonomy. The "Société du Développement," a program of action for Niger, is striving to reorient political and cultural structures and to secure nationwide participation in its efforts. Hutchison notes that the political borders do not match linguistic divisions, which presents a problem of considerable magnitude when determining policies for public and adult education. He closes by emphasizing that it is important for Niger to break the ties of its colonial heritage and firmly establish a unifying language other than French.

Viewed in its entirety, the present volume makes a significant contribution to international awareness and the promotion of intercultural understanding. Thanks to sophisticated advances in technology, the communication networks of the world are expanding at a rapid rate. Paradoxically, expansion has carried with it an information gap in international understanding that cannot be bridged by technology alone. Information often does not flow freely from one society to another and many groups remain isolated from the mainstream of world affairs for reasons other than technological ones. It is imperative that the linguistic, socioeconomic, and political reasons for this isolation be brought to light.

The collection of papers in this volume offers much to those specialists who are concerned with problems of language planning and related areas. It appears that certain characteristics recur from one communication situation to another. Yet we are far from the point where we can offer across-the-board solutions to the many interactional difficulties we face today. This volume brings us another step closer to the knowledge required for dealing with international communication problems.

PART I

THE PLENARY PAPERS

ONE

Language Policy and Global Interdependence

James E. Alatis
Georgetown University

I begin with a quick reference to the dazzling diversity of cultural expression around the world and the dramatically increased interdependence between various nations. This theme of interdependence has, of course, many variations, but a short glance at the economic structure of today's world reveals the fact that there is no radical independence in the life of any modern nation. Leonard Silk in an October 29, 1982, *New York Times* article ("Major question in elections: Blame for state of economy" A1, 24) wrote:

> The greater interdependence of the world economy has made it more difficult than ever for a single nation, even the United States, to act alone to attack one problem to the exclusion of the other. In using tight money and high interest rates to stop inflation, the Administration caused unemployment to rise not only at home but also abroad, as other nations raised interest rates to protect their currencies.
>
> High rates in the United States also made the dollar so dear as to hurt American exports, endangering pressures for protectionism. High unemployment world-wide endangers the entire economic and monetary system.
>
> Likewise, for a single nation to try to attack unemployment simply by stimulating internal demand can also be perilous, as the Carter Administration found in 1979 and the Mitterrand government in France and the Trudeau government in Canada have since learned. Solving unemployment and inflation together will require greater international policy coordination. (Copyright © 1982 by The New York Times Company. Reprinted by permission.)

Economic interdependency inevitably results in cultural interaction. Although it is generally true that no culture in the world is either wholly a recipient (and hence dependent upon others) nor totally a donor (and hence independent of others), America today enjoys a unique position in this regard. As an article entitled "What the world thinks of America" (July 11, 1983: p. 44–52) which appeared in *Newsweek* illustrates:

> The great engines of American culture drive on unimpaired through the recession, pouring out to the world 265 million servings a day of Coca-Cola and an infinitude of hamburgers embedded in a double infinitude of sesame-seeded buns. So thoroughly have some American products—such as hamburgers, cola drinks and blue jeans—

penetrated foreign nations that they are often regarded as part of the common cultural heritage of mankind, in the way that no one bothers to recall the British origins of what is now the standard Western business suit. Consider the Japanese child on his way from the airport to his hotel in Los Angeles, who was heard to exclaim with delight: "Look, Mommy, they have McDonald's in America, too." . . . (p. 44)

The great chaotic diversity of American culture extends its realm every time a television set is sold abroad. The set itself may have been made in Taiwan or Korea, but chances are most of the entertainment programs it shows will be as American as the Super Bowl, which this year was broadcast to 23 nations, from Thailand to Costa Rica. Indeed, the one type of machinery in which American exports reign supreme is plot machinery. Africans tune in "The Jeffersons" to view white American producers' fantasies of black American life; European connoisseurs of duplicity can choose between "Dallas" and "Dynasty"; the earnest Chinese can learn much from what one comrade from Szechuan Province referred to as that great "scientific and educational program from America, the 'Man from Atlantis'." (p. 46) (Copyright 1983, by Newsweek, Inc. All rights reserved. Reprinted by permission.)

However, exporting blue jeans and entertainment programs are not ends in themselves. The present interdependent structure of the world requires that, along with our products, we should project our values, intentions, and policies to the people of other countries and be aware in return of their values, intentions, and policies. We should, in other words, attain international understanding of a much deeper, more profound sort. The significance of such an understanding becomes clear only if we remind ourselves of the alarming nature of the cross-cultural conflicts that, despite the interdependence between various nations, continue to abound in our complex world. There is ample reason to believe that such conflicts can readily draw the superpowers into dangerously confrontational positions. At stake, thus, is not just the security of a particular country but the survival of mankind.

To show the effectiveness of cross-cultural awareness in creating constructive relationships between people of diverse cultural backgrounds, I refer to an article by Robert G. Harvey. The argument put forward in this article is that cross-cultural understanding of the kind that puts one "in the head" of a person from a different culture cannot be achieved through contact alone. One must be ready to respect and accept, and one must have the capacity to participate. To support his argument, Harvey gives an account of a Peace Corps experience in the Philippines, which shows how lack of appreciation on the part of Peace Corps volunteers for cultural differences caused disastrous consequences. According to Harvey:

During the first two years, four volunteers resigned and twenty-six others were sent home, usually by mutual agreement, because they were not able or willing to cope with the extraordinary psychological burdens of being Peace Corps volunteers. Some volunteers developed a "what's the use" attitude and failed to appear at school, or made short unauthorized trips away from their barrios. Withdrawal was sometimes followed in the same volunteer by extremely hostile behavior against the Philippine Bureau of Public Schools, Washington, and the Peace Corps staff. (Harvey 1976:48)

Harvey goes on to show that some volunteers did solve the culture puzzle:

A male volunteer from South Carolina, D, was as much admired by Filipinos and volunteers as any volunteer in the project. Almost from the first, he accepted people for what they were, learned the dialect, made friends, and seemed to enjoy that more than anything else. After two years, he wrote, "I consistently believed and followed a life based on getting away from all identity or entanglement with the Peace Corps. My reasons were . . . to figure out a little bit about what was going on in the Philippines, to see what was really significant in my own place, to try to understand life here, and to learn to function in a way that could be meaningful to me and the community. I burrowed into life here unmindful of anything but my community and involvement and survival." . . .

Although everyone had thought that he epitomized the ability of a volunteer to live deeply in the culture after just six months, he wrote toward the end of his third year, "I have continued to change here and have now sort of reached a point of being able to feel with others. This is different from understanding how they feel. I am able to be a part of them as they do things with each other and me . . . " D was a success in both Filipino and Peace Corps terms. (Harvey 1976:49)

These are among hundreds of examples which clearly illustrate the significance of cross-cultural understanding to peaceful settlement and to the creation of a genuine spirit of kinship among peoples of diverse cultural backgrounds. Yet despite the modern interdependency, and despite her position as the leader of the free world, there is ample reason to believe that the United States has major deficiencies in her cross-cultural awareness which detract from her competitive edge in business abroad, and seriously affect her defense efforts. In this regard, it is revealing to quote from "Selling America in the marketplace of ideas" (March 20, 1983:44), an article by Richard N. Gardner, whose four years on the front lines of European diplomacy as the United States Ambassador to Italy brought him to the conclusion that:

The British, the French, the Germans and the Japanese have long understood "public diplomacy" and have applied resources and intelligence to programs of information, education, and culture to assure the vitality of the "intellectual connection" between themselves and other societies. The United States has not. As long as this remains the case, we will lack the ability both to shape a foreign policy that takes account of the real world and to influence foreign countries in ways that are consistent with our long-term interests.

We will continue to bemoan the fact that people overseas are poorly informed about the nature of our society and our foreign policy—that so many students, workers, and intellectuals in Europe, Japan, and the developing countries are convinced that *both* the Soviet Union and the United States represent threats to their interests—and that American embassies and the American intelligence community are frequently taken by surprise by foreign developments (the collapse of the Shah's regime being only one dramatic example).

This is the real "window of vulnerability" about which we should be concerned—for it is contributing to the progressive political isolation of the United States. (Gardner 1983:44) (Copyright © 1983 by The New York Times Company. Reprinted by permission.)

From all this it appears that it is essential for us as a great nation to enhance our education for global perspectives with a focus on understanding how nations, cultures, and civilizations are all interconnected. We must try to acquire more knowledge of our interdependent world and to enlarge our awareness of the relationships between our self-interests and the concerns of other nations. I find it appropriate to emphasize global education because it aims at fostering "a capacity to perceive oneself, one's community, one's nation, and one's civilization as both culture borrowers and culture depositors who both draw from and contribute to a global bank of human culture that has been and continues to be fed by contributions from all peoples, in all geographical regions, and in all periods of history" (Collins and Zakariya 1982:4–5). It is only through the enhancement of a global awareness of this sort that we can hope to survive—or indeed, prevent—the holocaust that threatens the world today.

The single most important key to success in creating a genuine international understanding lies in a breakdown of the language barrier between nations. As specified in a report of the National Assembly on Foreign Language and International Studies: "international understanding and language proficiency have become essential in an interdependent world, where each country's survival depends on its ability to understand and cooperate with other nations. Issues of peace, economics, and global harmony hinge on the strengthening of ties among people of diverse cultures. International trade and domestic employment, energy resources and foreign markets, diplomacy and cross-cultural interactions all require greater understanding of how other people think and live. International understanding and cooperation become as pragmatic as redressing the balance-of-payments deficit, as humanitarian as dealing with global hunger and disease, as crucial as avoiding war, and as humanistic as promoting a world of fully educated women and men." ("Toward education with a global perspective" 1980:1).

It is also relevant to refer in this context to a special issue of one of America's foremost educational journals, *Change* magazine. The special issue, entitled "Educating for the World View" expanded on theories of international education, and interest was sparked by the report of the President's Commission on Foreign Languages and International Studies which elaborated on the current status and future requirements of America's expertise in language and international studies.

Naturally, the question of the importance of language learning to international understanding can be argued at length, and I do not intend here to dwell on the discussions contained in the *Change* special issue. What is of particular interest is the interrelation which is presupposed between language studies and international and intercultural exchange, understanding, and cooperation. One of the contributors to the issue, Harlan Cleveland, wrote of this interrelation in a manner which is all the more interesting to us because he is neither a linguist nor a language teacher, but a political scientist. He says:

> It is true that I have long been skeptical of the too easy assumption that linguistic skill, cultural empathy, and political acumen are likely to be found in the same

package . . . but while language learning is not a sufficient condition for cross-cultural understanding, it is a necessary condition of global perspective. It is especially useful if the language learning is embedded in a total experience, including the learner's immersion in a situation where everybody else already speaks the language the student is trying to learn. (Alatis 1981:14)

The creative potential of language as a means of building bridges of understanding between peoples of diverse linguistic backgrounds has been verified by various language scholars. Our own linguistic experience in the United States offers ample reason to view language teaching as a most powerful weapon which can help create the mutual understanding necessary for people to function constructively and beneficially in a multicultural world. The reference to the United States is especially important in this context because we Americans have been nurtured in our own multicultural development over the centuries by continuing infusions of immigrants from various parts of the world. These cultural and linguistic transfusions have provided the language scholars in the United States with invaluable sources of professional and academic investigations.

Thus it is on the basis of an accumulated knowledge and experience that we talk about the creative or, to be more precise, the humanistic function of language acquisition. The classic statement on the creative potential of language is that provided by William Riley Parker who, recognizing that "knowledge of a foreign language, whether slight or extensive, brings no automatic or certain sympathy with the people speaking that language," nevertheless contends that "foreign language study *speeds* and *increases* understanding when the desire to understand is there—speeds and increases sympathy when the germ is present" (Parker 1961:100–01). He states further that "foreign language study may, and often does (although there can be no guarantee), create the desire to understand, the germ of sympathy. It may, and often does, prevent *mis*understanding. Given good will, foreign language study makes possible that ready and more nearly perfect communication between peoples upon which mutual understanding depends. Given indifference, foreign language study makes possible, through better communication, the discovery of good will (Parker 1961:100–01).

This encourages us to subscribe to a philosophy of language teaching which defines the ultimate function of our profession as an attempt "to achieve an understanding as complete as possible, between people of different linguistic backgrounds" (Fries 1955:10). We strongly support the notion that learning a foreign language is a "liberalizing" experience because it serves to free one from the shackles, the restraints, and barriers imposed by such limitations as confinement to a single language. We insist that even the study of language *as language* is a humanistic study. That is, all the uses and manifestations of language and linguistic communication, in all their philosophic, social, geographic, and ethnic splendor are the basis of a humanistic discipline.

To apply the humanistic aspect of language instruction within the context of international relations, we must have a coherent and consistent language policy.

Without consistent and unified language planning, it is obvious that language instruction and its related fields will suffer from proliferation, duplication, and internecine conflicts that consume energy and prevent the creation of effective programs.

But is has been stated that the United States is generally seen as having no explicitly formulated national language policy. To quote Rose Hayden:

> For reasons historical and otherwise, the United States has no official agency, professional group, or any other organ which *regularly* [italics supplied] surveys and reports on language policy and practice. It may be one of the few nations in the modern world where an apathetic, if not hostile attitude has impeded consideration of the role of language in American society. (1975:13)

How can we, then, influence government attempts to formulate and implement a desirable language policy? To answer this question, we have to make a reference to the President's Commission on Foreign Language and International Studies. The work which both preceded and followed the Commission proved that, because the United States did not have an official language policy nor a "ministry" to attend to language-related matters, members of the academic and professional communities were the only people who could effectively move to fill the gaps caused by the absence of government support. As responsible language educators, we were quick to recognize that in order to be instrumental in gathering evidence and presenting the case for foreign language studies, we had to first put our own house in order. We had to strive to know ourselves as professionals and as a profession. We had to be a *unified* profession, masters of our own fate. If the language profession was to acquire and maintain the intellectual strength and political power necessary in these troubled times, a new concept of the professional and a new concept of a unified professional entity had to be created. We had recognized that jurisdictional battles were a waste of energy and frustrated the realization of our common goals. It was *we* who were being weakened, not the laypersons who did not know our history and did not understand our mission. We had often allowed laypersons to make decisions of a professional nature about our own profession. But now we know that the control of our profession by laypersons would become more and more entrenched if we failed in what was perhaps our most important educational mission, and that was the education of those congressmen, lawyers, and Supreme Court justices who conduct the important affairs of our nation. We had to learn to control OURSELVES and govern our own profession. We were not blind to the fact that only a unified professional entity would ultimately receive the backing of the majority of teachers, of the American people, and of the American government. We had to educate the general public about our profession; we had to establish and maintain machinery for protection of competent and ethical teachers; we had to abandon our own petty provincialisms; and we had to maintain and support only the most effective, and HONEST, professional organizations.

To achieve all this, we needed the political mechanisms and political will to initiate action on our behalf—to amend legislation where plausible, to make suggestions about regulations where necessary, and to create an awareness of our needs among policy makers where possible. It was precisely in response to the need for unity, organization, and initiative on our part that the Joint National Committee for Languages (JNCL) and its sister organization the Council for Languages and Other International Studies (CLOIS) were created.

As president of JNCL, I am happy to say that we are now thirty-one brave organizations—good and true—come together in a spirit of professional cooperation, determination, and commitment. We have a combined membership of over 200,000 language professionals in all areas of the field, including English and the other foreign languages, interpretation and translation, language learning technology (LLT), applied linguistics, bilingual education and the classics.

By focusing public awareness on the issue of foreign language training, the JNCL functions as a point of reference for the planning of national language policies and the identification of national needs in this area. Through its Washington office, JNCL is endeavoring to create a national constituency for the promotion of foreign language training while simultaneously linking foreign language and international studies with broader educational and global concerns.

CLOIS is really the "action arm" for the organization of JNCL and it provides the mechanism for linking the language-teaching profession with the international studies communities. It is registered under the federal Regulation of Lobbying Act as the medium through which to maintain contact with legislators and policy makers, to "educate" them, and to sensitize them to our concerns. CLOIS provides a full-time, paid, professional lobbyist in Washington working for our interests. It also serves as a primary source of information flow to and from policy makers, and it attempts to influence policies which are important to our constituents. It thus serves as a continuous source of timely and relevant information. Finally, it provides a resource for member organizations to develop or enhance ability of their internal-communications networks to influence legislation and policy at the national, state, and local levels. JNCL and CLOIS, in short, exist to promote languages and international studies, Teaching of English to Speakers of Other Languages (TESOL), and bilingual education; to facilitate joint action and discussion among the members; and to develop relationships with other concerned individuals and organizations in the public and private sectors of the nation.

In the course of the last few months, I have seen strong evidence that JNCL and CLOIS have come of age politically. Instead of offering information and opinions for consideration by lawmakers and executives, these national decision makers NOW SOLICIT the views and expertise of the JNCL/CLOIS Washington office. We are called to testify, we are invited to attend planning sessions on the Hill, and we are asked to endorse and support the decisions made daily in legislatures and executive agencies. As a result of our continuous efforts to sensitize the policy makers to our concerns, we have now new public laws which will have a great impact on the future of language education and international studies. To give only two examples: The Appropriations Bill for the Departments of Commerce, Justice and State (H.R. 5712) is now Public Law 98-411. Passage of this legislation is indeed a victory in that it includes $35 million more for international education and exchange programs than the last year's funding levels. The total funding for Fulbright, International Visitors, Humphrey Fellowships, Eisenhower Exchanges, Congress-Bundestag, and Private Sector programs is $130 million. Furthermore, $4.8 million has been appropriated for the Soviet and East European Research and Training Program. PL 98-411 also appropriates $18.5 million for the National Endowment for Democracy and sets funding for the Asia Foundation at $9.6 million.

Public Law 98-377 provides $350 million for math, science, and foreign language teacher training at all educational levels. At the elementary and secondary level, foreign languages may receive up to 15% of the specific funding allocated for teacher training. At the postsecondary level, at least 20% of the funds available are to be used for "cooperative programs among institutions of higher education, local educational agencies, State educational agencies, private industry, and private non-profit organizations . . . for the development and dissemination of projects designed to improve student understanding and performance in science, mathematics, and critical foreign languages" (1278). The law also includes a provision for a discretionary grant program in which 25% of the funds allocated for this program may be used for "the improvement and expansion of instruction in critical foreign languages" (1282).

Thus, thanks to our new political awareness and our professional unity, we have become a real, credible force in the area of language and educational policy and law. We now have a contact in every congressional district and we are working on developing the political process. At long last, we have developed the political mechanisms and political will to participate, actively and cogently, in the decision-making and budget-drafting processes at all levels: local, state, and federal. Now that we have learned to govern our own profession, we must use our influence as effectively as we can in order to shape a comprehensive national language policy which could greatly enhance the intellectual consistency and effectiveness of language and international studies programs, discouraging the disparate projects with overlapping, inconsistent, or conflicting goals and facilitating instead close cooperation between language and its neighboring disciplines.

To shape such a policy we must first try to formulate a coherent, workable outline of priorities. As stated in an American Council on the Teaching of Foreign Languages (ACTFL) position paper concerning "Foreign language and international education in the twenty-first century," these priorities must include each of the following stages of development:

1. Awareness: Renewed emphasis must be placed on the value of foreign language study as a basic in the humanities; there must be heightened sensitivity to the value of foreign language and international studies in the world of work; and there is the need for reaffirmation of the value of the humanities as a foundation for the fullest realization of the potential of each individual.

2. Involvement: Planning for the future must involve the public in the creation of a strategy for reaching goals which they value. Through involving large numbers of the public, many of the points which we continue to emphasize would be given far greater significance and support, as evidence is gathered to support the value of foreign lan-

guage as a primary or auxiliary skill in many areas of international business, industry, government, and the service professions, including the need in many communities for volunteer, multilingual language skill banks.

3. Implementation: Renovation of existing education programs will be required as the nature of desired outcomes is identified. Support must be provided for those in education who will face the problems of pre-service and in-service teacher education. Due to decreasing enrollments at all levels of education, tenure restraints and lack of turnover have predetermined the selection of teachers. We must create a plan which will be feasible when entrusted to our current teachers, and provide the training that will enable them to accomplish the task. (Scebold 1979:28)

In conclusion, political differences and trade conflicts traditionally have been the focus of international negotiations. In recent years, however, other issues have caused worldwide concern, including the depletion of the earth's resources, environmental protection, and the effects of scientific advances and ever-expanding technology on our way of life. These common concerns demonstrate that people of different nations must learn to cooperate in new areas in order to solve problems that affect all humankind; language is the key to such cooperation. In this context, language is not merely a verbal skill or a mechanical instrument for forming grammatically proper sentences, but a highly sensitive and sophisticated tool of human understanding and rapport between people whose background and experiences can be drastically different. Thus, all people have a stake in language study. Domestically, it can help to solve some of our most pressing national problems. Internationally, it can contribute to the maintenance of world peace and increase the probability for human survival in a nuclear age. As committed language educators, we have a moral obligation to combine our efforts to promote an integrative language policy which could ensure the achievement of these national and international objectives as its ultimate goal.

Continents once isolated by vast oceans are now only hours apart by plane and seconds apart by means of electronic communication. Developed and developing nations alike find themselves thrust together in efforts to solve old and new problems. In short, the world is shrinking and global interdependence is a historical reality with which we must contend in everything we do and think. Hence we need, as a profession and as a nation, to develop a language policy which reflects the urgencies of our times, which relates directly to the primary issues of our times, and which is influenced by the social imperatives of our times.

REFERENCES

Alatis, James E. 1981. Interdisciplinary approaches to language teaching. Rassegna Italiana Di Linguistica Applicata. XIII. (3). 3–17.

Collins, H. T. and Zakariya, S. B. 1982. Getting started in global education. Arlington, Virginia: National Association of Elementary School Principals.

Fries, Charles C. 1955. American linguistics and the teaching of English. Language Learning. VI (1–2). 1–22.

Gardner, Richard N. (March 20, 1983). Selling America in the marketplace of ideas. New York Times 44.

Harvey, Robert G. 1976. Cross-cultural awareness: Attainable global perspective. New York: Reprinted by Center for Global Perspectives.

Hayden, Rose L. 1975. In the national interest: International education and language policy. ADFL. 6. (3). 11–17.

Parker, William Riley. 1961. The national interest and foreign language. Washington, D.C.: Department of State.

Scebold, C. Edward. 1979. The annual report of the ACTFL executive director. Foreign Language Annals. 12. (L). 27–28.

Silk, Leonard. (October 29, 1982). Major question in elections: Blame for state of economy. New York Times A1, 24.

Toward education with a global perspective. 1980. A Report of the National Assembly on Foreign Language and International Studies. Washington, D.C.

What the world thinks of America. (July 11, 1983). Newsweek 44–52.

TWO

On the Value of Local Languages

Kenneth L. Pike
Summer Institute of Linguistics and University of Texas at Arlington

LIFE IS CONTEXT; AUTONOMY IS DEATH

A human being's first personal context is mother. She gives nourishment, care, and belongingness. To separate the baby from mother and all other surrogate care is death. Life can be initiated, and continue, only in context. A person's first social contexts include the hearing of language spoken around him—and, in our culture, to him. In the Mazatec culture of Mexico, however, my sister (who had lived among the Mazatec for some years doing language research and for whom Mazatec was her second language—next to English) wasn't able to speak Mazatec to the babies because the mothers always interrupted apologizing that the baby couldn't yet speak. But when Eunice switched to speak to them in English (socially appropriate in her own culture), the mothers didn't interrupt, but saw the babies respond to Eunice with gurgles of social joy. The mothers concluded that the babies were speaking English, and thus came to the generalization that babies learn English before they learn Mazatec.

In adult life, a person's self-image is often still closely related to his mother tongue, even when he has changed residence and achieved almost native capacity in that new language. Some years ago I was helping a colleague at the Summer Institute of Linguistics (SIL) analyze the tone system of the Binumaria language of the South Pacific area. The total population of the ethnic group was about 300, and it was dying out. People had begun to lose the will to live. Babies were dying of malaria or other diseases—why have more? Farming land was being encroached on by neighboring ethnic groups. But even more discouraging than that was the feeling of the Binumarias that they were being despised: some nonlocal people accused them of "not having a language" and, hence, of being scarcely more than animals. This has been done to other groups even by very educated people here at home. For example, one research man in Ann Arbor asked me, on my return from the area. "Such people don't really have a language, do they—isn't their speech something more like bird calls?" I said, "Well, what would you say of this word, in a preliminary analysis of one of these languages: *dopneralo* "give it to me," where *d* (an implosive stop) means "something small," *op* means "an object," *n* is "to me," *e* "give" (or so I thought at the time, although it turned out later that I was wrong and that that word had no stem at all!), *ral,* something like "actively you in the future," and *o* "indeed"; would you consider even such partially analyzed data to be like bird calls?"

But when my SIL (Summer Institute of Linguistics) colleague and his wife began to talk the Binumaria language, the people said, "Oh, we're really people, we have a language!" They came to that conclusion since it was now spoken by people who, in their eyes, had prestige. When, in addition, some pills began to save the babies' lives, that helped a great deal. And a further touch came when part of the book of Genesis was translated—including the genealogies. The people said, "Oh, so God knows the names of our ancestors!"—and in the light of their strong interest in that kind of history, it gave them courage to believe that help was possible. Their new confidence allowed them to resist loss of land, and to enjoy their families again.

One's self-image, when good, strengthens resolve and life. When damaged by harmful context, the person is damaged. Changes forced on a group, without its desire or consent, can hurt deeply. Adoption of a second language by a group, by their own choice, by their welcoming it for commercial or social reasons, may be a strength. But the same adoption under resistance may be at a heavy price.

LANGUAGE AFFECTS WORLD VIEW AND WORLD VIEW AFFECTS LIFE AND SOCIETY

It is not easy for us to move back in our imagination to a time and place where beliefs about the world were different from ours. Yet, once in a while, we find ourselves almost doing so. Recently, an SIL colleague (Andrew Sims, reported to me by Ed Travis) was working in the tall steep highlands of an island in the South Pacific. He brought some of the ethnic speakers down toward the coastlands to help in language analysis at a workshop. They had never traveled in automobiles, although airplanes were a common sight and they had just traveled to the coast in one. They rode from the airport toward the workshop site in a mini-van taxi. When asked what they thought of the car ride, their reaction was that they thought that the places to sit in it were nice, but that they couldn't help wondering, as they watched through the windows, at how strong the people were who were pushing the world past the taxi so fast! Just how different was their view from that of our own ancestors not too many centuries ago who thought that the sun was moving around the stationary earth? And how deeply can such views affect not only our view of the earth, but metaphysical matters? One's world view includes convictions about how one should treat one's neighbor. Should one be required, for social integrity, to take vengeance upon one's neighbor? Or should one be allowed—or encouraged—to forgive him? But how can you forgive if you can't talk? How can they be encouraged to live at peace with neighbors—instead of decimating each other's crops and families— except with words? One's psychological structure is affected by words of teaching, or explanation, of forgiveness; these, in part, come from a world view which is also affected by words. Words explode before cannons do. Talking and language are an integral part of peace. Perhaps this poem of mine will say it stronger.

POW! WHY?
He slew.
So now?
Must I do too?
I wish I knew.

A NATION MUST BE INTEGRATED THROUGH WORDS

It is not just the small ethnic groups interacting who are affected by words and word-worlds. Nations are affected also. For a nation with many small ethnic groups to be at its best in helping its citizens, it needs to be able to talk to them. In every government there are good people. In every society there is some legal flexibility allowing special help for those in need—the poor. And in all nations we will always have the poor with us, as Jesus—it seems to me—tried to tell us (Matthew 26:11). But how can men of good will, even with government power, help those to whom they cannot talk? How can they help them get legal protection, or learn to change their habits enough to survive the new perils brought in by an expanding population resulting from the kindnesses of using medicine to save their people from dying? How can they be helped to meet new social challenges brought in by companies searching for oil (for national survival) in areas previously largely ignored by modern industrialized society? Nations need words, just as neighbors and families do.

Integration of the individual with the nation requires that the local ethnic groups learn the national language. The lack of knowledge of the national language affects the success of government officials' attempts at getting them the civil rights technically available but practically unavailable to them otherwise. It also affects the strength of the nation as a whole due to a lack of access to its own people and their capacities to contribute to the nation. When a person learns to read and write in his own language, he can take pride in who he is. Then he is ready to tackle another— the national language—with more courage. And in time he learns to take pride in his nation, without losing his own identity; he has a continuing pride in that too. (For data on some bilingual programs for ethnic groups in Peru, see Tuggy, appendix in Pike 1979, and Larson and Davis 1981.)

FAIR TRADE FOR ETHNIC GROUPS REQUIRES BILINGUAL CAPACITY AND NATIONAL INTEGRATION

Among the Piro of Peru, years ago, I met the man who invented the number eight!—where previously (according to Esther Matteson) they could only count "one, two, not-two." In Papua New Guinea, before that country's independence, I met a police officer who, similarly, in his native language could count (as translated by him into pidgin English) only "one-fellow, two-fellow, plenty-fellow." Mathematics is not, like language, a universal of human culture. Yet how is one to trade, in a world where money is now used (instead of shells, for example), without the ability to recognize fair bargains? Or to know when one has, in fact, paid one's debts? Even in the USA we need lawyers to tell us about laws on our side, when people want to treat us unjustly; what if we had no lawyers, no books, no "hearing"? We need bilingualism in some of these places for national integration, for personal protection, economic well-being, and for contribution to the nation. These things interlock. We must not assume that it is good or possible for ourselves or others to be isolated. Autonomy is death, as I say here:

ALONE, KILLS ME
I cannot live
Apart from others—
Self would die
If goal achieved
Is isolation.
Let me be myself,
With you . . .
TALK to me!

WHAT, *ME* WRITE?

How astonished a person can be when he first sees a dictionary in his own language, if he has been taught that having a language means having a dictionary in it, yet his has been unwritten. It can even affect his evaluation of his own ancestry. But when the context grows broader, and he himself is first encouraged to write in his own language, that can encourage change and personality development and the flowering of hidden artistic gifts. "Bootstrap literature" is one label for literature produced by the ethnic group, as encouraged by various governments, with the linguistic and pedagogic help of members of SIL (Wendell 1982: viii–ix).

Using materials produced by local authors, Wendell tells us, reading skills can be introduced into isolated situations. The new author can be shown that reading can be exciting, and a variety of titles can be suggested to suit different preferences and skills. A self-sustaining cultural drive toward the literacy process can be started without an outsider to keep it going.

Wendell also (110–11) suggests for discussion various reasons why it is highly desirable to read and write in one's own language as well as in the national language: to communicate more easily with friends away from home; to express one's feelings; to obtain respect; to make it easier to become literate in a second language; to sense the emotional impact from books; to obtain information from books about travel, birds, needs, friends—and numerous other topics. Additional suggestions are given (116–17) also, to help the ethnic group develop its own literature.

I have tried to express in the following poem (Pike 1976: 127) how a person from a preliterate culture might feel, by comparing him to Lazarus, who was called back to life by Jesus (John 11: 17–44) after having been buried in a tomb.

PRELITERATE
I'm small,
Ignored—
No gun, bomb,
Pen, or tongue

To politic the world.

Weep for me!
No choice to grow—
Where's my identity?
You have yours—
   Or smash your world
   To claim it . . .

I'm just
Not seen
By mass of men
Important
In their eyes.
But God's?—
   The widow's mite?
   The 99th plus
   One?

I'll live by Him—
Not culture's baksheesh.
I count as man,
Not beast.
With groans unutterable
   He weeps for me,
Lazarus, bound
In wordless tomb
By culture's shroud.

MAKE HAPPY CHOICES UNDER HOSTILE CHANGES!

No alternative? Then no choice. Preliterate ethnic minorities may have but little choice when winds of change blow cold. The economy does not allow them to trade adequately, since they cannot keep figures; artistic growth is thwarted, since the old patterns are not rewarded with cultural reinforcement or economic support; religious beliefs are destroyed by events which fail to match expectancies or to protect in spite of prayers; one's children slip to squalor and sink into slime where former teaching fails to meet the needs; what can we say? I'll cry thus:

COLD CLOUDS
WHAT TO DO?
NO CHOICE FOR YOU!
HOW TO CHOOSE
WITH ALL TO LOSE
NOW CLIMATE
FREEZES YOU?
ACCEPT THE WARMTH
OF FACT AND FAITH
TO LOOSE THE BONDS
OF SOCIAL ICE

THAT BIND WITH TONES
AND TUNES OF WORDS.
LEARN TO WRITE!
CHANGE TO LIGHT!
GROW!

In some instances an ethnic group may choose to move directly into the writing and reading of the national language without going through its own local language. That is then their responsibility. But alternatives have to be provided. It requires the making available to them of opportunities—academic, social, national, spiritual. Under some circumstances, the responsibility for providing these alternatives will fall on government departments or on their schools; or, sometimes, it may fall on international organizations.

MEANING FOR MAN PUTS PERSON ABOVE FORM

Yet all programs carry dangers with them. A good emphasis may be overdone, and get out of balance. A deep need seen by the outsider may fail to meet the felt needs of the insider. That which is good for today may carry seeds of difficulty for tomorrow. The world is too complex for any man or government to expect progress without pain. Here, too, there are choices. Should we refuse to move, since no "insurance policy" is available which can eliminate partial failure along with partial success? No. We must keep on, and help one another in individual and governmental efforts to aid these people. Yet one other emphasis should be made, in my view: We should insistently put person above thing, personal dignity above program, personal structure above machine efficiency. We should be sensitive to the needs of a person in his deepest being, not just in his stomach.

If we ignore these factors, mere technical excellence of linguistics and bilingual pedagogy may fail to be as helpful as one had expected them to be. Troike (1978) discusses various such problems. He summarizes the work of Lambert, Tucker, and Cohen (21) showing how English-speaking children in Canada have continued to achieve at their "grade level in English even though they have received no instructions in it"—probably because they were not treated as a "dominated minority." But, the work of Skutnabb-Kangas and Toukomaa (20–21) found that if Finnish "children migrated to Sweden when they were of primary-level age, they fell within the lower ten percent of Swedish children in Swedish language skills"—but this did not happen" if they were ten to twelve years of age when they immigrated, and had had five to six years of education in their native language in Finland." This was probably due to the fact that the children belonged to dominated minorities. Best learning, Troike suggests, comes when children "are in no way threatened or demeaned by their being taught in another language"(21); and "success of bilingual education . . . may rest on matters far deeper and more fundamental than the merely linguistic"(22).

REFERENCES

Larson, Mildred L., & Patricia M. Davis. (eds.). 1981. Bilingual education: An experience in Peruvian Amazonia. Dallas: Summer Institute of Linguistics, and Washington, D.C.: Center for Applied Linguistics.

Pike, Kenneth L. [1967] 1976. Stir-change-create: Poems and essays. Huntington Beach, Calif.: Wycliffe Bible Translators.

_____ . 1979. Social linguistics and bilingual education. System 7.99–109.

Troike, Rudolph C. 1978. Research evidence for the effectiveness of bilingual education. NABE Journal 3.1.13–24.

Wendell, Margaret M. 1982. Bootstrap literature: Preliterate societies do it themselves. Newark, Delaware: International Reading Association.

PART II

OFFICIAL AND INDIGENOUS LANGUAGES IN NATIONAL POLICY MAKING

THREE

Introduction of New Writing Systems: The Turkish Case

Erika H. Gilson

Princeton University

INTRODUCTION

On August 9, 1928, the president of the young Turkish Republic announced at a public gathering that a new alphabet for Turkish had been developed. And, not quite three months later, a new writing system based on Latin graphs—a radically different system than the one in use up to that time—was indeed unanimously approved and legalized by the Grand National Assembly. Within five months of the first public announcement by the president, the new Turkish alphabet was the sole legal medium of the written and printed word in the land. To provide some perspective, the author of a *New York Times* article of the era compared the situation to the United States' adopting "suddenly the Greek alphabet to express itself phonetically in English." ("Changing alphabet obsesses Kemal." *New York Times* September 2, 1928 section II p. 8).

The present article will first attempt to introduce the cultural, social, and political setting which permitted such a drastic change to take place, then summarize developments in Turkey towards the establishment of the new alphabet up to the founding of the Republic in 1923. The second phase of development between the founding of the Republic and the passing of the Alphabet Law in 1928 will be examined in chronological order and greater detail to the extent available sources make it possible. A brief look at the manner of implementation immediately after the adoption of the alphabet and some concluding observations will follow.

HISTORICAL SETTING

In the early decades of the twentieth century, urgent priority was given in the world of Muslim Turks to the promotion of literacy among the people in underdeveloped national entities emerging after the political, social, and cultural convulsions of the age. Whether the emerging nations developed into independent republics such as Turkey, or whether they were eventually absorbed as minorities of various standing into other nations, such as the Soviet Union, those in authority perceived in all cases mass literacy to be the vehicle with which to enter into the mainstream of twentieth century civilization.

The sincere search for ways to achieve the ideal of a literate citizenry focused attention on writing systems in use among Turks and the systems' compatibility with the professed goals of modernization. The First Turcological Congress in Baku (Menzel 1927) was convened essentially to address language and literacy problems of the Muslim Turks. At the time, most were using writing systems based on the Arabic alphabet, a medium adopted with their conversion to Islam and in continuous use for probably at least one millenium (Mansuroğlu 1959). At the conference in Baku, the Arabic alphabet was again and again declared a prime obstacle in the quest for literacy (Menzel 1927: 173–199), a notion also strongly prevalent among Turkish intellectuals (Heyd 1954; Levend 1960; Rossi 1927; Yalman 1956). It did not matter what the political, social, or cultural motivations which directed the findings of very diverse educators and linguists might have been; these specialists were, in their reports and resolutions, in agreement that the Arabic alphabet, even with modifications or outright novel approaches to application, was not suited to adequately represent Turkish. The Latin alphabet, on the other hand, unencumbered by graph-related orthographic traditions, was considered best equipped to render a phonetically unambiguous writing system for Turkic languages.

Although Turkish had a long and rich history of written representation, the written language was not a joint possession of the people. Literacy rates were hovering between 5% and 10% in Turkey in the 1920s. (Başgöz & Wilson 1968: 85) It was not meant to be any different: the traditional literary language, referred to as Ottoman Turkish, was far removed from the spoken idiom so that the population at large had little practical use for it. In addition, the orthographic tradition for Ottoman Turkish was complex indeed as it contained three distinct writing traditions side by side: for Arabic and Persian borrowings, which made up a vast majority of the vocabulary; their respective historical orthographies; and the system developed for Turkish with Arabic graphs. This system was based on morphological and historical principles, so that a graph included in a written form might have no phonetic counterpart in the spoken language. The different morphemes attained their acoustic shapes in the mind of the reader upon visual recognition of a certain graph-sequence in a certain context; a useful shorthand perhaps, but necessitating much previously accumulated knowledge.

The Turkish language has eight vowel phonemes, whereas the Arabic system had evolved to accommodate the three vowel phonemes of Arabic. This caused underrepresentation of Turkish vowel phonemes which further complicated reading and comprehension by the introduction of an ambiguity factor. Literacy, then, depended on knowledge of Arabic and Persian—or careful memorization of the spelling of Arabic and Persian borrowings—and the ability to distinguish between borrowings and Turkish words in a running text, in addition to complete familiarity of Turkish writing traditions (Levend 1960: 51–60). These intricate orthographic traditions, however, were never considered to be a hindrance to acquiring literacy by those who sought it. Mastery of the written form was an end in itself since, at the very least, it signaled knowledge of Arabic and Persian as well as the literary tradition of Ottoman Turkish.

The concept of literacy is radically different in the twentieth century. It is socially desirable and economically essential that the written language be available to the whole population. To modernize politically and to progress technologically, the written language had to be "democraticized." What was needed was a tool to transform oral communication into written communication. It was held that a democratic writing system is one that is based on strictly phonetic properties of the language (Menzel 1927: 68), eliminating the need to devise an orthography: access to the written word is afforded to all without discrimination when they learn to use a simple tool, the phonetic alphabet. The time, energy, and expense spent on learning traditional writing systems could be better spent elsewhere. Serious reservations were also voiced about the suitability of the Arabic alphabet for scientific research and methodology, a notion already mentioned by Arabic scientists in the tenth and eleventh centuries (Togan 1969: 316).

In the process of nation building, the ability to mold and guide the population along set national goals depends very much on how literate the population is with which the leadership has to communicate. Literacy becomes the tool of persuasion to create and maintain national and ideological unity. Of course, literacy is also the prime vehicle for communicating opposing ideas and criticism.

Criticism in the days of nation building among Turkic peoples has invariably centered around questions of political—and more profoundly, cultural—identity: to many, a future outside of the traditional Islamic framework was simply unthinkable. And if political concessions had to be made, as in the case of the Turks under Russian rule, adherence to Islam and its visible outward sign, the Arabic alphabet (Lewis 1968: 426) became that much stronger. Even though the experience of the Ottoman Turks who had suffered under their very own caliphs is somewhat different, religion and the Arabic script nevertheless exerted a strong pull. The leadership of an emerging nation, determined to avoid perpetuation of excessive religious influence, was therefore confronted with the need to either desanctify the Arabic graphs, or introduce a new neutral medium. But even if reform movements to give the Arabic graph new phonetic capabilities had succeeded, the needs of a nation promoting literacy would not have been met: the printing technology at the time was wholly geared to Latin writing systems and could not easily accommodate the peculiarities of the Arabic script. Typesetting 612 basic forms was also a much slower process compared to handling about 70 for Latin systems (Türk Tarihi 1931: 255).

1860–1923: National Awakening

Dissatisfaction with the writing system and the need for change began to be reflected in newspaper articles, letters, journals, and pamphlets in the second half of the nineteenth century. At a conference of the Ottoman Learned Society in 1862 the problem was debated openly for the first time (Rossi 1927: 295). It should be stressed that the calls for reform were not restricted to any particular urban intellectual center. Faced with the challenges of the modern era, serious, educated men began to express the same reservations about the Arabic script in various parts of the Empire as well as in other Muslim lands (Menzel 1927: 175). The famous Azeri

Turkish playwright Mirza Fethali Ahundzade offered a proposal for alphabet reform which was discussed at the suggestion of government officials at a general meeting of the Ottoman Learned Society. The resulting resolution regarding reform stated:

1. Writing system needs to be reformed.
2. Proposed reforms of the alphabet are useful and appropriate, but do not alleviate inherent difficulties encountered in practical applications.
3. Proposed reforms cannot be accepted as they would doom Islamic Turkic classics to oblivion (Levend 1960: 156). (Translations from the Turkish are by Erika H. Gilson.)

These contradictory statements form the core of arguments surrounding alphabet reform throughout the period under discussion. Only one new element is added: adoption of a totally new alphabet.

Spoken Turkish has been written in different alphabets—Greek, Armenian, Syriac, Cyrillic, Latin—by Ottoman subjects of different ethnic groups who had their own writing systems. The fact that primary education seemed to progress faster among children of these subjects probably did not escape the attention of some of those concerned with educational development of Turkish children. From the fourteenth century on, there is a great amount of material compiled by Europeans of Ottoman Turkish in the Latin alphabet, transcribed according to their own different writing systems (Gilson in press). Especially in the nineteenth century, numerous grammars and language teaching aids for Turkish were published by French, Hungarian, and German writers among others, all representing Turkish in Latin graphs.[1] European dictionaries for Turkish always included a transcription of the entries to insure proper pronunciation, and often Turkish appeared in such transcribed forms only. Turkish intellectuals, grammarians, and lexicographers were certainly aware of these publications in which their language was rendered in a number of different ways with Latin graphs.

During this period various societies were formed, some under the direction of the Ministry of Education, to study alphabet reform problems (Levend 1960: 360–361). Prior to World War I several concrete proposals for a reformed orthography were in print (Rossi 1927: 297). The Albanian Learned Society, formed to promote literacy among Albanians, was affiliated with the Turkish societies. This society announced in 1869 the forming of a three-member committee to resolve the alphabet needs of the Albanians and to come up with a unified writing system acceptable to all Albanians, Christian as well as the Muslim majority. Up to that time, Arabic, Greek, or Latin graphs had been in use depending on religious convictions (Bourgeois 1913: 386–390). At a congress in 1879 in Istanbul, the society introduced the new "national" Albanian alphabet—which was based on Latin graphs—and submitted it to the religious authority, the *şeyhülislam,* for approval. The *fetva,* in response, de-

---

[1] One of the very first books printed by a Turkish printing press was the *Grammaire Turque* by Jean Baptiste Holdermann printed in Constantinople in 1730. All Turkish entries are given in the Arabic alphabet as well as in corresponding transcription.

creed that approval could never be granted, and it was furthermore stressed that tampering with the Arabic script in any way in the name of reform was sacrilegious (Levend 1960: 363–364). The Albanians proceeded with the "alphabet de Constantinople" and have been using it with minor changes ever since (Bourgeois 1914: 275–276). Although Albanian is not a Turkish language, the event is significant because this appears to be the first instance of a Muslim people accepting the alphabet of the "infidel" in the name of progress, in spite of strong religious exhortion. The events were covered and discussed in the Turkish press; a 1910 article argued that alphabet had nothing to do with religion and commended the Albanians (Levend 1960: 363). Yet articles in 1911 openly promoting adoption of the Latin graphs for Ottoman Turkish caused the closing of the journal where they had appeared (Levend 1960: 362). The same author, Kılıçzade Hakkı, was still being warned about writing such articles in 1923.

The ruling of the *şeyhülislam* also did not prevent Enver Paşa, the Minister of War, to order a "military alphabet" to improve communication in the military. It consisted of Arabic graphs, written separately, each corresponding to one sound (Alpay 1981: 33). It was introduced just before World War I, but had to be abandoned during the war years.

The immediacy of the war pushed alphabet reform discussions somewhat into the background. However, as the war progressed and defeat appeared inevitable—and particularly during the War of Independence—the arguments defending religious traditions appeared to be getting stronger: citing historical evidence, it was questioned rhetorically whether change of alphabet is in fact possible without change of language and religion (Levend (1960: 388). At the same time, those seeking a total break with the past introduced a new angle to their argument by pointing out that from a historical perspective, the Latin graphs are the same as Arabic ones since they both come from the same source, the Phoenician alphabet (Rossi 1927: 297).

In 1922, the Azeri Turks introduced a new writing system based on Latin graphs and began implementing it (Menzel 1927: 180). A *Denkschrift* was sent to the education minister of the provisional government in Ankara—receipt of which was duly acknowledged by telegram—and it was suggested that Ankara follow the example (Duda 1929: 442). Latin-based alphabets were being prepared for other Turkic languages of the Soviet Union: Uzbek, Kazak, and Kirgiz (Menzel 1927: 176). Those preferring to retain the traditional Arabic script introduced reformed orthographies, implemented for Tatar, Bashkir, and Crimean Turkish (Menzel 1927: 175).

1923-1928: National Preparation

With the founding of the Turkish Republic in 1923, the task of nation building became a more concrete endeavor. The time had come to make decisions and to act. Indeed, there was a lot of action: abolishment of the Caliphate, of the tithes, of polygamy, of the *fez*, the traditional headgear; the closing of *tekke*, the religious lodges; acceptance of the international calendar, of a new civil code based on the Swiss model; and the secularization of the new republic. Within five years, a courageous and purposeful revamping had taken place and the nation, aiming at a "modern'' future, was clearly beginning to emerge. It is noteworthy that the alphabet and language reform was not among the first slew of reforms. The first efforts were all directly geared to loosen the grip of religious institutions. The builders of the new nation considered the 1000 years' history and tradition a paralyzing weight; their responsibility rested with the future and they did not hestitate to make the liberating cut. They were quick to remind those calling on the Brotherhood of Islam that only a short while ago Muslim brethren all around had taken up arms against the Turks. The first time the alphabet question was put forward officially was during the Economic Conference in Izmir in February of 1923, when two workers' delegates from Izmir, referring to the adoption of the Latin alphabet in Baku, wanted to enter a proposal for similar action into the agenda for discussion. The motion was denied on grounds that it had nothing to do with economics, and later strongly denounced by the presiding official, Kâzım Karabekir. This seemed to rekindle interest and the issue was again taken up in the press, with the momentum clearly on the side of traditionalists (Duda 1929: 442).

Istanbul newspaper reporters met and discussed the situation with the president of the republic, Mustafa Kemal, in Izmir in 1923 asking that some change be initiated (Arıkan 1981: 9). Talk about reform and change had been around for some 60 odd years, and people directly affected in their profession by alphabet-related difficulties were getting impatient. Some publishers of influential dailies were openly advocating adoption of the Latin graphs (Jansky 1929: 162).

The alphabet question was brought up for the first time at the Grand National Assembly on February 25, 1924, by the representative from Izmir, Şükrü Saraçoğlu, during budgetary deliberations. Referring to the sums allotted to education, he asked why illiteracy on a large scale persisted in spite of large expenditures and efforts. His own answer was that the Arabic alphabet was the reason. He caused an uproar and was threatened with bodily harm (Ertop 1963: 64). This incident occurred just prior to the abolishment of the Caliphate on March 3, 1924.

A survey taken the same year by the education ministry showed that 96% of teachers were opposed to change in the writing system (Başgöz and Wilson 1968: 85).

The next official mention is a year later—February 28, 1925—again at the budgetary sessions. Saraçoğlu was now present as Minister of Education and refrained from taking any sides in the discussions (Levend 1960: 396).

On March 4, 1925, *Takrir-i Sükun*—the Law for the Maintenance of Order—was put into effect following the Kurdish rebellion in February of the same year. This law gave the ''government powers to suspend newspapers and try journalists who disturbed social peace'' (Karpat 1964: 272). Whether this law—which gave the government such control of all written communication—had a direct effect on how the alphabet question was handled in the press needs to be further researched. Discussions in print certainly continued. Some of the most eloquent defenses of the Arabic script were printed in the years when the law was in effect (Levend 1960: 366, 399). Yet the newspapers appear to have moved more securely into the camp of the government.

Nothing newsworthy appeared in the Turkish press regarding the alphabet question until the mention of the Turcological Congress in Baku which was held February 26 through March 6, 1926. Yet the *New York Times* of January 31, 1926 printed an Associated Press release in four eye-catching paragraphs under the heading "Roman alphabet for Turks, latest of Kemal's reforms" (section II, p. 1), stating that the national government had decided to introduce the Latin alphabet. This surprising announcement came prior to a statement by the Education Minister Mustafa Necati on February 9 defending the delay in the establishment of a language academy as announced by Prime Minister Ismet on November 7, 1925. Stressing the immensity of the task, the education minister asked for patience and understanding as "it would not befit the ministry to rush into an endeavor that is beyond its capacity" (Korkmaz 1963: 40). The education minister announced on March 22, 1926, the forming of a language commission to study the alphabet question and application methods (Duda 1929: 443). The *Times* article also preceded renewed interest generated by the Baku conference and a survey initiated by the daily newspaper *Akşam* on March 28, 1926, eliciting serious public comment on the alphabet problem from men of learning (Arıkan 1981: 5). Sixteen prominent intellectuals responded, of whom only three were in favor of the Latin alphabet (Duda 1929: 443).

In the official history book published by the Ministry of Education in 1931, the year 1927 and the first months of 1928 are given as the time a final decision was made and preparations started (Türk Tarihi 1931: 251). Naşit Hakkı Uluğ, then editor of the semiofficial Ankara daily *Hakimiyet-i Milliye,* also notes in his memoirs that, without any doubt, the leader of the Turkish revolution, Mustafa Kemal, had arrived at a decision regarding the alphabet sometime in 1927 (Uluğ 1973: 168). The press, now openly promoting the adoption of the Latin alphabet, began addressing itself to questions of methodology. There apparently was a consensus, at least as far as the press was concerned, that the high illiteracy demanded a concerted effort for reform.

Although preparations were supposedly quickening (Duda 1929: 443) and decisions imminent, nothing of interest seemingly made it into the Turkish press according to secondary sources. There is, however, a short article in the *New York Times* dated April 29, 1928, that the press, for the past two years, "had thoroughly exploited the feasibility of adopting Latin characters" and that adoption by Ankara was inevitable ("Turkey curbs move to force language," section III, p. 6). On the following day, another article in the *New York Times* featured the headline "Turks drop Arabic for our alphabet" (p. 21), mentioning that 15 years will be given by the government for people to adjust to the change. An editorial the next day, May 1, 1928 (p. 28), maintained that "the Turkish parliament has enacted a law to substitute" the alphabet and concluded with the statement that mechanical arguments, that is, difficulty with typesetting and typewriters for Arabic graphs, "have given powerful support to the cultural" arguments.

There was nothing in the Turkish press about imminent alphabet reform. There was an official announcement in the spring that the proposal to adopt the international, that is, Arabic, numerals was ready. The proposal was discussed on May 20, and was accepted—as the *New York Times* correctly reported on May 22, 1928 ("Turks adopt Arabic numerals," p. 2). During the discussions the matter of the alphabet reform was brought up and an explanation from the government for the seeming inertia sought. On June 3, the *New York Times* again reported "Angora bewilders by swift reforms: Casting Arabic overboard" (section III p. 1), yet the Council of Ministers is supposed to have agreed at a meeting on May 23 to form a language commission, the first step towards resolving the alphabet question. Six members were originally appointed to the commission, but the membership was enlarged to fifteen by the time the commission first met in Ankara on June 26, 1928. Mustafa Kemal personally supervised the selection of the members (Ertop 1963: 59) which consisted of four linquists, two civil servants, and three representatives. They were commissioned to decide on the matter of alphabet reform and present a workable solution. The daily *Milliyet* published the news the next day in its own version of a Latinized system. Postage stamps had also already been issued using Latin graphs in a French-based orthography for Turkish. Private commercial correspondence typed on European typewriters was also often conducted in transcribed form heavily influenced by French orthographic traditions.

Commenting on the work and deliberations of the language commission, Uluğ insists that if left alone nothing would have been decided for years; the national leadership had already made up its mind (Uluğ 1973: 170) and closely monitored the work of the commission (Arıkan 1981: 10). Uluğ further informs that Mustafa Kemal personally inquired about technical difficulties and possible complications during July of 1928, asking for realistic assessments from publishers (Uluğ 1973: 171). He was told that the semiofficial *Hakimiyet-i Milliye* could make the alphabet switch by the end of November at the earliest, definitely by the beginning of 1929 (Uluğ 1973: 176). Publishers of newspapers in Istanbul met and discussed their concern over financial implications of a switch in alphabet. Their concerns were relayed to Mustafa Kemal; mentioned in particular was the lack of available Latin type and the expense involved in shipment from Europe (Uluğ 1973: 172). The Education Ministry apparently had been avidly collecting all available type in Istanbul (Uluğ 1973: 174–175).

Although the role of the national leader, Mustafa Kemal, is still not reflected in the Turkish Press, the *New York Times* of July 11 reported that even "before the law makes it obligatory" Mustafa Kemal was setting another example with his first official use of the Latin letters in signing his photograph given as a gift to his newly appointed ambassador to Afghanistan ("Kemal uses Latin letters," p. 24). Events unfold rather swiftly from the middle of July on. The several different channels involved in the process more or less visibly all along seem to converge. On July 9, that is, barely nine days after the actual work sessions of the language commission were started on June 30, the press announced that the majority of the members voted for the Latin alphabet; that adoption will be guided by phonetic principles and will correspond to international sound-associations of the individual graphs (Duda 1929: 443).

The commission announced on July 17 that the timetable for conversion was five years. Prime Minister Ismet attended the meeting of the commission the following day, after which it was announced that all members were in total agreement and that a conference was scheduled to meet in Ankara in September to be attended by academicians, the press, government officials, teachers, the army, and literary societies, and that a final decision would be made at that time (Duda 1929: 444). The *New York Times* meanwhile, in another article on July 22, wrote again that "The Turk gives up Muhammad's script" (Magazine, p. 18), adding that ample time, 15 years, will be allowed for the growing generation to master the new alphabet.

At this time, more articles began to appear in the Turkish dailies in Latin letters, even though no approved system had been declared. The July 1 copy of *Cumhuriyet* has only international numerals and an occasional title in advertisements in Latin graphs, whereas the August 1 copy has a front page article *in Latin graphs* entitled "Toward the application of Latin letters in our language." A cartoon the next day in the same daily shows a child in front of a blackboard teaching his grandfather the new alphabet.

The language commission as called to join Mustafa Kemal in Istanbul on August 2 to continue its work there. At the meeting the next day the different groups of the commission met together and a "final official version" of the adopted alphabet was announced. The teaching profession now said that they would be ready in two years and that the total switch within the schools could be accomplished in four years, although Turkish classics would still have to be taught in the Arabic script. Yet, the *Cumhuriyet* of August 9 featured the following news on the front page: "Instruction in the primary grades will be in Latin letters this year." An order to that effect apparently had been issued according to the Minister of Education, Mustafa Necati (Uluğ 1973: 182).

The next event involved Mustafa Kemal for the first time with the public on this issue. He emerges henceforth as the true moving force behind the alphabet reform, openly taking full charge. On August 9, at an evening of entertainment arranged by the People's Party at the Sarayburnu Park in Istanbul, Mustafa Kemal addressed the audience towards midnight in what appeared to be a spontaneous manner. Referring to the new "Turkish alphabet," he personally called on his countrymen to accomplish their next important task, namely to learn the alphabet promptly and quickly, and to consider it their patriotic duty to teach it in turn to others. Illiteracy was to be eradicated in short order, now that they have "freed [themselves] from the script which held [their] heads in its iron grip" (Atatürk 1952: 256). The relatively brief address is often cited as the actual start of the alphabet reform. It had an electrifying effect on the general public, the half-educated and illiterates who up to that point had not been fully aware and involved in the process which, after all, affected them the most. Under the confident and decisive leadership of their national hero, with the goal clearly identified and the new "tool" at hand, the people set out enthusiastically to conquer illiteracy, much as they had followed him into battle before. The press throughout the country gave extensive coverage to the speech and the ensuing developments of the following months.

The first task was to prepare teachers. On August 11, courses were started at the

Dolmabahçe Sarayı for top officials of the nation, setting an example for all. The commission's members were to teach the personnel of the Education Ministry, and they, in turn, teachers under their jurisdiction. Simultaneously, anxious officials eagerly tried to outdo each other to be the first to begin with courses in their own district. Evening classes were started at municipal centers (Arıkan 1981: 37), for the army personnel, at the Istanbul Teachers College, and on Radio Istanbul (Levend 1960: 403). By this time, although the graphs were decided on, a writing system had still not been worked out. All kinds of teaching material was on the market, however each differed slightly from the other in the manner the graphs were applied to the language, and each was denounced as unofficial by the language commission (Duda 1929: 445).

There were frequent personal responses of Mustafa Kemal published in the press in the Latin alphabet; some were congratulatory messages, some simply acknowledged communication received, and others answered to criticism. To the criticism of the publisher of *Cumhuriyet,* Yunus Nadi—an ardent supporter of reform—in the August 17 issue of the paper that excessive haste in implementation would be harmful, Mustafa Kemal answered in the next day's paper, reassuring that there was no harm in speed once the alphabet and orthography had been established.

Lectures to promote the reform were given at the Istanbul University by a professor of psychology (Duda 1929: 445) and courses for editors, typesetters, and members of the judiciary were started. At this time, about 100,000 manuals for grade schools were published and 50,000 copies of the alphabet printed and distributed among members of the Assembly (Baysal 1981: 115). Telephone books, timetables, and advertisements were ordered to be changed to the Latin letters, and employers were asked to show preference for those who had learned the new alphabet (Duda 1929: 445).

Mustafa Kemal made an unannounced trip (Uluğ 1973: 185) on his yacht to Tekirdağ on August 23, the first of his many field trips as "schoolmaster" around the country to personally communicate with the people, explain and teach the new graphs—usually in front of a blackboard—and observe firsthand the reception the new alphabet was accorded in the land. He could point out with complete justification that even before official guidance and teaching, or a law that compelled them, people were forging ahead rather than waiting (Goloğlu 1972: 253). The newspapers were now swamped with news about the reform: the Fourth Conference of the Teachers Association resolved to work to fully implement the reform; some provincial offices announced use of the new alphabet (Arıkan 1981: 33); mayors instituted people's courses, and so on (Duda 1929: 445).

For three days meetings were held at the Dolmabahçe Sarayı on August 25, 27, and 29, with Kâzım Karabekir, who had strongly opposed the reform and who was now president of the Grand National Assembly, presiding. According to a *New York Times* report of August 31, others in attendance included the language commission members, ministers, army officers, 300 deputies, and students ("Kemal holds class to teach leaders the Latin ABC," p. 23). The previously announced conference for final decision making set for September was obviously rescheduled to an earlier date, as no other conference took place in September. The first two days were apparently devoted to working out the last problems of which there were still several (Korkmaz 1963: 44). On August 27, *Milliyet* published an alphabet list which included all graphs currently in use. The last day of the meetings was open to the press. The *New York Times* article of August 31 described the crowded session in the following manner: Mustafa Kemal and Ismet were seated "on the front bench while an instructor held forth before a huge blackboard for nearly five hours. At the end of the lesson the President made the deputies who have been opposing the adoption of the new alphabet mount the platform and state their case. Kemal then rebuked them" (cf. Rossi 1929: 38). At the end of the session Prime Minister Ismet made public the three-point resolution earlier accepted by the language commission (Uluğ 1973: 192) and proclaimed the onset of a literacy campaign:

1. In order to eradicate illiteracy in the nation, it is imperative to adopt the Turkish alphabet based on Latin graphs and abandon use of the (for Turkish) inadequate Arabic graphs.
2. The alphabet proposed by the commission is truly and resolutely the Turkish alphabet. It meets all of the needs of the Turkish nation.
3. Orthographic rules will be perfected as the language develops and according to prevailing national preference. (Levend 1960: 403)

Mustafa Kemal took time out during these sessions for another excursion into the country. He went to Bursa on August 26 (Ertop 1963: 63) to test the climate of a region that had shown some resistance to change in the past (Başgöz and Wilson 1968: 80). After the sessions were over, Mustafa Kemal personally thanked the mayor of Istanbul, its people, press corps, and intellectuals for their cooperation (Uluğ 1973: 196–197). He was continuously keeping in touch via telegram or mail with people of all social backgrounds—thanking, urging, reassuring, or explaining. These communications were well publicized in the press.

On September 1, Mustafa Kemal went on another teaching excursion, this time to Çanakkale, site of the victorious battle he led against the invading British forces in World War I. He was given a hero's welcome by an enthusiastic people who were ready and eager to learn and to please (Uluğ 1973: 194). He actually taught the new alphabet on these trips, noting several crucial instances of orthographic usage invented as aids but which caused difficulty or confusion in the process of learning.

On this day also, the director of the Pedagogical Department of the Ministry and member of the language commission, Mehmet Emin, was called back to Ankara to initiate the implementation process. The language commission was now asked to prepare word lists in alphabetical order based on existing Turkish dictionaries giving the "correct" new spelling in the Latin alphabet. A control bureau was established on September 2 and put at the disposal of people in commerce anxious to rewrite store signs and other public notices. The typewriter keys and their order were established. Courses for beginners and for the advanced were held throughout. On September 12, a municipal directive in Istanbul ordered that all civil servants were to learn the new alphabet by the end of October.

During these developments, the writing system was still evolving; no definitive version had appeared. On September 13, rules for usage of capital letters were established and announced. Inadequacies, unforeseen in the planning stages, manifested themselves during this initial application phase. In the second half of September, both Mustafa Kemal and Ismet were personally campaigning for the alphabet, traveling and teaching in the country. Mustafa Kemal stopped at Sinop, Samsun, and Sivas—the latter two towns closely associated with momentous events of the recent national history—before returning to Ankara. As a result of his observations he rejected certain aspects of the writing system, originally thought to be of phonetic value, as unnecessary handicaps. Thus, no hyphen was to be inserted between the root and suffixes and no special graphs were needed to indicate palatalization of consonants. These changes were incorporated into a directive by the Education Ministry on September 29. Mustafa Kemal sought a simple "national" alphabet that reflected the Turkish pronunciation (Steuerwald 1964: 121). Mustafa Kemal's personal interference resulted in elimination of graphs that were proposed by a language commission which was relying too closely on the phonetic distinctions the old writing tradition made. He also insisted that a single graph, rather than a graph-cluster, represent one sound.

By the end of September, five more members were added to the language commission in order to speed up the preparation of orthographic guides.

The secondary literature is relatively quiet about the activities of the month of October, although there were rumors that preliminary preparations for the legalization of the alphabet were taking place. In October 16, the undersecretaries met to prepare the draft of the Alphabet Law. The draft was accepted by the Council of Ministers on October 30, and by the People's Party on the 31 (Duda 1929: 447). A *New York Times* article of October 28 mentioned that public employees had to master the new alphabet within two months or lose their positions, suggesting that economic pressure was being applied ("Kemal spurs Turks to hasty erudition," section III, p. 8).

November 1, 1928, marked the beginning of the second session of the Third Grand National Assembly. The first session had dealt with secularization; the second was to "legalize the national will" by accepting the new alphabet (Türk Tarihi 1931: 254). Mustafa Kemal formally presented the draft at the end of his opening speech, after touching on matters of education: "I would like to bring up a subject which forms the foundation of all progress." In three concise paragraphs, he urged the Assembly to decide saying "(your) decision to accept and legalize the new Turkish alphabet will, by itself, pave the way for this country's progress" and stressing the national duty awaiting all to combat illiteracy and move onto victory—"no other kind of victory can create the same thrill" (Atatürk 1945: 345–346).

The reception on the floor was tumultuous, with many interruptions for applause. After a second speech by Prime Minister Ismet, a temporary committee of 15 members was formed to study the submitted draft. The same afternoon, the Assembly unanimouly voted for the draft which was then passed unchanged as Bill 1353, the

Alphabet Reform Law. According to this law, use of the new alphabet became mandatory in government and private offices the day it took effect and—by January 1, 1929—in the rest of the country, with the following modifications:

1. Protocols, court decisions, statements, and petitions by the public will be acceptable in the old alphabet until June 1, 1929.
2. Beginning December 1, 1928, all public signs, advertisements, and movie subtitles as well as all public and private communication, newspapers, books, journals, and so on will be in the new alphabet.
3. Until June 1, 1930, material already typeset in the old graphs can be utilized, and minutes of proceedings taken in Arabic graphs as shorthand.
4. Monies, securities, stamps, and other legal tender and documents remain valid until changed. (Alpay 1976: 22)
5. All instruction in Turkish schools will take place with the new Turkish alphabet. Use of textbooks in the old alphabet is prohibited. (Alpay 1976: 23)

The event was extensively covered in the press (Arıkan 1981: 10ff) and according to a *New York Times* report on November 1, datelined October 31 ("Kemal to broadcast speech to all Turkey," p. 15), it was to have been broadcast simultaneously to be heard all over the country.[2] After the acceptance of the bill, the Assembly voted to present Mustafa Kemal with a golden plaque embossed with the new alphabet as a token of the nation's gratitude (Gologlu 1972: 258).

The Alphabet Law was published in the official gazette on November 3, 1928, and went into effect immediately.

IMPLEMENTATION

As soon as the new law went into effect, authorities of the province of Istanbul announced that all civil servants would be subject to a literacy test which they could repeat once. The text consisted of a dictation of 15 sentences and a short reading. On November 10, the Assembly voted a sum of 600,000 TL to be made available for the implementation of the law, 200,000 TL of which was earmarked for importation of new types for the printing presses during the remainder of 1928 (Alpay 1976: 36). On November 11, 1928, the Council of Ministers agreed to establish "National Schools" which were to open on January 1, 1929. The opening date was proclaimed "National Education Day." Anyone between the ages of 16 and 40 and still not versed in the new alphabet by January 1, 1929, was obliged to attend evening classes held by the government in schools, mosques, coffeehouses, and other public places. Only those who had already passed an official exam were exempt. The courses had two sections, one for illiterates, lasting four months, and the other for those who knew the old alphabet, lasting two months. Places of business em-

---

[2] The first radio station in Turkey was established in Istanbul in 1927 by a private firm under government supervision (Karpat 1964: 275). No mention is made in the secondary literature consulted regarding this broadcast.

ploying more than 20 workers had to institute literacy classes and cover the expenses (Uluğ 1973: 211). Courses were also started in prisons, and traveling teachers were sent to remote areas without schools. The entire country was mobilized and sent to school. In addition to the 12,000 teachers recruited and the use of radio broadcasts for instruction, each literate person was to teach his illiterate fellow citizen ("Kemal to broadcast speech" *NYT* November 1, 1928, p. 15; "Turkish papers appear in new characters," *NYT* December 1, 1928, p. 1).

The newspapers had been gradually increasing the amount of columns printed in the new alphabet. Starting with the September 29 issue, *Cumhuriyet* had the title and on the average three out of six columns in Latin graphs on its back page. On December 1, 1928, newspapers—including *Cumhuriyet*—appeared in the new alphabet only as decreed. The *Cumhuriyet*'s size had shrunk to four pages from eight the previous day. The *New York Times* report of December 1 mentioned above read in part "people will be newsless until they learn (the new alphabet)." It also reported that the government was buying unsold copies for distribution around the country. Some dailies and periodicals had to stop publishing—some altogether, others temporarily—until they could cope with the switch (Alpay 1976: 55–56). Circulation dropped drastically: *Tasvir,* one of the largest papers, with a 14,000–15,000 circulation, dropped to 5,000–7,000 (Uluğ 1973: 213). Government subsidies were mentioned, but apparently were not granted until March of 1930, retroactive to cover 1929–1931. Only those papers that managed to publish without interruption were eligible (Uluğ 1973: 213). The crisis appeared to be over by 1930 and circulation soon passed the previous limits (Yalman 1956: 176). Dailies and periodicals published in Istanbul and Ankara amounted to 35 in 1923; the figure for 1933 was 230 (Uluğ 1973: 213). Because of the clause in the law allowing the printing of books that had already been set, book publishers did not experience financial losses due to the switch; there was, in fact, an increase of 25% in publishing activity in 1928 over the average of the previous two years (Alpay 1976: 52). The yearly average for the period 1923–1928 was 666 titles, for the period 1928–1933, 1259 titles (Baysal 1981: 130). The increase seems to be due largely to the fact that teaching material and aids of all kinds were in great demand.

On December 22, a directive was issued by the police instructing all who were illiterate between the ages of 16 and 45 to report to their district elders and register for courses. There are some indications that this was not welcomed in all quarters. A report in a Turkish newspaper on December 19, 1928, mentioned arrest of opponents of the new alphabet, and a few days later, there is further mention of unrest in Sivas due to religious convictions (Duda 1929: 449). The government denied the charges and sued the papers involved. The court proceedings were not followed in the press.

On January 1, 1929, the opening of the National Schools and National Education Day were celebrated with marching bands, speeches, and parades. The daily *Cumhuriyet* the next day had extensive illustrated coverage of the festivities. It was reported that in Istanbul, 1208 places of instruction were opened and 45,000 students registered on the first day. For the next weeks the newspapers were filled with articles and pictures of people congregating and learning. It was reported that demand for classes had exceeded all expectations and that it was impossible, therefore, to meet the demand.

A total of 20,489 classrooms were operating in 1928–1929 and 597,010 students were attending "National Schools" (Başgöz and Wilson 1968: 120). Some statistics are available for the first eight years, and they show a rather steep decline in number of classrooms and students, especially after the *Menemen* incident in October of 1930 in which a teaching officer was beheaded by reactionaries (Uluğ 1973: 211). Up to that time, in their first two years the "National Schools" had graduated about 860,000 students of which 266,515, or roughly one-third, were illiterate initially. Apparently only about 500,000 more students attended in the following six years so that the total for the first eight years is about 1.5 million graduates (Başgöz and Wilson 1968: 120–121).

The population figure in the 1927 census is 13,648,000, of which by conservative estimates one million are literate.[3] At the next census in 1935 the population was reported as 16,157,450, and the literacy rate—according to information gathered for the census—15.58%. Thus, the literacy rate between 1927 and 1935 had more than doubled. But that rate of increase was not maintained as the "National Schools" were being abandoned, or at least, drastically scaled down. Why this effort was not further pursued when it appeared to be successful needs to be researched.[4]

CONCLUDING OBSERVATIONS

There were others besides Mustafa Kemal who were concerned about the future of the Ottoman Turks, who dreamed about educating the people and reestablishing a Turkish identity (Lewis 1968: 236–237). Discussions of these problems seemed doomed to remain strictly in the academic realm as many prominent and sophisticated Turkish intellectuals thought well into the 1920s that the creation of a new writing system was an awesome and simply impossible task. Even usually astute European observers were flatly stating as late as 1927 that Turkey was not ready to follow the example set by Azerbaijan and abandon the Arabic graphs (Rossi 1927: 310). Rossi had to admit (Rossi 1929: 32) that he had neglected to take two elements into account, the revolutionary spirit and Mustafa Kemal. The change did

---

[3] The statistics were based on the Government Institute for Statistics publication *Milli Eğitimde 50 Yıl 1923–1973*, published in 1973. According to the figures, the literacy rate for 1927 is under 8%, rather than the generally quoted 10.6% (cf. Frey 1964: 218). This is further verified by Başgöz and Wilson who write that "not much more than five percent of the total population could write in Arabic" (Başgöz and Wilson 1968: 85). According to the UNESCO Statistical Yearbook of 1982, the literacy rate for Turkey in 1975 was 60.2% among adults aged 15 or over.

[4] The National Security Council issued a directive in 1981 reviving Atatürk's literacy campaign (Flemming 1981: 149). It could not be confirmed whether the concept of "National Schools" was also restored.

come and was instituted swiftly, once the leader decided on the question and made it his own personal campaign.

At what point Mustafa Kemal's final decision was made cannot be ascertained as yet. It is well known, however, that he was familiar with different writing systems for Turkish and that he tried his hand at these, perhaps as early as 1903, in private letters (Korkmaz 1963: 34). According to the memoirs of a companion, Mazhar Müfit Kansu, Mustafa Kemal dictated to him the evening of the final day of the Erzurum Congress, August 8, 1919, a list of his plans for the country. This list included as the fifth item the adoption of the Latin alphabet, prompting the incredulous companion to chide him for being a daydreamer (Altuğ 1981: 4). For the sake of the unity of the Turkish revolution which aimed at building a modern nation anchored in Western traditions, it was inevitable that the nation's writing, reading, and thinking tool had to conform also. Mustafa Kemal obviously saw the need for a lengthy incubation period before implementing this important reform which was to change fundamentally the whole structure of Turkish society. When he thought the time had come, a veritable *Blitzkrieg* in the name of literacy took place: prior deliberation, careful planning of the moves, gauging and manipulating the general climate through use of mass media, taking advantage of opportunity presented for a dramatic start, the call on all for mobilization, and the speedy, relentless push for victory.

It was a fearless campaign, with great risk to Mustafa Kemal's personal prestige. For the successful outcome, speed was essential, not only to forestall opposition from organizing—he also believed it would facilitate acquisition of the new writing system if no chance to procrastinate were offered to the public. Thus he strongly rejected any proposal for gradual change, using both Arabic and Latin graphs at the same time, because "at the end of five years, they will still be seeking out that half column of Arabic! Either in three months, or it will never get done" (Uluğ 1973: 171).

The new alphabet itself was straightforward, remarkably sensible and simple. It had indisputable advantages that enabled speedy implementation. Teaching the uneducated became not only possible but easy as well. It proved also to be a splendidly adaptable tool that has seen only rather minor changes since its acceptance (Steuerwald 1964: 7–9). In addition, the new alphabet was uniquely Turkish: no other writing system is quite like it although many share the Latin graphs. There were charges of lack of methodology. Indeed, the literacy campaign had started before any official final version of the writing system had been worked out. Whether this was deliberate or not, it turned out to be most helpful, since this trial-and-error phase allowed for input by those for whom the system was meant, the people. Switching to the Latin alphabet was a relatively simple matter for those who were educated since most had previous exposure to European languages. Modern Turkish literature does not present the alphabet reform as a traumatic experience, and no negative currents can be directly tied to it (Flemming 1981). Nevertheless, in contemporary Western reports, the "restrictive atmosphere" under which the reform is to have taken place is stressed, and the process is called a "parlamentarisch verhüllte Diktatur'' (Duda 1929: 316). An article in the *New York Times* of September 2, 1928, reads "mankind, especially the Turk, schooled in the whims of despotic Sultans, seems adaptable enough to religious and social changes" ("Changing alphabet obsesses Kemal," section II, p. 8). There is yet no definitive study on the subject as some of the archives apparently are still closed to research. However, it seems certain that, as had been warned in the 1920s, a writing system, if forced on the people, would barely survive five months (Levend 1960: 398). The people were responsive and ready; "it did not occur to anybody to ask where the law was" (Uluğ 1973: 185). The alphabet reform was a true revolution, reflecting in the end the national will as much as Mustafa Kemal's.

REFERENCES

Alpay, Meral. 1976. Harf devriminin kütüphanelerde yansıması. Istanbul: Edebiyat Fakültesi Basımevi.
————. 1981. Yazının işlevi ve harf devrimi. Dilbilim 6.31–38.
Altuğ, Yilmaz. 1981. Atatürk ve milli eğitim. Proceedings of the International Conference on Atatürk. Istanbul: Boğaziçi University Press.
Arıkan, Zeki. 1981. Türk yazı devrimi ve İzmir basınına yansıması. Proceedings of the International Conference on Atatürk. Istanbul: Boğaziçi University Press.
Atatürk. 1945. Atatürkün söylev ve demeçleri 1. Istanbul.
————. 1952. Atatürkün söylev ve demeçleri 2. Ankara.
Başgöz, İlhan, & Wilson, Howard E. 1968. Educational Problems in Turkey 1920–1940. The Hague: Mouton.
Baysal, Jale. 1981. Turkish publishing activities before and after the new alphabet. Anatolica 8.115–131.
Bourgeois, H. 1914. La question de l'alphabet albanais. Revue du Monde Musulman 28.275–280.
————. 1913. La question de l'alphabet albanais. Revue du Monde Musulman 25. 385–403.
Cumhuriyet. 1928. July 1, August 1, August 2, August 9, September 29, November 30, December 1.
————. 1929. January 2.
Duda, Herbert W. 1929. Die neue Lateinschrift in der Türkei. Orientalische Literaturzeitung 6.441–453.
Ertop, Konur. 1963. Atatürk devriminde Türk dili. Atatürk ve Türk Dili, 53–99. Ankara: Ankara University Press.
Flemming, Barbara. 1981. Literatur im Zeichen des Alphabetwechsels. Anatolica 8.133–155.
Frey, Frederick W. 1964. Education. Political modernization in Japan and Turkey, ed. by Robert E. Ward and Dankwart A. Rustow, 205–235. Princeton: Princeton University Press.
Gilson, Erika H. in press. The Turkish grammar of Thomas Vaughan: Ottoman Turkish at the end of the XVIIth century according to an English "Transkriptionstext." Wiesbaden: Otto Harrassowitz.
Goloğlu, Mahmut. 1972. Devrimler ve tepkileri, 1924–1930. Ankara.
Heyd, Uriel. 1954. Language reform in modern Turkey. Jerusalem: Hadassah Apprentice School of Printing.
Jansky, Herbert, 1929. Die "Türkische Revolution" und der russische Islam. Der Islam 18.158–167.
Karpat, Kemal. 1964. The mass media. Political modernization in Japan and Turkey, ed. by Robert E. Ward and Dankwart A. Rustow, 255–282. Princeton: Princeton University Press.
Korkmaz, Zeynep. 1963. Türk dilinin tarihi akışı içinde Atatürk ve dil devrimi. Ankara: Ankara University Press.
Levend, Agah Sirri. 1960. Türk dilinde gelişme ve sadeleşme evreleri. 2nd ed. Ankara: Türk Tarih Kurumu Basımevi.
Lewis, Bernard. 1968. The emergence of modern Turkey. 2nd ed. New York: Oxford University Press.
Mansuroğlu, Mecdut. 1959. Das Karakhanidische. Philologiae Turcicae Fundamenta 1.87–112.

Menzel, Theodor. 1927. Der 1. Turkologische Kongress in Baku. Der Islam 16.1–76, 169–228.

New York Times. 1926. January 31.

_____. 1928. April 29, April 30, May 1, May 22, June 3, July 11, July 22, August 31, September 2, October 28, November 1, December 1.

Rossi, Ettore. 1929. Il nuovo alfabeto latino introdotto in Turchia. Oriente Moderno 9.32–48.

_____. 1927. La questione dell'alfabeto per le lingue turche. Oriente Moderno 7.295–310.

Steuerwald, Karl. 1964. Untersuchungen zur türkischen Sprache der Gegenwart II. Berlin: Langenscheidt.

Togan, Zeki Velidi. 1969. Tarihte usul. 2nd ed. Istanbul: Edebiyat Fakültesi Basımevi.

Türk Tarihi Tetkik Cemiyeti. 1931. Tarih IV: Türkiye Cümhuriyeti. Istanbul: Government Press.

Uluğ, Naşit Hakki. 1973. Üç büyük devrim. Istanbul: Baha Matbaası.

Yalman, Ahmed Emin. 1956. Turkey in my time. Norman: University of Oklahoma Press.

FOUR

Adult Literacy Campaigns in a Multilingual Country: Official vs. Indigenous Languages

Fanny M. Argüello
Pennsylvania State University

INTRODUCTION

Every multilingual country through its educational system must make decisions regarding language issues; for instance, each must choose a language for instruction. If the state recognizes one particular language as official, then this language becomes most likely the sole instructional medium, and the other languages may or may not be taught in the schools as second languages. This naturally will depend on the status assigned to them. The criteria used in such cases vary from country to country.

In countries such as those in Latin America that emerged after a long colonial period during which Spanish took hold and native languages gradually disappeared or had been reduced to only the indigenous groups' actual use, Spanish was adopted automatically as the official language when the countries drafted their first constitutions. In spite of the high level of development and the great numbers of users, native languages such as Quechua, Mayan, Nahuatl, and so on, were disregarded and, in a sense, condemned to extinction along with the other cultural elements as a logical corollary to the oppression imposed upon those peoples. Nevertheless, language—unlike culture in general which becomes subculture—does not become a sublanguage of the dominant language (Albó 1977:5). Thus, in spite of the long impoverishment process, Quechua continues to be a language of its own. Only in the last half of the twentieth century have these "oppressed languages" (Albó's terms) and their users caught the interest of intellectuals, humanists, and government planners; this, in turn, has made possible a reinterpretation of the linguistic conditions of countries where a variety of indigenous languages are spoken. Thus, Ecuador—following México and Perú—has been redefined as a multilingual country. At the First Symposium on Bilingual Education held in Quito on October 15–20, 1973, Quechua was recognized as a national language and suggestions were made to the national government for policies that would ensure the rights of all indigenous languages to survive and develop within their own linguistic dynamics. Thus, Ecuadorian officials and scholars have begun to acknowledge the multilingualism problem and have accepted the challenge to educate all Ecuadorians in order to achieve national development; but it took five years before actual language planning was done. At last an adequate nationwide program toward the eradication of illiteracy among the indigenous population is being implemented.

Nineteen hundred seventy-eight marks the beginning of a new era for the culturally pluralistic Ecuadorian nation. The new constitution which was established in force in 1977 provides civil rights to all Ecuadorians regardless of their lack of knowledge of Spanish and their illiterate status. Nevertheless, in spite of the fact that indigenous languages have been elevated to a national status, Spanish continues to be the only official language. Therefore, every citizen has to learn it in order to be able to communicate and interact within the dominant culture as a member of a national community.

The final goal of the literacy campaign in the vernacular appears not to be an assimilationist Hispanization which would imply acculturation of the indigenous peoples, but a functional bilingualism to be achieved through a national bilingual-bicultural education program.

HISTORICAL VIEW OF THE LITERACY PROGRAMS

Literacy programs are, in fact, one aspect of the national education plan; therefore, they must be considered in this context. Education policies go hand in hand with national ideologies and socioeconomic factors as seen in the successive government decrees affecting popular education in Ecuador. The type and quality of educational programs have always depended on the demand created by the economic system and the sociocultural structure of the country.

In colonial times, only the elites had access to formal education; the rest of the population was kept illiterate or had limited access to a type of trade school where, in addition to training in manual crafts, the boys were taught reading, writing, and arithmetic. Women, of course, were kept ignorant. Education was in the hands of the church and was concentrated in urban centers. The medium was Spanish.

In the middle of the sixteenth century, however, a school—Colegio de San Juan Evangelista—was created in Quito to educate the Indians (Vargas 1965).

The independence brought very little change in the field of popular education. A few government decrees favoring education of the indigenous people became inoperative because they unfavorably affected the interests of the agrarian elites and the church.

During the administration of Garcia Moreno (1860–75) in the Christian Brothers institutions, special sections were established in order to prepare teachers for the rural communities including those of the Indians (Uzcátegui 1951:15).

With the establishment of liberal regimes, the country's education was secularized and placed under the direct control of the state; it also became mandatory for all children. Normal schools were created to prepare teachers. Protestant missionaries were allowed in the country for the first time.

In 1916, the first Catholic Cathequist Congress passed a resolution to meet the educational needs of the rural communities including those of the native Ecuadorians. These projects, including the government decree of 1919, never materialized (Moya 1975:271–2).

During the 1940s, in order to spread and improve the educational programs in the rural areas, *Normales Rurales* were established to train specialized teachers in a short time to fill the demand of the several hundred newly created rural schools. At this time, the first literacy programs were launched by the legislative decree of February 15, 1945. The "Unión Nacional de Periodistas" (National Association of Journalists) undertook the project for the Highlands; the Liga de Alfabetización Ecuatoriana did likewise for the coastal area campaign. These programs lasted until 1963 when, by executive decree, Emergence Law of February 6, 1963, the Adult Education Department under the Ministry of Education, was officially created. The National Literacy Campaign continued under the direction of this department as one unified government program.

The national government and UNESCO signed an agreement to carry out a Literacy Pilot Plan which lasted from 1965 to 1969. It functioned independently from the National Literacy Campaign.

The Andean Mission (1956–1973) sponsored by UNESCO and the government, created to foster and promote the economic development of Indian communities, opened several centers for adult literacy in cooperation with local schools.

Legislative Decree No. 021 of April 10, 1967, sanctioned by Executive Decree No. 143 of October 15, 1968, reiterated the statements of the 1963 decree and mandated that every educated individual teach literacy to at least three illiterates every year. Government and private institutions were charged with the responsibility of carrying out the National Literacy Campaign whose goal was to eradicate illiteracy in the shortest time possible.

In 1973, the University of Massachusetts began a project directed to educate women.

In 1977, a new constitution was established in force and the impact of the new laws upon educational goals has been tremendous, especially for the indigenous segment of the population. The Minister of Education announced the new literacy campaign's goals and objectives and appealed for national support inviting all Ecuadorians to take aggressive action toward converting the whole country into a school where every one of those illiterate, marginalized *campesinos*— "peasants"—could learn to become active, productive citizens (Plan nacional para la educación y alfabetización de adultos 1977).

As part of the agreements with the national government, Protestant missions maintained schools and literacy programs among several groups of the Indians on the Highlands, in the coastal area, and in the jungle. On April 23, 1980, the Oficina Nacional de Educación y Alfabetización was created by Executive Decree No. 118, thus centralizing all the efforts and programs related to the National Literacy Campaign for 1980–84.

Table 4.1 Illiterate Adult Populaton, 1950–1981

Source	Total Illiterate	Urban	Rural	Male	Female
1950—1st Census	815,464 = 44%	11.9%	44.3%	37.9%	53.3%
1962—2nd Census	799,535 = 33.4%	107,742 = 11.9%	691,793 = 44.5%	337,849 = 27.9%	461,686 = 36.9%
1974—3rd Census	965,490 = 26%	162,820 = 4.5%	802,670 = 22.2%	408,949 = 11.3%	556,541 = 15.4%
1981[a]	760,310 = 16%	142,558 = 3%	617,752 = 13%	332,636 = 6%	427,674 = 9%

[a]From Poveda 1981, pp. 3–4.

FACTORS FOR THE SUCCESS OR FAILURE OF LITERACY PROGRAMS

The evaluation of any educational program must take into consideration the agreed-upon goals and objectives, and measure the progress toward their achievement within a certain period of time. Goals and objectives of adult literacy programs are in direct relationship to the perceived needs and these needs, of course, can be felt and expressd by the illiterate themselves or by others such as the government, the church, and so on. The success or failure of these objectives has to be examined in the context of other intervening factors, a task that requires sophisticated tools to produce reliable qualitative and quantitative data. However, census data and personal encounters with the Indian communities can provide clear evidence of the persistence of the illiteracy problem. In the Ecuadorian case, in spite of almost 40 years of uninterrupted literacy programs and efforts in developing rural education, the number of illiterates is appalling, as can be seen in Table 4.1.

I will consider the four principles of national commitment, popular participation, coordination, and mobilization in my analysis of the literacy campaigns (The World of Literacy n.d.: 12–13). But first I will examine goals and objectives in relation to the interpretation of the concept of literacy.

The Concept of Literacy: Goals and Objectives

The 1950 and 1962 census define as *alfabeta* ("literate") any individual capable of reading and writing a simple paragraph in any language; it establishes the age of 10 as the year a person can be considered *alfabeta* or *analfabeta* "illiterate" (Hurtado 1969:186). According to these criteria, an indigenous individual who has learned the mechanics of reading and writing in Spanish—although he or she might not be able to understand what is being read—could be considered *alfabeta*.

This concept of literacy constituted the basic criterion for determining objectives and goals of the first literacy campaigns as well as for the elementary education available in the rural areas. Consequently, rural schools and literacy centers have been producing thousands of semiliterate individuals who, in the modern concept of literacy, cannot be categorized as literate.[1] Thus the figures provided by the census data are not truly accurate. The national picture is bleaker.

Although the preamble of the government decree of 1963, which mandated the execution of a nationwide campaign, reflected the spirit of the resolution adopted at the UNESCO Conference on Literacy, the objectives of this campaign did not change in practice from those of the previous programs; they continued unaltered until the 1970s. The results of the national campaigns before 1978 have not gone beyond the acquisition of basic reading and writing skills in Spanish. The overemphasis placed upon the possession of these skills in the official language

---

[1] It has not been uncommon to find Indian students reading and writing perfectly in Spanish, doing mathematical operations with six or more digits, and answering prelearned questions, but being unable to use Spanish to express their own thoughts or to communicate even at a low level. This memorization system prevails even today. I have encountered it during my latest visits to several communities.

failed to interpret the full meaning of the definition of literacy set forward by UNESCO, which clearly states that the acquisition of skills in reading, writing, and arithmetic should enable the individual to actively and effectively participate in the group's activities in order to promote his personal as well as his community's development (Literacy as a factor in development 1965).

In the case of the indigenous Ecuadorians, such goals can be reached only when the members of the community become capable of critically examining and evaluating their own culture and the surrounding Hispanic culture; only then may real development take place without endangering the survival of their native culture.

Unfortunately for the government and socioeconomic elites, literacy objectives were designed to develop human resources to a level of high productivity. Thus literacy has become a tool of control and a means to develop the economic system (Kozol 1980:55). Semiliterate masses can be manipulated for the realization of a dominant group's self-interests.

The few literacy programs carried out by several Protestant missions had one common goal: to enable the individual to read the Scriptures. Because of government requirements, as part of the agreements, missions had to establish schools in unpenetrated areas where the only inhabitants were native Indians.

Although these schools were for children, young adults were admitted also. In several locations, real adult literacy programs were carried out. The Church of the Brethren and the United Andean Mission achieved moderate success in their literacy programs of Calderón, Picalquí, and so on, perhaps because theirs were integrated into a complete socioeconomic development program for the Indian communities. The measure of their success, naturally, is linked to the growth of their congregations.

The more successful literacy programs have been those carried out by the Summer Institute of Linguistics (SIL) among the peoples of the jungle. Their main objective of translating the Scriptures into the native languages made it necessary to teach the Indians to read and write in their own language. In order to comply with the stipulations of the agreements made with the national government, they had to teach Spanish in their schools, thus creating the first bilingual programs.

Parallel to the Protestant efforts—actually on their footsteps—the Catholic Church has implemented educational programs in some Indian communities, but these have been mainly for children. However, a unique program directed to the adult Indian population in the Highlands has been established through radio. In the last five years, literacy programs using the radio have been implemented by the Salesian Mission for the Shuar people and by the Diocese of Riobamba for the Quechua speakers.

As we have seen thus far, objectives and goals of the adult literacy campaigns have been set up by the government and by religious institutions. It can be said that they have attained some success in reaching their goals. The Protestant churches have many more members among Indo-Ecuadorians than Hispano-Ecuadorians, and the government can claim credit for the decreasing illiteracy rates from 44% in 1950 to 16% in 1981. Contributing factors for this success are the involvement and support of the national government through its institutions, military and civilian, and private institutions and organizations.

National Commitment

The Ecuadorian government's concern for the eradication of illiteracy has been manifested in many ways: through declarations, decrees, and emergency laws. It has, as we have seen above, a long history. This involvement has grown stronger with every new campaign. In the 1940s, the government endorsed the campaigns but did not participate actively. In 1963, by creating a department under the Ministry of Education, the active participation of government began. Literacy was made compulsory for all adults between the ages of 15 and 50, and the cooperation of all national and local government agencies, public and private institutions, and organizations was made mandatory. In addition, budget appropriations were made, and specific means to acquire the necessary funds were established.

The 1967 campaign was officially inaugurated with an Executive Decree which mandated national involvement, invoking the principle that literacy is not only a right for all people, but it is an obligation of all literate societies to offer equal education opportunities for all their members so they can participate in socioeconomic, cultural, and political affairs. A five-year goal was set to achieve total literacy with the participation of all the Ecuadorian people. Anyone with a high school level of education had the obligation to teach literacy to three persons, and failure to comply with this law carried a 30 *sucres* fine. High school as well as university graduates would not receive their diplomas unless they had complied with this mandate.

The 1977 campaign began with a powerful manifesto from the Minister of Education in which he summarized the causes of illiteracy in Ecuador, and outlined the goals and objectives of the program. The new approach for the achievement of literacy is the concept that literacy is not an end in itself, but a means, an instrument of modernization which will help those marginalized individuals to better themselves. By becoming literate, the individual will acquire confidence in himself and his capacity; this, in turn, will help him regain his human dignity and develop a critical consciousness capable of assessing reality objectively and becoming responsible for his own future. The manifesto calls for all government agencies and private institutions to work together and transform the whole country into a *gran escuela*—"great school."[2]

The government's commitment has been evident although it has not always brought success. Some goals and provisions, unfortunately, have been unrealistic and, therefore, ineffective. For instance, the five-year goal set in 1967 could not be achieved because funds were insufficient. The Adult Education Department was unable to organize the campaign adequately for lack of qualified personnel, and the government agencies could not implement a law which affected a great number of

---

[2] The entire text of the Minister of Education's speech appeared in a special supplement published with the newspaper *El Comercio*, Quito, October 10, 1977.

citizens and institutions without an increase in the bureaucracy. In short, the government plans have been overly ambitious. They have not been able to achieve national will which has made the campaigns in Cuba, Brazil, and other places so successful (The World of Literacy 1977: 12).

Popular Participation

The participation of the target population is the missing principle in most of the campaigns in Ecuador. The urban population, for the most part, would be able to see the advantages of becoming literate, and this would motivate them to attend literacy centers, but the people in rural areas would find it more difficult to see the need to learn to read and write. For the Indian population—with a 70% rate of illiteracy (the highest in the country)—which has learned to live with all kinds of deprivations, discrimination, and exploitation, literacy campaigns are viewed as another attempt of the oppressive class to control them and to invade the privacy of their isolated lives. They have many times violently rejected government-imposed programs. However, a number of literacy programs have been initiated at the people's request. Some of these programs were run by Protestant missionaries who have been successful in convincing the Indians to accept a new way of life in which literacy can enhance their potential for success and spiritual enrichment (Muratorio 1983:520–25). Some of the programs of the Andean Mission were also implemented because the people wanted them.

In general, the literacy programs, as well as rural elementary education, have been designed without consideration of local conditions, the needs, and the cultural and social patterns of the target people; therefore, the programs could not be considered relevant or useful to them.

Coordination

The creation of the Oficina Nacional de Educación y Alfabetización represents the latest attempt to bring all the efforts from different ministries, institutions, and organizations under one centralized leadership in order to better coordinate the programs affecting the illiterate. For many years, this lack of coordination has caused a waste of funds and resources. There has been duplication of programs in the same community which caused confusion among the people. Sometimes, real rifts in the community were caused by rivalries started at different educational centers.[3]

Mobilization

Under the principle of mobilization, training of personnel, preparation of curricula and materials, and public support are examined.

---

[3] The traditional opposition of the Catholic church to any Protestant infiltration has caused certain Indian communities to have two schools, two literacy programs, and sometimes three or four, if the government happened to select that same community for an experimental program. The number in itself is not detrimental, but the fact they are in competition with each other is.

The training of teachers for the specified job of teaching literacy has been neither systematic nor adequate. Most of the instructors are elementary school teachers; other volunteers are required to undergo some training in workshops organized by the Department of Adult Education. The teachers working in Protestant organizations usually get training at the Alfalit centers. However, many times regular school teachers are charged with the responsibility of literacy classes without any additional training, but this does not constitute a crucial difficulty in the teaching itself. The real problem emerges from the lack of understanding of a different culture and from the inability to speak the indigenous language.

The materials used for the first two campaigns were those created by Frank Laubach. These syllable-based materials proved to be very efficient for teaching reading skills in Spanish and, with a few limitations, the method worked also for the Ecuadorian Quechua.[4] The very much needed follow-up materials by Laubach were scarce or nonexistent. Many of the texts used, even now, are filled with irrelevant materials. They do not reflect the reality of certain sectors of the population, and the language does not reflect the people's own dialect because they are written in a restricted code. The most recent texts have been improved but not enough to be really efficient. The three texts in Spanish published in 1982 show gradation in grammatical difficulties, but the vocabulary and themes are not always appropriate; for instance, the last of the three first readings of book one is an essay on the Rio de Janeiro treaty written in an eloquent manner and with elegant words. The newly literate are expected to become readers of regular newspapers, books, and the Bible. Very few succeed, and the rest may relapse and become content with being able to sign their names and be able to vote in national elections and thus avoid fines. The problem of diglossia has not yet been acknowledged, and neither has the existence of regional varieties. The fact that the great majority of the illiterate do not speak Spanish had just been acknowledged for the 1978 literacy campaign.

MOTHER TONGUE VS. OFFICIAL LANGUAGE

The Ecuadorian Constitution of 1945 explicitly specifies that Quechua or the indigenous language of the people must be used in addition to Castellano (Sec. 3, Art. 143). It has never materialized. However, an attempt was made then to fulfill this law by creating the *Normales Rurales* to train teachers specialized in rural education.

The curriculum in these schools required Quechua as the second language as well as a personal acquaintance with the Indian culture and communities. Most of the students were from small towns, although a few came from cities and from the mid-

---

[4] After I had demonstrated to the parents of my students the advantages of using Quechua in teaching, a group of mothers and several of the fathers who were illiterate asked me to teach them to read and write in their language. I adopted the Laubach materials to create my own charts and began my literacy classes. For follow-up materials, Biblical translations and songs and short stories written by the regular school students were used.

dle class. Unfortunately, a few years later these schools were, supposedly, up-graded and in the process they lost their original purpose. English was substituted for Quechua. Only a handful of those who graduated from those schools, such as myself, had the opportunity to work for Indian communities, at least for a short time.

The Educational Development Plan for 1973–77 expresses the government's concern for the illiterate indigenous population and outlines the efforts to be made in order to place education within the reach of those marginalized peoples, but nothing is said about the use of the mother tongue as an effective vehicle of instruction (Burneo 1982:79).

Among the recommendations offered to the government in the resolution taken at the First Bilingual Education Seminar 1973 were the officialization of vernacular languages and the use of vernacular at all levels of the education of the indigenous population (Burneo (1982:79–82). At least one of these recommendations has become a reality. Vernacular languages, along with Spanish, are indeed the media of the current literacy campaign.

It was evident during a panel discussion about development and socioeconomic change in Ecuador (1977) that the problem of implementing an educational program that would effectively promote the country's development, the needed changes in the social structure, and cultural enrichment while preserving the national cultural authenticity had made an impact on scholars and educated elites. The universities were ready to cooperate with the Ministry of Education in order to achieve the goals and objectives outlined by the latter which were in accord with the rights granted by the new Constitution, Title 2: Sec. 3: Art. 26–27, Chap. 2: e, and Chap. 15: art. 60.

The fact has finally been accepted that the mother tongue is the best medium of instruction since cultural values are better understood and explained in the indigenous language, and that any language can be used as a vehicle of modern civilization. Therefore, to achieve functional literacy, the mother tongue must be used first. Later, the official language should be introduced as a second language.

Since dialogue is the best way to reach the individual, his own particular spoken language has to be used, and this could mean a dialect of Spanish, or of Quechua, or a different indigenous language.

THE CAMPAIGN IN VERNACULAR LANGUAGES

In 1977, after several preliminary sessions, a committee of three members (an Indo-Ecuadorian, a Hispano-Ecuadorian, and a French specialist in adult education) was formed. This team worked out a plan for a literacy campaign in Quechua and Shuar. Dr. Tarlé became the official consultant of the National Literacy Campaign. Later, two agreements were signed (on January 31, 1978) between Pontificia Universidad Católico del Ecuador (PUCE) and the national government and PUCE and the University of Paris V on October 22, 1979.

The team was increased to nine members representing various regions and fields of specialization, thus taking into consideration a whole range of indigenous groups in order to determine particular needs as the team designed the program. It included three stages: Alfabetization, Post-alfabetization, and Introduction to Spanish. The first and second stages would be carried out completely in Quechua and Shuar, and the materials would be designed to give positive reinforcement to their cultural values, including their language, in order to build up their faith and confidence in themselves. Then, they would guide the new readers into a knowledge of modern civilization in the fields of health, laws of the country, agriculture, and so on. The third stage would be implemented only after the first two had been successfully accomplished and when the people were ready for a dialogue and interaction with the dominant culture without the danger of being lured into an ethnocide in the name of progress.

Status of the Vernacular Languages

There are more than 10 indigenous languages in Ecuador as can be seen in Table 4.2. Thanks to SIL efforts, all of them have been analyzed and put into a written code. Quechua, of course, was first written in 1585, and Shuar in this century. Quechua is the most widely spread, and it is also spoken in Bolivia, Perú, and parts of Argentina and Colombia which were originally part of the Inca Empire.

When the Catholic Church and the Spanish Crown decided to use Quechua as the medium of Christianization of all Ecuadorian Indians, many of whom did not speak Quechua at that time, the first grammar and vocabulary were written. The Spanish alphabet was used, and the Latin grammar was the model for describing the Quechua syntactic and morphological structures. Those first Quechua grammarians were pleased with and amazed by the degree of development of this Indian language in which they could express the most high spiritual concepts. Many Quechua grammars and dictionaries have been written and, depending on the authors' linguistic backgrounds, different graphemes have been used to symbolize its phonemes and allophones.

Table 4.2   Languages of Ecuador

Languages		Main Varieties	No. of Speakers[a]	Location
Spanish	(Official)	4 Regional	6,000,000	All over the country
Quechua		2 Regional	2,047,000	Highlands Jungle
	Shuar	2 Regional	40,000	Southern Jungle
Jivaroa				
	Achuar	1 Regional	2,500	Southern Jungle
Cofan		1 Regional	600	Northern Jungle
	Cayapa	1 Regional	4,000	Northern Coast Forest
Barbacoa	Colorado	1 Regional	1,600	Northern Coast Forest
	Coaiguer	1 Regional	600	Northern Coast Forest
Záparo				Jungle
Huaoroni			700	Northern Jungle
	Secoya-Siona		600	Northern Jungle
Tucano				
	Tetete	1 Regional	2	Northern Jungle

[a]These numbers are only estimated figures taken from a Summer Institute of Linguistics (SIL) map (Mapa étnico del Ecuador 1977).

After 400 years of contact with Spanish, borrowing has occurred and, because of the nature of the relationship between the two societies which has been characterized as dominant vs. dominated, the indigenous language has been slowly losing ground. Nevertheless, Quechua is now a language of its own; there is, however, an intermediate variety in which the syntactic elements of Quechua and Spanish morphemes have been integrated. This variety is spoken mainly by young adults and children, but it is despised by older adults and by those who have become Spanish speakers.

Quechua has regional varieties, which coincide with the Spanish varieties in some of the phonetic features, such as the realizations of the palatal lateral phonemes, but the major differences are found between the Highlands varieties and those of the jungle.

Shuar also has several varieties that belonged to two antagonistic groups, but since they have made peace and there is more interaction between them, differences can be systematically worked out.

The planners of the campaign have taken into consideration the linguistic as well as the sociocultural factors for the preparation of materials. Research, testing, and constant revision of materials and of teaching methods and techniques are the backbone basis of the literacy program. The CIEI, Centro de Investigación para la Educación Indígena, has become the language planning agency where decisions concerning the indigenous languages are being made.

Developing the Vernaculars

As indicated, all the vernacular languages have at least been reduced to graphization, and written materials in these languages are available. Quechua presented a problem because there were conflicting orthographic systems applied to this language. Therefore, finding an adequate system was the first task for the planners. Bolivia and Perú had already adopted a standard system for their varieties. However, that system was not appropriate for the Ecuadorian varieties. The team initially adopted a unique system which they said was in accord with certain cultural characteristics of the Indo-Ecuadorian Quechua speakers. One of the proposed innovations was the use of only one grapheme to represent all the homorganic phonemes: for example *i* would represent /i, y, j/, *w* would represent /u, w, U/. Thus [yaya] would be written *iaia,* and [wawa] would be *uaua* (Yanes Cossio 1980: 23–24).

Apparently these suggestions did not work and they were abandoned in favor of the more commonly used system, the one which is closest to the Spanish orthography. Thus [yaya] → *yaya* and [wawa] → *huahua*. There are definite advantages in adopting this system, the most important being economy, since one system will be adequate for both languages; this, in turn, will facilitate the transition from Quechua to Spanish. The two phonological systems are similar enough for this to be possible; the differences can be worked out by using conventional diacritics and other linguistic devices.

Planners also directed their efforts to the need for modernization. This implied the search for a process to expand the lexicon of the language with new words and expressions in order to handle new topics. A great emphasis has been placed on bringing back words that have fallen out of use and on combining Quechua morphemes to create new, but authentic, words. The last resort will be to use a loan word from Spanish. This zeal for authenticity has been carried a little bit too far at times, when a long cumbersome phrase is preferred to name something that could have been easily said with a Spanish loan word, such as *gobernador* instead of *markapak jatun apuk*.

Because of ecological differences between the habitat of the Highlands and the jungle Quechua speakers, each group has developed deep cultural differences. Therefore, the planners decided to use two linguistic varieties and not attempt to standardize Quechua any further for now. Materials are being prepared in both dialects. Materials for literacy are also now available in the Shuar and Cachi languages.

As the campaign progresses, new materials are being developed at the CIEI. The first experimental texts introducing Spanish as a second language are being tested now. The challenge of developing an instrument for the implementation of bilingual, bicultural education is now a reality. These materials, which will serve as models for those to be prepared for the regular school programs, are pedagogically organized to address those areas in which linguistic interference is anticipated.

CONCLUSIONS

The almost 40-year-old effort to achieve total literacy in Ecuador has been dominated by traditional, old methods of personal instruction in Spanish, the official language, thus perpetuating discriminatory practices against the indigenous peoples who did not speak Spanish. The narrowly conceived goals of literacy failed to achieve a real economic and sociocultural development of the people.

Well-intentioned efforts of the national government to aid the native peoples have failed because, in planning, the Hispano-Ecuadorians did not take into consideration the real needs and the cultural and social structures of the indigenous groups. Literacy programs imposed on the Indians were not integrated with other developmental programs.

The policy of Hispanization aimed at total assimilation of a few and isolation and exploitation of the masses who could not or would not abandon their inferior culture is not a workable solution. Linguistic and cultural isolation from the dominant society means psychological and social security for the deprived Indian.

If true integration of the indigenous people into the national society is to be accomplished, it has to be done after the pride, dignity, and confidence of the Indian people are restored to them and when the rest of us accept and respect their ethnicity. And I believe this process finally began when, in 1978, the national government and the PUCE signed the agreement to initiate the literacy campaign in

54   LANGUAGES IN NATIONAL POLICY MAKING

vernacular languages. Much has been accomplished already. The number of illiterate people has dropped to 9.56% in 1983, and the educational process of all the Ecuadorians (Hispanic, Quechua, Shuar, Cayapa, and so on) is moving on. There are many problems yet to be solved, but now it is not the government's coercive policies, but the people's will that is committed to achieve true literacy in which people, not as recipients but as knowing subjects, achieve a deepening awareness both of the sociocultural reality which shapes their lives and of their capacity to transform that reality (Freire 1970:452).

REFERENCES

Albó, Xavier. 1977. El futuro de los idiomas oprimidos en los Andes. 2nd ed. LaPaz, Bolivia: Centro de Investigación y Promoción del Campesinado.
Almeida, Jose. 1983. Política educativa y etnicidad, ed. Ecuador Debate, 2. 83–97. Quito: Centro de Arte y Acción Popular (CAAP).
Anderson, Darrel, & Niemi, John A. 1970. Adult education and the disadvantaged adult. Syracuse University Publications in Continuing Education and ERIC Clearing House on Adult Education.
Bataille, Leon. 1976. A turning point for literacy. Proceedings of the International Symposium for Literacy. Persipolis, Iran, 1975. Oxford: Pergamon Press Ltd.
Bernstein, Basil. 1973. Class, codes and control. Vol. 2: Empirical studies. London: Routledge and Kegan Paul.
Burneo Jaramillo, Cesar Agusto. 1982. El reto de la educación primaria para las comunidades quechua-hablantes de la Sierra Ecuatoriana. Loja, Ecuador: Universidad Nacional de Loja.
Cardinal, Harold. 1969. The unjust society. Edmonton: M. G. Hurting Ltd.
Charnley, A. H., & Jones, H. A. 1979. The concept of success in adult literacy. Cambridge: Huntington Press.
Coloma, Carlos. 1982. Hacia una política de investigación—La experiencia en el CIEI. Revista de la Universidad Católica 10, No. 34. 59–69.
Constitución Política de la República del Ecuador. 1964. Quito: Imprenta del Gobierno.
Decreto Legislativo No. 021. Registro oficial No. 202. 31 de agosto de 1967.
Decreto Ley de Emergencia No. 07. Registro oficial No. 377. 8 de febrero de 1963.
Desarrollo y cambio social en el Ecuador. 1979. Quito: Centro Andino de Estudios e Investigación.
Ecuador 1971. Ministerio de Educación Pública: Plan ecuatoriano de educación 1973–77. Quito: Editorial del Ministerio de Educación.
Escobar, Alberto. 1972. Lenguaje y discriminación social en América Latina. Lima: Colección el Ande y la Vida.
Fishman, Joshua, Charles A. Ferguson, and Jyotirindra Das Gupta (eds.) 1968. Language problems of developing nations. New York: John Wiley and Sons.
Freire, Paolo. 1970. Cultural action and conscientization. Harvard Educational Review 40 (3). 452–477.
Gumperz, John J. 1972. The communicative competence of bilinguals: Some hypotheses and suggestions for research. Language in Society 1. 143–54.
Haidar, Julieta. 1979. Problema en torno a la forma estándar del quichua ecuatoriano. Lengua y Cultura, 251–342. Otavalo: Instituto de Antropología.
Hurtado, Oswaldo. 1969. Dos mundos superpuestos: Ensayo de diagnóstico de la realidad ecuatoriana. Quito: Offsetec.
Kozol, Jonathan. 1980. Prisoners of silence. New York: The Continuum Publishing Corporation.
Laubach, Frank C., & Robert S. 1960. Toward world literacy: The each one teach one way. Syracuse: Syracuse University Press.
Literacy as a factor in development. 1965. Paris: UNESCO.
Mancias Chaves, Jorge. 1962. Estudio de elevación socio-cultural del indio. Friburgo: Frese.

Mapa étnico del Ecuador. 1977. Quito: Instituto Lingüístico de Verano.

Martin, D'arcy. 1971. Pedogogía y política: La educación de adultos en América Latina. Convergence 4 (1). 54–60.

Miño-Garcés, Fernando. 1982. Producción de materiales educativos para el programa de alfabetización y educación infantil en lenguas vernáculas. Revista de la Universidad Católica 10 (34). 71–85.

Montaluisa, Luis. 1980. El vocabulario general de la lengua quichua para el Ecuador. Revista de la Universidad Católica 8 (25). 99–115.

Moya, Ruth. 1975. Panorama histórico de la situación del bilingüismo y de la educación nacional. Proceedings of the First Inter-American Conference on Bilingual Education, ed. by R. C. Troike and N. Modiano, 265–83. Arlington, Va.: Center for Applied Linguistics.

_____ . 1980. Lineamientos para una política nacional de educación bilingüe. Revista de la Universidad Católica 8 (25). 69–85.

Muratorio, Blanca. 1983. Protestantism, ethnicity, and class in Chimborazo. Cultural transformations and ethnicity in modern Ecuador, ed. by Norman E. Whitten, Jr., 506–34. Urbana: University of Illinois Press.

Niemi, John A. 1974. Cross-cultural communication and the adult educator. Literacy Discussion 5 (4), 545–58.

Plan nacional de alfabetización de adultos. 1964. Quito: CCE. Ministerio de Educación.

Plan nacional para la educación y alfabetización de adultos. (10 de octubre de 1977). El Comercio: Sección especial. Quito.

Poveda, Carlos. 1981. Alfabetización: Manual de orientación, No. 1. Quito: Ministerio de Educación y Cultura.

_____ . 1983. El Programa nacional de alfabetización. Ecuador Debate, 2. 123–57. Quito: Centro de Arte y Acción Popular (CAAP).

Primer censo de población del Ecuador, 1950. (1960). Quito: Ministerio de Economía.

Salazar, Ernesto. 1983. The Federación Shuar and the colonization frontier in cultural transformations and ethnicity in modern Ecuador, ed. by Norman E. Whitten, Jr., 589–613. Urbana: University of Illinois Press.

Sanchez Pargo, José. 1983. Estado y alfabetización. Ecuador Debate 2. 59–72. Quito: Centro de Arte y Acción Popular (CAAP).

Segundo censo nacional de población y primer censo de vivienda. Vol. 1. 1962. Quito: Junta de Planificación.

Stutzman, Ronald. 1983. El Mestizaje: An all-inclusive ideology of exclusion, in cultural transformations and ethnicity in modern Ecuador, ed. by Norman E. Whitten, Jr., 45–94. Urbana: University of Illinois Press.

Tarlé, Gabriel. 1980. Función de las corecciones en la elaboración del material de alfabetización. Revista de la Universidad Católica 8, (25). 31–40.

Taylor, Anne Christine. 1983. God-wealtlh: The Achuar and the missions, in Cultural transformations and ethnicity in modern Ecuador, ed. by Norman E. Whitten, Jr., 647–76. Urbana: University of Illinois Press.

The world of literacy: Policy, research and action. (1977) Canada: International Council for Adult Education.

Uzcátegui, Emilio. 1951. L'obligation scolaire en Equateur. Col. Etudes sur la scolarité obligatoire, VII. UNESCO.

Vargas, José María. 1965. Historia de la cultura ecuatoriana. Quito: Casa de la Cultura Ecuatoriana.

Verner, Coolie. 1974. Factors in learning to read and write. Literacy Discussion 4 (4). 583–96.

Yanes Cossio, Consuelo. 1980. Sistema ortográfico para la alfabetización en la lengua quichua. Revista de la Universidad Católica 8 (25). 17–29.

_____ . 1982. Esquema del modelo de post-alfabetización. Revista de la Universidad Católica 10 (34). 49–57.

FIVE

ARABIC LANGUAGE ACADEMIES AS LANGUAGE PLANNERS*

Mohammed Sawaie
University of Virginia

INTRODUCTION

The purpose of this paper is to examine the role of the Arabic language academies in their attempts to engineer new developments in the Arabic lexicon. It focuses on the efforts of the academies to canonize ways for coining new terminologies pertaining to the scientific fields and technological advancements in the twentieth century. Additionally, it discusses (a) the extent to which these academies have been successful in their efforts, and (b) the reasons these academies fall short of their goals. This paper will explore the efficacy of these academies regarding their attempts at homogenizing the linguistic situation in a vast and linguistically diverse area.

THE ARABIC LANGUAGE ACADEMIES

At present there are four language academies in the Arabic-speaking world; namely the Arab Academy of Damascus (established in 1919), the Arabic Language Academy in Cairo (established in 1932), the Iraqi Academy (established in 1947), and the Arabic Language Academy of Jordan (established in 1976). In addition to these officially recognized and sanctioned institutions, we find in other Arab countries both governmental and nongovernmental agencies[1] whose main task is to Arabize and disseminate terminologies suitable for the modern society. It is worth mentioning that such committees were the forerunners of the existing academies in the Arab world.[2]

---

*Many thanks are due to Professor Arne A. Ambros, for useful comments that arrived as this chapter was going to press.

[1] Examples of these abound, as the Committee of Arabization in Tunis, the Sudan, Algeria. An office to coordinate Arabization in the Arab world has been set up in Rabat, Morocco. Periodic conferences are held for these committees, language academies, and other organizations. The first conference was held in Rabat in 1961, the second in Algiers in 1973, and the third in Tripoli, Libya, 1977.

[2] An example of this is the Arabic Language Academy of Jordan which developed into its current status from the Jordanian Committee for Arabization, Translation and Publishing, which was founded in 1961. A similar situation is true of the Egyptian academy. See Chejne, p. 104.

The Rationale for the Academies

Despite the gap in time between the establishment of the academies in Damascus (1919) and in Jordan (1976), the four academies share some common goals. Chief among these are the preservation of the Arabic language, its development to meet the needs of modern society in all domains of human knowledge, and the creation and standardization of scientific terms (Khalifa 1977). Other goals include the Arabization of terms from European languages, the revival of Arabic manuscripts, making an Arabic dictionary that provides information on the etymology of words and illustrates semantic shifts. Additionally, the academies express interest in scientific study of modern Arabic dialects (Madkur 1964:10–11; 122, 128, 139, 144).

In order to understand the insistence of at least two of these academies on the preservation of Arabic and on making it self-sufficient to meet the scientific and humanistic needs of modern day society, it is necessary to examine the sociopolitical and educational atmosphere in Syria and Egypt during the late nineteenth, and the early twentieth centuries. Syria during those periods went directly from being a part of the Ottoman Empire to being a French mandated territory. With the ascendancy of Turkish nationalism, Arabic was deemed a secondary language as Turkish became the language of instruction in Ottoman institutions. Later, when the French won a mandate over Syria, they, in turn, tried to impose French as the language of instruction at the expense of Arabic.

Egypt had an experience similar to that of Syria during the Ottoman rule, then during a short Napoleonic occupation and later during British domination. The language of instruction in elementary and secondary schools was English. There were also deliberate efforts to adopt colloquial Egyptian rather than classical Arabic as the language of science, journalism, and theatre (Madkur 1964:14). The imposition of foreign languages and calls for the adoption of colloquials to replace classical Arabic prompted the establishment of reform committees to examine the linguistic situation in Syria and Egypt, and to explore ways of remedying the linguistic deficiencies that Arabic demonstrated. The result was a demand for institutions similar to those established by the French and other Europeans, for the purpose of setting up linguistic academies concerned with preserving classical Arabic as a symbol for national and cultural unity among all Arabs.

The contact with the West in the nineteenth and the twentieth centuries revealed to the Arabs the wide disparity between the scientifically advanced West and their own less developed countries. This situation of backwardness was attributed mainly to a paucity of schools. Consequently, efforts concentrated on upgrading the few existing educational institutions, establishing new ones, and dispatching scholars to Western capitals to acquire the necessary sciences and technologies that would lead to the advancement of the Arab societies. (For detailed discussion of this, see Chejne 1969: Chapter 5.) The result of all this was a reaffirmation to the Arab countries of, among other things, the need for the necessary scientific and technical vocabulary in the Arabic language to express new ideas, entities, concepts, and so on.

Lexical Expansion

The encounter of the Arabic-speaking East and the European West made it imperative for Arabic to adopt new words for the newly acquired concepts and perspectives. As a result, a large number of words entered Arabic either in their original
forms, or through modified forms (i.e., by the substitution of Arabic equivalent)
taken from the literature, or through the coinage of Arabic words patterned according to the rules of Arabic morphology. This expansion in the lexical component was
mainly undertaken on the initiative of individuals, and hence it was ungoverned by
established principles, which rendered the results complicated and confusing.

The situation above is comparable to the situation that Arabic faced in the ninth
and early part of the tenth centuries when translation from Greek, either directly or
via Syriac, into Arabic was at its zenith. At that time, the predicament of coining
new words was solved by one of four methods. Each of these methods had its advocates and opponents; those concerned argued the pros and cons of using these methods and their merit in preserving the purity of Arabic, while trying to enrich it by
added lexicon. These four methods have been revived as possible ways of solving
the dilemma that Arabic was facing in the nineteenth and twentieth centuries.
Discussion of the three most important of these methods is in order.

Arabization (ta'rib).   This method simply means the assimilation or the adaptation of foreign words to the Arabic language patterns. There have been divided
views regarding this method of coining words. Some opposed Arabization on the
grounds that it would result in an overflow of foreign words that might change the
character of the language and consequently compromise its purity and integrity. For
example, in a modern context, the Arabic word *hātif* "telephone" is preferred instead of *telifōn* "telephone"; for "bank," the Arab word *maSraf*, and so on. Others
favored the use of foreign words in their original forms, arguing that this method
surely guaranteed and preserved the intended meaning. Additionally, they argued,
Arabic had tolerated foreign words in the past.[3] Finally, a third group offered a compromise solution by accepting foreign words as a last resort, after efforts had been
made to find their Arabic equivalents by using any of the other methods. The
academies of Damascus, Cairo, Baghdad, and Jordan have tended to adhere to this
view. Efforts at coining new terminologies have been the concern of individuals and
the academies. At times, the academies designate a specific task to groups of specialists in charge of coining terminologies in special areas of human knowledge,
such as agriculture and botany. The results of these commissioned tasks are published either in the journals of these academies or special pamphlets and mono-
graphs that these academies produce. Academies sometimes first publish their lists
of words, then request suggestions and reactions from the specialized readership.
Individual scholars not commissioned by the academy often still contribute to the

---

[3] For detailed discussion of how some leaders view the process of Arabization, see Chejne 1969, pp.
151–157, especially that of Al-Maghribi's. For a detailed historical study of ta'rīb, see Stetkevych 1970,
Chapter 3.

journals of these academies.[4] These efforts by individuals and academies have intensified in recent years, and efforts have covered words for nearly every sphere of human knowledge.

Analogical Derivation (*al-qiyās*). This method is used in the formation of words according to existing word patterns in the language. The Arabic language academies have widely encouraged this method as a means of expanding the Arabic lexicon and of enriching the language with new terminologies. The academies have sanctioned this method for the formation of nouns from verbs, and vice versa, and particularly for the adaptation of loan words to Arabic morphological principles. Historically, derivation from an existing root has been considered the most natural way for the language to increase its vocabulary. Arab writers and philologists pride themselves on this mechanism in the language because it enables one to derive words extensively from triconsonantal roots, whether real or hypothetical. It is a well attested fact that this method of word formation greatly enriched Arabic in the formative period of Arabic-Moslem civilization.

The Arabic language academies saw in this method of deriving new words from existing roots a powerful mechanism for enriching the language. Expressed differently, the academies consider *qiyās* a dynamic, formative mechanism which could create much-needed lexical items. Stetkevych (1970) illustrates this formative mechanism by citing the case of an amateur linguist, an engineer by profession, who offered a list of 196 lexical items, verbs and nouns, all derived from the root *Sahara* "to melt," applied to metallurgy alone. All of these items possess well-defined and usable meanings.

The analogical derivation method employs linguistic molds as the organizing principle. These molds extend themselves to verbs, nouns, active and passive participial forms, and verbal nouns. All newly coined words are to obey the morphological structure of these molds. The academy in Cairo approved in the mid-1930s a mold like *fiᶜālah* where the first, second, and third consonants are the three consonantal variables of triconsonantal verbs. This pattern denotes profession such as *Tibāᶜah* "printing," and *jirāHah* "surgery." Many nominal molds were the source of long debates, sanctions, rulings, and changing of these rulings. Thus the three molds *mifᶜal, mifᶜāl,* and *mifᶜalah* underwent lengthy discussions regarding whether to permit the analogical formation method to apply. Views among the Cairo academy members differed about this issue, with some supporting the application of new molds in the formation of nouns from transitive or intransitive, sound or defective verbs, while others were opposed to this stand. (For a detailed discussion of this, see Stetkevych 1970: 16, including footnotes 39–41.) These molds, despite all the controversy around them, have been widely used to coin new terminologies, especially in light of their precise inherent meaning. Examples of

---

[4] See the journals of these academies for various contributions from different scholars in specialized fields as early as the 1930s. J. Saliba, for example, has dedicated his work to the coining of philosophical terms.

new coinages according to these molds are *mijhar* "microscope," *miS^cad* "elevator," and so on.

Despite coinages for newly introduced entities or concepts, many coined words suggested by the academies did not meet with acceptance by the populace, and molds eluded such strict application. Consequently, academy members—as well as individuals concerned with coining new vocabulary—agreed to adopt the following three principles: First, emphasis must be put on the use of existing roots in the formation of new terminologies. Thus, *mijhar* "microscope" is a regular derivation from the existing verb *jahara*, one of whose meanings pertains to "bringing something to light." Second, older meanings of words in the language could be semantically extended to denote new concepts or situations, or archaic vocabulary could be revived to represent new meanings. The word *qiTār*, for example, at one time denoted a file of camels in tow as in a caravan. When trains were introduced to the Arabic-speaking world, through semantic extension, this word was adopted to signify "a train." Third, in case the other two principles cannot be met, descriptive paraphrasis, or translation of foreign terms, could be used in the derivation of new terminology. Thus "a jet airplane" expressed by *Tā?irah naffāthah* literally means "a plane that spews." This third principle, recognized by both academies as well as individual neologizers, contributed large numbers of compound words to Arabic. The reason for this could be attributed to the massive translation movement as well as to widespread journalism in Arabic-speaking countries. Many of these terms were direct translations from European languages, such as *al-jam^ciyyah at-tashrī^ciyyah* "legislative council or assembly." Many of these composites have other variants or failed to acquire sufficient currency. The result of multiplicity of terms, of course, can be the lack of the desirable semantic exactness.

The Arabic verbal system follows a rigorous scale of so-called derived forms that inherently have semantic connotations. Thus, the transitive Form I verb *jama^ca* "to gather" is related to the intransitive Form V *tajamma^ca* "to assemble," and to the intransitive Form VIII *?ijtama^ca* "to meet." In modern Arabic, formation of new molds for verbal forms is almost nonexistent. As a result, coining of verbal elements is done by (a) semantic extension, such as *SallaTa* "to charge with electric current," which relates to a classical meaning of power, or by (b) derivation from concrete nouns that have become accepted in the language such as *talfaza* "to televise," from the newly-accepted term *tilfāz* or *tilfizyawn* "television." This new verb is derived according to a quadriliteral mold that already is a part of the language's verbal patterns.

Two observations must be made regarding derived verbal forms. The first pertains to the attitudes of the language academies regarding the analogical approach to verbal derivation in Arabic. It is noteworthy that no substantial attempt was made by the academies to contribute actively to verbal neologism. Secondly, there was quite an impact of semantic extension on the classical verbal lexicon. This process resulted in a greater tendency toward abstraction because of the attempts to broaden the meanings of classical Arabic verbs. (For a detailed discussion, see Stetkevych 1970: Chapter 4.) A verb like *?inHadara* "to descend" denoted originally the physical act of descending. In Modern Standard Arabic, because of semantic extension, new meanings have developed. This verb is now also used figuratively to mean "to degrade."

Compounding of Words (*an-naHt*). This method of word formation, where a single word is derived from a string of words (usually in the form of a sentence), was used by classical philologists. When the need for new lexical items became acute, academies recognized this method as a partial solution for word coining. As with the method of Arabization, *naHt* met with some opposition. The method of analogical formation of words was strongly emphasized and encouraged as it was believed to be an integral part of Arabic word formation. *NaHt*, on the other hand, despite its usage to some degree, was viewed as characteristically Indo-European and a feature of agglutinative languages. Despite this opposition to *naHt*, it gained limited acceptability. There are two areas in which *naHt* is used in word formation. The first mainly pertains to abstractions. Words in this area are generally antonyms of their positive counterparts and always have the prefix *1ā- 'un-, non-'*. This prefix is equivalent to the negative particle *1ā*, which is often used with the imperfect tense, and in one case, as the absolute negative, with nouns. The other element used to express the same idea is *ghayr* "other than," an independent inflected noun normally used to form antonyms to positive adjectives. Examples having *1ā-* or *ghayr-* as prefixes abound. Thus we find *lādīni* "nonreligious" or *ghayr-dīni*. The *1ā-* and *ghayr-* as antonym-forming prefixes are interchangeable at times, a situation that produces doublets.

The second area where *naHt* is formative to some degree is the scientific and technical. Thus we get *betro-kīmāwi* "petro-chemical," *bar-mā?i* "amphibious," *kahro-maghnāTīsi* "electromagnetic."

Despite the fact that, theoretically, word formations could be unlimited numerically, words coined according to *naHt* are still limited in number and to the areas that were illustrated above. Word compounds tend to be restricted to one specialized area and it is conceivable that, owing to their restricted occurrence, nonspecialized language speakers are unaware of these lexical developments.

The Academies' Success and Problem Areas

The raison d'être for the four academies in the Arab world has primarily been the preservation of Arabic against the calls for the use of dialects as more expressive means of expression. It was recognized at that time that the means for preserving the language could be in lexical expansion in the spheres of science and technology, in the simplification of the grammar, and in orthography reform. The last two areas merit treatment outside the confines of this paper. The success or failure of these academies will be assessed here by their achievement, or lack thereof, in the area of lexical expansion.

Since the academies' inceptions, the question of coining new terminology to meet the needs of the new society has been of paramount significance. Through the

work of committees of specialized experts, such as committees for chemical, physical, biological, and diplomatic terms, these academies approved and published
terms in their specialized journals. According to Madkur (1964:60), the Cairo academy alone published 20,000 scientific terms between 1942 and 1964. Madkur
(1964:60) also records that the approved terms are approximatey two thousand annually.

In connection with this lexical expansion, we must mention the efforts by the
academies to compile dictionaries of approved terminologies for the purposes of
disseminating these new developments in the language. The Cairo academy published a new dictionary, *Al-mu^cjam Al-wasīT,* in two volumes in 1960–1962. Since
the establishment of these academies there has been a desire by academy members
to make available a dictionary for school use.[5] This dictionary, traditional in format
in that words are arranged according to their roots rather than alphabetically, contains items of modern usage.[6]

Despite their accomplishments, these academies fall short of their goals on many
counts. First, there is no guarantee that writers, in particular, and society, in general, pay any attention to these academies' recommendations, suggestions, approval, and disapproval of certain terminologies. Since the academies lack any authority to implement their edicts, their decisions are often inoperative.

Coordination of activities proved to be problematic to these four academies. The
political splits in the Arab world reflect themselves in other endeavors. Consequently, the work of these academies has been affected by political upheavals in that
region of the world. An example of this can be seen in the efforts to merge the Cairo
and Damascus academies during the (political) unity between Syria and Egypt,
1958–1961. Following the breakup the academies' merger also fell apart.

There has been a universal attempt among members of these academies to standardize the language as a language of culture. These efforts at unifying specialized
Arabic terminologies date back to the 1930s, when attempts were made to unify the
terminologies used in postal services in the Arab world, as well as medical, legal,
and engineering terminologies (Chejne 1969: 120). Despite all this, the academies
failed to coordinate their efforts and to agree on technical terminologies. In 1953
there was a call to establish a united academy of Arabic in order to coordinate the
work of academies existing at that time, especially with regard to the scientific-
technical terminology (Chejne 1969: 122). This call bore fruit in 1956, when a Conference of Academies of the language was held in Damascus (Chejne 1969: 122). Its
recommendations included the goals for which these individual academies were established, namely coining scientific and technical terms, simplifying grammar,
analyzing the relationship between dialects and classical Arabic, and compiling a

---

[5] See minutes of the meeting, *Bulletin of the Arabic Language Academy* 3 (1936): 33–34.

[6] It should be mentioned that the Cairo academy's insistence on arrangement by the traditional root
system did not prevent other lexicographers from compiling alphabetical dictionaries. See the dictionaries by Al-^calāyili and Mas^cūd.

dictionary. This conference formed a committee to coordinate the work of the individual academies, but the need for a Pan-Arab academy continues to be unmet.

This lack of coordination among different academies, and between the academies and other governmental agencies and professional groups, often results in a chaotic multiplicity of terms for the same object or concept. For example, the Baghdad academy coined the term *raqqāS* "pendulum," whereas the Cairo academy used *bandōl,* and the Damascus academy used *nawwās* for the same object. This multiplicity of terms could be attributed to many factors. First, the differences of the source languages, that is, French or English, where different terms are likely to be used. The Arab academies depended heavily on English and French in the coining of new scientific and technical terminologies. Second, the duality of terms in the source language contributes to a similar situation in the borrowing language (British English "electronic valve" vs. American English "electronic tube").

At the practical level, coining of words by the academies at times remains removed from the reality of actual use outside the academy walls. Due to the conservative attitudes of many academy members, the dynamism of societies, and the urgent needs to find appropriate terms for newly introduced objects, words coined by these academies many times do not meet with acceptance in society. The suggested word *jammāz* "a quickfooted ass" for "tramway" became an object of ridicule, as did *?irzīz* "telephone." By the time a decision was made by the academies as to which word to adopt, the words "telephone" and "tram(way)" were already in usage.

The Academies and Language Planning

Karam (1974) states that language planning could involve varied activities, ranging from the upgrading of a vernacular to a national language as in Indonesia, or the revival of a language that has not been in use as in Israel, or script replacement and purification of vocabulary as in Turkey, or lexical expansion as in the case of Arabic.

In order to assess in a satisfactory way the role of the academies in the Arabic language planning process, these academies must be viewed as the language planning agencies. The goals for these agencies have been explicitly specified as the preservation of Arabic (read "Classical") and the development of the necessary scientific and technical terminology in order to make Arabic a suitable medium for the modern Arab society. While these academies have shown some success in this regard, we notice that they fail to oversee two important and interrelated activities: implementation and evaluation. Implementation involves all activities germane to the execution of the goal, ranging from the actual coining of terms to their dissemination. In the same way, these academies seem to lack an evaluative device to monitor and assess the results of their tasks of coining new terminologies. The planning, implementation, and evaluation are iterative (Karam 1974). Detailed information regarding the language situation could be valuable for the planning of new items and their dissemination (implementation). Viewed from this conceptual framework, the language academies reviewed here are often not effective nor do they play a coherent role in a successful language planning program.

SUMMARY AND CONCLUSION

This paper has attempted to discuss the role of the language academies in four Arab countries regarding the creation of scientific and technical terminology. Three methods of coining lexicon that have been adopted by these academies are discussed in this paper. Analogical formation of new vocabulary, as opposed to the other two methods, seems to be favored by these academies. This is in line with their concern for the preservation of Arabic in its Semitic "garment." This paper has discussed some areas of success that these academies have achieved; additionally, it has pointed out several problems that these academies face. These problems include the existence of several linguistic centers in the Arab world; the lack of uniformity and standardization in the coined lexicon; little or no acceptance by the society of coined terms; the actual gap between the work of these academies and the public; and the conflicting approaches to the same linguistic problem by different academies. These academies do not constitute an integral part of a planning agency. In sum, these academies lack the authority for implementation and the evaluative procedures.

REFERENCES

Al-ᶜalāyili, ᶜAbdullah. 1963. al-marjiᶜ. Beirut: dār al-muᶜjam al-ᶜarabiyy.

Al-Juburi, Abdullah. 1965. al-majmaᶜ al-ᶜilmi al-ᶜirāqi (in Arabic) (The Iraqi Academy). Baghdad: al-ᶜāni Press.

Al-muᶜjam al-wasīT. 1960–62. Cairo: The Cairo Academy.

Altoma, Salih J. 1974. Language education in Arab countries and the role of the academies. Advances in language planning, ed. by Joshua A. Fishman, 279–313. The Hague: Mouton.

Blau, Joshua. 1981. The renaissance of modern Hebrew and modern standard Arabic. Berkeley: University of California Press.

Chejne, Anwar G. 1969. The Arabic language. Minneapolis: University of Minnesota Press.

Karam, Francis K. 1974. Toward a definition of language planning. Advances in language planning, ed. by Joshua A. Fishman, 103–124. The Hague: Mouton.

Khalifa, Abdulkarim. 1977. majmaᶜ al-lugha al-ᶜarabiyya al-urdunni fi al-mu?tamar (in Arabic) (The Jordan Arabic language academy at the conference, Tripoli). al-lisān al-ᶜarabi 15:3 19–22. Rabat, Morocco.

Madkur, Ibrahim. 1964. majmaᶜ al-lugha al-ᶜarabiyya fi thalāthin ᶜaman (in Arabic) (The Arabic language academy in thirty years). Cairo: al-hay?atu al-ᶜāmmah li-shu?ūn al-maTābiᶜi al-?amīriyyah.

Masᶜūd, Jubrān. 1977. rāi'd al-Tullāb. Beirut: dār al-ᶜilm li-lmalāyīn.

Masliyah, S. 1982. majāmiᶜ al-lugha al-ᶜarabiyya wa majamaᶜ al-lugha al-ᶜibriyya: wa waDᶜ al-muSTalaHāt al-ᶜilmiyya wa al-fanniyya: dirāsa muqārina (in Arabic) (The Arabic language academies and the Hebrew language academy. Coining of the scientific and technical terms: A comparative study) Al-Karmil 3. 97–114. University of Haifa.

Rubin, Joan, & Bjorn H. Jernudd (Eds.). 1971. Can language be planned? An East-West Center Book: The University Press of Hawaii.

Stetkevych, Jaroslav. 1970. The modern Arabic literary language. Chicago: The University of Chicago Press.

APPENDIX 1: SOME SPECIAL PHONETIC SYMBOLS USED IN THIS PAPER

A lower case c raised above the line = voiced pharyngeal fricative.

D = emphatic d
S = emphatic s
T = emphatic t
H = voiceless pharyngeal fricative
q = voiceless uvular stop

Vowel length is marked by ⁻ placed above the vowel.

PART III

LANGUAGE PLANNING: THE INTERFACE WITH MINORITY GROUPS

SIX

English for Immigrants: An Analysis of Governmental and Private Attitudes toward, and Support for, ESL in Canada

Roger E. Gannon

Glendon College, York University
Toronto, Canada

In this paper[1] I propose to describe and analyze the conditions under which adult immigrant learners of English and their teachers function. Although the English-language education of child immigrants is a very important issue in Canada today, it is such a large one that the two areas cannot possibly be covered in the present paper. I shall therefore confine my attentions to adult English as a Second Language (ESL) education in Canada. The paper consists of four parts: a brief historical introduction, an examination of ESL conditions as they existed in 1980–81, a discussion of a number of more political issues underlying these conditions, and a review of recent developments.

ATTITUDES TOWARD IMMIGRANTS AND THE RISE OF ESL EDUCATION

If nothing else is known about Canada, at least it is known that it is a country of immigrants. Immigration in the past forty years approximately has declined, in comparison with the heady, relatively unrestricted days of immigration prior to World War II; nevertheless, during this period approximately three and a half million immigrants/refugees have entered Canada (Lanphier 1980: I). The majority have settled in Ontario. While there is always a danger in generalizing, I think a generalization may legitimately be permitted with respect to the attitudes of Canadians to this influx of immigrants. The official and unofficial ideology of the "Anglo-Saxon"-dominated country was, until recently, unmistakably assimilationist.[2]

---

[1] Much of the present paper is based on conversations with Professor Ian Martin of Glendon College, York University, convenor of a December 3, 1980 symposium entitled the Provision of ESL to Adult Refugees from Southeast Asia, and with Professor Nicholas Elson of York University, chairman of a number of important committees in the field of ESL education in Canada. I have also drawn extensively on a Position Paper issued by TESL Canada as a consequence of the symposium (TESL Canada 1981) and on notes made while I was participating in the December 1980 symposium.

[2] This assimilationist attitude often showed itself in violence, especially towards groups difficult to assimilate, e.g. Chinese, Japanese, and East Indian, groups which today are referred to as part of the visible minority. In 1907, for example, there was an infamous riot in Vancouver in which Japanese and Chinese residents were terrorized and their windows smashed.

Officially, at least, with the federal government's introduction of a multiculturalism policy in the mid-1970s, the ideology of assimilation disappeared. Outside of government, however, there is still a considerable opinion that assimilation is the only answer to Canada's perceived racial/ethnic problems. Such a view is particularly strong among people from older generations with a "British connection," though it is also held by some recent immigrants themselves.[3] Until recently—indeed as late as the 1960s—the school system attempted to assimilate the children of immigrants/refugees as rapidly as possible. Attempts to assimilate adults were less direct. Nevertheless, it was made very clear to them that they were expected to conform to the accepted ideologies and that serious deviations from the prevailing norms were unacceptable. (For a succinct summary of Canadian attitudes toward immigrants, see McLeod 1979.)

Interestingly, prior to 1945, there is little evidence of any attempts, governmental or private, to initiate special instruction in English for immigrant children; the prevailing method was to put the children in a classroom and to treat them, pedagogically, as though they were native-born. There were no texts which could be classified as ESL texts in the modern sense of the word. During the same period, adults received even less help formally with their English. The results of such nonaction can be seen and heard in every city and town of Canada today. Many adults who immigrated prior to the introduction of readily available ESL classes have never acquired fluency in the English language; there are those who are difficult to understand and those who do not write or speak English at all. In some cases, such adults did not have a need for English: certain communities became, for all intents and purposes, self-supporting (though with a limited number of bilinguals for external contact) where there was no need for them to develop a command of English in order to live. The Chinese community in Toronto is a good example; many older Chinese do not speak English at all. It should also be remembered that, until the post-war period, many immigrants settled in rural areas where there would have been less demand for English than in the cities to which immigrants have increasingly gone in the past 40 years.

The post-1945 influx of immigrants and refugees to Canada marked the beginning of government involvement in ESL instruction. Activity was concentrated chiefly in Ontario and British Columbia until quite recently, but even here it was not until the mid 1960s that ESL instruction and ESL teacher training began to expand rapidly. A few illustrations will make the point:

- The first teacher training course for ESL teachers was not introduced in Ontario until 1961 (by the Ontario government's Citizenship Branch).
- It was not until 1964 that the federal government agreed to include ESL in its subsidized training program.

---

[3] Certain immigrants from non-British backgrounds have chosen to assimilate as rapidly as possible—often changing or anglicizing their names in the process—and to support such a policy as the only feasible one in a country of mixed ethnic and racial origins.

- It is interesting to note that until 1964 there had been no special classes provided for immigrant children in the public schools of Ontario and that the Citizenship Branch of the Ontario government had to cope with numerous day-school students arriving for daytime adult language classes.
- The first ESL conference in Ontario was not held until 1967. It was organized by the Ontario government. It has now been taken over by the Association of Teachers of English as a Second Language of Ontario (TESL Ontario). (Martin 1972)

The years 1967 to 1983 have, however, seen a veritable mushrooming of courses for students and for teachers of ESL across the country, the universities have become involved in teacher education (child and adult ESL), professional associations for teachers have sprung up in the majority of the provinces and a national association of teachers was formed in 1978. As a result, the acronym (T)ESL (Teachers of English as a Second Language) is no longer the stranger that it was to the teaching profession and educational administrators. Even federal and provincial ministers, including some not directly concerned with ESL education, have begun to hear the name ESL and to appreciate its implications for their ministries.[4] While the past 15 years or so have indeed been "revolutionary" ones for the ESL profession and for the students it serves, there are still extremely serious problems in the system that prevent the introduction of universally top-flight courses for adult students of ESL. Most of the remaining paper will be devoted to detailing these deficiencies and to looking at the proposals made, and actions taken, to remedy them.

AN EXAMINATION OF ESL CONDITIONS IN 1980–81

In 1979, Canada began to open its doors to refugees from Southeast Asia, especially Vietnam, the so-called "boat people." This exodus of thousands of Vietnamese, Chinese, Khmer, Lao, Hmong, and others had a profound effect on the ESL scene in Canada, more profound than the arrival of thousands of Hungarian refugees in 1956.

As in the past, the various governments and the population at large responded well to the emergency. But as in the past, too, much of the the effort was of an ad-hoc nature, since no established network of federal, provincial, and municipal offices set up to anticipate and coordinate refugee assistance existed. The various public and private institutions scrambled—and scrambled magnificently—but it *was*

---

[4] Jim Fleming, Minister of State for Multiculturalism was reported in the *Toronto Star* ("Immigrant women 'shadows' " March 21, 1981 p. A17) as deploring the condition of immigrant women and recognizing that their lack of English played a key role in their isolation in a speech to the National Conference on Immigrant Women held in Toronto on that same day. The Minister of Employment and Immigration and the Minister of State responsible for The Status of Women also addressed the conference and devoted almost four pages of a 12-page prepared speech to the importance of language training for immigrant women.

a scramble and in the initial months there was considerable confusion.[5] Slowly the situation sorted itself out and large numbers of government and privately-sponsored refugees began to head toward various parts of the country. At the same time, it was becoming more and more apparent to the ESL profession as a whole and to a number of concerned government officials that the delivery of ESL services needed a drastic rethink and overhaul. It took an emergency such as the one in 1979 to dramatize what a number of ESL people in the ESL profession had been complaining of for years.[6]

Thus, after months of preparation, a symposium, jointly sponsored by two teachers' associations—TESL Canada and TESL Ontario—was held in Toronto in December 1980 as part of the annual TESL Canada conference. This symposium examined the provision of services to the Southeast Asian refugees who, by then, numbered approximately 60,000. During the one-day symposium, which was attended by more than 200 people (mostly academics, ESL teachers, and government officials), it became quickly apparent to the delegates that the problems emerging from the various discussions and papers, while of immediate concern as problems for the Southeast Asian refugees, were really the problems of ESL education and immigrant policy in general. Thus, the results of the symposium, which have taken the form of a number of different reports, including recommendations and meetings with the federal and provincial ministries responsible in their various ways for aspects of immigrant policy, have been to call into question—and to make proposals for remedying—the supply of language and related services to immigrants as a whole. After the symposium a number of committees, representing various ESL professional associations, began to work on the data accumulated at the symposium and to gear up for meetings with federal and provincial ministries. The data revealed an alarming number of problems which can be viewed under five headings:[7]

1. Funding and administrative problems
2. Classroom and classroom-related problems
3. Teacher training and related problems
4. Support facilities problems
5. Reception, assessment and placement problems

To understand these problems fully, the reader should have some knowledge of the general ESL picture in Canada and I am, therefore, permitting myself a short digression to provide this necessary background. When the boat people began to arrive in 1979, the provision of ESL services to adults was unsatisfactory. Despite

---

[5] During the period September 1979–April 1980, I acted as a consultant on ESL education to the then Ontario Ministry of Culture and Recreation (now Ontario Ministry of Citizenship and Culture) and witnessed the confusion first-hand.

[6] Mary Ashworth, while discussing the state of ESL in Canada wrote: "And last, but not least, who is going to put pressure on the three levels of government, municipal, provincial, and federal to see that services to immigrants are adequate in terms of quality and quantity?" (Ashworth 1975:15).

[7] These divisions follow closely those utilized in TESL Ontario (1981).

the introduction of Adult ESL instruction in the post-1945 period, 90% of residents in Canada whose mother tongue was neither French nor English were functionally illiterate (TESL Canada 1981: 14). The period 1945–1979 had witnessed the birth of the concept of ESL education and a steady development in the quantity and quality of teachers and courses. Yet such efforts were obviously not producing citizens who were equipped to participate fully in Canadian society. Deprived of a real capability to operate in English, these people were, for all intents and purposes, second-class citizens—a semidisenfranchised population, numbering in the millions, in a country of approximately 24 million.[8] This is a revealing statistic in a country apparently dedicated to the concept of democracy and equality of opportunity! In addition, these immigrants/refugees/residents had no language rights guaranteed to them. The Official Languages Act of 1969 talks of the equality of the two official languages—English and French—but ignores the needs of second-language learners of the two languages. A position paper of TESL Canada quotes approvingly a complaint from the Elections Steering Committee of the ESL Association of British Columbia (B.C. TESL), which describes the discrimination (however innocent) contained within the Official Languages Act:

> The "Official Language Act" (sic) gives equal recognition to French and English as the official languages of Canada. It follows then that access to any and all of the institutions in this nation requires that each individual acquire one or both of these languages. One third of our people speak a language other than French or English and many of these adults and children need official language instruction (English as a Second Language or French as a Second Language) and are being denied this basic right. The current policy of the federal government is to only fund short-term programs for newly arrived *adult* landed-immigrants. A great number of immigrants in need of instruction depend on the educational resources and policy of the province in which they live; the *right* to official language instruction becomes a matter of luck. (TESL Canada 1981:17)

Such linguistic and social discrimination was hardly calculated to foster smooth integration and to forestall alienation.[9] Put bluntly, the situation in 1980–81 smacked of a form of separate development, a form of linguistic apartheid. Even the new constitution (brought back from England) and Charter of Rights and Freedoms offered no solace.[10]

---

[8] This lack of English sometimes has tragic results. A case reported in the *Toronto Star* ("Woman's hospital death brings call for probe" February 7, 1981) (Page AI) described the death of a 68-year-old Arabic-speaking woman who died in agony in hospital because she spoke no English and therefore could not communicate her pain and its source. It should be noted that the hospital did not attempt to use the services of a translator or bilingual relatives!

[9] A survey conducted in Toronto concluded that Spanish-speaking women were forced into low-paying factory jobs because of their inability to function in English. It also observed that the women were isolated from social agencies because of their lack of English and were falling into debt as they acquired goods on credit as status symbols, as compensation for their marginal lives—the marginality in part at least attributable to their lack of English—and as an attempt to show that they were integrating into the community (Latin American Community Centre 1980).

[10] Canada acquired its own Constitution and Charter of Rights and Freedoms in 1982.

Administratively and financially, adult ESL education was dominated by two ministries of the federal government: Employment and Immigration Canada and the Department of the Secretary of State. Employment and Immigration Canada (CEIC) through its Manpower division purchased student places in provincial adult ESL programs (in community colleges) for newly-arrived immigrants/refugees, determined thereby the length of courses, and was responsible for deciding who among the new arrivals could take a Manpower course. Such courses were set up for "breadwinners" with the principal aim of helping the adult immigrant find work, which in practice usually meant finding work as soon as possible. The content of the courses was, therefore, job-oriented and there was relatively little cultural content. A second type of course, funded by the Secretary of State, was more cultural and offered instruction to enable new arrivals to qualify for citizenship. A newly arrived immigrant/refugee was normally streamed into one of these two types of courses and rarely was given the opportunity to take both. As the Position Paper of TESL Canada put it:

> Far from having a policy which provides opportunities for newcomers to be exposed to language training based on both rationales, we have an either-or policy overwhelmingly favouring market affiliation over cultural adjustment. (TESL Canada 1981:23)

The two types of courses referred to above dominated the adult ESL scene in 1980–81. However, there were other courses available to newcomers: some funded by federal/provincial grants, others by provincial monies alone, and yet others supported by volunteer agencies, especially church organizations. These were nearly all part-time courses. We are now in a position to return to the problems that existed in 1980–81.

Funding and Administrative Problems

The Lack of Coordination of Services.   Although there were many courses and programs offered to adult ESL students across Canada, there was very little coordination of the services provided by government, industry, and volunteer agencies/groups. The result was a considerable duplication and waste of time and resources; the wheel was constantly being reinvented in the ESL community. There was a need for measures that would encourage the circulation of information and resources and that would lead to the rationalization and integration of programs at local and provincial levels within a comprehensive approach. The Position Paper of TESL Canada advocated a leading role for TESL Canada as a clearing house for information on "all aspects of language-training for adult immigrants and refugees" (TESL Canada 1981:V). The Position Paper was also critical of the federal government's inability to put its own house in order. While observing that the federal government's immigration policy deserved "rather high marks" (TESL Canada 1981:6), it went on to criticize the lack of any effective collaboration between the major cogs in the adult ESL wheel, namely the CEIC and the Department of the Secretary of State. It also criticized the lack of coordination and collaboration between ministries at the provincial level (e.g., in Ontario, the Ministry of Citizenship and Culture and the Ministry of Education) and between federal and provincial governments, castigating the prevailing resettlement policy as "a patchwork of intergovernmental agreements which passes for a policy and a serious impediment to rational manpower planning for the 80s" (TESL Canada 1981:6).

The Lack of Any Principle of Universal and Equal Access to Funding and Training for Students and the Problem of Insufficient Funding.   The federally-sponsored language programs in 1980–81 had a number of major weaknesses, which produced considerable inequity in the provision of services and led to students being forced into the marketplace and society in general without sufficient English. Among these flaws were the following:

1.   Students were given insufficient time to acquire the necessary English to enter the workforce with confidence. Though course lengths varied across the country, 24 weeks full-time was a length commonly found.

2.   Not only did students in general suffer from the inadequate amount of tuition time, but immigrant professionals with specialized skills such as doctors, dentists, nurses, and engineers were given even less chance to acquire sufficient English to enable them to pass the necessary professional examinations and to practice their profession. Twenty-four weeks was simply not enough time.[11]

3.   The federal government distinguished between (a) government-assisted newcomers and (b) privately-sponsored newcomers. Both groups were, in general terms, eligible for "breadwinner/job-market" courses and "citizenship/culture" courses. Privately sponsored immigrants/refugees could enroll in the above courses if there was space available, and have their tuition paid. However, they were not given a living allowance. Consequently, many privately-sponsored newcomers received no government language training, either because they could not afford to attend classes or because there were no places. In addition, there were other barriers to access: women with male breadwinners in the family were not eligible for job-oriented courses; conversely, their menfolk frequently could not attend culture/citizenship courses because they were held mainly during the day and because they were either working or attending "breadwinner"-type courses. Moreover, the "dependent wife" who needed to work for the family to survive economically was often unable for logistical reasons to attend culture/citizenship courses (held mainly during the day) and was denied access to the job-oriented courses because, by government definition, she was not the breadwinner. She, thus, frequently received no formal linguistic or cultural training and was liable to be "exploited due to (her) lack of English and information about labour practices" (TESL Canada 1981:24).

4.   Officials within the CEIC had too much discretionary power in making decisions about the future of newcomers especially as to whether they should receive

---

[11] The Ontario government introduced Medical English classes for 55 foreign medical graduates in conjunction with Canada Manpower in 1971–72. However, ESP (English for Special Purposes) courses have not become a regular, well-funded feature of the adult ESL landscape in Canada.

language training or not. Thus, pregnant women were sometimes denied entry to ESL classes or official support was withdrawn on the assumption that the women would be quitting the workforce. In addition, it was up to officials, with no language-training qualifications and using no formal tests, to decide if a newcomer had sufficient English for entry into the workplace. If it was judged that he or she had sufficient English, language training was denied. In a similar vein, if a new-comer took work requiring no English or was judged capable of doing so, he or she was often denied language training on the grounds that he or she had no linguistic deficiency. Such a ''work-centric'' policy was extremely unfair and short-sighted: newcomers were often denied sufficient language training (or all language training) to enable them to qualify for the job for which they either had the necessary, or most of the necessary, qualifications, or which as novices they wished to train for. In general, little or no thought was given to the long-term language needs for such people, nor to the waste of talent that was frequently the result of such policies. The Position Paper summed up the situation as follows: ''This Manpower definition of 'sufficiency' is an extremely minimalist one and leads to some very unhealthy social consequences. It implies a hierarchy of job-slots, the bottom rung of which are so menial and/or so tied down to an immigrant language ghetto that a functional level of English for these jobs is zero. Therefore to countenance that such a definition of 'sufficiency' could be applied by a Manpower counselor is to acknowledge that our Manpower policy, in its language training aspect at least, fosters the existence of bottom-rung jobs ('the jobs Canadians don't want') filled by illiterate immigrant workers without English competency and prevented by Manpower from acquiring it'' (TESL Canada 1981:37). The very lack of formal criteria for deciding whether an immigrant/refugee had sufficient English for a particular job (and here I am leav-ing aside the whole question raised above of whether it is equitable, democratic, or socially useful ''to push a person into the first job that comes along'') invited and inevitably produced inequitable treatment, while at the same time placed an unfair burden on the counselor responsible. As if this procedure was not arbitrary and bad enough, nowhere in the regulations was there provision for appeal.

5.   Equity was also lacking in the actual furnishing of courses. The agencies involved adopted a policy whereby courses were provided as long as there were sufficient enrollees. This minimum-number policy had the effect of denying lan-guage training to a number of immigrants/refugees, especially those living in subur-ban and rural areas. There is a certain irony here in that governments, federal and provincial, have attempted to encourage newcomers to settle in the countryside as well as in the big cities—to spread the load as it were—and to lessen the chances of ethnic and racial tensions developing. Those boat people who did go to the suburbs and countryside found support systems relatively nonexistent, compared with those in the city, and there has been a tendency for such people to move into the cities.[12]

6.   In a very real sense, too, there was no academic equity for the newcomer

---

[12] Taken from my symposium notes.

within the classroom. It became quite apparent at the December 1980 symposium, and subsequently in the discussions held by the various TESL associations, that there were no uniform levels of proficiency and that no coherent standards existed from institution to institution.

7.   Women, as we have noted, were particularly discriminated against by the federal government's policies, but there were also two other groups who did not receive equitable treatment: certain young adults and senior citizens. A number of youths arriving from abroad "fell between the gap" of the provincial school-leaving age and the age at which immigrants could qualify for the adult Manpower training allowance and, therefore, were denied much needed English-language training. Senior citizens suffered because language learning was for them an especially difficult task, whether the learning environment was of a formal nature or not. The Position Paper saw the need for special types of classes for this group which would pay special attention to their learning styles, interests, and needs. It also advocated particular consideration for housebound senior citizens and research into " 'Seniors' language learning and cultural adjustment" (TESL Canada 1981:27).

The Lack of a Coordinated Research Policy.   In 1980–81, Canada did not have a coordinated research policy which could act as the backbone of a well-coordinated approach to the teaching of ESL.

Classroom and Classroom-Related Problems

Vocational ESL.   In its recommendations to the various parties involved in the provision of ESL services in Canada, the Position Paper proposed a two-stage program for newcomers consisting of an "initial reception programme with orientation, cultural adjustment and functional language-learning objectives" (TESL Canada 1981:23), and a second stage consisting of a range of options of a vocational type. It further recommended that "all newcomers should qualify for stage I and be given equitable consideration for stage II" (TESL Canada 1981:29) and that earlier immigrants, what the Position Paper calls "the backlog population" (TESL Canada 1981:49), should have the same opportunities as newly-arrived immigrants/refugees. The Position Paper also foresaw an immigrant/refugee "following a sequence of programmes selected from stage II options, the selection based on a large range of such program considerations as intensive vs. part-time; general purpose vs. general vocational vs. occupation-specific; location at a training institution vs. on the job; skills-upgrading/adaptation vs. skills-acquiring; achievement-tested vs. non-tested, and so forth. As well, these programs could be, wholly or partially, funded by one or more of the three levels of government, singly or jointly, and may involve the employer, a labour organization or a professional accrediting body" (TESL Canada 1981:52).

The above recommendations were a "global" response to the problems perceived. However, the fact that it was recommended that the program should continue to have a vocational stage did not mean that vocational ESL, that is, the Manpower "breadwinner" courses in Canada, was free from classroom-type problems. Far from it. There were a number of weaknesses including the following:

1. Courses were offered in insufficient numbers.
2. Classes contained too many students for effective teaching to take place.
3. Courses frequently contained students of mixed occupation, thereby effectively nullifying the aim of the classes.
4. Courses rarely had a work experience component. As a result, the integrating aim of the courses was considerably reduced.
5. Programs were offered at times that made it difficult for shift workers to attend.
6. Few work/school programs existed that allowed students the flexibility to leave and enter the programs as work opportunities dictated.

Literacy training.   When the Southeast Asian refugees began to arrive in Canada in 1979, it soon became apparent that a number of them were illiterate, and attempts were made to accommodate this problem. Yet the problem was not entirely new; in the past immigrants had arrived with few or no literacy skills. The events of 1979 merely made it more difficult to ignore this aspect of ESL education and to brush aside the fact that the federally funded programs were organized in such a way that it was almost impossible to deal with the illiterate. Teachers had the almost impossible job of teaching literates and illiterates in the same class.[13] The influx of boat people highlighted the need for a special program with specialized teachers, separate from the regular ESL programs, which would enable illiterate students to become literate and to enter the regular programs at the appropriate time.

Alternatives to the Formal Classroom.   Manpower programs tended to be offered full-time, six hours a day. This presented problems for a number of people including:

• The handicapped
• The housebound
• Shift workers
• The elderly

There was clearly a need for more self-study courses, correspondence courses (with tapes), telephone tutoring, buddy systems, TV ESL programs, radio courses, and bilingual phrasebooks.

---

[13] Johnson (1981:23) describes the (Vietnamese) illiterate and the attendant teaching/learning problems thus: "Handicapped by undeveloped visual and kinesthetic skills, they find the mere copying of letters and words painfully difficult. Unable to use a bilingual dictionary, they cannot look up the meaning or spelling of words, they cannot make notes and they cannot review any of the work studied in class."

English in the Workplace Programs. In 1980–81 there were a number of English in the Workplace programs (EWP) operating outside the formal classroom, mainly in factories. Such programs, while catering to an urgent need, suffered from a whole range of problems:[14]

1. They were too few, given the need: large numbers of immigrants in the workplace had, for a variety of reasons, never received any, or had received insufficient, language training. (The backlog population).

2. There was no government-industry-wide coordinated effort to solve the problems of workers with insufficient language training. Indeed, there was no government policy on this form of education, whose inception in the area of ESL was of recent date.

3. Funding was precarious; grants tended to dry up after an initial period and programs often sank into oblivion to the disappointment of those waiting to get into the class. What was lacking was long-term commitment from government, unions, and management. There was (and is) talk in EWP circles of the need for an industry-wide educational levy but this was (and is) highly controversial.

4. Teachers complained that they were given insufficient time to prepare what was in effect an ESP—English for Special Purposes—course.

5. Part of the problem in number 4 could have been removed by the use of already-prepared and appropriate materials but, for the most part, these did not exist.

6. It was very difficult for teachers in certain circumstances to meet the demands of workers, unions, and management as to what the course content should consist of.

7. Workers found it difficult to concentrate, especially if the course was held at the end of the working day.

8. A common complaint from teachers centered on the problem of student levels; teachers were often obliged (by various circumstances) to teach mixed-level classes, thereby reducing efficiency.

9. Programs were invariably too short and could not be expected to meet student needs.

10. Workers who were laid off tended (for a variety of reasons) not to attend class.

11. Most programs contained no evaluation mechanism. There was a need for evaluation, since many employers needed to be convinced that ESL education for their workers was indeed good for business.

Teacher Training and Related Problems

Teacher training. From the professional's point of view, ESL teacher education in Canada was a hodge-podge of differing standards, where standards existed at

---

[14] Problems discussed here synthesized from TESL TALK (1982).

all. There was a need for ESL teacher training guidelines to be established in each province and for there to be some standardization of these requirements. Moreover, many teacher training programs in Canada contained no provision for ESL training/ specialization. The lack of standards alluded to above enabled (or forced) many institutions to employ untrained teachers as ESL teachers. ESL for some administrators was still in 1980–81 the ugly sister of the teaching profession; they felt that ''anybody could teach ESL.''

Materials development and distribution problems.   Canada suffered from a lack of ESL resource centers and specialized materials. Resource banks, readily available and national in scope, simply did not exist. It was hard work for the ESL teacher to discover what was available and what was about to become available. In this respect, there was a very real need for a central resource service to which teachers/consultants, educators/officials, and publishers could have ready access. As to materials, Canadian materials were in the minority and frequently dated. British and American texts abounded. There was a need for more Canadian content and books aimed at the Canadian reality. In particular, there was a need for more ESP materials, especially vocational ESL texts.

Support Facilities Programs

While such topics as day care would seem to be outside the scope of this paper, I would draw the reader's attention to the words ''Support for ESL'' in the title. It is the writer's view that effective ESL training cannot be provided unless the immigrant/refugee is accommodated in those noneducational areas that will have a major effect on whether he or she will be able to learn English. I make no apology, therefore, for looking at a number of external factors that are material to the general well-being of the immigrant/refugee. Here there were a number of problems:

• There was insufficient support, in terms of money/personnel, being channeled to ethnic agencies who provided counseling (vocational and personal) and resource and referral information.
• New immigrants/refugees often feel isolated; there was a need for the establishment of social centers designed to prevent loneliness and depression and to encourage social integration.
• Newcomers with little or no English frequently need the help of translators. While government and other agencies did provide translation and interpreter services, they were insufficient.
• The lack of sufficient day care services (a general social complaint) prevented certain mothers from attending language classes. There was a need for these to be provided by institutions offering classes.
• There was a need for more community education regarding the immigrant, his or her needs, lifestyle, and so on, to prevent friction in the community.
• Little was done by CEIC offices to help newcomers solve their employment problems. One of the recommendations resulting from the December symposium

addressed this lack and proposed that CEIC offices be responsible for "preparing a detailed file for each potential employee stating short- and long-term goals based on past experience and education, and helping him or her to achieve these goals" (TESL Ontario 1981:12).

•   Another recommendation proposed the institutionalization of Employer Awareness Programmes (TESL Ontario 1981:12) to help sensitize employers to the needs of the immigrant employee.

•   A number of immigrants experienced problems getting to courses; this was especially true in the countryside. They lacked transportation or the funds to travel. There was a need for aid to facilitate teacher and/or student travel so that the principle of equal educational access could be maintained.

Reception Assessment and Placement Problems

Problems occurred in the boat people crisis of 1979 that could have been prevented, or at least mitigated, if the Canadian government had established orientation programs in Southeast Asian refugee camps. It would seem appropriate that the federal government should consider institutionalizing a program to provide for any future emergencies; such a program could include orientation to Canada (initial reception; survival English skills; information of a more general nature about Canada— geography, cultural life, customs, taboos, and so on—and would have to establish "hit teams" ready to leave at short notice for the particular trouble spot. What happened in 1979 was that the reception process in Canada became overwhelmed and the initial integration process suffered as a result.

THREE UNDERLYING ISSUES

Government Policy and Worker Supply

A cynic might well maintain that the policy of federal/provincial governments was a deliberate attempt to maintain a steady stream of compliant workers for jobs that native-born Canadians refused to accept. He or she could argue that the points system of immigrant selection[15] was partially a smokescreen set up to convince Canadians and the world that Canadian immigration policy, while demanding, was fair and equitable; that once here many well-qualified immigrants with little English found the points system to have little relevance: he or she could point to the obviously inadequate language training programs for these people and for aspiring but unqualified immigrants as evidence of a cynical introduction of inequity from the very beginning of the immigrants' stay. The above "proofs" are hardly primary, concrete proofs. We need more damning evidence of a literary kind. But there are simply no memos, nor indeed policy papers, which suggest that the policy in force in 1980–81 was a deliberate attempt to create and preserve a "lumpen proletariat."

---

[15] Under the points system, potential immigrants are awarded points for various attributes sought by the Canadian government; professional qualifications and knowledge of English or French are two areas in which potential immigrants are evaluated.

Nevertheless, leaving all thought of cynical conspiracies aside, it can be stated that the weaknesses exposed in this paper are either testimony to the low-level priority which ESL education seemed to occupy in the minds of the various ministries responsible for immigrant training/reception or to an incredibly incompetent bureaucracy. History suggests that it was the former—that the erratic and unorganized growth of adult ESL education together with a low-level interest on the part of government produced the problems. It is also quite possible (though this obviously cannot be documented) that governments responded to two strong ideological "undercurrents" in Canada: the belief that the country does "more than enough" for immigrants simply by accepting them and the belief that, as English was one of the official languages of Canada, immigrants "should have no problem picking it up." If these undercurrents did influence government thinking, then the language training programs could be seen as a compromise between perceived educational needs and political/ideological pressures.

Whatever the reasons were in fact for governmental policies, the results were, as we have seen, most unfortunate for students. They were also, in my view, bad for the country as a whole: according to a number of specialists in the field of worker education, ESL education improves industrial productivity, reduces absenteeism, leads to fewer industrial accidents and less waste, and produces greater job flexibility (Richer 1982:72f). However, despite the above claims, there may be drawbacks for employers. After all, a more enlightened worker, cognizant of his or her contractual rights, may be a mixed blessing as far as an employer is concerned. Further, certain employers have expressed to the writer, in private, the view that they will be unable to attract workers to do their menial work at minimum rates if workers achieve a good command of English and thereby become eligible for better-paying jobs. This view is of considerable interest, since at least one writer has claimed that the practice of maintaining a steady supply of workers who barely speak English and who can be paid the minimum wage is a

> costly proposition [since the] widespread availability of low skilled workers puts a damper on the motivation of Canadian industry to innovate. If the product can be produced economically by combining out-of-date technology with low paid labour then many employers will not invest in technological upgrading. The result, however, is self-defeating because the failure to innovate results in low productivity growth in the aggregate and eventually the replacement of Canadian production with imported production. The bottom line is a reduction in the overall potential standard of living. At present productivity growth is a major Canadian problem. . . . It is projected that productivity during the 1980's will increase by only 0.5 per cent annually. One of the reasons for this decline is that Canadian business spends less on research and development than most other countries. The availability of a large pool of poorly educated and trained people certainly contributes significantly to the problem. (Adams 1982:10)

English-Language Level and Industrial Accidents
Statistics Canada does not classify industrial accidents according to ethnic origin. Nongovernmental statistics are also lacking in this area. Statistically, therefore, any claim that there is a link between knowledge of English and the likelihood of an

industrial accident remains unproven; such a claim, or perhaps the term belief would be more appropriate, exists among EWP teachers. Support for such a belief can be found in an article referred to earlier in this paper in which Roy Adams states that the functionally illiterate worker is "more likely to be forced to accept jobs which are inherently dangerous, thus assuming a much greater risk of injury and disease" (Adams 1982:10). It is hard to quarrel with such a statement; moreover, it is hard to deny that an illiterate or poorly comprehending ESL worker is more likely to have an accident than a literate worker (all other things being equal), since such linguistic handicaps are likely, for example, to result in a worker misreading, or failing to understand at all, a safety warning in a factory or a caution or instruction from a supervisor with resulting injury to him or herself.

English-Language Level and Unemployment

A recent Canadian report (Lanphier 1980) demonstrates convincingly that the "ESL immigrant" is behind, indeed considerably behind, the average in labor force participation and job status. This should not surprise us if we accept the view that we need language to function fully in society and if we recognize that Canadian employees have for years put a premium on educational level, including language ability. This having been said, it would be foolhardy to claim that the present socioeconomic position of the "ESL immigrant" is attributable solely to linguistic/educational deficiencies.

EVENTS SINCE 1980–81

In an earlier part of this paper, reference was made to the various follow-ups that took place after the December 1980 symposium. I shall detail these here for the sake of completeness and to assist others who may wish to do research in this area:

•   In February 1981, the newsletter *Contact* of the TESL Association of Ontario issued an early report on the symposium.

•   In the same month, the Greater Metropolitan Southeast Asian Task Force (of Toronto) issued its report.

•   In April 1981, the TESL Association of Ontario's English as a Second Language/Dialect (ESL/D) Action Committee published a condensed version of the recommendations which resulted from the symposium and which appeared in a more detailed context in the Position Paper published by the TESL Canada Action Committee in December 1981. These recommendations addressed the problems cited in this paper and others not discussed.

•   In May 1981, a brief was presented to government officials in British Columbia by Directions ESL in cooperation with agencies serving immigrants entitled *Immigrant Settlement Services in Vancouver*. It was subsequently used by the TESL Canada Action Committee in the drawing-up of its Position Paper of December 1981.

•   In the spring of 1982, TESL Canada's newsletter published *Six Principles. The Provision of ESL Training to Adults. Towards a National Policy*. This was based on the Position Paper of December 1981.

Since the above events, provincial TESL associations and the national association have been actively attempting to promote the cause of adult ESL, ever mindful
of the deficiencies outlined in this paper. The TESL Association of Ontario, for
example, has been active through its Action Committee in responding to a *Consultation Paper on The Delivery of English as a Second Language Instruction in Metropolitan Toronto* (Rigby 1982) and in responding to a 1981 Ontario government
report—*Continuing Education: The Third System*—which was notably silent on the
question of ESL/D education! In a subsequent statement on the report, the Ministry
of Education took up a number of issues brought to its attention by the TESL Association of Ontario. It spoke of "ensuring 'appropriate support, coordination and direction . . . to meet the needs of adults' through part-time or short-term programs in
several areas including ESL and literacy" (*Contact* 1983:2). The report of a joint
task force set up by the Secretary of State and the CEIC to look into immigration
settlement and integration of newcomers was published in April 1983. As the newsletter *Contact* reported,

> In line with the TESL Canada position paper, the report proposes a two-stage reception
> process, the first relating to 'survival' language and orientation, the other focussing on
> more advanced and specific language. The document proposes a strong federal leader-
> ship role in immigrant settlement and integration, with responsibilities divided be-
> tween Employment and Immigration Canada (CEIC) and the Department of the Secre-
> tary of State. CEIC would be responsible for developing and maintaining an enriched
> settlement package related to initial adjustment. This would address basic access needs
> of immigrants in language training, orientation, information and referral, health care,
> assessment and counselling for employment. The Multiculturalism Programme, Secre-
> tary of State, would be responsible for ensuring 'the maintenance and viability of an
> effective voluntary support of settlement/integration programming.' Language training
> is seen in the report as an 'essential and interdependent element of the settlement/
> integration process. A global language training policy for all adult Canadians, mi-
> grants, and permanent residents' is seen as 'a long term goal.' (*Contact* May 1983:2)

The chairman of the ESL/D Committee of TESL Ontario goes on to say that "the
exact status of this report is unclear at the present time" (*Contact* May 1983:2).
However, if the report's findings are implemented in a positive spirit, ESL education for adults in Canada should undergo considerable improvement.

At the same time as the TESL Canada association is contributing input to the
ongoing discussion on adult ESL education, provincial associations are doing their
own follow-up to the task force report. To quote the newsletter *Contact* once more,
"Each association is attempting to get input at the provincial government level, as
well (sic) meeting with local CEIC officials on the report. There is a lot of work to
be done if we are to get an effective language training settlement and integration
policy into place in the near future" (*Contact* May 1983:10).

To sum up, in December 1980, the symposium on The Provision of ESL to Adult
Refugees from South East Asia was, in a very real sense, the watershed f or adult
ESL education in Canada. Since then, governments, as we have seen, have begun to
respond but, like many a governmental process, the pace has been slow. Perhaps

necessarily so, since the changes required to alter the present unacceptable situation would be costly. In a time of budgetary restraint, considerable unemployment, and increasing bankruptcies, it is perhaps understandable that governments, mindful of the prejudice towards immigrants, especially in times of unemployment, are moving cautiously and without fanfare. Only time will tell whether the governments had any long-term intention of responding to the recommendations of the various groups of ESL teachers and others. Undue delay will only lend credence to the cynical interpretation of government policy that was discussed earlier in the paper. Governments have little time left to prove their good faith is more than words: at the time of writing, the conditions described for the period 1980–81 have remained unchanged to a disturbing extent. Thus, the recommendations of the TESL Canada Position Paper for government action remain, with a few exceptions, recommendations.

Other recommendations were directed at the profession itself and at individuals (e.g., potential textbook writers). To date, there has been little movement from these quarters either, principally, it should be said, because professional association efforts have been directed at pressuring government—a logical enough step since the major problems in ESL education need government solutions.

REFERENCES

Adams, Roy J. 1982. The functionally illiterate worker and public policy. TESL Talk 13(4). 9–16.

Ashworth, Mary. 1975. Today and tomorrow in ESL. TESL Talk 6(1). 1–15.

Contact. 1983. Newsletter of association of teachers of English as a second language of Ontario (TESL Ontario) 10(1) (February and May issues).

Directions ESL. 1981. Immigrant settlement services in Vancouver. A brief to government officials. Vancouver.

Government of Canada. 1983. The recommendations of the Secretary of State—Employment and immigration Canada review of immigration settlement and integration policies and programs. Ottawa.

Greater Metropolitan South East Asian Task Force. 1981. Report. Toronto.

Immigrant women "shadows." (March 21, 1981). Toronto Star. A17.

Johnson, Mary. 1981. Literacy for newcomers with little formal education. TESL Talk 12(1), (12)2. 23–25.

Lanphier, Michael C. 1980. Ethnicity and occupation prestige ranking: Sociodemographic and regional perspectives. Toronto: Institute for Behavioural Research, York University.

Latin American Community Centre. 1980. Latin Americans in North York (unpublished manuscript).

Martin, Carson. 1972. History of TESL in Ontario. TESL Talk 3(3). 3–10.

McLeod, Keith A. 1979. Schooling for diversity: Ethnic relations, cultural pluralism and education. TESL Talk 10(3). 75–90.

Ontario Government. 1981. Continuing education: The third system. Ontario.

Richer, Judy. 1982. Workplace language classes: The management factor. TESL Talk 13(4). 72–82.

Rigby, Edna (Committee Chairperson). 1982. Consultation paper on the delivery of ESL instruction in metro Toronto. Toronto.

TESL Canada. 1981. Position paper: The provision of English as a second language (E.S.L.) training to adult newcomers: Six principles toward a national policy. Ottawa.

———. 1982. The provision of ESL training to adults. Six principles towards a national policy. TESL Canada Newsletter. 2(1). 1–12.

TESL Ontario. 1981. Recommendations from the Symposium on South East Asian Refugees. Toronto.

TESL Talk. 1982. English in the workplace. 13(4).

Woman's hospital death brings call for probe. (February 7, 1981). Toronto Star. A1.

SEVEN

Communication: Perspectives from the Developing World

D. P. Pattanayak

Central Institute of Indian Languages, India

Language and communication are both communal in character. Both have one thing in common: "sharing." Sharing means jointly participating in an act, an event, or an experience. Through language human beings share meanings. In communication they share information. It is only through the sharing of common pursuits that human groups are formed. Thus language, which is the medium of information and experience, transforms itself into the message. It is in this sense that the medium is the message.

The same message can be given in different languages as much as different messages can be given in the same language. A single message can also be presented in different styles of one language to communicate to different audiences. In the Alitalia "vomit bag," the inscription—*chiudere arotolando, close by folding, fermer en pliant, durch zusammenrollen schliessen, cierare enrolando, fechar enrolando*—is a good example of the same information given in many languages. This is aimed at the pluralistic Europe. The clientele of the airlines drawn from different countries is given the opportunity to share the information in the language at their command. If it was written only in one language, then the information would not have communicated itself to those who do not know that language.

The same message presented in high and low styles of a single language can lead to restrictive communication as one or the other may not be accessible to the others. Thus, in Arabic, where high and low varieties lead to diglossia, the high variety has great symbolic and ritual value but little or narrow communicative value to the large majority of Arabic speakers in the world. Here is an example of a message getting blocked because of the medium. A different example of the message being blocked by the medium is the cyclone warning given in Telugu to the coastal Andhra region in India. The warning spoke of the velocity of wind per hour, the expected tidal wave, and the moving eye of the storm. The message did not communicate itself partially because of the nature of the message and partially because of the newness of the register employed. It did not inform people of the expected consequences. Thus it will be seen that as ignoring dialects, sociolects, styles, and registers of a single language may macerate the regional speech patterns, imposition of a single code in a multilingual society may similarly block sharing of information and force people to learn the one language through which information is offered or they must do without that information.

86

Sharing the same language does not necessarily lead to communication, but sharing a language is a precondition to communication. Thoreau wrote in 1854, "We are in great haste to construct a magnetic telegraph from Maine to Texas, but Maine and Texas, it may be, have nothing important to communicate" (quoted in Abel 1981:4). Today's mass media people have to learn a lot from this. By sheer coverage through a network of electronic media, communication potential is created, but communication cannot be taken for granted.

Sharing can be seen from yet another perspective. By state ownership or chain ownership of information media and information-gathering and distributing agencies, facts are actually and potentially manipulated. People are then asked to share the variety of truth dished out to them, and consequently erosion of democratic values takes place. When different languages gather information independent of one another and see the same phenomenon from the vantage point of different perspectives, there is scope for democratic dialogue leading to a consensus. In this sense many languages are a better defense of democracy than one.

It is a strange contradiction that the developed countries with their monolingual orientation are in favor of audience fragmentation in terms of programs and publications, but they are unwilling to concede audience fragmentation in terms of languages in multilingual countries, although in the first case it is narrowcasting and in the latter case it is broadcasting. In the West, the new technology, with the introduction of home information retrieval systems, has induced "erosion of the common data base." As more and more people share less and less data base, the consumer cost is likely to push the power section out of the high technology information circuit. As Elie Abel predicts, "We may, in short, confront the prospect of media segregated by economic and social class: over-the-air broadcasting for the masses and the newer technologies for the classes. The affluent would be better informed than they are today; the lower orders could be even more less informed" (Abel 1981:8).

With 10% of the world population enjoying 90% of the world energy and 90% of the available radio frequency, it is not at all surprising that the developing world is information-starved. The media segregation feared by Elie Abel has already taken place between the developing and the developed worlds. It has taken place within nations in the developing world and it is growing at an accelerated pace threatening saturation of communication for a few and deprivation for many. The developing world—which has a low percentage of literacy and is burdened with colonial languages—suffers from tremendous underaccess to the print media. With almost 80% of the total news flow emanating from the West-based major transnational agencies, there is only one-way bombarding of information. This can be seen in the context of a single developing country. In India, "taking all the modern media of communication into account, it can safely be stated that their reach is not more than 20% of the population" (Madan Gopal 1980:87). Whether it is from the developed to the developing countries or from the elite-controlled media to the masses within a country, one-way dialogue is not communication. It has been called a transfer of information that is auxiliary to communication. Under these conditions terms like "Communication Age," "Information Society," "Global Village," and

"Technotronic Era" are indicative more of a life style which handles and manipulates information as commodity. No wonder that in the present day world the media is segregated on the basis of social class and the use value of communication in an interactive world is forgotten.

The technology of communication has overshadowed communication and almost paralyzed thought and action. Asimov's prophecy, "The twenty-first century may be the great age of creativity in which machines will do the common place work of humanity, and human beings are free at least to do things that only human beings can do—to create" (1980:10), is a good example of such paralysis of thought. The biggest flaw in the logic of such arguments is that they seek to divorce work from thinking. Instead of eliminating drudgery in mechanical work they seek to eliminate work itself. It is often forgotten that creative consciousness develops by doing, by learning and sharing through experience. The packaged consumer-specific information delivered at the doorsteps of those who can afford it narrowcasts the data, anesthetizes the surrounding, and undermines culture.

Jack Goody's observation, "Culture after all is a series of communicative acts, and differences in the mode of communication are often as important as differences in the mode of production, for they involve developments in the storing, analysis and creation of human knowledge, as well as the relationship between the individuals involved" (1977:37), assumes importance in this context. As the editorial of Media Development (1980) says, "Information and Communication are much more than 'commodities' or 'consumer goods', a concept promoted by the West. They are essential needs for persons-in-community and communities of persons." The importance of communication for culture cannot be more emphatically stated.

Cultural practices do not communicate their secrets easily. Many social scientists who have studied the anthropology of agriculture have suggested that the rural peasant is too steeped in traditional practices and taboos to accept innovations. In Bengal in certain areas after the Amon crop, the land is kept fallow during summer. This is quoted as a wasteful practice that is due to prevailing taboos. The farmers have generations of wisdom behind them. From experience they have found that if the land is not permitted to dry up then it is prone to the attack of pests. Therefore they balance between short-term and long-term benefits. It has been found that many farmers who keep their own land fallow grow summer crops on other people's land through commercial arrangement. Thus what appeared to be ignorance and taboo now appears to be a wise and cautious approach to new technology.

Like culture, language is also a multilayered phenomenon. In a single language area, language variations in terms of regions, social classes, situations, and the topic and conflict of discourse create problems for communication. In a multilingual area, besides these, the complementary use of many languages for specific communicative tasks adds another layer of complexity. Social scientists, whether they come from the dominantly monolingual West or from the multilingual world imitating the mode of Western development, tend to consider this complexity in language use as inconvenient, uneconomic, and a burden. It is no wonder that in the 31 Commonwealth countries over 1000 languages are struggling to maintain their identity (Pattanayak 1981a). The multilingual, multiethnic, and multicultural world consisting of Asia, Africa, and Latin America—which has a colonial past and is constantly under pressure to adopt a colonial language for modernization and development—is caught up in the contradictions of imposing monomodels on plural societies.

It is a well-known fact that "34 industrialized countries of the world with only 30% of the population produce 81% of the world's book titles" (Narenda Kumar 1982). When only 3% of the world's expenditure on research and development is spent in the developing countries and the research is a pale replica of the developed world, this is only to be expected. With over-the-air communication controlled by the rich and the powerful and 800 million illiterates solely dependent on it, it does not take much ingenuity to see that the communication flow is controlled, manipulated, and unidirectional.

The world linguistic spectrum can broadly be divided into two bands—linguistic colonialism and linguistic neocolonialism. Every country in the world contains both of these in different measures. Linguistic colonialism is defined by a relationship of dominance and subordination. Linguistic neocolonialism can be characterized by the argument in favor of the neutral colonial language in the interest of national integration and national development of multilingual countries.

The developed countries of the world pursue the path of linguistic colonialism within their national boundaries. They seek to impose the dominant language on the minorities and expect them to melt their identities and become one with the majorities. They back linguistic neocolonialism in the multilingual and multiethnic developing countries. The basis of both is a simple language acting as the emblem of a nation state and determining and guiding economic, political, and cultural developments.

It is argued that in the context of development it is not linguistic heterogeneity which is problematic but the social context of the use of many languages which is problematic. This is a clever ruse first to establish a distance between language and its context and then deemphasize the importance of language. Why either language or its context of use should be considered problematic is not clear. There is only one explanation. Linguistic monism is assumed to be problem-free and linguistic pluralism problematic by the proponents of the above view. Naturally, communication with the people speaking many languages receives low priority.

The world "development" spectrum can be divided into two bands, one threatened with death and semistarvation and the other suffering from overconsumption and threatened by the growing consciousness of the other half of its miseries and the causes of it. The mutuality of dependence between the two worlds is such that one gets impoverished and the other enriched due to one another. The unequal distribution of resources not only creates a relationship of dominance and subordination between the two worlds, but also creates "two mutually autonomous and organically separate communication boundaries" (Agrawal 1982). Those investigating a North-South dialogue for a new economic order as well as a new international information order talk of survival of both worlds. While survival in the South is on the basis of minimum needs, survival in the North is on the basis of a maintaining of the privileges and the status quo. Linking both the survivals in any discussion on the improvement of the lot of the developing world amounts to scuttling the discussion even before it began. As Hamelink rightly observes, "In order to survive we do not need a new world order that delivers us 'one world.' We are, however, in urgent need of new relations between nations: relations based upon the vital differences and upon the systems adequately embody such differences. The new international information order has to be the order of many different worlds" (1980:6).

REFERENCES

Abel, Elie. 1981. Looking ahead from the twentieth century. Communications in the twenty-first century, ed. by Robert W. Haigh, George Gerbner & Richard B. Byrne, 1–9. New York: John Wiley & Sons.
Agrawal, B. C. 1982. Communication structures in India; A case study of television. Mimeo. Ahmedabad, India: ISRO, Space Applications Center.
Asimov, George. 1980. The permanent Dark Age: Can we avoid it? Working in the twenty-first century, ed. by C. Stewart Sheppard & Donald C. Carrol. New York: John Wiley & Sons.
Editorial. 1980. Media Development, Journal of the World Association for Christian Association 27: 4.
Goody, Jack. 1977. The domestication of the savage mind. Cambridge: Cambridge University Press.
Hamelink, Cees. 1980. The NIIO: The recognition of many different worlds. in: Media Development, Journal of the World Association for Christian Association 27: 4.
Madan Gopal. 1980. Reaching rural India. Mass media in India 1979–80. Publications Division, Ministry of Information and Broadcasting, Government of India.
Narendra Kumar. 1982. Cultural imperialism and Third World publishing. MEA 109/XP. New Delhi: External Publicity Division, Ministry of External Affairs.
Pattanayak, D. P. 1981a. Communication structure in commonwealth countries. Literature related to commonwealth studies: Access, dissemination and use, pp. 97–104. Australia: La Trobe University Library.
_____. 1981b. Multilingualism and mother tongue education. New Delhi: Oxford University Press.

EIGHT

The Politics of Language Status Planning: 'Normalization' in Catalonia*

Kathryn A. Woolard
University of Pennsylvania

In the movement for Catalan national autonomy during the period of Spanish redemocratization since 1976, the status of the Catalan language in its native territory has been a principal issue. With the attainment of a new Spanish Constitution in 1978, and especially of a Statute of Catalan Autonomy in 1979, some people of Spain and Catalonia thought this issue was settled. Both documents address the language question, and in combination they appear to guarantee full official status for both the Catalan and Castilian languages in Catalonia.

Nonetheless, efforts toward a kind of language planning dubbed "linguistic normalization" have been central in the program of the new Catalan government. In June 1980, the general director of linguistic policy for the governing body (*Generalitat*) of Catalonia convened a group of sociolinguists and political representatives to outline a "Charter of the Catalan Language." The meeting was reported under the news headline "New law for Catalan in nine months," and the director hoped to have a bill presented to the parliament by September and possibly enacted by January 1981.[1]

In fact, nearly three years were to pass before the proposed law materialized. The Law of Linguistic Normalization in Catalonia was approved by the Catalan parliament in April 1983, although even then it could not take immediate effect because the constitutionality of two clauses was challenged by the Spanish government. But, once cleared by the Spanish Constitutional Tribunal, the law would provide an explicit legal framework designed as a step toward "normalizing" the linguistic situation in Catalonia.

While the term "normalization" does not make it immediately apparent, this law and the public campaign that accompanied it are a kind of language status planning

---

* This article is partially based on fieldwork conducted in Barcelona and supported by a Social Science Research Council doctoral fellowship. The opinions and conclusions reported here are mine and not those of the Council.

[1] Interview with Aina Moll, July 22, 1980, p. 5. Page numbers of interviews are from author's transcription of tape-recorded material.

rather than corpus planning (Kloss 1969). As Cobarrubias has pointed out, most research in language planning has been concerned with corpus planning. The problems of status planning are not as clearly defined and may be of an even greater complexity (1982:5).

In the Catalan case, one of the most important elements of status planning is a process that we can call persuasion. One of the best known models of language planning is that of Haugen (1969), in which he identifies four stages: (1) norm selection, (2) codification, (3) implementation, and (4) elaboration. At first glance, the process I am calling persuasion appears to be an aspect of Haugen's implementation stage, but the situation is not in fact so simple. In Catalonia, there are feedback loops between the norm selection and implementation stages, and a cyclical model may be more appropriate than Haugen's linear one. Persuasion serves as a mediating process between these stages, for the rhetoric of persuasion not only encourages the acceptance of norms but actually defines them through interpretation, and prepares the ground for further evolutions in norm selection as well.

In order to understand the purposes and tactics of Catalan language planners' persuasive efforts, it will be useful to sketch first the historical and sociopolitical context in which these steps were initiated.

THE SETTING

As more people are becoming aware, Catalonia is one of the newly-autonomous communities of post-Franco Spain. More than this, however, it is a once-independent, historic nation which at the height of its glory in the thirteenth and fourteenth centuries dominated the Mediterranean, and which has its own distinctive Romance language, Catalan. Catalonia was joined to Castile through the marriage of Ferdinand and Isabel in the fifteenth century, but it did not lose its political personality under this arrangement until the beginning of the eighteenth century, and it has never completely lost its distinctive linguistic character.

The economic and social structure of Catalonia has also long been distinctive on the Iberian peninsula. Catalonia is now home to some 5.7 million inhabitants, or nearly 16% of the Spanish population (Recolons et al. 1979), and its capital and governmental seat, Barcelona, is one of the largest and most important industrial-urban complexes in Spain. Catalonia does not fit the typical profile of minority regions in centralized states. Although as a periphery it has often suffered political subordination and linguistic-cultural repression from the center, it has not experienced the economic lag so often characteristic of such regions. Rather, the introduction of industrial capitalism in Iberia was actually led by Catalonia, and most of Spain still lags significantly behind it. Although currently beset by economic crisis, Catalonia is still one of the richest and most industrially developed communities of the Spanish state. Its inhabitants have traditionally enjoyed privileged economic status in comparison to other regions, even as they suffered repression in other ways.

The economic disequilibrium between Catalonia and other areas of Spain gave rise to a second peculiar feature which distinguishes Catalonia from the territories of most Western minority languages: a primarily non-native working class. As industrial growth spurted in the early twentieth century, monolingual Castilian speakers immigrated from impoverished regions of the south of Spain to fill positions as manual laborers. This immigration was suspended during the years of the Spanish Civil War in the 1930s, but postwar recovery brought some one and a half million more Castilian-speaking immigrants into Catalonia, most of them members of the undereducated, unskilled, and illiterate rural proletariat. At the present time about 40% of the population are immigrants, and at least half of the population is Castilian-speaking. This figure reflects actual change in the demographic base of Catalonia, rather than linguistic shift on the part of the autochthonous population. Moreover, the Castilian-speaking population is heavily concentrated in the lower socioeconomic statuses of the community, with over 80% of the unskilled and semi-skilled labor force being immigrants (Sáez 1980).

The history of threatened status and official repression for the Catalan language is a long one. Castilian began to make unofficial inroads into Catalan-speaking territory through its elites as early as the seventeenth century, and official inroads began to be carved in the early eighteenth century. Catalan, however—never displaced as the vernacular language of Catalonia—underwent a successful literary and public revival in the late nineteenth and early twentieth centuries, accompanied by the economic and political pushes of the growing industrial bourgeoisie.

Despite a temporary reversal under the Spanish dictatorship of Primo de Rivera in the 1920s, the Catalan language achieved its greatest modern strength as the coofficial language of an autonomous Catalonia under the Second Spanish Republic, 1931–1939. At that time it had achieved a widely-accepted standardized form and became an important medium of administration, education, and information.

After its losses in the Civil War, however, Catalonia underwent not only the social and demographic change outlined above, but the most systematic linguistic and cultural repression it had yet experienced. Catalan was displaced from public and official spheres by force of law, and Castilian enjoyed a nearly 40-year reign of exclusive official status and almost exclusive use in formal and public domains. With Catalan absent from schools, government, business administration, and the information media, Catalans experienced an enforced diglossia and most became functionally illiterate in their native language.

The death of Franco in 1975 signaled the beginning of the end of the exclusive Castilian-language reign in the periphery, as well as the beginning of reorganization for the state as a whole. By the Statute of Autonomy of 1979, Catalonia regained its status as an autonomous community, similar (but not identical) to the status it had enjoyed in the Second Republic. As an "historic" community, Catalonia along with the Basque country was one of the first communities to be granted such status under the new government. Although the entire Spanish state has now been reorganized through the recognition of autonomous communities, Catalonia views its situation as distinct from that of regions such as Andalusia, Murcia, or the Castiles; its recent gain is seen as the recovery or reconstruction of a past status rather than as a new development.

The Statute of Autonomy grants Catalonia considerable but not absolute authority to administer its own affairs and define its own character. Such administration and self-definition take place within the framework of the Spanish state and constitution, and thus it is also within these limits that language planning takes place.

THE LEGAL STATUS OF THE LANGUAGES

As I have noted, some people imagined that with the passing of the Statute, the linguistic question was settled. However, there were several different notions of exactly how the question was settled, and what the results were. The day after passage of the Statute, an immigrant told me that the vote meant that "everything"—radio, television, cinema, schooling—would now be in Catalan. "That's what the Statute says," she informed me. Yet others believed that very little in their immediate world would change, because they believed that the documents mandated equal status for the two languages, a scrupulous official bilingualism.

In actual fact, the Spanish Constitution (Article 3) states in reference to language matters that: (1) Castilian is the official language of the state. All Spaniards have the obligation to know it and the right to use it; (2) The other languages of Spain (*lenguas españolas*) will also be official in the respective autonomous communities, in accordance with their Statutes; (3) The richness of the distinctive linguistic modalities is a cultural patrimony which will be the object of special respect and protection (author translation from Spanish).

Three points in this constitutional charter give rise to interpretive difficulties. First, some have noted a subtle distinction between the obligation to know Castilian—in itself clear enough and one of the constraints on Catalan policy—and the right, but not the obligation, to use it. Secondly, the constitution makes separate mentions of official status for each language, and never makes a straightforward and explicit statement of coofficiality. And lastly, it is unclear whether the special respect and protection it mandates for the "distinctive linguistic modalities" should be interpreted as enabling special affirmative action programs for minority languages.

The Catalan Statute of Autonomy (Article 3) states that (1) Catalan is Catalonia's "own" language (*llengua pròpia,* literally "proper language," in the sense that we use the term "proper name"); (2) Catalan is the official language of Catalonia, as is Castilian, which is official in all of the Spanish state; and (3) The *Generalitat* guarantees the normal and official use of both languages, and will adopt the means necessary to ensure that they are known, and will create conditions which will permit them to achieve full equality with respect to the rights and duties of citizens of Catalonia (author translation from Catalan).

The Statute introduces several new areas of vagueness, and thus of confusion and conflict over correct interpretation. Most problematic is the meaning of "proper language" in relation or contrast to "official language." No definition is given and there is no legal or popular precedent for interpreting these terms. Moreover, the meaning of "normal use," "full equality," and "necessary means" is not at all clear, nor is it clear who is entitled to decide these questions.

Taken together, the Constitution and the Statute can be interpreted as chartering at least three very different arrangements for sharing the official status granted. Contention hinges primarily on two points: the meaning of "proper language," and the intent of the special protection clause in the constitution. Catalan sociolinguists, like many others, recognize two principles for establishing language rights: the territorial and the individual (Ninyoles 1976). Accordingly, we can read the Constitution as establishing a kind of territorial-based privilege for Castilian, since it makes clear the obligation to know Castilian while no such obligation is maintained for Catalan. Within this interpretation, Castilian dominates because it is the territorial language of Spain, but measures are provided to honor and protect the individual rights of Catalan speakers.

In contrast, one can read by "proper language" in the Statute that Catalan is to be given territorial preeminence as the language of the autonomous nation, while the individual rights of Castilian speakers are to be honored on a more ad-hoc basis. And lastly, the two documents can be read as instituting a scrupulously bilingual policy in which the two languages are fully coofficial and therefore, in a sense, not completely autonomous from one another. Wherever one official language is found in public institutions, acts, and documents, then the other shall also be found. Not only would this imply the copresence of the two languages in all official communications, it might be seen to imply the institution of parallel systems for such public undertakings as education.

Each of these interpretations has been invoked either explicitly or implicitly by some group of supporters. The view that territorial supremacy for Castilian is mandated, with subordinate protection of the individual rights of Catalan speakers, seemed to emanate from Madrid in the early days of autonomy. In the state-run education system, for example, Castilian was the unmarked medium of instruction, with a long and complex procedure established by which schools could demonstrate consensus and apply for certification as Catalan-medium institutions.

The contrasting position, that Catalan must be given territorial supremacy in Catalonia, was endorsed by a group of Catalan language professionals in an essay asserting that the language was unlikely to survive under any other arrangement (Argente et al. 1979). This essay provoked a round of public discussions in 1980 as well as considerable response in print, and it came to be viewed as summarizing the Catalan territorialist position.

Lastly, the third possible position was represented in 1981 by 2300 Castilian-speaking intellectuals and professionals residing in Catalonia, who issued a "Manifesto: For equality of linguistic rights in Catalonia" (March 12, 1981). The manifesto protested the discrimination against Castilian speakers which the signers claimed could be found in the Catalan government's cultural and linguistic programs. The manifesto's authors characterized such actions as clearly unconstitutional, and called for the establishment of the permanent, fully-official bilingualism which they saw mandated by the Constitution and the Statute. Such bilingualism would entail the establishment of parallel institutions for education and equal distribution of public monies across Catalan and Castilian-language activities.

THE FAVORED INTERPRETATION

It is within this framework of ambiguity and conflict that we can turn now to examine the actual choices that have been made by those in charge of Catalonia's official policies and the strategies they have chosen for achieving their goals. It should be clear that a choice had to be made, and that no choice could fully and ultimately please all interested parties. Thus, in analyzing both the programs and persuasive tactics of Catalan policy and revealing the manipulative aspects of the language planning campaign, my purpose is not to criticize on any ethical grounds. Any decision and any program would have involved manipulation of symbols and groups for the management—exacerbation or diminution—of conflict. Our interest is in seeing how the Catalan language planning forces have done this, so that their eventual success or failure can be understood.

Not surprisingly, given the difficult social circumstances, the official program is characterized by extreme caution. Nonetheless, two important decisions have been made. The first is a decision to base the ultimate goal, the end point toward which planning is directed, on the territorial principle, buttressed by historical justifications and philosophies which equate a nation and a language. By this principle, Catalonia must ultimately be identified by a single language as the normal language of relations in society, and that language must be Catalan. The place of Castilian is as a second language. Although this goal is seldom articulated explicitly in official public statements, it is the position held by those charged with shaping and carrying out linguistic policy: the general director of linguistic policy, the director of the linguistic normalization service, the members of the sociolinguistic working group, and many others who have been involved formally and informally in the planning process. In the initial outline of a Charter of the Catalan language, the working group agreed that the long-range goal is application of the territorial principle and unique official status for Catalan (Torres 1980: 2). In an interview, the general director stated similarly that the planning goal is to arrive at territorial status for Catalan, saying that this is what is meant by "proper language." She sees the desirable role for Castilian as a complementary second language which is used to unite the people of Catalonia with those of the other autonomous communities.[2]

In no sense is the enhancement of the status of the Catalan language conceived as a deliberate means of enhancing the social status of speakers of Catalan. Timothy Reagan notes that status planning decisions almost inevitably favor one group over another (1983:150). In some areas of minority group subordination, this is the desired consequence of language planning. But in Catalonia, even the most convinced adherents of Catalan territoriality see this group favoritism as an undesirable side effect. The status of native Catalans is already elevated in comparison to the mass of Castilian speakers in the community, a fact to which all parties are considerably sensitized. Because of its association with socioeconomic superiority, in fact, Catalan is already the prestige language of the region in important ways (Woolard 1982, forthcoming).

---

[2] Interview with Aina Moll, July 22, 1980, pp. 22, 30.

This has been a critical condition for the second decision that has been made. That is the decision to treat the achievement of the ultimate goal as a process involving several transitional stages (taking place over the span of a generation) rather than as a fact to be created by fiat and implemented in one stage. Thus, while planners take history rather than current demography as the charter for choosing the endpoint of the planning process, they do take the current demographic situation seriously as the starting point. The general director, Aina Moll, stresses that her planners cannot act as if the complicated sociolinguistic situation did not exist. She believes that a program to make Catalan the language of all Catalans within 20 years should be acceptable to all.[3] This position allows planners to capitalize on and reshape the considerable degree of political sympathy for the Catalan cause which still exists among working-class Castilian immigrants, created largely by the equation of Catalanism with antifascism and democracy during the Franco years. Moll recognizes the need to eschew contrastive or confrontational tactics which would erode this sympathetic base and polarize the population.

Language planning toward the ultimate goal then takes on various short-term goals, and each of the other major possible alternative goals is subsumed in this process: first, the guarantee of individual Catalan rights within a dominantly Castilian atmosphere; then a fully bilingual transitional period; then a period of preference for Catalan within official bilingualism; and only then the sole official language policy. These consciously planned stages appear to parallel the stages through which Quebec has passed in its language policy from the 1969 Act to Promote the French Language in Quebec through the Official Language Act of 1974 to the 1977 Charter of the French Language, Bill 101 (Cobarrubias 1982:13).

THE POLITICS OF PERSUASION

With the chosen goal of status planning in mind, we can turn now to examine the persuasive process by which it is to be achieved in spite of the threat of conflicts. The first issue that is of interest within this program of transitions is the rubric under which the entire proceedings occur. "Normalization" or "linguistic normalization" is a term that is no more traditional or transparent in Catalan or Castilian than it is in English. The phrase was first introduced into Catalan sociolinguistic discourse in 1965 by the Valencian sociolinguist Lluis V. Aracil (Vallverdú 1979:5). Significantly, it is the term that has been taken up not only by sociolinguists, but by the government, political parties, and popular commentators as well, and it is now the most popular native term for the planning process.

Aracil first introduced the term in a cybernetic model of the interaction of language and society. He viewed normalization as a type of negative feedback or self-correction in the system, whereby a deficit in the social functions of language introduced by changing external conditions (political intrusion of the Spanish state in the Catalan social system, in this case) provokes a reorganization of the linguistic func-

---

[3] Interview, July 22, 1980, pp. 20, 24.

tions of society in compensation, to bring the system back into its original alignment. This he saw as an ideally "normal" reaction for the maintenance of the system. Neither purely social nor purely linguistic, normalization consists of a two-pronged attack in Aracil's model: linguistic-cultural change to develop the functions of the language, and sociopolitical change to reorganize the linguistic functions of society (Aracil 1982).

The term normalization appeals to Catalan planners because it captures the extralegal aspect of planning. As Vallverdú points out, normalization can be seen as more comprehensive than either "standardization" or "language planning." Both of these terms seem to emphasize the official and the legal aspect of language change. Normalization, on the other hand, implies not only a process, but a process that emphatically goes beyond legal processes. Normalization cannot be accomplished by decree but depends on the support, cooperation, even the initiative of the populace to make the situation "normal." Measures by decree are not only antidemocratic, but unproductive, especially given the demographic split of Catalonia (Vallverdú 1979). Since much of the demand for the Catalan language traditionally comes from the left, supporters can be made comfortable with the planning process when its emphasis lies so heavily and self-consciously on the efforts of the normal folk and the masses.

Thus the first significant appeal of the term is its implicit encompassing of the populace and the legal apparatus in a collective process. This emphasis is seen in the principal slogan of the campaign, "Catalan belongs to everyone" (El català, cosa de tots). As Moll has said, a collective will is an indispensable condition for Catalanization in the long run. "This will happen only if Catalans want it, and when I say Catalans, I mean all those who live in Catalonia, original Catalans and immigrants alike" (author translation from Catalan).[4] Again, due to the nearly 50–50 linguistic split in Catalonia, this is not empty rhetoric but pragmatic politics. The problem becomes one of persuading all Catalans, original and immigrant alike, to cooperate in this effort. Other features of the concept of normalization aid in this persuasion.

A second feature of the term which is especially appropriate to the purposes of Catalan supporters is essential in Aracil's model: the return to some prior state. In all of the Catalan rhetoric, regarding language as well as other aspects of nationalism, the emphasis is one of recovery (recuperació). It is said to be a return to an earlier, more natural and normal state that has been thrown out of balance by external intervention. Here it is the Francoist government which is cast as the intervener, the factor which displaced Catalan from its "normal" roles in public domains, rather than the shift in the population base.

Such appeals for recovery rarely address the issue of what state is to be recovered, when that state existed, or exactly what form it took. The most immediate positive antecedent available is that of the autonomous community under the Second Spanish Republic. But in many senses that short-lived adventure was the anomaly in modern Catalan history. And while it does serve as a fragile charter for cur-

---

[4] Interview, July 22, 1980, pp. 24–25.

rent demands, it is hardly the model to which many wish to appeal. Even under the
Republic, Catalan had only coofficial status rather than acknowledged legal predominance in its own territory, and it had no official recognition state-wide.

The historical situation which is to be recovered is therefore most often left
unspecified. Instead, "normalization" seems to imply that there is some normal
state for natural languages in literate societies that, unless deformed by political intervention, will normally be used for all available sociolinguistic functions in all
social domains. Limitation to a restricted set of domains is abnormal and not the
equilibrium the system normally seeks.

The choice of the term "normalization" carries an implicit legitimizing charter
for Catalanization. The term presupposes, sets as a condition for all action, the fact
that the current situation is "abnormal." If one is against normalization, then one is
by implication for abnormality. Although intervention may—indeed must—be consciously organized and is therefore in a sense artificial, it is in the service of a normal balance chartered in an unspecified way by natural forces and history. Even
special protection and compensatory measures then become appropriate, as is seen
in the public campaign slogan, "Normalization = restitution = compensation"
(author translation from Catalan) (Department de Cultura de la Generalitat de
Catalunya 1983:50).

The term normalization also has great persuasive utility because of its lack of
specificity regarding the ultimate goal of the normalization process. It does not carry
with it a single clear image of what normalcy might look like. In contrast, a term as
transparent as "Catalanization" may be too threatening to the Castilian-speaking
population, implying possibly assimilation and the loss of its own language.
"Recatalanization," on the other hand, while stressing historicity and recovery,
may seem too narrow to Catalan defenders, since it may be interpreted as applying
only to those individuals who have abandoned Catalan or those domains where it
was formerly used. The vagueness of the term normalization allows each supporter
to accept the most congenial reading.

In a weak reading, the object to be normalized is the Catalan language—that is,
the goal is to make it normal and acceptable for Catalan to be used for all possible
social functions. The point here is simply vertical extension of the domains of Catalan, putting it on an equal footing with Castilian in Catalonia. Such a goal may
imply certain affirmative action programs in cultural and communication media, but
these are only compensatory tactics in such a model, necessitated by the historical
institutional weight of Castilian to create the same prestige for Catalan and increase
its use in public and official domains. Normalization also carries a note of
normativization, and one can imagine that it refers primarily to corpus planning to
modernize Catalan. Thus, the main target as well as the main beneficiaries of normalization may in this view appear to be Catalan speakers themselves, who must be
encouraged to acquire and to use a correct, appropriate, and standardized Catalan
and extend it to domains where they are accustomed to using Castilian.

On the other hand, the object of normalization may be the linguistic situation,
and/or the society itself. The implication in this sense is that aspects of the current
situation are abnormal: for some, that it is abnormal to have a bilingual society,

especially when that society is identified and distinguishable principally—if not exclusively at this point in time—by its "own" language. A nation whose distinctive national language is not superordinate to other languages in the territory is abnormal.

This is, in fact, the position taken by current planners. Moll holds that "a language is an instrument of communication, and one is enough. Where there are two, the situation is perforce abnormal" (author translation from Catalan).[5] This belief is reinforced by the current sociolinguistic wisdom about diglossia and the impossibility of maintaining a situation of functional redundancy. Moll: "Either you have to divide them up by convention, or one will always end up on top of the other" (author translation from Catalan).

To normalize the society in this sense, then, not only must there be vertical extension of the language in question—elimination of diglossia, acquisition or recovery of high domains of use—but also horizontal extension of its use, to other social groups in the territory who do not currently use the language for any purpose. Castilian speakers do become a primary target to be acted upon.

The usefulness of the term, of course, lies in its ability to merge these various meanings and obscure the differences among them. Different groups who espouse distinct goals, or might do so if led to think about them, may all be persuaded to subscribe to or at least tolerate normalization. And, while both vertical and horizontal extension may be intended, the extension of the language to a sector of the population which has never used it is cast as a return to some normal state of the past. There was, after all, a time when nearly the whole population of Catalonia did use and identify with Catalan, and the current demographic situation is reinterpreted in terms of this past. Through this historical reinterpretation, Catalonia no longer seems to be confronted with new conditions which offer the possibility of new solutions.

Vagueness and ambiguity in the terminology of the planning process therefore provide much of the rhetorical capital for the persuasive process. However, the images through which the campaign has been communicated to the public are also significant. Of greatest interest is the figure who personifies normalization in government-issued materials.

This personification is "Norma," a cartoon character of a fair-haired little ten-year-old girl. The *Generalitat* has widely disseminated bilingual fliers and posters of Norma, as well as a series of comic strips in which Norma admonishes, cajoles, and instructs other characters in proper language use and attitudes. In the first mailing, colorful foldout fliers depicted a large bilingual population, hopefully awaiting the arrival of the little girl who just keeps saying "Catalan belongs to everyone." The balloon comments are lightly amusing, and are variously in Catalan, Castilian, and sometimes both languages—modeling a normal bilingual population which gets along well, enjoys mutual understanding, and shares the happy anticipation of the arrival of "La Norma."

---

[5] Interview, July 22, 1980, p. 29.

In this clever and likeable symbol we find the feminization and infantilization of normalization, which serves to greatly reduce the threat implied. Norma encourages the population toward acceptance and support of the normalization campaign by depicting visually, thus emphasizing the impact of, the weakest and least threatening readings of ''normalization,'' even while the course may be steered toward a more powerful ultimate goal.

Beyond the fact of Norma herself, what she has to say is also instructive. For in her childlike lectures to her peers and to adults, she does not discriminate among targets. In many of the cartoons, she chides Castilian speakers to realize that they at least understand her, and to make efforts to speak the language. But almost as often, it is Catalan speakers that she instructs in proper use of Catalan, avoidance of Castilianisms, and extension of Catalan to formal domains of use. She even occasionally corrects her friends' Castilian as well as their Catalan, showing her respect for the proper use of the Castilian language. Thus Norma defuses the tension that mounts when Castilian speakers feel themselves to be the only or principal targets to be ''normalized.'' The happy but firm little figure is designed to accustom the population in the gentlest manner possible to the normalization project in Catalonia.

The gentleness of this extensive campaign is matched by the caution of the new language law. Most of its text is devoted to establishing simple parity for Catalan in government administration, education, and the communications media. While it does provide for the creation of special institutions to foment both use of and knowledge about Catalan, these are compensatory rather than preferential measures.

The Spanish government was quick to spot any clauses which implied greater official authority for Catalan than for Castilian. One of the constitutionally-challenged articles provided for publication of official acts of the Catalan government in both Catalan and Castilian. However, it specified that where there is conflict between the texts, the Catalan version will be viewed as correct and binding. The Spanish government explained that it challenged this clause because it accords to the legislative body a privilege which belongs to the courts, that of interpreting the law; this explanation was obviously meant to minimize the political import of the challenge. However, it was a similar clause in Quebec's Official Language Act of 1974 that was a turning point in the history of status planning there (Cobarrubias 1982:13). There can be little doubt that both parties in the Catalan case have found this example instructive.

The current law must be seen as just a transitional point in Catalan planners' schema. But the public campaign for normalization, more than just a means of implementing the transitional goals, serves to prepare the ground and build a base for future policy maneuvers in which Catalonia may have to push on the limits set by the Spanish Constitution. Given the recursive nature of this process, it is too early to say whether or to what extent the public campaign for normalization has succeeded. It will take at least a generation to know if the ultimate goal of territorial supremacy is achievable.

Assessing the success of the normalization campaign to date, Moll (1982) contrasts earlier explosions of discontent, such as the Manifesto, with the much quieter response more recently, and concludes optimistically. But cynical Castilian defenders have suggested that the two-year delay in bringing legislation to the floor of the parliament was a deliberate strategy to erode opposition (Vallejo, Lopez, and Mañueco 1983). Moll writes that "with all the people of Catalonia unanimously supporting normalization, one can no longer speak of discriminations" (1982)(author translation from Catalan). To the extent that this is the case, it is in large part due to the strategic ambiguity of *both* the normalization effort, and the very concept of normalization itself.

REFERENCES

Aracil, Lluis V. 1982. Conflicte lingüístic i normalització lingüística a l'Europa nova. Papers de sociolingüística, ed. by Lluis V. Aracil, 23–38. Barcelona: La Magrana.

Argente, Joan et al. 1979. Una nació sense estat, un poble sense llengua? Els Marges 15. 3–15.

Cobarrubias, Juan. 1982. Language planning: The state of the art. Progress in language planning, ed. by Juan Cobarrubias, 3–26. Berlin: Mouton.

Department de Cultura de la Generalitat de Catalunya. 1983. La campanya per la normalització lingüística de Catalunya 1982. Barcelona.

Haugen, Einar. 1969. Language planning, theory and practice. The ecology of language, ed. by Anwar S. Dil, 287–298. Stanford: Stanford University Press.

Kloss, Heinz. 1969. Research possibilities on group bilingualism: A report. Quebec: International Center for Research on Bilingualism.

Manifesto: Por la igualdad de derechos lingüísticos en Cataluña. (March 12, 1981). Diario 16, Disidencias 17. Madrid.

Moll, Aina. 1982. El difícil i llarg camí de la normalització lingüística. Avui, October 21.

Ninyoles, Rafael. 1976. Bases per a una política lingüística democràtica a l'estat espanyol. València: Quaderns Tres i Quatre.

Reagan, Timothy. 1983. The economics of language: Implications for language planning. Language problems and language planning 7 (2). 148–161.

Recolons, Lluis et al. 1979. Catalunya: Home i territori. Barcelona: Editorial Blume.

Sáez, Armand. 1980. Catalunya, gresol o explotadora? Notes sobre imigració i creixement. Immigració i reconstrucció nacional a Catalunya, 25–42. Barcelona: Editorial Blume.

Torres, Joaquim. 1980. Esborrany de 'carta de mesures per a la normalització de l'ús del català.' Barcelona: Unpublished manuscript.

Vallejo, A., Lopez, I., & Mañueco, J. P. 1983. La emigración castellana; crónica de dos genicidios. Madrid: Editorial Riodelaire.

Vallverdú, Francesc. 1979. La normalització lingüística a Catalunya. Barcelona: Laia.

Woolard, Kathryn A. 1982. The problem of linguistic prestige: Evidence from Catalonia. Penn Review of Linguistics 6. 82–89.

_____. Forthcoming. The politics of language and ethnicity in Barcelona, Spain. Stanford University Press.

PART IV

LANGUAGE AS A CULTURAL, POLITICAL, AND SOCIAL MARKER

NINE

Human Rights: An International Linguistic Hyperbole

Klaus K. Obermeier

Battelle Columbus Laboratories

Is not peace, in the last analysis, a matter of Human Rights? (J. F. Kennedy)

The purpose of this study is to investigate the linguistic use of the term *human rights*. In particular, I propose to give an account of what politicians and human rights advocates mean (or don't mean) when they use the term in speeches and articles. The major problem that anyone dealing with human rights faces is that it connotes and even denotes different things for different nations and their representatives. Moreover, the concept of *rights* and its attribute *human* conjures up different meanings for laymen and researchers as well as for politicians and human rights advocates.

THE CONCEPT OF A RIGHT

According to the current literature a right can be interpreted as a second party duty where A's right against B and B's duty to A stand in the relation of an obligation on B's part to warrant A's (moral) right (Brandt 1959). Feinberg (1970) contends that a right implies a valid claim to something and a valid claim against someone. Thus the concept of a right has, in general, three components: the person (thing?) that holds a specific right, the person that grants or redeems the right, and the right itself.

Human rights are rights held by individuals either as absolute rights or prima facie rights. The latter type are rights that can be overridden by other more important considerations (Martin 1980); this possibility, however, does not imply that the right which has been overridden vanishes.

METAPHYSICAL CONSIDERATIONS

The most common context in which human rights are subject to metaphysical considerations concerns the relationship between the individual and the society he or she lives in. The function of society for the individual can be characterized in two different, totally opposite concepts.

As Thoumi (1981:181) points out: the concept of society can either mean "an association of free individuals who belong to the society because it is convenient to do so, or as an entity in which each individual is assigned a position or function to maximize a concept of social well-being.''

In the first case, each individual will have more freedom and must rely on his own capabilities more so than in the latter case. The choice between these two possibilities always depends on the metaphysical conviction of the individual. It is worth noting here that this distinction is the basic difference between democratic and communist societies, the former allowing more freedom for the individual, whereas the latter demands more discipline and loyalty towards the state.

METAETHICAL CONSIDERATIONS

Another very important aspect of human rights is the metaethical consideration. Can it be shown or proven that something is morally good or bad, right or wrong? A number of so-called noncognitivist human rights theorists (Machan 1980) deny the possibility of a proof by claiming there are no certainties in the field of values. For there are no true or false beliefs about values, but only better or worse decisions and choices (MacDonald 1967:54). The opposite point of view—the cognitivist one—strives for normative definitions of human rights to be implemented by society (Rand 1968, Mack 1977, Gewirth 1971): individuals have rights when, for some reason, a collective goal is not a sufficient justification for denying them what they wish, as individuals, to have or to do, or not sufficient justification for imposing some loss or injury upon them (Dworkin 1977: xi).

It should be obvious by now that the term human rights not only has the potential to be misinterpreted but also to be abused for reasons of "realpolitik." Unless a common denominator for the meaning of human rights can be found, its use will be limited to mere rhetoric and polemic. In the following analysis of speeches dealing with human rights, the denotation and connotation will be delineated.

The data for my study consisted originally of about 40 speeches and articles dealing with the human rights issue. Out of these 40, I chose to investigate about 10 .extensively. Since two common themes recur in all the speeches I looked at, it seems feasible to group them accordingly into those that consider human rights as moral values and those that view human rights from an ideological standpoint.

HUMAN RIGHTS AS VALUES

As could be seen from the discussion above, human rights is not an analytic term but rather an evaluative one (McCamant 1981). Coupled with the notion of morality, it can be used to condemn people or nations for different convictions concerning morality and human rights.

> Our commitment to human rights must be absolute, our laws fair, our national beauty preserved; the powerful must not persecute the weak, and human dignity must be enhanced. (258)
>
> Peoples more numerous and more politically aware are craving, and now demanding, their place in the sun—not just for the benefit of their own physical condition, but for basic human rights.

> Our moral sense dictates a clear-cut preference for those societies which share with
> us an abiding respect for individual human rights. (Carter 1977:259)

The reference to an absolute commitment evokes the impression that we are dealing
with a clearly defined concept, since we only commit ourselves to something that
has been clearly defined previously. Along these lines Scoble and Wiseberg
(1981:167) conclude that "there is today an almost universal, yet inarticulate and
just unjustified, assumption that there is a single correct level of analysis for examination of human rights progress and violations *and* that the level is that of the
nation-state."

The idealistic nature of human rights becomes evident when basic human rights
are contrasted with physical conditions. Again, Carter is, like many others that talk
about human rights, convinced that human rights is an issue removed from the immediate reality and that it does not pertain to physical, that is, living conditions
directly. The mentioning of politically aware peoples that are demanding basic human rights supports this claim, since political ideas (e.g. human rights) start out as
abstract concepts that might eventually be realized.

After establishing an absolute commitment on the basis of political awareness,
Carter tries to invoke the moral sense to justify value judgments with respect to
certain societies that do not follow the same standards. The verb *abiding* transforms
the rather vague allusion to a moral sense into a law-like notion (e.g. law-abiding
citizen). The focus of basic human rights has changed to individual human rights. It
is obvious that in Western societies individual rights are more clearly defined than
rights for groups or nations; moreover, individual rights vary from nation to nation;
they are bound by the culture. Mentioning individual rights gives the audience a
much broader basis for identifying with this plight for respecting their personal
rights or privileges.

A further implication of this statement is that there are societies that do not share
the same respect for human rights, thus putting societies that do share it in a morally
superior position. Thus human rights is no longer a political question but a question
of ethics and morals. It is in this speech that Carter gives us a preview of what lies
ahead with respect to the human rights issue: human rights as moral values to be
used as political arguments in a clash of ideologies.

The importance of morality is emphasized in the following excerpt of a speech
by David Owen, former Secretary of State for Foreign and Commonwealth Affairs,
delivered to the Diplomatic and Commonwealth Writers Association:

> Equally, the Communist countries must recognize that concern for human rights is not
> a diversionary tactic but an integral part of foreign policy in the western democracies.
> Of course we have to balance morality with reality. The art again lies in striking the
> right balance. This is a subject on which I welcome and seek to stimulate discussion
> and debate.
>   This is not an excuse for dodging the issue: it is the means by which we try to draw
> the fine line between measures that stand a chance of being effective and those which
> will spark counter-productive reaction. (1977:372)

Human rights is seen as a matter of morality that the communist countries are liable to neglect. Morality has to succumb to goals of "realpolitik." Owen condones the trade-off between morality as an idealistic concept and "raison d'état" as a pragmatic force. The role of politicians is to solve an ethical issue on the basis of socioeconomic considerations. To put it rather bluntly: Human rights are considered as long as they don't cost anything. On the other hand, paying lip-service to ethical values improves the image of a nation considerably.

A more severe result of the "moral equals human rights" theme is that naturally people draw the inference that those who do not adhere to human rights in an arbitrarily given form do not have any moral or ethical values. The next step is, of course, to claim that nations which do not have ethical values are not as valuable or good as nations that do, that is, Western democracies are better than Eastern communist countries. In this context, I would like to refer back to my previous discussion on p. 106 in which the disagreement on values is moved to a higher (metaethical) level: only under the admittedly brute-force assumption that normative definitions are accepted can we claim that there are certainties in the field of values. This, however, does not solve the problem in the least; it only moves it to a still higher level of abstraction.

It is common knowledge that Lenin made his opinions about values and ethics explicit. He contended at various times that people will witness the decay of values in societies that adhere to ethical considerations of this sort. However, he certainly did not mean by that that humans do not have intrinsic values (e.g., life and its manifestations). He was referring to the values that "capitalistic" societies conferred upon their members, such as private property, amassing of material wealth to the exclusion of others, and so on. Thus it is very important to realize that values and ethics are connected to the form of society in which a person lives. As a result, human rights do not exist in the abstract, in isolation from society (Kudryavtsev 1976).

The mitigating process of human rights as a moral issue vis-a-vis "realpolitik" is also addressed by A. Cecil, Chancellor of the Southwest Legal Foundation, in a speech delivered to the Rotary Club of Dallas, Texas. The subtitle reads: *Selective Application. Danger of Self-Righteousness.*

We live in an imperfect world, and it is not surprising that charges of selective morality have been leveled against the human rights policy recently proclaimed by President Carter. As a result of the actualities of power politics, only small countries of little strategic importance are being rewarded by having a growing share of our military and economic assistance channeled to them when they respect human rights of their people, or are punished by restrictions on the flow of assistance when they curtail human rights. (675)

Our renewed interest in human rights is not a consistent or fundamental tenet of our foreign policy when different standards are applied. . . (675)

Because of misleading assumptions, the issue of human rights may affect adversely not only our relations with our totalitarian enemies but also those with friendly governments. One of these assumptions is the belief that left-wing totalitarian governments are more "humane" than right-wing totalitarian regimes. (675)

> We are running the danger of setting up double standards for the manner in which we respond to violations of human rights whenever we try to strike a balance between morality and reality. (676)
>
> Human rights is a moral issue, and religious traditions emphasize the dignity of man. (1978:678)

The term "selective morality" and the mentioning of different standards are rather harsh criticism of the Carter government. They verify the previously seen theme of exploiting the human rights issue for political expediency. The progression in Cecil's speech seems to go from considering human rights from a political stand-point to viewing it as a matter of ethics that is beyond politics and instilled in every human being per se. His allegation thus follows the same reasoning we have seen in Owen's speech: there is something (God-)given about values, and all the societies that do not cling to this eternal system are considered to be deviant in an ethical and social sense. A further piece of evidence for the charges of selective morality is found in former Ambassador to Argentina R. Hill's speech to the Argentine-American Chamber of Commerce:

> As for tactics, and here we return to Argentina, the obvious problem is that different national situations and varying U.S. interests dictate employing different strategies with different countries. But such flexibility on a moral issue like human rights imme-diately makes the U.S. vulnerable to charges of hypocrisy. (Hill 1977:615)

The contention that when it comes to a clash of U.S. interests and human rights, the former have to dictate what is to be done shows that the human rights issue has been used as a political propaganda concept, alluding to ethics when, in reality, power is at stake. Moreover, in numerous other speeches, human rights often falls victim to ethnocentricity in that it is connected with deep-rooted national value. There should be no doubt that human rights have different meanings for different nations; thus C. Vance's statements to the National Association for the Advancement of Colored People:

> Our policies must reflect our national values. Our deep belief in human rights—political, economic, and social—leads to policies that support their promotion throughout Africa . . . One of Africa's principal concerns is that its basic human needs be met. (1977:643)

What this says is that the United States will help Africa as long as it adheres to the same values that the United States has; on the other hand, the concession that its basic human needs be met reflects that assumption that there are Africa-specific needs that might not figure prominently in the United States due to affluence or other factors. The undercurrent of Vance's statement is, however, that no matter what needs Africans have, they have to be in line with American principles in order to be supported by the United States.

Thus the line of reasoning that human rights depend on ethical and moral consid-erations is confounding the issue of metaethics and politics, in that moral convic-tions are not subject to political approval, or at least should not be. From the discussion above a common theme seems to develop: although human rights is supposedly an issue of morality, politicians use it to cherish or put down political systems on the basis of there being one concept, one value for all people that is unequivocally accepted: human rights as an absolute measurement of human well-being within a society.

Moreover, the form of government determines the nature of the relationship between state and individual as far as rights are concerned. It is often the case that the different rights which an individual has are neglected (e.g., socioeconomic rights in the United States). It is also the case that individual rights derive from different sources (e.g., social rights derive from ideological considerations). Along with misconceptions concerning the diversity of rights come misconceptions about the nature of rights: which rights protect the individual vis-a-vis the state and vice versa. Thus to treat human rights as an abstract and esoteric concept, only to be manipulated by politicians for their motives, is missing the significance of talking about and dealing with human rights.

HUMAN RIGHTS AS PART OF AN IDEOLOGY

In the previous section, human rights was considered to be a moral issue. Speakers tried to integrate it into a more comprehensive framework, thus transcending ethics and leading into politics and ideologies. In this section, we will look at evidence for the claim that human rights are often equated to Western democracies only with the exclusion of Eastern countries. If this turns out to be true, human rights is but a figure of speech within ideological controversies.

> One of those constructive forces is enhancement of individual freedoms through the strengthening of democracy, and the fight against deprivation, torture, terrorism and the persecution of people throughout the world. The struggle for human rights overrides all differences of color, nation or language. . . . The battle for human rights—at home and abroad—is far from over. . . . If we are to serve as a beacon for human rights we must continue to perfect here at home the rights and values we espouse around the world. (Carter 1981:227)

Human rights are no longer viewed as a matter of morality but as a rather militant expression of disagreement between two parties. The battle-metaphor suggests that there will be a winner and a loser at the end. The metaphorical use of *fight* and *battle* is setting the stage for a more deeply felt conflict: democracy on the one side and possibly communism on the other side. Democracy is mentioned as a constructive force, thus implying that although there may be other constructive forces too, democracy might be the most effective one. The metaphorical use of words is carried further by referring to the United States as "a beacon for human rights." Beacon is usually associated with light, guidance, and a higher vantage point. By implying that the United States has the potential to function in this capacity, Carter again implies that the form of our society is the ultimate reason for this privilege. Moreover, a beacon is often the only help for seafarers (at least in the preelectronic age), thus the implication is that the United States has the function to direct the promotion of human rights throughout the world, at the same time promoting democracy as the substrate for human rights.

Along the same lines, human rights is interpreted by Buergenthal, Dean of the Washington College of Law, in a speech given at The Pan American Development Foundation and Meridian House International:

> The current Administration falls into a similar trap. Its spokesmen criticize and reject a strong human rights policy because they see it as having purely moral but very little, if any, political significance. They view it as a propaganda tool. (414)
>
> A sound human rights policy provides the U.S. with an ideology that distinguishes us most clearly from the Soviet Union and seriously undercuts the ideological appeal of Communism. (415)
>
> To suggest that we are imposing our values on others by promoting human rights in other countries, be it against totalitarianism or oppressive regimes, is to reveal one's arrogance and ignorance. (1981:415)

What Buergenthal is saying is that human rights should be considered as part of an ideology; however, to equate human rights with value judgments is missing the point. There should be a clear-cut line between the imposing of values on others and the promoting of human rights. What Buergenthal termed "intervention by associa- tion" (1981:415) expresses the commonly advocated notion that the way allies of the United States deal with human rights reflects on the stand of the United States on the issue at hand. What is called for is clearly a notion of human rights independent of the form of government.

To safeguard oneself against such allegations of equating human rights with de- mocracy, politicians take great pains in disclaiming that they use human rights to promote democracy, a procedure that often leads to inconsistencies in their speeches:

> We are determined to encourage the free movement of people and ideas and respect for human rights . . . Abuses of human rights, wherever they occur, are the legitimate subject of international concern. The dignity of man stands on values which transcend national frontiers. And in the democracies of the west it is inevitable and right that foreign policy should not only reflect the values of society, but that those who conduct foreign affairs should respond positively to the weight of public opinion and concern. In Britain we will take our stand on human rights in every corner of the globe. We will not discriminate . . .
>
> We recognize that the issue of human rights is only one strand in the complex east/ west relations. (Owen 1977:372)

By singling out Western democracies, Owen does indeed discriminate against the communist nations. In this speech, the progression from the morality to the ideol- ogy theme can be witnessed. The use of the words "dignity" and "transcend" evokes the eternal ethics that by association are only upheld by democracies. That politicians realize the discrepancy in their contentions is proven by Owen's state- ment "We will not discriminate," when, in fact, he has already done so in the pre- ceding lines.

It is not uncommon practice in speeches to associate the East with the negative connotation, while associating the West with the positive one. In a speech to the Commonwealth Club in San Francisco, former U.S. Supreme Court Justice Arthur Goldberg referred to

> our outrage at the incidents which occurred in the East in direct contravention of the Final Act and in profound disregard of its provisions in the area of human rights and fundamental freedoms. (1978:520)

I will now present an account of one of Breznev's speeches to the Communist Party of the Soviet Union Central Committee on the occasion of the new draft constitution of the U.S.S.R.:

> It is known that the present constitution provides for a broad complex of social and economic rights of fundamental importance for the people. However, we are well aware of how their content has deepened and how much richer and weightier have become the material guarantees behind them. All this is reflected in the new draft constitution. While, formerly, it granted the general right to work, that is now complemented by the right to choose professions, occupations, and jobs in accordance with the vocation, abilities, professional training and education of the citizens and, what is no less important, with due account of the social needs. (1977:548)

In this excerpt we find the notion of a right is more restricted in contradistinction to the propagandistic style of the previous speeches. What Breznev tries to spell out here is the obligation on the part of the state to provide for its citizens. Another aspect of this definition of a right as basic as the right to work is that, in the United States, socioeconomic rights are neglected; thus the role of the state with respect to rights is different due to the different ideologies.

Whereas Western democracies ordinarily do not spell out basic human rights, communist countries have to due to their form of government. It does not surprise us that Breznev proclaims a further right that we take for granted:

> The draft also speaks about one right of Soviet citizens which is not in the present constitution. I am referring to the right to housing, which will be provided more and more fully as the housing program is implemented through state assistance to cooperative and individual housing construction. Our new constitution is one of the first in the world to proclaim that vital human right. (p. 548)

The viewpoint of a Soviet citizen concerning the implementation of his rights is also determined in the constitution:

> The draft constitution proceeds from the assumption that the rights and freedoms of citizens cannot and must not be used against our social system. (p. 548)

Thus this constitution has two functions: to protect the individual, and to incorporate the citizen into the structure of the state. The use of human rights in this context is more operationally defined and pragmatically motivated. If the citizen wants to enjoy his or her privileges, he or she has to contribute in due course. The striking feature of this and other Breznev speeches is the lack of recourse to ethical and moral issues with respect to human rights. The rights of the individual are conferred by the government on the citizen: human rights do not exist in the abstract. As Kudryavtsev (1976:199) puts it: "There are no human rights in the abstract, in isolation from society. A right is an opportunity guaranteed by the state to enjoy the social benefits and values existing in the given societies." Thus, the same right has a different content or function in different societies.

Although Western statesmen often associate human rights policies and their observance with democratic nations, they do so to support their own political system and moral values. The contention is that human rights are observed provided that people adhere to the respective form of government. The use of the terms *human rights* and *democracy* becomes circular. Can we, on the basis of the political situation in the U.S.S.R., for instance, expect that human rights have the same status as in the United States? The answer is no, since their political system and constitution do not allow for the same role the individual plays in such a society as in the United States. When both forms of government are compared side by side, we will see a dialectic clash that has its effects particularly in the area of responsibilities (rights) of the individual towards the state and vice versa. Moreover, the criticism of communist nations by Western democracies is based on an idealistic understanding of rights. In most speeches, human rights are referred to in the abstract, only mentioned as a catch word, without being defined.

CONCLUSION

As we have seen throughout the discussion of the use of human rights in speeches, human rights, for the most part, are discussed as if they were dependent on the particular society (political system); at least, this seems to be the view of Western statesmen. Human rights become associated with a particular form of government (e.g., democracy). The common denominator of human rights is that every government claims to honor human rights, while postulating that political systems different from their own do not. In the East bloc nations, every right has to be spelled out, since all those rights are conferred by the state upon the individual. Thus, to compare human rights on the basis of the form of society in which the individual lives is like comparing apples and oranges.

Human rights activists add to this seemingly empty denotation (due to the lack of a common basis) a variety of connotations: ideological, moral, economic, and religious ones (if human rights are derived from God's power). The argument that a particular form of government lends itself better to implementing human rights is somewhat circular and such reasoning is used by the United States (as seen in the aforementioned speeches) as well as by the U.S.S.R. whose appearance before the Human Rights Commission of the United Nations caused Professor C. Tomuschat (Bonn, West Germany), a member of the Human Rights Commission of the United Nations, to remark that on behalf of the Commission there exist neither socialist, capitalist, nor developing countries, but only states which ratified the human rights convention and which, by this very act, are obliged to obey the contract. No nation can claim to satisfy the rules and regulations by simply referring to its own form of government.

In conclusion, I would like to stress that due to the conceptual and metaphysical bias of human rights, the term is used metalinguistically as an analogy for the relation of the individual to the state or government. Although politicians and human rights advocates use the term, it remains semantically and pragmatically empty if it is not considered within the given context of a nation and its philosophy. Within the context of a particular society, or as part of an operational definition (see Breznev's speech) human rights is conceptualized according to the intentions of persons or institutions which use the term in a specific situation. What is behind the disagreement on the semantic and pragmatic side of human rights is the adherence to diametrically opposed political systems that define the role of the individual within the society and, subsequently, his rights.

If the meaninglessness of the lip service paid to human rights is not realized, misinterpretations and ill-advised polemic will continue to prevail.

REFERENCES

Brandt, R. 1959. Ethical theory. Englewood Cliffs, NJ: Prentice Hall.
Breznev, L. 1977. Address to the Soviet Union Central Committee. Vital Speeches 43 (18). 546–551.
Buergenthal, T. 1981. Human rights and the U.S. national interest. Vital Speeches 47(13). 414–416.
Carter, J. 1977. Inaugural address. Vital Speeches 43(9). 258–259.
———. 1981. Farewell address. Vital Speeches 47(8). 226–228.
Cecil, A. 1978. Human rights. Selective application. Danger of self-righteousness. Vital Speeches 44(22). 674–678.
Dworkin, R. 1977. Taking rights seriously. Cambridge: Cambridge University Press.
Feinberg, J. 1970. The nature and value of rights. Journal of Value Inquiry 4. 243–257.
Gewirth, A. 1971. The Normative structure of action. The Review of Metaphysics 25. 238–261.
Goldberg, A. 1978. Human rights and the Belgrade conference. Vital Speeches 44(17). 519–521.
Hill, R. 1977. Argentina today. Vital Speeches 43(20). 612–615.
Kudryavtsev, V. 1976. The truth about human rights. Human Rights 5. 193–199.
MacDonald, M. 1967. Natural rights. Philosophy, politics and society, ed. by Peter Laslett, 33–55. Oxford University Press.
Machan, T. 1980. Some recent work in human rights theory. American Philosophical Quarterly 17(2). 103–113.
Mack, E. 1977. Natural and contractual rights. Ethics 87. 145–153.
Martin. R. 1980. On the justification of rights. Philosophy in action, ed. by G. Fløistad. Paris: Le Seuil.
McCamant, J. F. 1981. A critique of present measures of human rights. Development and an alternative. Global human rights, comparative measures and NGO strategies, ed. by V. P. Nada. Boulder, CO: Westview Press.
Nada, V. P. 1981. Global human rights, comparative measures, and NGO strategies. Boulder, CO: Westview Press.
Owen, D. 1977. Detente, Helsinki and human rights. The British view. Vital Speeches 43(12). 369–372.
Rand, A. 1968. Man's Rights. Reprinted in Readings in introductory philosophical analysis, ed. by John Hospers, 364–385. Englewood Cliffs: Prentice Hall.
Scoble, H., & Wiseberg, Laurie. 1981. Problems of comparative research on human rights. Global human rights, comparative measures and NGO strategies, ed. by V. P. Nada. Bouder, CO: Westview Press.
Thoumi, F. 1981. Human rights policy. Basic needs and economic implication for LCD's. Journal of Interamerican Studies and World Affairs 23(2). 177–201.
Vance, C. 1977. U.S. policy toward Africa. Vital Speeches 43(21). 642–645.

TEN

Language Strategists in India*

Brian Weinstein
Howard University

During his successful campaign to become chief minister of the State of Andhra Pradesh in southern India, N. T. Rama Rao was asked about the importance of the type of new and purely regional and ethnic political party he headed. His response revealed the continuing and growing role of language as a cultural, political, and social marker in the world's most linguistically diverse nation. He said that parties should be organized according to region, particularly if regions are linguistically defined (Ramaswamy 1983:24). His subsequent election in January 1983, along with that of Ramakrishna Hegde in neighboring Karnataka State, pushed the dominant national Congress (I) party out of all southern states and territories except for Kerala. In March the leaders of the ruling state and linguistically-based parties of Andhra Pradesh, Karnataka, Tamil Nadu, and Pondicherry met to institutionalize their shared interests by creating the Southern Council of Chief Ministers which intends to press the central government "for more decision-making powers and a greater share of federal funds" (Claiborne 1983: A24). These efforts at political and economic decentralization, which been temporarily stopped by the election following the death of Mrs. Gandhi, may necessitate a further differentiation of Telugu, Kannada, and Tamil linguistic identities from the Hindi-speaking north in the years to come.

Concurrent demands by some Sikhs in the Punjab for greater autonomy, efforts in Assam to resist the influx of non-Assamese, and demands elsewhere for the exclusive use of local languages rather than Hindi, English, or other regional languages prove that language persists in India as a potent instrument for politicians at the center and in the states. The forces at work could change the relationship between the states and the central government in the years to come.

These political elites cannot by themselves fashion language into a symbol of identity and an instrument for government operations and education. They need the assistance of politically committed and innovative writers, poets, translators, singers, and other artisans who have proven their importance since the beginning of

* Thanks to a fellowship from the Indo-American Fellowship Program I spent most of 1981 in India where I was affiliated with the Central Institute of Indian Languages, Mysore. I am grateful to CIIL, its directors, Dr. D.P. Pattanayak and Dr. E. Annamalai, and to the American Association of Indian Studies in Delhi, Madras, and Calcutta. I alone am responsible for the interpretations and conclusions.

115

the independence movement and since the start of many reformist movements. Not all linguistic innovators were or are politically inspired. Purely aesthetic motives and the desire for self-expression are probably paramount for most. Those who have been committed to assisting political elites through change in language form should be called "language strategists." The networks to which they belong legitimize and diffuse their innovations so that they can be used for political purposes if political elites so desire. The alliance of cultural and political networks sharpens or creates a sense of linguistically-based nationality or ethnicity. Therefore, the study of language strategists and the means used to disseminate their ideas and choices in India is one way to understand the link between language change and the political developments represented by the growing regional loyalties in South India.[1]

LANGUAGE AS A MARKER IN INDIA

Almost every type of group in the world's second largest country has been defined at one time or other on the basis of language despite the importance of other markers such as religion. During this century people have been told that a variety of language is the symbol of a caste, a class, an ethnic group, a region, religion, or all of India. Their leaders have explained that they must pursue their interests through a defense of the language; that they must perceive themselves as different from people using languages defined as different; and that they must conform to certain linguistic usages to be a loyal member of the group. The leaders demand the use of the variety in education and government and insist that certain other languages be excluded.

Tamil Nadu in the southeast and West Bengal in the northeast are states where one can observe these phenomena. While many centripetal forces operate within India to pull these two states toward the 20 other states, important centrifugal forces pull them toward particularism and local loyalties. Conflicting interests within each state influence relations with the center as well.

India's highly developed infrastructure of railroads, motor roads, airlines, and telegraph and postal systems pull all regions together. The economy is reasonably interdependent and it is recognized that the best government jobs are in the federal or union service. Hinduism, the religion of the vast majority of Indians, tends to unite although there are many varieties and no central hierarchy to ensure conformity. Pride in the freedom movement culminating in national independence in 1947 is widely shared by Bengalis and Tamils as well as other Indians. The many heroes of that struggle—Mahatma Gandhi, Jawaharlal Nehru, Tilak, and many others—belong to all Indians. The late Prime Minister Indira Gandhi, astutely appealed to all elements of the population in an effort to remain in office and forestall division.

At the same time, opposing forces provide a context favorable to efforts aimed at sharpening local identities. Madras, Madurai, and other cities have long been important centers of cultural and political activity in the south. The state or region is

---

[1] I have dealt with language strategists in detail in Brian Weinstein, *The Civic Tongue: The Political Consequences of Language Choices* (New York: Longman, 1983), pp. 62–78.

perceived by many as the most important arena for politics. Key political parties are purely state-based such as the Dravida Munnetra Kazhagam (DMK) and the All India Anna Dravida Munnetra Kazhagam (AIADMK), each of which uses the term *Dravidian,* meaning "southern" in its name. The Self-Respect Movement, a purely Tamil affair, pitted non-Brahmans against Brahmans and also focused attention on local affairs. In West Bengal, Calcutta, the former capital of India, was the home of important political, cultural, and social movements before independence and today boasts a vibrant cultural life overshadowing New Delhi, the current capital. Calcutta's book publishing industry, for example, is very dynamic. Like Tamils, the Bengalis tend to look at local politics as most important. The Brahmo Samaj movement pitted reformist Bengali Hindus against conservative Bengali Hindus. Although the ruling party, Communist Party of India-Marxist (CPI-M), is not restricted to West Bengal, Bengalis consider it to be their own and take pride in recalling other Bengali radicals such as Subhas Chandra Bose who competed with Gandhi and Nehru for leadership of the nationalist movement.

Tamils and Bengalis joined hands in 1958 at a meeting held in Calcutta to protest plans that Hindi would become the only national language used in central government administration. C. Rajagopalachari, a Tamil Brahman serving as governor of West Bengal, denounced the so-called "Hindi fanatics" who should "concentrate on their own states. When they succeed, let them come to West Bengal or Madras" (Official Language 1958:208). In the West Bengal State Assembly, the chief minister B.C. Roy said at the same time that no single language "should be forced upon any other linguistic areas in the country" (Official Language 1958: 224). Efforts in the 1960s to make Hindi the only link language, thus replacing English in communications between states and the center, were met with rioting and resistance, particularly in Tamil Nadu. State government officials appear to oppose the spread of Hindi: educational policy in Tamil Nadu and West Bengal has minimized the usefulness of Hindi and English while emphasizing Tamil and Bengali. Bengalis and Tamils are now known for their language loyalty. Mallik reports that of all Indians they in particular prefer radio programs in their own language to Hindi or English, for example (Mallik 1982:146). Tamil and Bengali literacy, while is higher than literacy in the Hindi-speaking areas of the north, provides a large reading public for the numerous and popular Tamil and Bengali language newspapers, books, and magazines. Although Hindi films are increasingly popular, the Tamil and Bengali film industry is very important.

Both Bengalis and Tamils have experienced a splitting up of their territory forcing a redefinition of identities. In 1905 the Bengalis were split into a predominantly Hindu and a predominantly Muslim state by the British who feared growing radicalism. Although the two states were reunited, they split again in 1947 with the creation of Pakistan. These experiences challenged intellectuals and politicians to redefine themselves and their constituencies either in religious or linguistic terms. Discrimination against Muslim Bengalis in Pakistan—including the choice of Urdu as the sole official tongue—muted the religious basis for loyalty and raised language to a new level of acuity which led to the independence of Bangladesh.

Although many intellectuals in southern India campaigned for the unification of Bengal after 1905, they questioned administrative frontiers which put Telugus, Tamils, Kannada, and Malayalam speakers together. As war began in 1914, Telugu speakers called for separation. In 1920, the Congress movement approved the goal of linguistically-based states, and it used regional languages in its own discussions and deliberations at the regional level. After independence, party hesitation on this issue sparked Telugu and Marathi agitation. The State Reorganization Commission was appointed to discuss the matter in 1953; it suggested some reorganization of state boundaries, and in 1956 new linguistic states came into being. Tamil Nadu with a majority of Tamils was created alongside Karnataka with a Kannada dominance and Andhra Pradesh with the Telugus in the majority. The movements, the debates, and the drawing of new lines sharpened ethnic and linguistic sensitivities.

The religious conflict leading to the creation of Pakistan had a linguistic aspect which continues to affect India. Although the masses of northern Indians spoke a language influenced by both Sanskrit and Persian, Muslim and Hindu elites attempted to convince them that they must use two different languages, Hindi in the Devanagari or Sanskrit-based script or Urdu in the Persian script depending on their religion. This effort sharpened the differences between the two populations (Brass 1974). It contributed to a steady "purification" of the languages meaning a removal of Sanskrit-based words from Urdu, which was declared the official language of Pakistan even though the majority of Pakistanis could not speak it, and the removal of many Persian words from Hindi. Bengali writers in particular, and on both sides of the frontier, felt pressure to remove the so-called polluting elements from their poetry and prose. Few creative writers have been able to avoid being swept up in political and social changes of all kinds. Some consciously decided to contribute to them by helping make a form of language a marker for a community.

ROLE OF WRITERS IN MAKING LANGUAGE A MARKER

At the end of the nineteenth and the beginning of the twentieth centuries' population movement, greater individual freedom, secular and Christian education, new classes and changing senses of identity subsequent to the coming of the British, urbanization, industrialization, the integration of India into worldwide commerce, and the rise of the liberation movement released new creative cultural forces. Poets who had been employed to amuse a rural aristocracy or to remind Indians of the virtues of the gods and goddesses moved to cities or emerged from newly prosperous merchant families to write for newspapers read by an increasingly literate public. With a sense of themselves as a secular rather than as a sacred intelligentsia, several wished to participate in some way in efforts to promote "universally valid values" in their homeland (Mallik 1982:120). Those who were convinced India must be more secular, democratic, and egalitarian participated in the struggle to reform their society and to liberate their country, then locked in the grip of European imperialism.

Because language was their principal instrument or weapon, they began to realize its deficiencies for the new purposes and audiences they envisaged. For example, they perceived diglossia to be a problem: the spoken language of the masses differed markedly from the language of the educated which was used in literature. They were unable to learn how to read and write without an expensive education program. New styles and forms of communication closer to the spoken forms would have to be developed. Moreover, poetry dominated, and prose was poorly developed; lack of punctuation, long sentences, spelling irregularities, and other problems made the written language difficult to print by machine and difficult to read quickly. Many languages had no widely accepted standard, and combinations of letters also made printing cumbersome.

Tamil

Among the Tamils, writers born into high and prosperous middle castes began to perceive their mother tongue as an instrument for social and political change. Their goals varied, particularly between Brahmans and non-Brahmans, but they owed their inspiration to one man who began the process of linguistic innovation for purposes of social change and who was therefore the first language strategist.

Robert Caldwell, missionary with the Church of England, lived from 1814 to 1891. He spent most of his productive life among the Tamils serving as what has been called a "change agent."[2] Change agents, who introduce sharply innovative ideas into a society, are most often marginal with one foot in another society or way of life. They are better able to objectify their milieu than those who are fully integrated in a community and have had no experience outside it. Caldwell, who was born in Northern Ireland, spent most of his life promoting Christianity in southern India for the same reasons that motivate other missionaries and because he saw a need for social change. In his own words, Hinduism was "one of the chief obstacles that exists to progress of every kind . . . its disappearance from the scene and the peaceful extension of Christianity instead would be as life from the dead" (Caldwell 1874:14). As abusive as the statement is, it also reflects a greater commitment to social change than to saving souls, and that is what is important about Caldwell.

This British pastor's desire to change Indian society, particularly the lives of the poor, led him to study all forms of Tamil and its two-thousand-year-old literature. From an intense examination he concluded the Tamils possessed an original culture about which they themselves were unaware. Tamils appeared to believe their language derived from Sanskrit or was inferior to it. They also thought English was the only tongue suitable for the modern world. Caldwell believed Tamil learning should be rejuvenated through linguistic change introduced by Tamil scholars themselves. Logically, therefore, he opposed Brahman and Sanskrit dominance and promoted Tamil literature and the type of language understood by the masses. An accomplished historian, linguist, and writer, he published a history of the district in which

---

[2] These terms and subsequent terms concerning diffusion come from Rogers, Everett M. and F. Floyd Shoemaker, *Communication of Innovations: A Cross-Cultural Approach,* 2nd ed. (New York: Free Press, 1971).

he worked and a comparative grammar whose influence is still felt more than a century later. The latter, his *Comparative Grammar of the Dravidian or South Indian Family of Languages,* was first published in 1856, and it is currently available in somewhat revised form at the University of Madras Press.

Caldwell's introduction to this large book provided the basis for a Tamil-led renaissance which revived the language by altering its form and renewing its literature by making it relevant to a changed society. He asserted and proved to scholars' satisfaction that the South Indian or Dravidian languages were separate from North Indian Aryan languages, that "Tamil is probably the oldest and most highly cultivated member of the family" and that it could "flourish" without the assistance of Sanskrit (Caldwell 1875: 4, 49). The idea that any Indian language did not develop out of Sanskrit and could develop further by depending on its own resources was revolutionary. Such an idea undermined the authority of those who knew Sanskrit best, the Brahmans, and it promoted a sense of separate identity, particularly as Caldwell urged young Tamils to study and use their language rather than English or Sanskrit. He openly doubted that his own mother tongue, English, or any language other than Tamil could serve as a medium of education for the masses.[3]

In order to influence Tamil thinking, these ideas would have to be accepted or indigenized by Tamil "innovators." In the process of diffusion of new ideas and products, the innovator is the individual who recognizes the importance of what has been proposed by the change agent and makes it his own. Unlike the change agent, he or she is not marginal to the society, but he or she does have a superior intellect and high status. He or she adapts and begins to propagate the new idea along a network of friends and colleagues.

Among the Tamils there were doubtless several intellectuals whom one could call innovators in the nineteenth century, but the most important was P. Sundaram Pillai (1855–1897) who wrote and then paid for the publication of a play called *Manonmaneeyam* or *The Story of Manonmani* in 1891. Pillai came from the area where Caldwell worked and must have known him. He belonged to a non-Brahman caste, the Vellalas, many of whom, like his father, were part of an expanding middle class because of their land holdings and new commercial ventures. After his solid Tamil education he went to an English school, was awarded a B.A. degree, and taught in an English medium school in his home area. He also wrote on Tamil themes for English language publications.

In the play, his most important work, Pillai makes no reference to Caldwell although the influence of the cleric is obvious in the introduction. Pillai asserts forcefully that "Tamil is not inferior to any language" (Pillai 1973: 27). But, he adds, Tamil must be rejuvenated by finding and publishing the treasures of ancient times and by developing new forms to suit the present exigencies. In this regard, it is significant that the subtitle of his play means "A Modern Play."

---

[3] For a more detailed discussion of the Tamil renaissance, see Brian Weinstein, "India: Planners and Poets," in *Praci-Bhasha-Vijnan Indian Journal of Linguistics, 10*(1), Jan.–June 1983, pp. 47–76.

More important than these remarks—or even than the play itself—is the invocation to the Tamil language he wrote. It is customary at meetings and in books by Tamil authors to begin with a prayer, and P.S. Pillai did not fail to open with a poem to God. He then innovated by dedicating a second poem to Tamil. In two stanzas of six lines each he sang the praises of ancient but vibrant Tamil claiming incorrectly that other Dravidian languages came forth from his mother tongue. Then he made an invidious comparison with Sanskrit: "You have not gone out of use in the world nor been destroyed nor corrupted as Sanskrit has been" (Pillai 1973: 41). He added that he wished to serve "Mother Tamil" through his writing (Pillai 1973: 43).

The link between Pillai and others along what appears to be a network of friends, intellectuals, teachers, and middle-class members of non-Brahman castes is quite clear. Pillai's ideas were taken by Maraimalai Adigal (1876–1950) who played the role of "early adopter." Early adopters are strong opinion leaders with relatively high status likely to influence teachers and others close to the masses. Adigal belonged to the same Vellala caste as Pillai, and the two men met in 1895 after Adigal read the play. Pillai, the older and more distinguished man, then helped his young admirer obtain a position as a Tamil teacher. Adigal was also a devout Saivite Hindu which gave him further legitimacy as a loyal Tamil since this branch of Hinduism is particularly associated with South India. Some of his friends and his son-in-law founded the Saiva Siddhanta Publishing Works to promote the Tamil language, Saivite religion, and non-Brahman values. They also published Adigal's books.

In his speeches and many publications, Adigal went further in the promotion of Tamil than Caldwell and Pillai though he gave credit to both for many of his ideas. Like them he complained that Tamil needed rejuvenation and that it must be done without reference to Sanskrit, but then he openly attacked the Brahmans who, he claimed, were northern invaders in disguise. They had brought many evils to the south among which Sanskrit was high on the list. He proposed that rejuvenation must include a purification of Tamil by removing Sanskrit words and replacing them with Tamil words drawn from ancient texts. He launched the Tanittamil or Pure Tamil Movement in 1916. Coincidentally, some of his friends and fellow Vellalas launched a political movement the same year, the anti-Brahman Justice Party. Although Adigal belonged to no political movement, the political and cultural organizations complemented each other and reinforced each other's actions.

The Pure Tamil Movement and the Justice Party—linked by family, caste, class, and friendship ties—institutionalized the anti-Brahman sentiment building among members of prosperous middle castes who resented Brahman control of infant industries and the civil service positions open to Indians. The non-Brahman goals were to replace Sanskrit and Brahmans at the top of the prestige ladder and to win power in the political system as the British allowed greater Indian participation. Their class consciousness was not hidden. In 1916, a leading non-Brahman and head of the Justice Party, Dr. T.M. Nair, made clear that non-Brahman meant the rich Vellalas and related castes. According to Irschick, he "urged a policy of nonviolence, with leadership in the hands of the landed aristocracy" (Irschick 1969: 47). They were joined by E.R. Ramasamy Naicker or "Periyar," as he was affectionately called. Periyar broadened the social and linguistic concerns of the non-Brahmans and appealed to lower-caste and lower-class Tamils by founding the Self-Respect Movement and DK or Dravidian Party.

Adigal spread the purely linguistic and cultural message while Periyar and others proposed political and social goals. He traveled about southern India and Ceylon lecturing and meeting teachers to tell them they must first Tamilize their name and use his new words. Thus, he made contact with what is called the "early majority" of neighborhood opinion leaders. Unexpectedly for him, they did not accept all his ideas, at least in the short run.

A barrier to the Pure Tamil Movement's innovations was that the masses of people were unfamiliar with the old Tamil words he introduced. They had absorbed Sanskrit words into their spoken language and were not unhappy with them. A journal Adigal published was not popular, and many writers mocked his promotion of obscure Tamil expressions in the name of purification. They continued to use "Manipravala" or Sanskritized Tamil. K. Kailasapathy, a more contemporary scholar, accused Adigal of following a "retrogressive" or undemocratic approach which failed to recognize that the real problem of Tamil was not Sanskrit words but "traditional diglossia" (Kailasapathy 1979: 35). It was the work of another politically committed linguistic innovator which began to close that gap. He was C. Subramania Bharati, now recognized as one of India's greatest modern poets.

Unlike his contemporary, Adigal, Subramania Bharati (1882–1921) was born into a Brahman family in the same district where Caldwell worked. His poetic talents revealed themselves early, and he began a traditional career by working for the local rural *zamindar*. In charge of the lord's library, he read Indian and Western authors such as Walt Whitman and Shelley, whose blank verse style surprised the young man and led him to experiment with it. Because of his Brahman background and Sanskrit training, he was suspicious of the non-Brahman purifiers and promoters of the Dravidian ideas of Caldwell. Nonetheless, he lived in the context of reawakening for which Caldwell deserves substantial credit.

In his reading, Bharati must have studied P. Sundaram Pillai's play, but others such as Arumuga Navalar and S.B. Ramalingar were probably of greater influence. They began using a simple syntax in their poetry, but they tended to deal with religious themes exclusively. Such themes were not easy for the masses to understand even if the texts were read aloud. Although they began to take some words from the spoken language, Annamalai reports they did not spell them as they were pronounced, thus making it difficult to understand without training (Annamalai 1981: 14). Bharati went further than they or Adigal did by working through form to make Tamil a better instrument and symbol by simplifying it, by drawing the high literary variety closer to the spoken variety so that literacy and comprehension would be easier. This linguistic change would help politicians bring the masses into the movement for independence.

Bharati should be seen as an early adopter and language strategist who provides an important link between sacred and secular poetry, between poetry and prose, rural life and urban life, colonialism and independence. A devout Hindu, he said he worshipped all Hindu gods and refused to be identified with any regional variety of the religion. If he had a favorite, it was Kali, a goddess most popular in Bengal. He traveled about northern as well as southern India participating in Congress party deliberations. Within his own Tamil society he rejected caste and class distinctions by discarding symbols of Brahman identity and by associating openly with lower castes and classes, an important taboo in those days.

After his travels and extensive reading of Indian and Western literature, Bharati began experimenting with new poetic forms which would, he thought, be easy to understand, particularly by new literates. According to Dr. G. John Samuel of the International Institute of Tamil Studies, the classical poetry Bharati first studied used words, similes, metaphors, and references unknown to the common people. Only the lords and Brahmans could understand. Bharati took the stories, metaphors, songs, and rhythms he heard from fishermen, workers, beggars, peddlers, and others he met along the roads and began to integrate them in both his sacred and his secular poetry. The change of form made Tamil poetry accessible to more people.[4]

Another characteristic of classical poetry which barred easy comprehension was that it used long sentences. According to literary critic C. Kanakasabapathy, each traditional verse of four lines was one sentence recited without pause. Bharati took the four-line stanzas and broke them into eight using short concise phrases making them easier to read and recite.[5] To further facilitate reading, understanding, and memorization, Bharati indicated that his poems should be sung to certain well-known folk songs and *ragas,* the classical melodies. Like Adigal, he had the urge to communicate his ideas to a large public, and he was able to do it as a journalist, a poet who presented his works to a public audience in Madras, and as a Congress supporter.

Bharati's first job after leaving his home area was in Madras with the first and most important Tamil language daily newspaper, *Swadesamitran,* which had been founded near the end of the nineteenth century by Brahmans. Although the daily had a circulation estimated at only 850 in 1904, it was very influential. The British considered it the most important newspaper in South India and certainly in Madras, the main city of the south. It supported "the cause of political and social advancement" dealing regularly with "educational, agricultural, and industrial problems." The editors were reportedly pleased by the Japanese victory over the Russians, an English official noted in 1905, because they perceived it as a victory of Asia over

---

4 Interview, Madras, April 10, 1981.

5 Interview, Madurai, April 15, 1981.

Europe. Other newspapers took their cue from *Swadesamitran* and even reprinted its stories in their own columns, the British complained.[6]

Bharati's job was the translation of English articles into Tamil, and this daily exercise helped him develop a prose style. Because the newspaper had to appeal to the large public to survive, the style and writing had to be clear and interesting. Bharati had to write so that some thousands—not one lord—could understand. Otherwise, he would have lost his position. He later explained that this work helped him simplify his developing prose style: "I had to find direct Tamil equivalents to ideas expressed in English in order to convey them without distortion and in interesting ways to the Tamil people" (Va Ra 1944: 21). (Translations from the Tamil are by Brian Weinstein.) The poet opposed purism and Dravidian separatism which was developing. He threw himself into the struggle for independence from Britain and social reform within India using his pen as a weapon.

Bharati began publishing poems and prose in a new style in *Swadesamitran* and then in his own newspaper. By simplifying the vehicle, Tamil, expanding its vocabulary to express modern ideas and using language to express the concerns and thoughts of the oppressed, he wished to make Tamil into a symbol of identity for all and an instrument of radical change. Through simplifying form he facilitated an understanding of the message which was not always political. He wrote on religious themes, and his greatest work is a love story. Through the use of common and familiar themes from everyday life, human experiences, and the classics of Indian literature, he increased the usefulness of Tamil and raised loyalty to it. In his own newspaper, *Bala Bharata or Young India,* he made his message explicit by calling for a revival of Tamil literature, increasing pride in the language and political change. He wrote in 1907:

> The greatest creation of a nation is its language. National revivals almost always begin with language revivals. There must be life in the vernaculars. There never was a great man, who was not trained to think in his mother tongue. (*Bala Bharata* 1907:19)

Tagore and other Bengalis with whom Bharati was familiar had preached the same message, and Bharati urged Tamils to take inspiration from Bengalis fighting the British in Calcutta. Inspired by Bengali writers, he wrote poems and songs to commemorate dramatic events such as the arrest and trial of Tamil patriots. Supporters of these individuals took Bharati's songs and sang them in the streets, the courtrooms, and the prisons. When the British forbade the publication of some of Bharati's songs and essays, they naturally became more popular.

Bharati's premature death at the age of 39 ended a highly productive career and robbed him of the fame waiting for Rabindranath Tagore, another giant of twentieth century Indian literature. A network of friends who shared his linguistic and political ideals promoted his poetry and prose works, however, pointing out that they

---

[6] "Report on the native-owned English, vernacular and Anglo-vernacular Press of the Madras Presidency . . . for the year 1904," in National Archives of India, Home Department (Confidential) September 1905, Public Part B, No. 232, pp. 15, 34, 53.

must be considered as much more than political diatribes. They included literary critics, poets, and freedom fighters who told teachers, students, workers, and the masses about him.

The literary critic, Va Ra, was the most important. He edited *Manikkoti,* an avant-garde literary review in the 1930s. In it he promoted the ideas of Bharati with respect to style and kept his name before a younger generation of creative writers. Its influence endures 50 years later (Kennedy 1980:17). Bharati Dasan, who had known Subramania Bharati and was with him when he died, wrote poetry along new lines and taught school children about these innovations. He belonged to a non-Brahman caste and later associated himself with the Self-Respect Movement and DMK political party in the 1930s, 1940s, and 1950s. Bharati Dasan was probably less innovative in form than Subramania Bharati, but his powerful poetry calling for political and social change made him quite popular.

A very interesting collection of Bharati Dasan's poems was published in 1938. In the first forward, the non-Brahman political leader E. V. Ramasamy Naicker praised Bharati Dasan as the messenger of social reform. In the second forward Va Ra, a Brahman, took pains to insist on the link between Bharati Dasan and Subramania Bharati:

> Gandhi's writings and [Subramania] Bharati's poems give life to humanity. The songs found in this work have been written by Bharati Dasan. The very fact that he had assumed the pen name of Bharati Dasan [or slave of Bharati] shows that he belongs to the lineage of Bharati directly. That he belongs to the race of life poets is evident not only from his name, but from his poetry as well. (Kunjitam 1938:12–13)

Thus, a political leader and a literary critic legitimized Bharati Dasan's work and tied it to a tradition of linguistic and social reform.

Va Ra was correct in making the link. In one of the poems Bharati Dasan wrote, following Subramania Bharati, that "Tamil words must be written in an easy style." "We must enrich Tamil." We must use a Tamil "which all people can understand without anybody's aid" and "If one Tamilian is devoid of education because he is poor, all people here must be ashamed" (Kunjitam 1938:12–13). Periyar was also correct for the DMK political party, which came to power in Tamil Nadu in 1967, and made Bharati Dasan its poet laureate ensuring that Subramania Bharati's ideas would be carried to the "late majority" or masses of people. An invocation to Tamil also became part of modern politics when it was decided to open political meetings by reciting it. All these actions institutionalized the alliance between linguistic change and political change.

Even after the independence of India, the introduction of Tamil as the medium of instruction from primary school to college, simplification and expansion of prose styles, and purism have continued. In the last 30 years, written and spoken varieties of language have moved closer together and people tend to accept the original pure Tamil in their verbal communications despite the earlier hesitations (Annamalai 1981:12–13). M. Varadarajan or Mu Va (1912–1974), who wrote novels, taught linguistics, and served as vice-chancellor of Madurai University, is given credit for blending the two trends of purification and simplification. Mu Va was respected by the non-Brahmans and the Saivites who had earlier diffused Adigal's ideas. He belonged to the Mudaliars, another prosperous non-Brahman caste similar to Adigal's Vellalas. He taught Tamil courses and believed that Tamil should change; his motto was "That which is useful will live. The useless will fall. . . . " And he agreed with Subramania Bharati that "everything from government to dance and song must take place in the language which a majority of the people of the land speak. If it is not so, it will prove to be bad for the country" (Balasubramaniam 1976:71, 89–90).

Mu Va also believed a reform in the script would help simplify Tamil, and he joined with other scholars and Periyar, the leader of the Self-Respect Movement, to write a book on the subject. In his own chapter Periyar wrote: "If a language is to be learned easily, the characters of the language should be easy to write and few in number" (Periyar et al. 1980: 9). In order to facilitate literacy and printing, he suggested reducing the number of separate characters from 216 to 38. Of particular concern to him were the "compound letters" formed out of parts of two different characters. These compounds must be memorized separately. He insisted the basic characters could be used although words would be slightly longer. Printing and learning would be easier. In 1978 the government of Tamil Nadu accepted a few of his suggestions, but not all printers and writers have accepted them. The absence of copyeditors and the decentralized nature of the printing industry mean there are problems in standardization. Newspapers add to the confusion by using their own spelling.

The most popular daily newspaper in Tamil Nadu is *Dina Thanthi* which is directed at new literates and has a circulation of 350,000. The founder published a style handbook in which he instructed his writers to use very simple sentences with a maximum of ten words. Sanskrit words must be avoided unless common speech accepted them. Editors must split words so that they have no more than eight letters even though this has not been accepted by others. His reasoning was that people who do not read and write well will have difficulties with long words and long sentences, an idea of Subramania Bharati. The spoken language is the basis for articles which concentrate on local news without much attention to national or international events.

Dina Thanthi writers coin Tamil terms to take the place of English terms. First, they put the English equivalent in brackets and then, they drop the English term after they are convinced people understand the Tamil word which may not correspond with a term coined by someone else. Unlike the writers discussed here, *Dina Thanthi* has studiously avoided taking a position on politics. The form of language used promotes mass participation by providing access to information and thus the newspaper is committed to democratic ideals whether or not it proclaims them.[7]

In general there is probably less debate about language form today than previously. The relative status of Tamil, English, Hindi, and other languages is dis-

---

[7] Information about this newspaper came from an interview with Dr. Shantha, Madurai University. She wrote her PhD dissertation on *Dina Thanthi*. Interview, Madurai, April 18, 1983.

cussed, and politically committed poets like Tamilanban, novelists like T. Janakiraman, film script writers, and song writers use their messages rather than their form to convey a political idea. They all assume that communication to the many is necessary in a language they understand. Although knowledge of English is considered essential for a good position, no important creative writer except for the very gifted R. K. Narayan writes in English. Tamil has won in both a literary and political sense.

Bengali

The modernization and politicization of the form of the Bengali language are similar to the development of modern Tamil. The process is also better known to non-Indians because the Bengali renaissance took place in India's most important city, Calcutta, and could boast scholars and poets admired in Europe and America. The most important "change agent" in the renaissance was also a British missionary, William Carey, a Baptist who arrived in Calcutta in 1793. Like Caldwell, he spent most of his subsequent life in India absorbing himself in Indian culture, and today even the most nationalistic Bengali writers give him credit for laying "the foundation of Bengali prose" (Guha 1981:1).

Along with other missionaries, Carey set up a mission at Serampore. Because he obtained a printing press, he could publish materials, including his own translation of the New Testament, into Bengali. In 1801 he joined the staff of Fort William College in Calcutta where British civil servants were trained in Indian languages, including Bengali. Carey's responsibility was to teach Bengali and to prepare materials in it. The difficulties of diglossia and the absence of prose forms forced him to innovate.

Prior to Carey's experiments with Bengali, most poetry was written in a heavily Sanskritized form making it incomprehensible to the masses. This pedantic language, called Sadhu Bhasa, was not a useful instrument for mass mobilization. Unlike Tamil, Bengali is based on Sanskrit or evolved from forms of Sanskrit. Because most poetry served a religious purpose, and because most people believed Bengali was not suitable for serious matters, a heavy Sanskrit content was inevitable (Ghosh 1948:118). As the society changed in ways similar to South India, people began to feel the need for a prose form and an accessible secularized poetry to serve their more modern interests. New words and new styles were needed to express the phenomena. Printers wished for a standard spelling. Unlike traditional Tamil poetry, the Bengali verses were too short for modern writers. The rigidly observed rules of rhyme prevented flexibility. How to create meaningful sentences was a problem. For example: "Subordinate clauses, so necessary in prose writing, were rare" (Clark 1970: 23).

Carey and his Bengali colleague, Pancanan Karmakar, invented the new forms which were to open the door for further innovations. They wrote textbooks in Bengali for the students at Fort William. For this purpose they had to enlarge the vocabulary which they did by writing down words from the spoken language of Calcutta as well as from other Indian languages and English. They did not feel constrained to

use Sanskrit only. In 1801 Carey published a Bengali grammar and finished his famous *Dialogues,* a series of prose conversations between typical Bengalis of very
different statuses. This work has been widely praised by Bengalis and others as an
authentic, respectable reproduction of spoken Bengali in written form. It served to
advance prose forms (Kopf 1969:53-56, 72-80, 93-94).

As a missionary, one of Carey's obvious purposes was to touch the so-called
"heathen" with the Gospel, and the best way to do it was through their mother
tongue. In addition, he shared with Caldwell the belief that missionaries must do
more than save souls. They must help people in their earthly lives. His own humble
birth into a peasant family and his conversion from the Church of England into the
Baptist religion must have meant he was interested in the common man and woman,
but unlike Caldwell, he worked in urban areas among rather fortunate civil servants
and urbanites.

An Indian innovator and language strategist continued Carey's work. He was the
very famous Rammohun Roy (1774–1833). Like Subramania Bharati, Roy rejected
his own exclusive Brahman status traveling as a young man to different parts of
India studying religion and languages. He obtained a position working under a
former student of Carey, made considerable money in association with the British,
studied English and Christianity with his British associates, and read widely. The
resulting prosperity and intellectual whetting permitted him to devote most of his
time to literature and language and religion after 1815 (Mukhopadhyay 1979:
17-37).

Roy began to write in a Bengali prose which had been influenced by Carey, and
he, too, prepared a grammar. In 1815 he published a Bengali translation of Hindu
scriptures, originally written in Sanskrit, in an effort to prove that in its pure form
Hinduism was monotheistic. Thus, use of the vernacular form and religious reform
were wedded in Roy's thoughts and work.

For the rest of his life he engaged in efforts to reform the Hindu religion to which
he always remained faithful. These undertakings were made through a Bengali
prose he helped develop. In 1817 he denounced *sati* or "widow suicide." He wrote
about Christianity portraying Jesus as an ethical leader rather than as a divine per-
sonage. In 1828 he founded the Brahmo Sabha, which gave birth to the Brahmo
Samaj reformist Hindu association. An important precept of these organizations was
that all Hindus should understand the holy works previously written only in Sanskrit, and this meant they must be translated into the people's Bengali. Such action
undermined the status of the Brahman priests, the guardians of Sanskrit, and helped
raise Bengali to a symbol and instrument of modern life (Kopf 1979: passim).

In 1821 Roy began to publish his own Bengali newspaper. As in the case of
Tamil, the need to write clear prose quickly for a limited space forced changes in the
form of Bengali. English naturally served as a model for simplification, punctuation, and vocabulary. The newspaper gave authors an audience other than the rural
lord and forced them to aim their words at a relatively large and impersonal audience. Professional secular-oriented writers were encouraged, and some of them belonged to the Hindu reformist movements started by Roy. They committed them-

selves to modernize society and religion through explicit messages to the public and through innovations in language form. Eventually the "class of literati which had functioned universally as the articulators of a heritage gave way to the intelligentsia who functioned to interpret change" (Kopf 1969:111).

Possibly the most important journalist contributing to this change was Vidyasagar, a Sanskrit scholar or pandit turned Bengali journalist. He was most productive from the 1840s through the 1870s. T.W. Clark, a careful observer, admired "his ability to combine the sonorous phraseology of the Sanskrit element in the Bengali vocabulary with that fluency and ease of comprehension which two generations of journalism had succeeded in inculcating" (Clark 1970:33). He and journalists writing for the reformist Brahmo Samaj newspaper introduced punctuation marks and experimented with subclauses. As yet, however, the novel had not appeared. It emerged with the nationalist movement.

Bankim Chandra Chatterjee (1838–1894), a Brahman like Roy, was also a civil servant after obtaining his B.A. from Calcutta University. (He was the first graduate of the university.) He openly belonged to no movement, but his writings showed a desire to promote equality between men and women, an antipathy to the exploitation of peasants, and a deep love for Mother India. As a civil servant in the pay of the British Crown, he could not afford to attack imperialism unambiguously. He called on Indians to take pride in the nation, to unite themselves, and to fight for their rights within the system. He felt ambivalently about radical changes in Hinduism and in the relationship with Great Britain, but others interpreted his works as a call for independence (Mukhopadhyay 1979:110-125).

In 1865 Bankim Chandra began publishing the first of his 14 novels in serial form, and it proved a success. What appealed to Bengalis was his portrayal of them as a strong people with a clear identity and definite goals in life. This contradicted colonial stereotypes. In 1880 he published his most famous novel, *Anandamath*. Although the readers could not find a call for revolution in this work, they understood they must love India, Hinduism, and Bengalis. In this story, a person called Bhabananda, leader of a band of men attacking government troops, sings a song called "Vande Mataram" (or "Bande Mataram") which means "Bow to the Mother." The first stanza glorifies a strong, beautiful, and free India:

> Mother, I bow to thee!
> Rich with thy hurrying streams,
> Bright with they orchard gleams,
> Cool with they winds of delight,
> Dark fields waving, Mother of might,
> Mother free. (Bhattacharya n.d.:19)

Bhabananda explains the meaning of the song to his followers: "To us, our native India is the only mother. We have no parents, no brothers, no wives or children, no home and hearths; we only have our Mother . . ." (Bhattacharya n.d.:20). The singer continues "Who hath said thou art weak in thy lands when the swords flash out in seventy million hands." He concludes:

Loveliest of all earthly lands,
Showering wealth from well-stored hands!
Mother, mother mine!
Mother sweet, I bow to thee,
Mother great and free! (Bhattacharya n.d.:22)

Bankim Chandra facilitated the reading of his work by a large audience by avoiding the most difficult Sanskrit words and expressions. He proposed a prose form by moving his writing closer to the spoken language than his contemporaries, but did not close the gap completely (Clark 1970:73). Today's readers, accustomed to even less Sanskrit, find his prose quite Sanskritized, but then it seemed innovative. At the end of the nineteenth century some scholars criticized his Bengali-Sanskrit mixture. They also disliked his neologisms and derivations from English and applied the epithet "Guru Condali" to his language. The very uncomplimentary word means "Brahman-Sudra" and implies a polluted, unclear hodgepodge.[8]

Bankim Chandra's song was disseminated to political activists and the masses after his death by another innovative writer who supplied the link between ideas and innovations of the nineteenth century and the twentieth. He was Rabindranath Tagore (1861–1941), India's premier language strategist and "early adopter" or "early majority." Tagore synthesized linguistic innovations with the message of reformist Hinduism and radical nationalism.

Tagore was born into a landholding Brahman family of considerable wealth, and his grandfather had been a friend and associate of the reformist Rammohun Roy. Tagore was thus part of the Brahmo Samaj network whose members would imitate his writing style as well as his message. He grew up in an environment already favoring the Bengali language and internal reforms. The use of certain forms in language and his messages promoted the ideas of independence from the British which had not been an idea of the Brahmo Samaj.

The future Nobel Prize winner studied Bankim Chandra's novels and loved his song which he sang at a meeting of the Congress movement in 1896. Through his efforts Bande Mataram became the official song of the nationalist movement. By 1905 students sang it in schools and in the streets, and an organization called Bande Mataram Sampraday or Society to Propagate Bande Mataram Ideas was founded (Mukherjee and Mukherjee 1957:11-13). In 1906 Bengali nationalists Aurobindo Ghose and Bepin Chandra Pal, a member of the Brahmo Samaj network, founded the *Bande Mataram* newspaper. In South India, Subramania Bharati—who welcomed Bepin Chandra Pal to Tamil areas in order to spread the nationalist message—translated the song into Tamil and sang it on the Madras beach, a favorite meeting place for people of all classes. It was discussed and sung in Calcutta coffee and tea houses where Bengalis of all castes and classes meet.

In 1905 the Bengali intellectuals were mobilized into the Swadeshi or "own-country" movement after the partition of Bengal by the British. Followers of the

---

[8] Suhas Chatterjee, Interview. Santiniketan, September 20, 1981.

movement struggled to undermine British control of the economy by setting up their own shipping company, banks, and other institutions while boycotting British products. They promoted the Bengali language in their own new schools.

Leaders were obliged to appeal to the masses to support these efforts, and this necessitated increased use of a variety of Bengali that people would understand. Newspapers and magazines appeared in the spoken rather than the literary and Sanskritized variety. One daily called *Sandhy,* with a circulation of 7,000 in 1907, used a prose described as "the language of the streets." It was known for "its vitriolic and often vulgar abuse of the feringhee [foreigner] and all who aped his ways" (Sarkar 1973:259). The newspaper unhesitatingly also called for independence.

The movement did not reach its economic or political goals, but it gave new life to the modernized and spoken Bengali. It also pushed Tagore permanently into a leadership position for he had written patriotic songs learned by the militants. He warned against forgetting the rural areas and insisted on using the dialects of villagers so that they, too, could participate. On his advice, theater performances in towns and villages dealt with political themes in the spoken language. He pointed out that the rural theatrical companies or *jatra* were excellent vehicles of politicization of the countryside, and he asked his friends in urban areas to prepare materials for them. British authorities fully realized the importance of the rural theater, and in 1907 the director of criminal intelligence asked if he could suppress plays. One company, he reported, played "Matri Puja" or "The Worship of the Mother." "In it the country is described as being plundered by the foreigners who while robbing the people of their money best them in exchange." And, he added, "Matangi, the goddess of war, is eagerly preparing herself for war" (National Archives 1908:1).

Tagore extended his network and influence in 1907 as chairman of the first annual literary conference called to discuss developments in Bengali, during the Swadeshi movement. The conference was organized by the Bangiya Sahitya Parishad or Bengali Literary Academy, founded in 1894 to promote the modernization of Bengali and its extension into all domains of society. The conference blended the political goals with literary goals while giving institutional support to efforts to purify Bengali of non-Bengali words and to replace English with Bengali in education.

For the Academy leaders, who included university teachers—important in the chain of diffusion of innovation—Sanskrit had too much influence over Bengali. They complained that Bengalis were ignorant of "the thousands of words of which the origin cannot be distinctly traced to any Sanskrit source, but which are used by the people in their daily speech and are constantly to be met with in works both in classical and modern Bengali literature" (Bangiya 1915:6). The association began publishing word lists to encourage a non-Sanskritized Bengali.

Tagore was interested in de-Sanskritization insofar as it facilitated learning the language and legitimizing the life and culture of the masses. As early as his seventeenth year he had begun to alter Bengali spelling to draw it closer to the spoken language, called Cholit. The advice was not easy to follow. According to one observer, writers took a word such as *karchi,* meaning "I am doing" in the Cholit, and tried to substitute it for the Sanskritized and longer *karitechi* from the literary language, but they spelled it in an unbelievable 36 different ways (Ghosh 1978:13).

Rabindranath's prestige soared after he received the Nobel Prize for Literature, and his ideas on spelling were studied seriously. He had founded a university at Santiniketan, and its publications were supposed to follow Tagore's views. Unfortunately, neither the publication department nor Tagore himself was completely consistent, particularly with respect to indicating long vowels and short vowels. Another distinguished writer, S.K. Chatterji, professor of linguistics at the University of Calcutta, disagreed with Tagore.

Some standardization took place after the 1936 publication of spelling rules by the Calcutta University Spelling Reform Committee whose creation had earlier been urged by Tagore. At least the university adopted one set of rules and even took upon itself the standardization of student names. Spelling is still a problem, partly because of the compound letter problem which in English would be "ħ" for "th."

Nonetheless, since independence, the Bengali language has spread throughout the public educational system, and the CPI-M government of West Bengal embarked in 1981 on a program to remove English as a subject for the earliest grades in primary school. The most important Bengali daily newspaper, *Ananda Bazar Patrika,* with a circulation of about 500,000, has taken up the challenge of spelling.

The person who chose and shaped its popular style has been Santosh Kumar Ghosh, de facto editor from 1959 to 1981. He was hired to increase circulation which he did in large part by changing the form of language from literary to spoken.[9] His goal was to "attract and trap a reader with a language and style he can read and like." His motto was to use active verbs, avoid nouns, put the kernel of the news in the first sentence or paragraph, and employ short, lively words. He proposed the separation of combined letters similar to Periyar's work with Tamil.

Government publications continue to follow the 1936 rules, and a dictionary was prepared by Raj Sekhar Bose, a member of the 1936 committee. Other scholars are preparing a new edition at Jadavpur University in Calcutta. In the Legislative Assembly all debates at present are in Bengali, but some members reportedly have difficulty reading and writing Bengali probably because they were educated in English medium schools. The transcript of the debates must be prepared first in English and then translated into Bengali, which, civil servants report, is spelled differently from the Bengali used in the Writers' Building or center of government operations. Without a corps of copyeditors who follow set standards, the private publishing industry accepts an individual author's spelling. These problems are not so serious.

Today, diglossia is not perceived as a problem in West Bengal. Bengali is now more modern, because of writers and government, and it is thus an effective instrument and a valued symbol of a people. In education the government follows a two-language formula, namely, Bengali for Bengali mother tongue speakers and a link language, most often English, as the second language. Government decisions

---

[9]   Interview with S.K. Ghosh, Calcutta, September 17, 1981.

confirmed the status of Bengali. Language strategists beginning with William Carey developed the corpus.

Strategists Today

Other regions and newly self-conscious groups are experiencing political and linguistic efforts at identifying language with communities. Many observers report it is rather the government language planning agencies, not individual writers, who take most initiatives in these regions and among these groups. This assertion seems unlikely to me, and I believe if one examines current party activity in Andhra Pradesh, Karnataka, and elsewhere, one can find the language strategists and their networks.

In Karnataka, for example, writers have called for the use of Kannada in government and education. They have complained that their people have a low regard for the language and claim they work to increase language loyalty. Many are also committed to political and social change. Efforts to remove Sanskrit words have increased in the last few years, although linguists have pointed out that is likely to be more difficult for Kannada than for Tamil.

One writer, Chandrasekhar Kambar, playwright and lecturer at Bangalore University, uses the spoken rural form from northern Karnataka, his home area, in his very popular productions. In one of his most widely seen plays, *Jo Kumar Swami*, modern, nonreligious themes concerning government hesitation to promote land reform are dealt with. Relations between the rich and the poor in Karnataka are examined, and in a popular language.

The author pointed out to me that the play was first performed by a professional company in Bangalore in 1972 and lasted about two hours. In ways he says he does not understand, village amateur companies began to perform it, but they expanded the production to about eight hours. The additional six hours were filled with local incidents, jokes, and village conflicts making the play even more relevant to each village. The year 1972 is important for a political reason because, Dr. Kambar reported, that was when Chief Minister Devaraj Urs, a non-Brahman, urged non-Brahmans to unite for political goals. He also opposed Sanskrit and Brahman influence in Karnataka education.[10]

Concern with Sanskrit in school curricula in 1983 seems strange to Europeans and Americans who regret the near disappearance of Latin, Greek, and Hebrew from educational programs. For non-Brahmans in India, the still-important place and prestige of Sanskrit in religion and education reflect and legitimize Brahman prestige, power, and wealth. Efforts to promote spoken language and to organize against Brahman influence have naturally brought forth a reaction in South India. Highly placed members of the caste have said that all India must recognize that "Sanskrit was the bedrock of Indian culture" and it should be maintained as a required subject in schools ("Govmt aid to Sanskrit study urged" June 21, 1981:13). R. Venkataraman, a Brahman Tamil in Mrs. Gandhi's cabinet, has said "that San-

---

[10] Interview with C. Kambar, Bangalore. February 28, 1981.

skrit had served as the language of national integration in the past" and should be promoted for that reason today ("Revive Sanskrit for cultural unity-RV" June 22, 1981:1). Many southerners view Sanskrit as a wedge for northern Hindi, which uses the Devanagari script of Sanskrit. Efforts of central government language planners to draw Hindi close to Sanskrit vocabulary alarm non-Hindi speakers for whom Hindi is becoming increasingly difficult to learn. It also alarms northerners who believe the voluntary acceptance of Hindi will contribute to national unification.

Sanskritization of Hindi and active promotion of Hindi encourage state political leaders to solidify their constituencies. Using the occasion of the public celebration of the ninetieth birthday of the late Bharati Dasan, the Chief Minister of Tamil Nadu, M. G. Ramachandran, urged people to protest rules concerning knowledge of Hindi for promotion in the armed forces. He warned that "all political parties should raise their voice in unison against such a move" ("Why Hindi for army promotion?" May 2, 1981:1). MGR, which he is called, is also able to use his fan clubs, organized while he played in films, to support his election and his views on language or any other subject. By the late 1970s he claimed he had 5,000 such clubs (Hardgrave 1979:124). In 1981 the MGR Fans Association "condemned [the opposition] DMK for its participation in the official languages committee which toured the Indian embassies abroad to assess the progress of Hindi . . ." ("MGR fans assail CBI action" May 28, 1981:1).

Social change has also continued within the regions and linguistic communities, and this has created new literary possibilities, needs, and interests which may facilitate the emergence of language strategists and new political elites from previously silent communities. The non-Brahmans who emerged and continue to emerge from earlier movements of social change are now being accused by intellectuals emerging from lower economic strata and from the Scheduled Caste, "Harijan," or Untouchable community of trying to prevent them from climbing the ladder of regard, power, and wealth. Intellectuals have come out of the Untouchable communities of Maharashtra, Karnataka, and Andhra Pradesh and have started the Dalit or oppressed literary movement which uses the spoken languages of the lowest strata in Indian society. These varieties of language are perceived as extremely vulgar by other Indians. According to Dr. Uttam Bhoite, a scholar at the University of Pune in Marahashtra,

> Dalit is an explicit protest against linguistic standards, but it is not designed to win favor with non-Dalit people. On the contrary, the movement is exclusive and inner directed; it is not interested in shaping Marathi literature as a whole but in creating a Dalit literary tradition of which the Dalit castes and classes may be proud.[11]

A Dalit writer in Karnataka confirmed the observations in Pune. He now insists on using spoken Kannada of his community:

> The cultured, educated language has a limited vocabulary. Untouchable dialect has a richer vocabulary. I cannot give up my language. If I do, then I cannot continue to

---

[11] Interview, Pune, March 13, 1981.

write. In my books I use the Untouchable dialect throughout. Outsiders cannot use it so well; nor can they effectively write about Untouchables as we can. The insider's view is best.[12]

These words reflect a desire to create symbols for the lowest strata, to reserve a special place for the writers who claim to represent them, and possibly to provide a weapon for political organizers. A Telugu Dalit poet, Bhohi Bhimanna, has achieved distinction in Andhra Pradesh and is a recognized literary leader. It remains to be seen if his work will serve political purposes by identifying a variety of Telugu with a social group, but it has already helped raise the pride of Untouchables.

These Kannada and Untouchable writers, like their Tamil and Bengali predecessors, use the form of language to assert the validity of a culture and to assert its utility to the users of that variety. The form is as important as the subject matter, if not more. Realization that a language has dignity and that it can be understood in a written form increases pride in it and self-respect. Pride in the language makes it a potential symbol or marker of a community; modernization of the corpus makes it into a potential instrument of action. How it is actually used depends on choices by political elites trying to discover issues to arouse the masses, to build a constituency for themselves, and to find an effective method of communicating with these people. In other words, language strategists can help political leaders, including a man like N. T. Rama Rao, Chief Minister of Andhra Pradesh, who himself wields language skillfully, mobilizing masses of people. Watching men and women seeking power and change while studying the language strategists who provide the weapons is one way to understand the link between language change and sociopolitical development.

REFERENCES

Annamalai, E. 1981. Simplification of language: An aspect of modernization of Tamil. Unpublished manuscript.

Bala Bharata or Young India. 1907. Archives of Tamil Nadu.

Balasubramaniam, C. 1976. Perunthagai Mu Ya [Great Man Mu Va]. Madras: South India Saiva Siddhanta Works Publishing Society.

Bangiya Shahitya Parishad. 1915. The Bangiya Shahitya Parishad: A record of twenty years. Calcutta: BSP.

Bhattacharya, Bijanbihari (Ed.) n. d. Ananda-math by Bankim Chandra Chatterjee, translated by Jitendranath Chakrabarti. Calcutta: Brindaban Dhar.

Brass, Paul R. 1974. Language, religion and politics in North India. London: Cambridge.

Caldwell, R. 1874(?). Christianity and Hinduism: A lecture addressed to educated Hindus. London: Society for Promoting Christian Knowledge.

Caldwell, Rev. Robert. 1875. A comparative grammar of the Dravidian or South-Indian family of languages. 2nd ed. London: Truner.

---

[12] Interview with M.N. Javaraiah, Central Institute of Indian Languages, Mysore, July 7, 1981.

Claiborne, William. (May 6, 1983). 4 Indian states seek to trim New Delhi's powers. Washington Post, p. A24.

Clark, T. W. (Ed.). 1970. The novel in India: Its birth and development. London: George Allen and Unwin.

Dimock, Edward C., Jr. (Ed.). 1967. Bengal literature and history. East Lansing: Asian Studies Center, Michigan State University.

Ghosh, J. C. 1948. Bengali literature. London: Oxford.

Ghosh, Manindra Kumar. 1978. Bangla banan [Bengali spelling]. Calcutta: Asha Prakashani.

Govmt aid to Sanskrit study urged. (June 21, 1981.) Indian Express (Madras), p. 13.

Guha, Pathik. (August 31, 1981.) A pioneer remembered, Amrita Bazar Patrika (Calcutta).

Hardgrave, Robert L., Jr. 1979. Essays in the political sociology of South India. Delhi: Usha.

Irschick, Eugene F. 1969. Political and social conflict in South India: The non-Brahman movement and Tamil separatism 1916–1929. Berkeley and Los Angeles: University of California.

Kailasapathy, K. 1979. The Tamil purist movement. Social Scientist VII (May 10). 23–51.

Kennedy, Richart Stanton. 1980. Public voices, private voices: Manikkoti, nationalism and the development of the Tamil short story, 1914–1947. Unpublished Ph.D. dissertation. University of California, Berkeley.

Kopf, David. 1979. The Brahmo Samaj and the shaping of the modern Indian mind. Princeton, N.J.: Princeton University Press.

_____. 1969. British Orientalism and the Bengal renaissance: The dynamics of Indian modernization 1773–1835. Calcutta: Firma K. L. Mukhopadhyay.

Kunjitam, T. S. (Ed.). 1938. Bharati Dasan kavitaigal [The poems of Bharati Dasan]. Cuddalore: T. S. Kunjitan.

Mallik, Yogendra K. 1982. South Asian intellectuals and social change: A study of the vernacular-speaking intelligentsia. New Delhi: Heritage.

MGR fans assail CBI action. (May 28, 1981). The Mail (Madras), p. 1.

Mukherjee, Haridas, and Uma Mukherjee. 1957. 'Bande Mataram' and Indian nationalism (1906–1908). Calcutta: Firma K. L. Mukhopadhyay.

Mukhopadhyay, Amal Kumar. (Ed.). 1979. The Bengali intellectual tradition: From Rammohun Ray to Dhirendranath Sen. Calcutta: K. P. Bagchi.

National Archives of India. 1908. (1–2). (January) 1. New Delhi: Home Department, Political A.

Official language of the Indian union. 1958. Tamil Culture VII (2). (April) 208.

Periyar, E.R., Dr. Mu Varadarajan, and T. P. Meenakshisundaran. 1980. Ezhuthuch cheerthirutham [Script reform]. 4th ed. Madras: Periyar Self-Respect Propagation Foundation.

Pillai, Rao Bahadur P. Sundaram. 1973. Manonmaneeyam (Naveen natakam). 3rd ed. Madras: South India Saiva Siddhanta Works.

Ramaswamy, Cho. January 16–22, 1983. The actor-politician and politician-actress. in Sunday, p. 24.

Report on the native-owned English, vernacular and Anglo-vernacular Press of the Madras Presidency . . . for the year 1904. September 1905. National Archives of India, Home Department (Confidential) Public Part B. No. 232.

Revive Sanskrit for cultural unity = RV. (June 22, 1981). Indian Express (Madras), p. 1.

Rogers, Everett M. with F. Floyd Shoemaker. 1971. Communication of innovations: A cross-cultural approach. 2nd ed. New York: Free Press.

Sarkar, Sumit. 1973. The Swadeshi movement in Bengal 1903–1908. New Delhi: People's Publishing House.

Va Ra. 1944. Mahakavi Bharatiar [The great poet Bharati]. Madras: Shakti Karayaalayam.

Weinstein, Brian. 1982. Noah Webster and the diffusion of linguistic innovations for political purposes. International Journal of the Sociology of Language 38. 85–108.

_____. 1983a. The civic tongue: The political consequences of language choices. New York: Longman.

_____. 1983b. India: Planners and poets. Praci-Bhasha-Vijnan Indian Journal of Linguistics 10 (1). (Jan–June) 47–76.

Why Hindi for army promotion? (May 2, 1981). The Hindu (Madras), p. 1.

ELEVEN

Foreign Languages as a Means of Attaining Political Ends*

E. Luther Johnson

Courtland International, Ltd. McLean, VA

In the field of international relations the impact of language is not always understood or sufficiently analyzed. The prominent actors in this field—the "nation-states" (a term that is used in international relations to express an entity)—are characterized by a number of features, such as political structures within an area with delineated geographic boundaries, their economy, population size, culture, mores, sense of history, and language, or, in some cases, languages. In addition, a common feeling of unity and nationalism, sometimes expressed as patriotism in the context of one's own country, imbues the population either naturally or through emphasis from political institutions. In this context, sentiments about one's own or someone else's language can reinforce this feeling. This feeling of nationalism contributes to the cohesiveness of a nation-state. These various factors combine synergistically to form nation-state power, the scope and impact of which are difficult to measure except in general terms.

In the international arena these nation-states tend to lead a competitive existence, and their interests and goals come into contact with those of other nation-states, inasmuch as few of them can function exclusively within their own borders. Conflicting interests require adjustments, which can be reached amicably or hostilely, rapidly or slowly, when considered advantageous, appropriate, useful, or self-serving. Moreover, other nation-states or international organizations may aid and assist in resolving conflicts when requested to do so.

In international relations the matter of language is rarely addressed, and if it is, it is usually within the context of nationalism, although it is a basic ingredient to the cohesiveness of a nation-state. The reason for this is perhaps because political messages tend to stress content rather than the vehicle of transmission. However, language definitively reinforces the boundary around the inhabitants, and when this boundary does not coincide with that of a nation-state, frictions tend to result, as

---

*The author wishes to express his gratitude to Billboard Publications, Inc., 1515 Broadway, New York, New York 10036, for permission granted to extract from *World Radio TV Handbook,* 37th edition, 1983, the information contained in Table 11-2 on language broadcasts by major powers.

when a nation-state contains several language groups or when the latter straddle an international border, exacerbating domestic tranquility.

The interests of a nation-state are often expressed as political goals, usually designated foreign policy goals when directed outside its borders, when a nation-state hopes to attain specific ends. In this essay politics will be defined as a process of applying various means to reach a value-centered end (Lerche and Said 1963:2-3), and the use of foreign languages will be addressed as one of reaching such ends. Since this essay deals with the international area only, all permanent domestic language issues, such as multilingual communities or language planning within a state, are excluded. While this would at first glance, appear to exclude the use of language as a means of reaching political goals abroad, there are still indicators to examine which show that language does affect political goals directed abroad. When the terms ''language'' or ''foreign language'' are used in this paper, it is, thus, only when applied to an international issue across an international border.

In the international scene actual and perceived levels of power allow some nation-states to dominate more than others, which also has a bearing on language factors in terms of their perceived usefulness. It is well known that world languages such as English and French also tend to dominate, if for no other reason than that millions speak those languages. A more balanced view of language in general, from a political and foreign policy viewpoint, may be obtained by examining its relationship to various centers of power in the international sphere. In order to identify these loci of power it is advantageous to form a matrix where the columns identify the Western, Communist, and Third Worlds, and where the rows represent first nation-states, then nongovernmental international organizations, and finally individuals (see Table 11.1). By including two major categories outside the nation-state system, further insight into language-associated factors for political goal attainment across

Table 11.1   Language Impact on Goal Attainment

	Western World	Communist World	Third World
Nation-States	Superpower	Superpower	Emerging Superpower
	Former World Powers	—	—
	Early World Power	—	Early World Power
	Other Small Powers	Other Small Powers	Other Small Powers
Nongovernmental International Organizations	Multinational Corporations	—	—
	Religious Organizations	—	Religious Organizations
Individuals	Long-term: Emigrants	Long-term: Emigrants	Long-term: Emigrants
	Medium-term: Guest Workers, Students, Businessmen	Medium-term: Students	Medium-term: Guest Workers, Students, Businessmen
	Short-term: Businessmen, Tourists	Short-term: Businessmen, Tourists	Short-term: Businessmen

international borders can be gained. By using this conceptual approach for analysis, it will become clearer which of the nine fields of the matrix contain language-associated foreign policy or political goals. With this conceptual mapping approach, language-related issues can be examined and analyzed on a row basis, followed by a final section of comments and conclusions.

FOREIGN LANGUAGES AS MEANS FOR NATION-STATES TO REACH POLITICAL GOALS

When considering the importance of foreign languages on the level of those political institutions on the nation-state level which deal with counterparts in another nation-state in matters of mutual interest, one can differentiate between two levels of importance: a primary level and a secondary level.

Within the context of this paper the secondary level is of lesser importance, as it is ascribed to governments interacting mostly on the diplomatic level, where foreign language considerations do not, or rather should not, interfere, hinder, or constrain accomplishments. All governments realize the importance of intercommunication, whether it is in Latin, as in bygone days, French, English, or other mutually agreed-upon languages. Here language is a tool available to, and a part of, established methods of operation: the foreign language, by itself, is not, or should not be, a critical component in the foreign policy process or foreign policy goal formulation. Language problems can exist in terms of insufficient capabilities among involved personnel. Further, a desire among members of an international organization, consisting of nation-state representatives, to have their language included as an official language, creates administrative and financial burdens and delays, as personnel in the United Nations or the European Economic Community can verify. However, the success or failure of their official endeavors is usually not dependent on foreign languages.

There are areas in nation-state political goal attainment where the consideration of one or more foreign languages becomes important, because not taking them into account will make a political effort less effective or irrelevant. Empirical data on these areas are sparse, but one good indication of nation-state interest can be derived from their policies in foreign broadcasts. This situation prevails among nation-states in the Western world, the Communist world, and the Third World, when these nations wish to transmit their message abroad. While nation-states claim that they do not interfere with internal matters of other states, a double standard is found in this context, as many nation-states do want to inform inhabitants in other countries. Which foreign languages a nation-state chooses and which audience it selects as target become quite significant.

World Powers and World Languages

For mass audiences the world languages tend to dominate. Among these the English language dominates perhaps the most, if for no other reason than the sheer number of English-speaking people throughout the world in addition to its frequent use as an official language. This dominance is reinforced by two nation-states, the United States and the United Kingdom. The latter was a former world power up to World War I, when a slow eclipse began as the United States gained in stature, and the English-speaking power center shifted to the United States. This power shift was completed after World War II, when the United States emerged as one of the two superpowers. With the influence in foreign affairs exerted by both these nations and the use of English by many millions of people, this language continues to dominate because of convenience, the spread of scientific knowledge and technological advances published in the English language, and so on. Additionally, many international activities, which are conducted by international agreement, use English exclusively, such as air traffic control which requires pilots and air controllers to speak English on international routes.

However, both the United States and Great Britain have comprehensive broadcasting services which differ in modi operandi. The independent-minded British Broadcasting Company (BBC) attempts to minimize government direction and claims to have 100 million listeners. This broadcasting service is judged by one writer to be the sole remnant of the image of a major world power with fewer vested interests than it once had (Osnos 1983). Perhaps because of this divestiture the BBC is able to be more forthright, as Great Britain's influence has diminished, but the institutionalization of the BBC over the years may also have helped to create a protective wall around its objective reporting. In contrast, the United States has three broadcasting services: the Voice of America (VOA), Radio Free Europe, and Radio Liberty (RFE-RL). The first mentioned service can be looked upon as a counterpart to the BBC, while the other two are targeted against East Central Europe and the USSR, respectively. While English is used in broadcasts directed to worldwide audiences, a number of less common languages are used to reach specific groups. Table 11.2 lists the foreign languages used in broadcasts by the BBC and the VOA, while Note 3 at the end of this table indicates the languages used by RFE-RL. Because of the uncommonness of many of the languages used in the broadcasts of the latter two, the problems of finding language-qualified replacements for retiring staff personnel have increased (The Board of International Broadcasting 1983:23).

The other superpower, the USSR, also broadcasts in a large number of foreign languages, as shown in Table 11.2. It does duplicate those used by United States' governmental agencies, but there are also broadcasts in other languages, which indicate attempts to influence the inhabitants in other parts of the world. In addition, it must be remembered that the USSR expends considerable energy in jamming. The director of the VOA has stated that the USSR spends more to jam Western broadcasts coming into the Soviet Union than the United States allocates for the entire VOA worldwide budget (Tomlinson 1983).

While the United States has localized broadcasts in less common languages in Eastern Europe, the USSR has also, as stated, certain geographic regions which it considers important for political influence. Since propaganda is considered to be an essential facet in influencing Soviet citizens as well as foreigners, it is interesting to note that the USSR broadcasts in various African languages and local languages of

Table 11.2 Language Broadcasts Beamed Abroad by Major Powers

	US (VOA)	UK	France	West Germany	USSR	PRC
To Europe						
Albanian	x	x			x	x
Armenian	x					
Azerbaijani	x					
Bulgarian	x			x	x	x
Czech	x	x		x	x	x
Danish					x	
Dutch					x	
English	x(w/w)	x(w/w)			x(w/w)	x(w/w)
Estonian	x					
Finnish		x			x	
French		x	x		x	x
Georgian	x					
German		x	x	x(w/w)	x	x
Greek	x	x			x	x
Hungarian	x	x		x	x	x
Italian					x	x
Latvian	x					
Lithuanian	x					
Macedonian					x	
Norwegian					x	
Polish	x	x		x	x	x
Portuguese	x	x	x	x	x	
Romanian	x	x		x	x	x
Russian	x	x		x	x(w/w)	x
Serbo-Croat		x		x	x	
Slovak		x		x	x	
Slovene	x	x		x	x	
Spanish			x	x	x	x
Swedish					x	
Ukranian	x					
To Africa						
Amharic	x			x	x	
Bambara					x	
English	x	x	x	x	x	x
French	x	x	x	x	x	x
Fulani					x	
Hausa	x	x		x	x	x
Malagasy					x	
Ndebele					x	
Portuguese	x	x	x	x	x	
Shona					x	
Somali					x	
Swahili	x			x	x	x
Zulu					x	
To the Middle East						
Arabic	x	x		x	x	x
Farsi	x	x		x	x	x
Dari	x			x	x	
Turkish	x	x		x	x	x

Table 11.2 (*continued*)

	US (VOA)	UK	France	West Germany	USSR	PRC
To Central Asia						
Russian	x					
Uzbek	x					
To South and South East Asia						
Assamese					x	
Bengali	x	x		x	x	x
Burmese		x			x	x
English	x	x		x	x	x
Hindi	x	x		x	x	x
Indonesian	x	x		x	x	x
Kannada					x	
Khmer	x				x	x
Lao	x				x	x
Malay		x			x	x
Pushtu	x	x		x	x	x
Tamil		x			x	x
Thai	x	x			x	x
Vietnamese	x	x			x	x
Urdu	x	x		x	x	x
To Far East						
Cantonese		x			x	x
Chaochau						x
Chinese	x	x		x	x	x
Japanese		x		x	x	x
Hakka						x
Korean	x				x	x
Mongolian					x	x
Nepalese					x	x
Tagalog					x	x
To Latin and Central America						
German				x		
Portuguese	x	x	x	x	x	
Quechua					x	
Spanish	x	x	x	x	x	x
To North and Central America						
English				x	x	x

Note 1. (w/w) signifies worldwide broadcasting.

Note 2. In addition to languages shown, the USSR also transmits to South Asia in Gujarati, Marathi, Oriya, Punjabi, Sinhalese, and Telugu.

Note 3. In addition to languages shown, the U.S. also transmits through Radio Free Europe-Radio Liberty (RFL-RL) in Armenian, Azeri, Belorussian, Estonian, Georgian, Kazak, Kirghiz, Latvian, Lithuanian, Russian, Tajik, Tatar-Bashkir, Turkmen, Ukranian, and Usbek to the USSR; in Bulgarian, Czech, Hungarian, Polish, Romanian, and Slovak to Eastern Europe.

Note 4. The information in this table is derived from the *World Radio TV Handbook* 1983, by permission.

the Indian subcontinent, giving a rather clear indication of the influence this nation wishes to extend to these areas. As an example, one can look at the broadcasts in Zulu from the USSR—the only country to broadcast abroad in this language. The Union of South Africa has internal difficulties with its various ethnic populations, and its national policies have led to a continuous problem of coping with racial strife. Strategically, one of the world's most important waterways follows the coastline of this nation, which adds to foreign interest in this area, and the broadcast in Zulu allows the USSR to insert its own arguments into contentious issues. The USSR, of course, has its own nationality problems which do not prevent it from focusing on those outside its borders. Its sensitivity to these matters is demonstrated by the efforts to jam Western broadcasts directed at these nationalities.

While both the VOA and the BBC broadcast in English for worldwide listening, Radio Moscow does likewise in both Russian and English. This combination shows Soviet realization of the usefulness of English, but it also presumes worldwide interest in Russian in spite of the fact that the size of the foreign audience that understands Russian is miniscule by comparison. The motivation for this approach could reflect the perceived need to put Russian on a par with other world languages as well as a need to maintain Russian as an important symbol of superpower status. The latter argument can be reinforced by noting the various levels of importance Russian has taken on in the USSR since the 1917 revolution. Since then the Russian language has reached a level where it is now subject to glorification and attributes such as "spiritual" and "mystical" (Kreindler 1982:18), a situation reminiscent of the context of the word "Volk" in Nazi Germany, hopefully without the same disastrous consequences. Thus, there is here a situation where domestic policy considerations are of such importance that they assume foreign policy overtones.

In the nation-state row of the matrix, the superpowers dominate with English for the Western world and Russian for the Communist world. Straddling the latter and the Third World is the immense area of the Peoples Republic of China (PRC), which can qualify in some respects as a superpower, particularly in the aspects of geography and population. In spite of the many millions who speak Chinese, or more correctly, the many dialects of Chinese, the PRC does not as yet measure up industrially to the USSR and Western nations. Its influence abroad is so far essentially regional as it does not broadcast in Chinese to worldwide audiences. The areas targeted for listening show a tendency to broadcast to overseas Chinese and to non-Chinese-speaking listeners in borderland areas in South and Southeast Asia and the Far East. Significantly, the PRC does not broadcast to Soviet Central Asia in the local languages spoken there. This nonuse of language factors to further political aims reflects perhaps a shortage of personnel and facilities, a desire to not exacerbate tension along the Sino-Soviet border, a belief that transmissions from another Communist country to that area are not cost effective, or a concern for Soviet retaliation in some unspecified or undesired way. The "other" China, the Republic of China (ROC), maintains a much smaller foreign language broadcast service, as would be expected, and it appears to engage in a certain amount of competition with the PRC in the Far East by including, as an example, such relatively unknown and obscure dialects as the Hakka group in Southern China.

Former World Powers and World Languages

The next tier of language importance are lesser nations with languages which still rate among the world languages, namely French and German, both in the Western category. Both languages are survivors of nation-states which, in the past, were powerful and recognized as such around the world. Moreover, they developed industrially during the last century, and both were colonial empires with worldwide economic and military interests, which tended to expand the influence of their languages as well.

The French contemporary stress of culture in the foreign policy context is well known as is the French judgment of the value of the French language. Perhaps this contemporary value judgment, imputed to the language, is a continuation of the feelings associated therewith by the French because it preceded English as a world language. It was the language of diplomacy for several centuries, and it still continues to function in that role to a lesser degree at the present time. Moreover, the French believe that their language is the best vehicle for expressing clarity and logic, which may or may not aid in expanding its influence abroad. Radio France International transmits in the well-known world languages, which would appear to place constraints on expanding the influence of the French language abroad. However, there are at least two other aspects to the use of French in international relations which are unique to this language in a foreign policy context. The result is that the French have perhaps succeeded better than any other nation, outside of the English-speaking fraternity, in using their language as a tool for reaching desired ends. English-speaking nations do not have to emphasize English to the same extent as the French, because of the sheer numbers of people who speak it and the desire of so many foreigners to learn it. The French, on the other hand, "have to try harder," if they wish to maintain and expand the influence of their language.

The first one is the Société Financière de Radiodiffusion (SOFIRAD), a public enterprise which is, reportedly, coordinating and directing commercial radio stations, particularly offshore radio stations, for the purpose of promoting French industrial products. Among its activities it is noted that the radio transmissions in the Middle East have become extremely popular. A company has been established in New York to distribute French programs on cable TV with local sponsor support and advertising (Boyd and Benzies 1983). This is an effective and profitable way to meld the propagation of French language and culture with commercial interests abroad.

The other unique aspect of the emphasis on French abroad is the language-based "francophonie" movement, a bridge-building mechanism among French-speaking people and political elites outside metropolitan France. While this is a much more amorphous entity than the above-mentioned SOFIRAD, it provides a framework for maintaining and expanding French culture and language, and for maintaining ties to France through various elites, such as former colonial administrators, language teachers, journalists, and publishers (Weinstein 1976).

As a practical matter, one should remember that Western languages in excolonial countries would be maintained to varying degrees as the new national administrations would come into existence because of the need to carry on managerial functions. Moreover, even if disliked, the old colonial language would provide national cohesion among separate language groups in the new nation, particularly when the geographic areas inhabited by these groups cross international boundaries established by colonial powers. This situation is equally applicable to English and to a lesser degree Portuguese and German. With these considerations in mind one can question the long-term efficacy of the "francophonie" movement, but as long as the members of this movement can discern advantages to maintaining a French language and cultural bond, it should endure. In the area of political goals the member nation-states would expect advantageous economic relations, access to educational institutions, increased flow of scientific and technical information, and, in general, amicable relations with France in order to modernize their countries.

This trend towards preserving a colonial language can be countered by phenomena such as the expansion of Swahili in East Africa, although this is confined more to internal national policy than external. This development shows a desire for Africanization and an attempt to open up the political process to local citizens who do not know English.

The second world language with a firm basis in a nation-state of the nonsuperpower category is German which was also a colonial language, but of a much lesser magnitude than others. On the other hand, Germany, and in the contemporary context West Germany, has attracted attention as a center for advanced education and scientific development with the added aspect that a knowledge of German would be necessary to take advantage of its resources. West Germany also has an external broadcasting service, the Deutsche Welle, broadcasting in some 32 languages in order to inform listeners abroad comprehensively about political, cultural, and economic events in Germany and to show German opinion on important questions (Prinz 1983), a goal that attempts to project Germany abroad. This organization also broadcasts in German to listeners on a worldwide basis.

Early World Powers and World Languages
The third tier of world languages consists of Spanish and Arabic, which differ from the former in that while they are spoken by many millions of people, the latter live in a number of nation-states, thus eliminating any particular political center for the language. However, these nation-states tend to be contiguous, with the notable exception of Spain. The foreign policy impact of these two languages tends to be less than other world languages from the point of view of foreign language broadcasts, since none of them has the vast networks of the nations discussed above.

Regarding Spanish, one must remember that the spread of this language was accomplished by a nation that enjoyed great power status at the time of its overseas' conquests. It developed into a colonial empire, where evolution has aided the retention of the language, a type of Spanish permanent counterpart to "francophonie," at least insofar as Latin and Central America are concerned. For the non-Spanish-speaking world, the foreign broadcasts tend to use world languages only, with only six Spanish-speaking countries doing so, and only Spain broadcasting in Spanish for worldwide coverage. There are a few exceptions, such as Ecuador transmitting in Czech and Mexico in Japanese, the latter undoubtedly for economic goal realization. While many Spanish-speaking nations do not broadcast abroad, it should be remembered that many of them may not have the resources available to do so, or consider the return on such an investment not cost effective.

Arabic has certain elements in common with the Spanish language situation. Centuries ago the expansion of Islam led to an extension of the geographical coverage of Arabic as well. Apart from the religious aspects, the secular feeling of nationalism associated with a language did not emerge until the beginning of the last century as a type of protest against the despotic rules of the Ottoman Empire (Fellman 1973). Currently only six Middle Eastern countries broadcast abroad in Arabic, while in North Africa all do with the exception of Tunisia.

Thus, the two languages have political characteristics in common. Spanish was spread by conquest and used for proselytizing. It was maintained by colonial rule which succeeded in creating a permanent Spanish language foundation. Arabic was also "exported," as it were, in a similar manner but at a much earlier date, and it was not until modern times that it was forged into a useful political tool in that it assumed the character of an "anti-colonial" weapon. Both Spanish- and Arabic-speaking governments do not seem to stress language broadcasts for audiences outside of those regions where these languages are spoken, which is not unexpected, considering that most of these governments represent nation-states in the Third World where resources are limited.

Languages and Nation-States without Worldwide Influence

A useful approach for surveying this area is to isolate particular target areas and audiences within the three geographic regions on the nation-state level of the basic investigation matrix for this paper.

Within the Western world all nation-states in North America and Western Europe transmit in a number of languages. Outside the expected goals of providing information of a cultural, economic, or political nature to foreign listeners and readers in the major languages and languages spoken in neighboring countries, there are a few discernable language aspects that can be related to specific political goals beyond the broader ones of a nation-state selling itself abroad, as it were.

Specific examples of this situation can be found among the irredenta created by the results of past conflicts between and among European nations. Underlying the Basque problem in Spain and France is a strong language factor which perhaps is reinforced by the unique characteristics of the Basque language. Similarly, the German-speaking minority in South Tyrol, or Alto Adige, can contribute, indirectly, language aspects to occasional difficulties between Austria and Italy.

While Eastern Europe abounds in irredentist sentiments reinforced by language demands, these problems have been subsumed by domestic language policies in the contemporary setting. Between World War I and World War II they did exist in the international arena, and language issues did acquire strong political overtones, as they tended to unify minority groups who wished to maximize their political goals with those of a neighboring country. One unique example remains in this area. The government of Communist Albania, without friends or alliance members both in the East and the West, apparently believes it is necessary to broadcast abroad in more than twenty languages, including the major world languages discussed above as well as Albanian for neighboring groups and North America.

In the Third World the borders from colonial times cut through tribal territories in many instances which should create irredentist language issues similar to those in Europe. So far the African and Asian nations have exhibited little interest in modifying borders to account for these situations either by force or by negotiation. The recent elevation to nation-state level of excolonies could account for the lack of emphasis on this matter and very likely the language minorities involved may not want—or do not have the power—to bring irredentist problems, including language problems, to a head. However, many of these nations engage in language planning within their borders, which falls under the cognizance of domestic political issues.

LANGUAGE ISSUES INVOLVING NONGOVERNMENTAL INTERNATIONAL ORGANIZATIONS

It is customary to divide international organizations into governmental and nongovernmental international organizations. The former, composed of nation-states, have to provide language facilities in order to be able to function, as discussed earlier within the nation-state context, but language considerations are not generally of primary importance for political goal attainment. Exceptions do occur, such as increasing the stature of Arabic at the United Nations or the praxis of making a new member's language official in the European Economic Community. Such developments will naturally increase the management burden of acquiring additional translator, interpreter, and publications staff with concomitant political decision making among the members for additional budget support which easily can become a contentious issue.

Beyond the governmental scope there are two major categories of nongovernmental international organizations where language capabilities can be critical to goal attainment: multinational business organizations and religious organizations. While the latter category may seem inappropriate in this paper, the definition of politics as a process for goal attainment includes all goals, religious as well as secular. Moreover, because of the different nature of the goals of these two categories, language standards and language requirements vary considerably.

In international business the large multinational corporations predominate. They are based in the industrialized world and are typically United States, Japanese, British, Dutch, French, German, Swiss, and Swedish. Among these there are a few dozen giants who tower over the others. Except for the Japanese, the languages of the headquarters of these large business organizations are European, with English, French, and German in the lead. Among the latter, English dominates from the combined immense economic power, geographical size, and influence of the English-speaking world as well as the fact that the largest number of organizations are based in this area. Thus, language can assume the same level of importance as among nation-state governments, in that language capability becomes secondary to the economic goal of profitable business. However, while this attitude might prevail on the management level, there is still a need to take local language into account on the local sales level if there are to be any. More often than not, one can expect that it is local management that has to be proficient in the language of corporate headquarters, not the other way around, in spite of the efforts of many businessmen to learn the local language of their sales area.

This situation tends to reinforce the use of world languages. It is the local managers who have to cross the language barriers for the purpose of hiring personnel, developing marketing, coping with local regulations, and attempting to deal with imposed advertising phraseology to fit local language and local culture barriers. The examples of the latter abound: ESSO's efforts of "putting a tiger in your tank" in a number of languages during the 1950s, and later on General Motors' attempts to market "Nova" model Chevrolets in Spanish-speaking countries.

The large international religious organizations provide an entirely different insight into the use of language, since goal attainment here includes communication with individuals in their own language. Examples include the efforts of missionaries to learn at least one foreign language, and the change in the Catholic Church from holding mass in Latin to doing so in a local language—although mass can still be heard in Latin in Vatican City broadcasts (Frost 1983:146).

The World Council of Churches (WCC) has devoted a study to language issues within its organization. It realized that the predominance of English created a handicap for many member churches as well as insensitivity among those who speak English and frustration among those who do not. However, practical considerations— such as finances—impose limits, and organization publications are published in English and variously in French and German. Through a WCC policy of encouragement and subsidization many member churches have their publications translated. Moreover, participants in meetings are encouraged to express themselves in any of the working languages which appear to increase as time progresses, to include English, French, German, Russian, and Spanish, as an attempt to prevent the attachment of an "ecumenical" label to any one language. With growing realization for the need to cope with the language situation the problem of terminology ensued, which the WCC Language Service has addressed by starting to prepare an "ecumenical terminology" index in English (as a departure language), French, German, and Spanish, with the concomitant problems of defining terminology and attempting to place boundaries around technical expressions and religious concepts. Additionally, the WCC holds language seminars, for example, in Africa and the Caribbean area to enhance interpreter and translator capabilities (WCC undated).

A comparison with the WCC approach to language can be accomplished by noting the language policies of another world religion, Islam. The Islamic States Broadcasting Services Organization (ISBO), "enjoyed by 42 Islamic states" (Frost 1983: 60), is an intergovernmental organization, but its language policies are of interest in this context, when it is realized that religion, state, and society are intertwined in the Moslem world. Since the accepted version of the Koran is in Arabic, this organization plans to give appropriate Arabic language lessons by radio, using member state broadcasting facilities, with commentary and explanation in English for those in English-speaking areas and in French for those who reside in French-speaking areas (Farrag 1983).

Consideration of the language factor in goal attainment in the area of nongovernmental organizations tends to be centered in Western organizations. A comparison between the goals of these organizations and those of nation-states is interesting: language factors increase in importance as the goal to reach an individual's attention increases. Moreover, the need to use world languages as a crutch in this process is apparent.

The Communist world cannot be addressed in this context, inasmuch as its very nature does not allow any nongovernmental organizations to exist outside the nation-state framework, although a Communist state may allow certain of its activities to participate in them, as evidenced by the Russian Orthodox Church's association with the WCC or the modus vivendi with the Catholic Church.

The Third World also exhibits a paucity of activity in the nongovernmental area as well, which may change as resources increase and economic development continues. Evidence of this can already be seen in the activities of ISBO, discussed above. However, a trend in this direction can be expected to evolve slowly, as many nation-states still have to concentrate on nation building.

THE INDIVIDUAL'S GOAL ATTAINMENT IN AN INTERNATIONAL SETTING

In the field of international relations the individual, as a private person, enjoys little recognition. As everyone, with the exception of a minority of unfortunate stateless persons, is a citizen of some nation-state, the latter's rules and conventions with other nation-states tend to influence an individual's activities beyond the borders of his or her nation-state. Nevertheless, individuals speak in many tongues, and their movements across international borders contribute to languages having an impact on the individual's goal attainment, perhaps not so much directly as indirectly. Moreover, this influences the political goals of nation-states and, as discussed above, of nongovernmental organizations as well. However, there are some phases of individual's activities that deserve attention, since they relate to the latters' attempts to reach a goal or a political end. In addition to the regional breakdown of the West, the Communist area, and the Third World, it is also convenient to divide individuals' activities into long-term, medium-term, and short-term goal attainment, and they tend to cut across all three geographic areas.

Long-term individual goal attainment involves those who emigrate to another country for a variety of reasons, such as better work conditions, escape from political persecution, or avoidance of high taxation. Many, if not most, of these individuals do not know the language of the nation of their new home. This language barrier can impact on local political matters. There may be a need to provide language instruction in a number of languages or to provide for multilingual instruction in schools, usually after a time lapse during which political pressure builds up until needs begin to be satisfied. If they are not satisfied, these problems will increase to a point that nonindigenous groups will evolve and expand in isolation from the remainder of a nation-state's population. Even though these emigrants do not expect, or even wish, to return to their original homelands, cultural ties may extend into successive generations, with some nationalities following this trend more than others. In this context it is interesting to observe how many European nations broadcast in their own language to North America where the great immigration stream ended in the interwar years. For instance, among the smaller powers Albania, Bulgaria, Czechoslovakia, Finland, Hungary, Italy, Portugal, Poland, Romania, Sweden, and Switzerland broadcast in their native language, or languages in the case of Switzerland (Frost 1983, passim). Significant in this enumeration is the high number of East Central European nations which have sent sizable minorities to the United States and Canada, and which have totalitarian political systems which will add ideological overtones to their broadcasts.

The medium-term category of individuals encompasses those motivated by employment opportunities in another country. They move there and return home after retirement, which may terminate as a result of an individual's decision or that of the host government through political and economic considerations. The most populous example would be the flow of migratory workers—or guest workers—particularly in Europe, but also in the United States and the Middle East. This medium-term period can last many years, or occur daily as workers commute over a period of time in border areas. In most cases, migratory laborers are in another country at host government acquiescence and even encouragement, the United States government being a notable exception. As is the case of members of the long-term group, previously discussed, accommodation of language questions has to be considered, particularly since many individuals resist learning more of the host language than is absolutely necessary. This translates into such matters as language issues involving schooling, ghetto-type living, and provision of multilanguage forms for bureaucratic management in order to accommodate diversity. From the host nation-state point of view these issues may be viewed as domestic problems, rather than foreign issues, but from the point of view of the individual, it is a process of attempting to exist in an alien environment, which requires him or her consciously or unconsciously to decide on individual goals, what they should be, and how to attain them.

The final group, the short-term individuals, include tourists, students, and businessmen who visit another country for a few days, weeks, or years. For some there is a goal to learn a foreign language, or be exposed thereto, before arrival at their destination, perhaps some attempt to learn while there, or even after their return home. For tourists language goal maximization can be questionable. Tourist travel is generally undertaken for pleasure, leisure, or cultural curiosity, but language interest may be a motivation. This latter consideration may be very minimal, in view of the number of people who participate in group travel simply to overcome the language barrier—an example of nonuse or unwillingness to use a foreign language.

Table 11.3   International Tourist Travel 1980 (in excess of one million)

Country	Notes	In 1000 Units	Country	Notes	In 1000 Units
France	TF	30100	Portugal	TF	2708
USA	TF	22500	Singapore	TF	2562
Spain	TF	22500	Sweden	VF	2485
Italy	TF	22194	(Hongkong)	TF	2279
Austria	TA	13879	Ireland	TF	2265
Canada	TF	12426	Thailand	TF	1847
Great Britain	VDF	12393	(Puerto Rico)	TF	1679
West Germany	TA	11288	Jordan	VF	1636
Switzerland	TA	10650	Tunisia	TF	1602
Hungary	TF	9413	Brazil	TF	1498
Romania	TF	6742	Morocco	TF	1425
Belgium	TF	6700	Egypt	VF	1253
Yugoslavia	TA	6410	Norway	TH	1252
Poland	TF	5664	Iraq	VF	1213
USSR	VF	5590	Columbia	TF	1210
Bulgaria	VF	5486	Bahamas	SDF	1181
Czechoslovakia	TF	5055	Argentina	TF	1120
Greece	TF	4796	East Germany	TH	1067
Mexico	TF	4145	Uruguay	TF	1067
Netherlands	TA	3840	Israel	TF	1066
Denmark	TA	3500	Venezuela	TF	1003

Note 1. SDF—Stopover departures at frontiers
Note 2. TA—International tourist arrivals at all means of accommodation
Note 3. TF—International tourist arrivals (not including group travel)
Note 4. TH—International tourist arrivals at hotels and similar establishments
Note 5. VDF—Visitor departures at frontiers
Note 6. VF—International visitor arrivals (including group travel)
Source: World Tourism Organizaton: Regional Breakdown of World Tourism Statistics, 1981 Edition.

Instructive in this context is a review of which countries attract tourists, although there are no statistics at present to show if language had an impact. Table 11.3 indicates that it is the Western nations with world languages that attract tourists, with France in the lead. However, in terms of aggregates by language, English-speaking countries lead. Thus, English, French, German, and Spanish predominate overwhelmingly. Further, there are no statistics available to indicate the native languages of the travelers who may, in many cases, travel to a country where the same language is spoken, such as a German visiting Austria, or a Belgian France, and vice versa. It is also interesting to note the number of travelers in Communist Eastern Europe, considering the constraints imposed by these governments. Here it is perhaps considered "safer" to visit "fraternal countries."

In terms of the last row of the matrix outline for this article, individual efforts to exceed language barriers appear in all three world regions: West, Eastern Europe, and the Third World, except for tourism where the Third World lags considerably. To what extent an individual includes foreign language considerations in goal attainment cannot, of course, be expressed very well in general terms, although the application of sophisticated statistical techniques may aid in answering this question. As part of a mass movement across international borders, the individual has a negligible impact, except for those who have to deal with persons crossing borders. The reverse of this observation is that if various political institutions were to ignore the foreigner and his language barriers, more chaotic and contentious situations would result.

COMMENTS AND CONCLUSIONS

As this survey has shown, world languages dominate in international relations. For a language to dominate, there should exist a nation-state, or nation-states, with very large populations which, inhabiting large territories, have a strong economic base, a history of empire, and a belief that foreigners will benefit in some manner, intangible or otherwise, from knowing the language, as well as a belief among the foreigners that this is so. This list of criteria points up the differences between English, on the one hand, and Chinese, on the other, where one billion plus individuals speak a language that carries little influence abroad, except as one of the official languages of the United Nations and spoken there by a small number of people. Among the world's populations, the perceived need to learn Chinese is minimal except for overseas Chinese.

While noninterference in the internal affairs of another nation is a basic rule of international conduct, all nation-states have issues in common that require resolution, which is generally reached through the conclusion of treaties and international agreements. In the language field, this paper has examined the use of broadcasting as a tool to gauge how a nation-state projects its message into the territory of others for whatever purposes and goals it considers important. While this can be considered interference in the affairs of other nations—and the USSR most certainly believes this, judging from its jamming efforts—there is still international agreement on the allocation of frequencies to avoid chaos in the airways through the International Telecommunications Union (ITU), a specialized agency under the United Nations.

In the above list of criteria the economic factor was cited, which is a basic consideration for all nations that broadcast. In all cases the resources devoted to broadcasting are minimal when compared to the yardstick of a national budget or a nation's gross national product. The additional expenses for language accommodation of tourists, in the form of signs, guidebooks, and so on, are also minimal by comparison, which points up a certain juxtaposition of a desire to broadcast in one's own and other languages with the decision to spend minimal amounts in doing so. In this context, it is interesting to note that the Nippon Hoso Kyokai—Japan's state radio—recently announced that it plans to expand its overseas' programs to the point that it will expect to rival those of the BBC in 1987 (Waves of Joy 1983), a case where the economic base most certainly is adequate, but where the perception abroad of the need to know Japanese most certainly does not parallel the perceived need to know English which supports the BBC's popularity. But perhaps Japanese aggressiveness and ability to sell its aims in a number of languages will change this situation.

Among the nongovernmental organizations, the matter of resources takes on another aspect. Of the two categories observed above, the international business community will allocate language resources in local economies to the perceived extent needed to sell their products. The religious organizations, on the other hand, must consider language factors from an entirely different viewpoint, since communication on the individual level is critical to goal attainment. Likewise, in this context, the cost and effort for an individual to acquire a second language can become counterproductive, since he or she can surely be expected to object if the religious message is not received in his or her own native language.

The individual—either as a listener to a radio broadcast from abroad or as a visitor to a foreign country, regardless of duration, for business or for pleasure—will resist penetrating language barriers unless he or she has a personal interest in foreign languages, or the incentive, in terms of profit or promotion, is such that the effort of undertaking this is considered worthwhile. Such an assessment can also be based on pure emotional evaluation, where world languages often are given a negative rating based on past historical developments in terms of conquest or ideologies, such as antiimperialism. Apart from this aspect, there is also a fear that the apparently continuous advances of world languages, in this case notably English, will tend to diminish cultural differences and make life less intellectually rewarding for the non-English-speakers (Valéry 1975). Moreover, the spread of a world language, such as English, can corrupt other languages with whole new international vocabulary systems, as can be expected in the ever-expanding field of technology—computer terminology being an excellent example—to the degree that the national heritage of a local spoken language becomes affected (Schumacher 1974).

Thus, one notes that world languages dominate the world scene; they are associated with large and affluent nation-states, past and present; they show no signs of losing their impact; and they can be resented by those who do not speak them, unless their utility can be demonstrated on a personal level. As nation-states increase in power and stature, the influence of their languages can be expected to increase concomitantly.

REFERENCES

Board for International Broadcasting. 1983. 1983 annual report. Washington, D.C.

Boyd, Douglas A., & Benzies, John V. 1983. SOFIRAD: France's international commercial media empire. Journal of Communication 33 (2) 56–69.

Farrag, Ahmed, Secretary General, The Islamic States Broadcasting Organization. Personal communication, August 17, 1983.

Fellman, Jack. 1973. The role of language in forging national identity: Arabic in the Middle East. Monda Lingvo-Problemo 5. 99–103.

Frost, J. M. (Ed.). 1983. World radio TV handbook. 37th ed. London and New York: Billboard Publications, Inc.

Kreindler, Isabelle. 1982. The changing status of Russian in the Soviet Union. International Journal of Sociology of Language 33. 7–39.

Lerche, Charles O., & Abdul A. Said. 1963. Concepts of international politics. Englewood Cliffs, N.J.: Prentice-Hall.

Opubor, Alfred E. 1972. Language and the communication of power. Monda Lingvo-Problemo 4. 65–72.

Osnos, Peter. 1983. BBC rules the world's air waves. Washington Post, July 26, A12.

Prinz, Karl. Federal Republic of Germany Embassy, Washington, D.C. 1983. Telephone conversation with author, August 5, 1983.

Rosenblatt, Ángel. 1975. Nuestra lengua en el mundo. Yelmo 24. 7–8.

Schumacher, Nestor. 1974. Étude onomasiologique d'un vocabulaire politique: Le vocabulaire européen. Meta 19 (4) 197–202.

Tomlinson, Kenneth Y. 1983. America's stifled voice. Washington Post, February 20.

Valéry, François. 1975. Langues et vie économique. Les langues modernes 69 (1) 45–47.

Waves of Joy. 1983. The Economist. August 27, 26.

Weinstein, Brian. 1976. Francophonie: A language-based movement in world politics. International Organization 30. 485–507.

World Council of Churches. Undated. The language policy of the world council of churches, 1971–1978. Position paper. Geneva.

World Tourism Organization. 1982. Regional breakdown of world tourism statistics, Edition 1981. Madrid.

TWELVE

The Art of Japanese Negotiation*

Don R. McCreary
University of Georgia

Robert A. Blanchfield
E. I. du Pont de Nemours, Inc.

INTRODUCTION

Negotiation is an art whether cross-cultural or not. The artistic element refers to three levels that simultaneously occur: linguistic, comprising the actual spoken artifact; interactional, comprising the personalities and how they mesh; and the transactional, comprising the negotiating needs, and the relative power of the participants.

Each participant or party has something to give and wants to get something the other party has. This "something" may be considerably more than just currency exchanged for product. In a monocultural negotiation, shared values may allow a negotiation to conclude successfully. On the other hand, interactional difficulties or personality clashes can sidetrack the negotiation as may transactional difficulties or proposed changes in power relationships that go against a corporate self-image. The linguistic outcome of these difficulties in the United States is cursing, raised voices, or silence signaling rejection, and a loud and clear *no!*

A skilled American monocultural negotiator can analyze these factors, ameliorate wounded feelings, flexibly negotiate other options to satisfy corporate transactional needs, and achieve a linguistic outcome of positive responses culminating in a final, "Yes, you've got a deal!"

This same sensitive, flexible, and understanding negotiator may fail in his art when confronted with a bicultural situation. Shared values are no longer available as principles for his psychological and business transactions to rest upon. The linguistic outcome of his desire to achieve agreement may superficially resemble the agreement process of culminating "yeses," and yet utterly fail to produce any progress, or it may result in silence which is interpreted as rejection.

A lack of information about the differing negotiation styles and confusion on how similar certain strategies may be is the primary weakness a negotiator takes overseas.

---

* We wish to gratefully acknowledge the contributions of Yoshimoto-san, Saito-san, and Kayko-san.

We will attempt to redress this lack for Japanese-American negotiations, not only from the American point of view, but also address the Japanese needs for information and understanding.

Negotiation with the Japanese is extremely time-consuming, frustrating, and confusing for the American businessman. The negotiation of contracts between Japanese and American companies is complicated by and dependent upon several constructs unique to the homogeneous Japanese people and culture. Three constructs, *amae, haragei,* and the pragmatics of negotiating are particularly crucial. The most fundamental of these is *amae,* a social hierarchy of dependency relationships which influences Japanese negotiators in their communication strategies. Negotiating advantages often ensue since the American side does not understand and becomes frustrated and impatient. A secondary linguistic construct is *haragei,* a unique, culturally based schemata of negotiation strategies employed in business and political circles, utilizing paralinguistic cues coupled with half-truths or superficially misleading verbal arguments with multiple semantic readings. These strategies, when used with Americans, create an atmosphere of seeming acceptance with relatively great confusion and correspondingly low comprehension on the U.S. side. Americans, in turn, have their own form of *haragei,* called brinkmanship. This again creates negotiation difficulties. A third area, the pragmatics of formal negotiation in Japanese, concerns the patterns of discourse peculiar to negotiations in regard to speaking versus writing, colloquial versus formal language, responsibility spread in decision making, and translation-interpretation difficulties. Excessive politeness in the formal style of the Japanese language, combined with the natural politeness of the Japanese people, is the lubrication that allows these strategies to achieve smoothly mutual agreement that is win-win, that is, both sides *feel* they have won.

Phatic communication, the communication and build-up of personal trust, must be included from negotiating day one. Conversation, seemingly about nothing of consequence, that is, family backgrounds, likes and dislikes, and employment history, tests the foreign negotiator's trustworthiness, how much respect and credibility is due him, and how much he is committed to a long-term outlook.

The problem we are attempting to throw light upon, specified by the managing director of the Japanese Federation of Economic Organizations in a speech on October 28, 1982, is the following:

> Trade problems between Japan and its western trading partners are exacerbated by other factors such as asymmetries in negotiating styles, different policy-making processes in the field of trade, an amplifying influence of the mass media and an imbalance in the flow of information and inadequate personal exchanges.

DISCLAIMER

The information in this paper concerning discourse in actual negotiations was taken from negotiations that occurred between Fortune 500 companies. The first-hand knowledge and recollections of the negotiators *for each side* form the primary data base, additionally supported by newspaper and magazine articles and numerous books on Japan and Japan-U.S. business practices. Experiences living in Japan, buying and selling various goods, negotiating salary levels and job responsibilities, and negotiating with a Japanese wife for seven years form the supportive data base.

Since the interactional or personality-matching variable is relatively important in any negotiation, care should be taken in generalizing this information to all Japanese-U.S. negotiations. Some general principles concerning cultural differences and differences in communication strategies and linguistic interpretations will be true for many negotiations. Others may possibly apply only to these specific negotiations. Still other points may be true only for the personalities involved. Remember, people are people.

REVIEW OF LITERATURE

Any review of literature regarding Japanese-American negotiations must be necessarily brief because several constraints on the publication of negotiation proceedings exist. Antitrust and antimonopoly fears, combined with perceived needs to maintain secrecy regarding financial matters and product information, reduce the possibility of a complete account of a negotiation. Behind-the-scenes maneuvering or intracompany negotiating also multiplies the difficulty of rendering the actual process in terms understandable to those outside the respective companies.

Nevertheless, a few articles and book chapters concerning principles of general negotiating strategies have been published.

The most useful is Yoshi Tsurumi's chapter, "Social Relations and Japanese Business Practices" which cites eight causes for negotiation breakdown in Richardson and Ueda's *Business and Society in Japan. Never Take Yes for an Answer* by Masaaki Imai includes the title statement and "never take a smile for yes" as advice. John Graham's "Brazilian, Japanese and American Business Negotiations" details several variables in those three nationalities' monocultural styles. Howard Van Zandt's "How to Negotiate in Japan" recommends increased knowledge regarding linguistic ability and negotiating style differences.

No article contained any theoretical framework or sociolinguistic advice based on detailed negotiations, but instead included points to be aware of, such as the importance of relative roles and status for Japanese negotiators. Many books on Japan, among them Christopher (1983), Masatsugu (1982), and Pascale and Athos (1981) lend cultural support for various points. Doi's *The Anatomy of Dependence (1971)* is the primer on *amae,* and Matsumoto's *Logic of Haragei (1975)* brought that phenomenon into Western public awareness. Books on Western negotiation, including Karrass's *The Negotiating Game* (1970) and Coffin's *The Negotiator* (1973) provide information on the American perspective on bargaining. Linguistic works applicable to the field of negotiation include: Goffman's *Strategic Interaction* (1969) and *Forms of Talk* (1981), Sacks, Schegloff, and Jefferson's work (1974) on discourse, and Grice's (1975) work on conversational implications. T. F. Mitchell's "The Language of Buying and Selling in Cyrenaica: A situational statement" (1975), is a discourse analysis of the style of negotiating in the Libyan marketplace according to the principles of Firthian linguistics.

FIRST PRINCIPLE—*AMAE* (ACTIVE INTERDEPENDENCE): AN INTERACTIONAL STRATEGY

Amae is a word the Japanese use to initially describe the feeling of dependence a child feels towards its mother. This feeling is thought to develop into adulthood with the maternal relationship being supplemented by other adult relationships, actively interdependent.

An employee may *amaeru* (the verb form) to his employer or presume upon his benevolence and the employer may recognize it, feel acceptance of his dependence by extending his benevolence, and allow the employee to take liberties or otherwise act spoiled and receive attention. In the vertical relationships of Japanese society, this phenomenon is widespread.

Within negotiations, *amae* creates several difficulties not understood well by Americans. One complication concerns regurgitation of a previously "settled" point. Since lower-level managers may *amaeru* with their superiors, they may raise objections without fear of being reprimanded in their attempt to reverse an upper-management decision. Responsibility spread through the corporate family via *amae* also lessens this fear. The decision maker, in turn, does not immediately reject the new considerations, but instead may be benevolent and satisfy his employee's demands if they are reasonable and rescind the agreement even though this may anger the Americans and endanger the entire negotiations. The key for the Americans here is understanding the underlying process allowing the regurgitation—*amae*. From the Japanese perspective, regurgitation of a "settled" point by the Americans needs to be understood in light of the formal, legalistic manner in which contracts are written and signed. Before the written contract is hammered out and formally agreed upon, Americans see nothing wrong with going back and trying to change a point. What the American may not understand, though, is this reversal of agreement may seriously damage his credibility and trustworthiness in the eyes of the Japanese.

Amae via Group Interactional Interdependence

How does this phenomenon manifest itself in negotiations? The typical Japanese negotiating team is exactly that, a team. It may, but does not necessarily, even have a captain or a "quarterback." Not so in the Western cultures. Westerners always have their "chief negotiator," the single person who makes the final decision.

In negotiations with the Japanese, the person or persons doing the most talking might be the senior and the highest ranking members of the negotiating team. That however, does not mean he or they are the decision formulators. Not only are they not, they do not want to be, and will resist being forced into such a position. If arbitration is required, the senior man may assume such a role, but not "happily," and only after confrontation has set in.

The decision formulating members of the Japanese negotiating team are members of that team for a very specific reason. They know more about some details that will probably come up than their seniors and the seniors count on them contributing to the best group decision. An actual example may best illustrate what happens under Japanese group dynamics:

A negotiation between two manufacturing companies was well underway. The sale had been "made," so agreed both sides. The implementation details were being discussed and the contract wording was being set, on an almost word-for-word basis. Part of the implementation detail dealt with the quantity of annual shipments of product from Japan to the U.S. over a ten-year period. Economics are cyclical and both sides wanted maximum flexibility with minimum commitment.

The Americans proposed a conventional "maximum/minimum" schedule of shipments with limits probably greater than might be caused by recessions and recoveries, and the senior Japanese team member quickly accepted.

Immediately, a junior team member, who had previously not uttered a word, jumped to his feet, said a few words to the senior members, and went to the chalkboard. The negotiations stopped.

Following perhaps a half-hour while his position was laboriously, yet meticulously, chalked and expanded with examples (in English!), he spoke to the group, both sides. His point was in one respect quite minor, as it did not significantly alter the original proposal. It did, however, specifically mold the contract terms to fit the inventory management constraints of his company and most importantly, he wanted all to understand why.

The earlier acceptance of the American proposal was rescinded and negotiations resumed only after all agreed with the young man. By allowing him to speak, the seniors allowed him to "presume upon their benevolence" or *amaeru*. Although time was spent on a long explanation that did not change the original American proposal, a broader understanding of the problems in implementing the proposal was achieved.

Amae is one of several factors in the amount of time consumed in the decision-making processes involved in all of the points in a complex negotiation. The process known as *nemawashi* builds consensus throughout the Japanese group from the bottom up to implement a decision, and the formal agreement paper known as *ringisho* requires a stamp of approval from every department head, although the initial decision is often made at the top. This consensus building takes time, but can be more efficient and even faster than American top-down decision making. The American negotiator, not used to such a drawn-out "touch all the bases" process, and not fully informed by the Japanese as to how many hands the agreement must pass through, may become impatient and prematurely change the points, thus *short-circuiting* the Japanese consensus.

Amae, then, does test the Western negotiator's and the home office's patience. The U.S. company's slowness in deciding crucial points and particularly in implementing the agreement will also test Japanese patience since all the American bases have not been touched during the negotiation phase.

Amae may work to create difficulties in a third way: when the Japanese negotiator expects to be able to *amaeru* to the American side or when he expects the Americans may *amaeru* to him. This expectation is related intimately with the personality interactions, and the way in which transactional processes are being carried out. Japanese feel that *amae* is a universal human quality extending into adulthood. However, the potential for *amae* disrupting a negotiation is recognized in an old proverb, *amae wa yurusarenai "amae* is not allowed." Nevertheless, *amae* is operating in many transactions.

Cross-cultural problems may then occur when the American, not realizing he has somehow acted in accordance with a Japanese cultural construct, receives a uniquely Japanese treatment, such as acceptance of his dependency. Then a change in the negotiating environment might occur as the Japanese misconstrues the American's position. The Japanese, in turn, often try to play a "big brother-little brother" (United States-Japan) game (a frequent analogy for Japan which used to be "father-son" 20 years ago). In the 1990s, it may become the "twin brother" analogy, where the more "powerful" company in the U.S. has to fend off constant requests for concessions or give-aways, even though the Japanese company may be just as "powerful" internationally.

Then, for the Japanese negotiator, his recognition of the American perception of his *amae* towards the American side may be twisted to fit his own cultural expectations and the potentially resulting rebuff by the Americans may discourage and/or confuse him enough to cause negotiation breakdown or stalemate.

Amae may also play a part in the first meetings and in after-hours entertaining, an adjunct to most negotiating done in Japan. The strength of the relationship between negotiators, development of personal trust, mutual respect, and credibility are crucial from the first bow and handshake on. This trustworthiness may continue to develop or may wither after each negotiating session ends. The importance the Japanese place on this personal knowledge gained while relaxing in restaurants and clubs varies from company to company; but there is no doubt that if a close relationship of personal trust and respect can be established, the negotiations will go more smoothly. In purely Japanese negotiations, the nighttime entertaining is considered an essential part of the total process, where political and business deals are overtly ignored verbally, but realized conceptually and routinely cemented.

A purely mechanical facet of negotiation that *amae* relates to is the seating arrangement. Since the Japanese negotiating team is truly a team, they sit along the length of the table with the senior man (possibly only a representative of upper management) in the middle. The men on his right and left have the authority to negotiate the deal, with others further away from the middle also having power to sway the negotiations as in the prior example.

This style is virtually the opposite of the American where the decision maker frequently sits at the head of the table. This change can lead executives into addressing only one Japanese, the one they think has the "real" power, thus failing to recognize that power is shared via *amae*. See also page 173, "Insisting on detailed decisions with high-level executives."

SECOND PRINCIPLE—*HARAGEI* (INTUITIVE COMMUNICATION): A TRANSACTIONAL STRATEGY

The word *haragei* (acting (*gei*) on guts (*hara*) alone) perhaps came from the tightening of the stomach muscles, a natural physiological reaction in vitally important situations, for example, the possibility of being decapitated in the feudal period of the samurai warrior. Today, this fear has been replaced by the fear of losing millions of dollars of business.

Haragei is known by the man in the Tokyo street as a communication strategy that is used by politicians and upper-level management in big business in Japan. One of the key factors in this strategy is silence over an indetermined length of time that varies according to the situation. This is not empty silence, but rather is a discreet meta-message, the Japanese *ma* or "pregnant silence." Japanese businessmen who use *haragei* must be sensitive to the *ma* or meta-message and must also be able to feel the empathy between the people involved. Logic, cogent verbalizing, or articulation of specific points is out of place. "Top (Japanese) salesmen of stocks and bonds often turn out to be shy talkers . . . Emphasis on logic often results in less emphasis on sensitivity or the intuition needed for business *haragei*" (Matsumoto 1978:4).

Another key to *haragei* is its situational nature. It is more likely to occur in crucial "win or lose" (live or die, in feudal days) situations where stalemates or termination may occur. Matsumoto (1978) divided it into two varieties, "hot" and "cool," based on this situational nature, cool being less crucial.

Euphemistic, overly vague language is another hallmark of this strategy, for example, *so desu ne* (semantically equivalent to "silence"), *shō ga nai* "it can't be helped," *zenshō shimasu* "I'll do my best," *hai, hai* "yes, yes" (although no agreement is implied), and *saa* or *maa* "well" (with possible disagreement). These superficial phrases provide cover for symbolic meta-messages and other verbal artistries.

> The Japanese movie, *"Kareinaru Ichizoku,"* dealing mainly with the probable collusion between big business and politics in a merger of city banks (an actual story), portrays a vivid example of how *haragei* works cozily in a sensitive business talk in a cozy room of a restaurant.
>
> The plausible harageistic dialogue in the movie goes like this: the Finance Minister *hara*-talks: "A beautiful rock garden." (Introduction.) The president of a city bank *hara*-answers: "Yes." The Minister: "Only one huge rock." (Analysis: It's a shame. A merger is needed.)
>
> The banker: "I'm afraid, yes." (I'm glad you said that. I can cooperate, if you engineer the merger.) The Minister: "I want another rock that matches the garden." (You know the going rate or unit of the political donation is 100 million yen, don't you?) "Yes. I'll manage to get another one." (I'll see to it you get the payment of an additional 100 million yen.) (Matsumoto 1978:10).

Body language and other paralinguistic features may accompany the pregnant silence or symbolic phrases, such as increased (searching) eye contact, constant smiling (only a facade), audible exhalation of breath through the nose (resignation), forced exhalation as an extended sibilant in *saa* (disagreement), sucking in the breath through the teeth (consternation or worry), or even closing the eyes (consideration—not sleepiness!). For Japanese negotiators, Fast's *Body Language* (1970) would be a good reference for most American nonverbal communication. Since silence is often a favored way of indicating rejection in the West, the

American negotiator may modify his point to the benefit (and pleasant surprise) of the Japanese.

> Western negotiators may jump into that pool of silence, sometimes to their regret. Howard Van Zandt, who spent seventeen years as ITT's top manager in Japan, recalls how the head of a Japanese firm did nothing when a contract was presented for his signature. Van Zandt's ITT boss then hastily sweetened the deal by $250,000. Says Van Zandt: "If he had waited a few more minutes, he would have saved the company a quarter of a million dollars." (Greenwald 1983:42)

If the American negotiator is not amenable to any negotiable changes, which he thinks the silence is calling for, he may become angry or impatient or both. This reaction may also surprise and/or confuse the Japanese.

Some negotiators claim that *haragei* should never be used with non-Japanese, but they are wrong. How can deeply embedded cultural features such as forced exhalation or inhalation of breath be completely controlled? And how can a Japanese executive turn from domestic dealings to international meetings and always remember that silence or ambiguous euphemisms may be interpreted negatively by the other side?

Americans also use *haragei*, but they do not name it with a commonly known word as the Japanese do. John Foster Dulles, President Eisenhower's secretary of state in the 1950s, probably came closest to naming it in his coining of "brinkmanship" which also occurs in a "do or die" situation just prior to possible stalemate or breakdown of communication. Matsumoto calls this "hot" *haragei*.

In "hot" *haragei* used in favorable situations, possible adverse consequences are hinted. An example of "hot" *haragei* as practiced by an American negotiator follows:

During an actual negotiation with a Japanese company routinely purchased from, one of the buyer's objectives was a lower price. When the buyer felt the Japanese team had reached their stalemate point, he said, "I have four short questions. How much product did you expect to supply to us this year? How much product have we already purchased?" (The amounts were the same, but it was then the month of August.) "How much additional product do you hope to sell to us yet this year? What will you do with the product you have probably already made without further orders from us?" (He strongly expected they had neither outlets to consume it nor any new, near-term markets.) They received the unspoken threat (which was nc more than a bluff). The price was lowered to where the buyer wanted it and the four questions were never answered. The questions that did not even seek answers in the stalemate were examples of "hot" *haragei* or "brinkmanship."

This "brinkmanship," in a nonlethal form, was practiced by Prime Minister Sato in his talks with President Nixon over Japanese textile exports to the United States. Before leaving Japan, he announced to the Japanese press that he would use *haragei* on Mr. Nixon. In the meetings, when confronted with a difficult point which he could not concede to, he said "yes" a lot, smiled, and said, *Zenshō shimasu* "I'll do my best," but otherwise kept silent. The President, interpreting the smile and the Japanese expression as agreement with the U.S. position, considered his point won. His insensitivity to his counterpart's communication strategy as well as to the Japanese domestic political pressure on Mr. Sato led him to ignore the prime minister's political sensitivity which created a turn for the worse. Several months later, when Japanese exports continued to increase, he became angry and issued a unilateral order without any consultation with the Japanese to close U.S. markets to Japanese textiles. The Japanese textile industry was seriously weakened in the early 1970s by this and gradually lost its market position both in the U.S and domestically to other Asian imports. Prime Minister Sato thus made a serious diplomatic mistake which hurt a segment of his industry and population through the use of this potentially confusing communication strategy.

However, once the American businessman is attuned to or sensitive to the cultural differences, he may perceive certain Japanese strategies wrongly as uniquely Japanese rather than as a shared value that really exists. These perceived values are more important than any real value that may exist. For example, Americans may occasionally make communicative demands that require a little mind reading— more so with spouses, but in business too.

One of the communicating partners must intuitively uncover the other's true intent. This must occur daily in marriage all over the world! Time, of course, is a necessity here since the euphemisms such as "yes, I'll do my best" cannot be readily understood until the speaker has had a chance to "do his best." So *haragei* generally is a learned appreciation of the other's intent. When this slowness creates impatience or worse, conflict, negotiation cutoff (or divorce) occurs. Communication without complete verbalization is potentially risky in any culture but occurs always. Mind reading without a shared personal history is difficult, to say the least. In Japanese-United States negotiation, it may occur on both sides. The Japanese need to recognize that U.S. culture considers this to be a "hot" or provocative strategy and does not name it or recognize it as a common communicative strategy. The American needs to recognize that Japanese culture names this phenomenon and considers it appropriate as an intuitive and emotional means of public or private communication. In the words of Mitsuyuki Masatsugu, "anyone who can neither read another person's mind nor let the other person read his mind is not worth a damn in Japan" (Masatsugu 1982:202).

Tacit understanding or the conveyance of information from mind to mind called *ishin denshin* is a central process in *haragei*. The homogeneity caused by almost total isolation makes this tacit understanding workable and useful for the Japanese. The advantage in relying on tacit communication lies in the strict vertical relationships. For example, in the feudal samurai society—a vassal was largely forbidden to speak up to a samurai—both inferiors and superiors made their intentions known through *haragei*. Conformity, homogeneity, and lack of contrasting thought processes allowed *haragei* to work. In today's Japanese society, continued homogeneity—less than 1% of the population is non-Japanese—and conformity of thought and action throughout the populace based on similar vertical structures continues to make *haragei* a workable process. If the negotiator for the upstart company X is forbidden by social constraints from directly expressing his company's view of hidebound blueblood company Y, he must use *haragei* to some extent. Likewise, the negotiator for company Y, in a superior position, may not wish to talk down or may not be able to dictate to X, so he, in turn, also uses *haragei*. Since they both understand their relative strength both on the interactional and transactional levels, the linguistic outcome is partly governed by *haragei*, rather than verbal communication alone.

This leads us to a second type of strategy—"cool" *haragei*. "Cool" *haragei* was the type employed by the finance minister and the banker with symbolic language. "Cool" *haragei* is a technique that accomplishes agreement without any direct, overt, or cogent verbalizations or actions. Multiple meta-strategies are attempted utilizing euphemistic probing and bluffing. The negotiators need savvy and intuition to make it work consistently. Both Americans and Japanese do it; only the Japanese label it. Confusion or misunderstanding may result, but, on the other hand, a negotiator may get more than he actually expects or deserves via this technique.

In favorable negotiating situations, the concession that will conclude the agreement is said. In an offhand manner (for Americans) it is mentioned briefly, and just once, generally out of context, for example, in discussion of a minor point or tangential matters.

For example, Prime Minister Nakasone and his various ministers have over and over defended their trade position, their tariffs, their market's openness, and their need to maintain active and fair international trade. But only once have they publicly mentioned their want, a want which would significantly rebalance United States-Japan imports and exports. They are eager and want to buy American softwood (pine and others) and Alaskan oil at the going price. This eagerness is not overt in verbalization or action, however; they don't make any direct demands since a demand would attract attention—a violation of *haragei*. *Haragei* is being tried, but we are not sensitive enough yet to realize there is a solution to an expanding problem.

The prohibition on direct, overt, or repeated demands is reflected in another tenet of "cool" *haragei:* don't come on strong. Consider the following dialog between an agent (M) of the Mitsubishi Corporation, Japan's largest, and a bank manager (B).

M: It looks like we need your umbrella.
B: When it isn't raining?
M: It's threatening.
B: You must be kidding. Yours is an enormous *shosha* (trading firm) and it wears a big financial coat. You don't need an umbrella.
M: What would you say to a loan request from us for working capital? Our client manufacturers need it for capital spending.
B: (Remains silent, but M understands a meta-message, i.e., Please drop hints as to why Mitsubishi needs our money so badly.)
M: We're dealing with all kinds of Japanese corporations. We might even ask you to let us make a payment to a shipbuilding corporation near your home office, using your facilities on a regular basis from now on.
B: I'm afraid our bank is not qualified to meet your future financial needs. (Implied question: Why don't you ask the Mitsubishi Bank, which is your mother bank, if you're so sure about your payment schedule.)

M: I'm not changing the subject, but I understand you're interested in the foreign exchange business. We're a trading firm. So we can be of some help to you.

B: (Remains silent, never agrees or disagrees, just wears the same old smile . . .)

(Matsumoto 1978:3)

In this conversation, neither the Mitsubishi agent nor the banker reveals much of the *honne* "truth" of their respective situations. The banker does not overtly express interest in the loan or directly ask why Mitsubishi needs a loan from a smaller bank. Instead, through his silence, he attempts to extract more information from the agent. The agent, however, refuses to divulge any pertinent information that could help the banker decide, and meta-bluffs by offering an inducement to do business unrelated to the loan.

The banker's subsequent refusal is interpreted as a request for more *honne* or "true reasons," which is met by another tangential response, and a second offer unrelated to the loan is made with an implied threat since Mitsubishi is powerful enough to not only help banks in the foreign exchange market, but also to effectively prohibit their involvement. The banker's final silence is an indication of his understanding of the probable difficulty of the loan and a willingness to wait until more relevant information is preferred. He knows that Mitsubishi is the largest company in Japan (the *tatemae* or "surface truth"), but he wants to know the *honne*, the true financial status related to the need for the loan.

This conversation of bluffs and hedges is not exclusive to the Japanese; Americans and Europeans can play it as well, although the use of silence as a probing answer to a question or polite request is certainly uncommon.

Based on Matsumoto's series on *haragei*, we may summarize them in an eleven point list of rules:

1. Be euphemistic, eschewing logic or reason.
2. Be sensitive to empathy.
3. Keep the message vague and ambiguous.
4. Let silence talk and language be silent.
5. Don't tell the truth.
6. Don't seek the truth.
7. Don't publicly disagree.
8. Don't be legalistic.
9. Play it artistically and wholeheartedly.
10. Don't attract attention.
11. Don't come on strong.

LINGUISTIC (ARTIFACTUAL) OUTCOMES

Western negotiation depends on agreement or disagreement to produce progress or regress. American negotiators may find that the Japanese do not satisfy their needs in this regard. Japanese negotiators, on the other hand, may find the Americans too blunt, impolite, or at worst, unacceptably rude.

In the Western world, particularly in those countries using the English language or the English logic thought pattern, negotiators quickly become aware of the value of the positive expression. The most simple and most clear is the word "yes." In any Western world negotiation, the term means either I agree with you or (at least), I understand you. In fact, the skilled negotiator knows one of the best ways to win a crucial point is to work his opponent into a series of "yes" responses. At the instant of the crucial point, even should the opponent wish to reply "no," he now is faced with the difficulty of going against his already expressed logic. Maneuvering the opponent into agreeing with you is a tried and true tactic.

This is simply not the case in Japan for several reasons:

Leading the Japanese to agreement on a crucial point frequently involves considerations quite apart from the familiar logic sequence. Getting them to disagree with the negotiator is crucial in order to become closer personally. Disagreement requires personal trust to reveal their true position. Polite agreement involves no lowering of the mask over the self.

The Japanese are exceptionally polite. They respond more quickly and more frequently than even called for in a dialogue, be it a negotiation or not. And, their expression is *hai*. It means anything from "I agree with you" to "I'm aware and I heard you." Of these two extremes, the latter one is dominant and is the source of the semantic sensitivity trap.

So frequently the American negotiator feels he has won his point, because the Japanese negotiator has responded very positively, or so the American thinks. But what is wrong is what the American thinks, not what the Japanese said. In most cases the Japanese man was being nothing other than polite. If he said "we accept" or "we agree," the American has won his point. If the Japanese person said *hai* or "yes," there is probably much more discussion to take place.

Misinterpretation of *hai* "yes" by Americans is an often cited problem, providing the title of a book, *Never Take Yes for An Answer* (Imai 1975). *Hai* generally is equivalent to "uh huh" or "I'm awake and listening to you." If it is really "yes" then much more elaboration and follow-up, including getting the agreement in writing (even on small points), needs to be done. The constant smiling is misinterpreted, too. The "smile" is not one of agreement or even happiness, but is often another signal of politeness or just a masking of true feelings.

When the Japanese do agree, they are often doing so for the sake of politeness, an outgrowth of *amae* or passive dependency. In fact, they are so polite (disarmingly so), they effectively take away some of the American's individualistic confrontational strategies and predispose them to act in a pleasant and agreeable manner. In a psychological study, Japanese commented on "What I am like in interpersonal relations" with statements such as, "I try to be as polite as possible," "I try to behave according to my role and circumstances," "I pretend to be cool and calm, even when I am not, I rarely show my true self," "I don't say all of what I think," "I try to keep the conversation happy and pleasant." "I use words that won't hurt anybody," "I try not to disagree," "I try to agree even when I don't," "I escape difficult questions," "I try to behave smoothly," and "I always smile when I talk" (Barnlund 1975: 57–58).

The Japanese are only maintaining their relationships—they are not "yes" men although the frequency of *hai* sometimes wrongly leads the American to assume they are. *Ee,* another more colloquial version of "yes," may also be heard infrequently between Japanese, but probably not directed toward the American negotiator, since it would be considered somewhat impolite.

This brings up the problem of formal vs. colloquial levels of speech occurring in negotiations.

The Japanese negotiating team is very polite throughout all stages in a negotiation, even when discussion of a topic becomes "heated." However, when directly speaking towards an inferior (any lower-ranking employee on the team), a Japanese will suddenly switch to colloquial levels. This means that most pronouns, certain nouns, verb forms (even the root occasionally), and the structure of the sentence can change. For example, in breaking for lunch, a *buchō* "manager" might ask the Americans *Onaka ga sukimashitaka?* "Are you hungry?" *Anatatachi wa watashitachi to issho ni gohan o tabemashō ka?* "Won't you eat with us together?", and then ask (tell) his subordinates *hara ga hetta* "I'm hungry" *nani ka kuu* "Let's have something to eat" *omaetachi, mo* "You all, too." Thus, *Anatatachi = omaetachi, to issho ni = mo, watashi-tachi = ∅, tabemashō = kuu, gohan = nanika, ka = ∅, onaka = hara, sukimashita = hetta*—so every content word has changed.

This switching can become a problem for the negotiator trained to negotiate in or at least able to comprehend Japanese. By switching artfully, the Japanese negotiator can conceal some of his meaning and essentially carry on a private conversation in front of the supposedly bilingual Americans. On the Japanese side, negotiators tend to be as skilled in English; they are conversant, read well, can write points of negotiation in English on the blackboard, and can listen with good comprehension. American negotiating team members, then, can never have private conversations in front of the Japanese, but instead must always ask to caucus in another room. One potential danger exists when the American is fooled into thinking the Japanese doesn't understand, simply because he does not say much. A similar Japanese mistake can be made with a newer breed of American negotiator who has lived in Japan and perhaps worked in Japanese companies. Since so few Caucasians bother to go beyond simple phrases in Japanese, the Japanese negotiators may feel secure in working out sensitive points (or building a consensus) right in front of the Americans. If enough details, that is, numbers, quantities, dates, and so on, can be picked up despite the colloquial level and constant elimination of subjects, objects, and other Western language necessities, the American can listen in and gain an advantage by simply sensing their "bottom line."

For the monolingual negotiator, interpreters can cause a frustrating experience at times since points are generally explained by members of the Japanese negotiation team in a wordy fashion due to the demands of formal Japanese and the demands of *amae.* They are talking to the other Japanese principally, to the interpreter secondarily, and to the English-speaking Americans not at all. The upshot of this is a tenminute stretch of discourse condensed by the interpreter into one minute's worth of the most important points which the American negotiator must know in order to proceed. What was lost could have provided information on the difficulty or ease of negotiating the point and other information on the social dynamics within the Japanese negotiating team. One solution is to hire a simultaneous interpreter, but Japanese-English simultaneous interpreters are very rare, exceptionally busy, and extremely expensive. An additional problem concerning interpreters concerns their degree of independence. In many cases, the Japanese company will provide one of its own employees as an interpreter for the American side. As an employee of the Japanese company, he may consciously or even subconsciously want to put his company at an advantage. If the interpreter is an employee of the American company, some guardedly pessimistic, or overly optimistic, slanting of the Japanese point of view may also take place, also making the negotiators' jobs more difficult. From the interpreter's point of view, preparation time, pertinent documents, and introductory talks with both sides (separately) on the nature of the deal would greatly help the interpreter and improve the quality and speed of interpretation. However, fears regarding personal trustworthiness, security, antitrust, and proprietary information regarding products prevent this from being done as often and to the extent it should be done.

Another linguistic area of potential negotiation frustration is the seeming inability of the Japanese to say "no." In the vertical relationships Japanese form, "no" can hurt the supplicant's feelings and could not be expressed directly to a superior for fear of mutual embarrassment. The maintenance of long-lasting, stable personal relationships is of the utmost importance, and "no" can damage them, so it is not said. In the closest family relationships, *chigaimasu* or *chigau* (colloquial) meaning "It's different" is used to replace "no." The intent is the same, but the force is only tangential compared to the directness of "no." This is one of the few times an honorific (*masu*) ending is used in a family relationship, another indication of the severity of disagreement. In Japanese business conferences, *chigaimasu* is also used to express a company's viewpoint (Cullison 1983), as do Americans in, "We see this in a different light," or "Our view is somewhat different." Again, Americans can be rather euphemistic when they want to be.

In business situations, *musukashii desu* "it's difficult," is perhaps the most common way of saying "no." "Difficult" in this case really means "impossibly difficult." This phrase may be grossly abbreviated to *chotto* which means "a bit" or "a little," which stands for *chotto muzukashii* or "a little difficult." *Chotto,* then, functionally means "a great deal" or "very much" (difficulty), and in this way contains a need for *ishin denshin* or "intuitive communication" (also defined as "telepathy") to be read correctly.

Other expressions for "no" requiring *ishin denshin* on the part of the listener include *saaa* while exhaling forcefully and optionally scratching one's head. *Saaa* is generally translated as "I don't know" or "I'm not sure" for many situations, but should be read intuitively for many more situations as, "I really can't agree with you on this point." The forced inhalation of breath through clenched teeth is another paralinguistic phenomenon indicating difficulty or disagreement which may or may not precede *chotto* or *muzukashii* or both together.

One common organizational technique of saying "no" oft-quoted in newspaper accounts of both economic and diplomatic negotiations is the formation of a "study group" or "high-level review board or committee" to consider the problem (Cullison 1983). In the conference room, *Mo sukoshi kangaemashō* "Let's think about it a little more" or *ato de sodan shimashō* "Let's discuss that later on" or *Jaa, kangaemasu* "Well, I'll think about it" are precursors to the formation of a "study group." The postponement of a decision may be a hidden "no" or it may only be a need to build a consensus. This requires understanding on the U.S. side. If the point is truly negotiable, a study group to review the point will be formed, but if recent history is any guide, they are often not formed and the various phrases, pronouncements, and so on, are only a strategy to avoid saying "no" and to please the American side. "When a Japanese avoids saying yes or no clearly, it is most likely that he wishes to say no" (Masatsugu 1982:190). In order to solve this problem, the following points could be tried: When a Japanese does not want to say no ask him for more information and he should tell you. Probe a little more—don't take him at his "word" initially. If the probing leads nowhere, ask a third party, perhaps those who provided your introduction, to sound out their true position. *Assuming* their words mean what our use of them does is the *greatest* source of negotiating breakdowns.

Another way to say "no" is via a proverb. The Japanese are fond of using proverbs, both English and ancient Japanese, or Confucian sayings in business situations. For example, "Words cut more than swords" or "An able hawk hides its claws" (Be humble). These may require some situational *ishin-denshin* intuition as well to correctly interpret.

Addressing the "no" problem from the Japanese perspective, the American tendency to say "no" too readily is considered rude, although the Japanese anticipate Americans will have no problems being very direct. The "Japanese usually refuse to interact with others when they are given a straight 'no' " (Matsumoto 1978:3). When confronted, the Japanese tend to either withdraw and become silent or "blow up" verbally or even physically, although this is rare. If the American's "no" is also combined with anger, table thumping, or ill-considered language, the Japanese are likely to use postponements, delays in orders, even cancellation of the deal "to get back" at the American company. The negotiator is seen as a representative of his company more than as an individual expressing his own personal needs as well. A lack of personal trust or credibility results from bluntness, poor language, (which can include verbal mistakes from poor preparation), or hemming and hawing from not having enough authority. Similarly, rudeness in gestures, manners, and cursing can kill a Japanese company's desire to do business with the American company, regardless of how responsibly the next negotiator may act. Avoid bluntness or rudeness, or negotiation termination is imminent!

Ten Semantic Sensitivity Traps

1. We understand: *rikai dekimasu* = appreciate or understand; *wakarimasu* = understand or know (but may not agree).

   I take note of what you just said, or just, I hear you.

2. We're thinking along parallel lines: *heikōsenjō no kangaekata* = Parallel lines never meet, nor will we.

3. (We agree) in principle: *Gensoku to shite* = We will abide by the agreement 95% of the time (the remaining 5% due to acts of God).

4. A gentlemen's agreement: *shinshi kyōyaku* = A much stronger agreement than a legal contract; unbreakable except for acts of God when witnessed by a respected third party.

5. Company: *kaisha* = Community or family in which a Japanese can immerse his individual self.

6. Democracy: *minshushugi* = Rule by a 51% majority, but relatively weak because consensus is not achieved.

7. I am sorry: *sumimasen* = I will not or cannot reply—or possibly "no" in some negotiating situations.

8. You're very good at Japanese: *Nihongo wa ojōzu desu* = You can barely put two words together, but I am flattered.

9. Maybe: *tabun* = Maybe (or maybe not).

10. We will review this: *Kore o kentō shimasu* = We might review it or we may shelve it.

NEGOTIATION APPROACHES

Americans tend to take the aggressive approach in negotiations. They start with high aspirations, ask for more than they expect to get, and back off slowly until a common ground is found with the adversary. The Japanese tend to be counterpunchers, and they frequently wait for the "other side" to declare its position before they start revealing theirs. They generally do not ask for much more than they expect to get, but they offer less than they are ready to give. Early on, the Japanese, who will have prepared for the negotiations just as much as you, may identify some points you expect to discuss as being "nonnegotiable." That does not mean the point is nonnegotiable. What it means is a combination of two things: First, it is a very important detail and second, the authority to negotiate it has not been delegated—yet—to the negotiating team.

   Actually, the Japanese are being quite nice to you in so identifying these "nonnegotiable" points. What they are really telling you is should your negotiations resolve all other problems to the satisfaction of both parties, the issues that will make or break the deal will be those earlier identified as "nonnegotiables." They will be negotiated—last.

   Stalemates and impasse situations will arise or you will get very close to them. Americans should and do expect such a possibility. Frequently the Americans simply stop negotiating when they happen, and chalk up the failure to "nothing ventured, nothing gained." The Japanese differ in that they anticipate such will occur, and they (a) like we, make concessions and (b) unlike we, are quite prepared for compromise. The Japanese value a compromise highly. They feel that should one get the better of another without a compromise, the other will plan revenge. Although they do not express their attitude about negotiation outcomes as "win-win," they carefully measure the value of what they are giving for what they are getting, and if these do not balance reasonably, there is no deal.

A DOZEN COMMON MISTAKES

The basic message in this paper is there is nothing totally mysterious about negotiating with the Japanese. However, in negotiating with them, there are many mistakes that can be made, most of which fall under the general heading of miscommunications. The first eight titles quoted are taken from "Negotiations with Japanese Firms" (Tsurumi 1981:306–31).

Slicing the Pie Before It Is Baked

Japanese sense the Americans try to do this immediately. One way of looking at the negotiating process is to visualize it as two parties meeting to make something happen that does not today exist—like baking a loaf of bread or a pie. Both sides of course want to have their fair share of that pie when it is baked, but trying to slice it this way or that before everyone knows what was involved in making it is a mistake. If a cooperative relationship is replaced with an adversary relationship, the negotiations may collapse. While this mistake is one the Japanese ask us not to make, it is a bit in conflict with how they go about the negotiation process. Americans usually start with how they, the American side only, perceive the "big picture," the woods, or that part of the whole they are willing to let the other side see.

The Japanese start with the pieces, the trees, and they deal with them one by one. The Japanese are using their approach to (a) get some potential stumbling blocks out of the way, and (b) to test your reactions. Of these two, the second is the most important. They feel that formal agreements somehow arrived at without mutual, developed trust are doomed to failure. The initial get-togethers to build trust through phatic communication are crucial to avoiding this mistake and the following one.

Selling the Deal, and Not the Seller

Unlike in the United States where legalistic and contractual bondings are prevalent, in Japan the basis of honoring agreements is personal trust. Americans are sure to signal their untrustworthiness when, during the course of the negotiations or after, new circumstances are revealed that lead to position reversals or regurgitations. That's the way the Japanese see it. In contrast, Americans have no qualms about switching gears, should the road change. Americans also tire very quickly when the Japanese start regurgitating something—as they frequently seem to do, apparently without cause or justification—as we view it as a useless waste of time rather than as a product of *amae* or the *ringisho* system. Neither side is totally right or wrong and neither side is very different. The way to avoid this problem is to set some negotiating game rules at the outset permitting both sides to reconsider and change positions as necessary, before the final agreement is made. Changing positions after the agreement is reached is a lot of work and it can be real trouble because the Japanese feel it signals American untrustworthiness for the future of the agreement as originally reached with the Japanese. However, conditions change and when they do, "agreements" should be renegotiated.

Ignoring the Hidden Economics of Japanese Business Relationships

The Japanese distribution system is quite confusing to Westerners and impacts many negotiations. The American should determine early if what he wants the Japanese to do is going to, in an important way, require the Japanese to alter their relationships elsewhere. If it will, the American then has a much, much more difficult task ahead than previously anticipated, as the Japanese vertical system is difficult to disturb without causing trouble for the Japanese, who may have depended on one supplier for many years—building up a strong social and personal relationship with him—not just a business relationship. A small price advantage is not enough to offset this.

Letting Lawyers in on Your Negotiations

Bear in mind that the bottom line for the Japanese is that the inclusion of your lawyer tells the Japanese you do not trust them, or are not sure of yourself, or both. A lawyer can be consulted privately, but never in front of the Japanese negotiators. Lawyers are felt by the Japanese to steer negotiations into adversity rather than the cooperation they prefer.

A similar communications mistake is the overuse of logic. The Japanese feel logic is a bit cold, sterile, and impersonal—those using too much of it lack feeling and humanity. The Japanese prefer the intangible and nebulous approach. "Cool" *haragei* contains elements of such an approach.

Disagreement made public before a court of law is regarded by the Japanese as shameful and is to be avoided at all costs. Japanese tend to see the plaintiff as greedy, while the defendant is apt to be regarded as guilty before tried. Any form of struggle is to be made preferably outside of law court. This psychological trend of the Japanese people is so strong it can sometimes be taken advantage of in international negotiations (Yoshimoto 1983).

Lack of Semantic Sensitivity

American firms would benefit considerably from developing a cadre of their own managers who speak Japanese and know something about Japanese culture. Yes, both. One without the other is no good. When Americans hear such expressions as "we will consider this" or ones similar to them, they must pause and think carefully before they conclude they understand what the Japanese meant. When they are not sure, they must ask the Japanese to explain what they meant. Examples of this miscomprehension of Japanese expressions are abundantly available. An everyday source is the newspaper article that tells how the Japanese are not doing what we thought they said they would do.

Insisting on Detailed Discussions with High-Level Executives

High-level executives are frequently absent—on the Japanese side—from the negotiation table. Mid-level executives are often delegated the strategic decision-making authority that only top American management enjoys. When the high-level Japanese executives are there, they are generally not there as "chief negotiators," but rather only to arbitrate, should that become necessary. Attempting to negotiate with them runs the risk of making the Japanese person quite uncomfortable. In addition, doing so is downgrading to those who have been delegated the negotiation responsibility. The high-level executive most likely will not have many of the negotiation background materials in mind. Thus, you might embarrass him badly.

Rushing the Negotiations

Be patient! Americans feel it takes an eternity for Japanese to make up their minds. On the other hand, the Japanese feel it takes forever for Americans to implement decisions once agreement is reached. Both are right. The Japanese feel the implementation steps are so important, they prepare them in advance. Unfortunately, they do not realize that in America, the decision making and the implementation processes are handled separately. Good communications from both sides will enable both Japanese and Americans to understand this, a priori.

Assuming Lasting Stability of the Agreement

As some Japanese perceive a joint venture, the agreement is a "marriage." But the Japanese also recognize that all marriages are not always peaceful or everlasting. They must be repaired periodically through mutual understanding and action. Divorces happen in both countries, and agreements are broken because of mutual feelings or the failure of one or the other party. However, many compromises are possible, and the Japanese are ready by nature to try them. Formal procedures for periodic reviews are recommended to increase the prospects for stability of Japanese-American agreements (Tsurumi 1981:311).

Holding Private Discussions in an Attempt to Override the Group

One or more individuals on the adversary's side may feel your position is right or best, and may even tell you. That, however, does not suggest the individual will risk the ill-will of his group by trying to sell his group on your argument. He may be able to do this quite naturally and effectively, but you should not ask him to try. First of all, he will have great difficulty telling you "no," and secondly, he will not appreciate at all the position you have forced him into.

So Relaxed the Feet Go on the Table

While in general the Japanese admire the relaxed approach Americans frequently portray, the American tendency to raise their legs and place their feet on a conference table or a desk leaves a very poor impression on the Japanese. Remember—shoes are extremely dirty things which do not even touch domestic Japanese floors! While thinking clothing, please remember to dress conservatively.

Failure to Follow Up

At the end of a negotiation, regardless of where one is in the negotiation process, one should not fail to confirm where he thinks he is, in writing. Failure to do so misses the opportunity to get early agreements on some points in writing, and runs the risk of having to rediscuss what had already been agreed upon. Writing can counter the nebulous areas or clarify items where *haragei* and/or *amae* may have been operating.

Sending the Wrong People

Women are not welcome at the Japanese negotiating table—except for serving green tea, snacks, and lunch. They are, by and large, excluded from management in Japanese companies. The day when a woman can negotiate as an equal with a Japanese man is still in the future. Letting the America wife go along on the after-hours entertainment rounds could also be mutually embarrassing. Young men (under 35) are also unacceptable if they are to negotiate alone with executives much more advanced in years (and experience), since the elder Japanese could be insulted. Inexperienced negotiators, or negotiators convinced of their own cultural and personal superiority, need to be replaced by those willing to demonstrate the understanding cooperation and patience necessary to achieve agreement. Once the Japanese clearly recognize an "American superiority complex," they may tell the negotiator so to his face, and the negotiations will be adversely affected.

TRAINING FUTURE NEGOTIATORS

A training program should be developed to teach Japanese and American negotiators strategies leading to success. For those concerned only about the stylistic differences and unconcerned about the language barrier, training sessions similar to the American Management Association's seminars could be implemented with leaders experienced in cross-cultural negotiation or at least well-read on the topic. The executive and his interpreter could both attend to their mutual benefit.

For the executive concerned with the difficulties of interpretation and willing to work to achieve a basic proficiency in the other language, one linguistic factor is working to his advantage—the technical vocabulary is generally the same in most fields. A personal advantage is also evident—if negotiation training could be combined with foreign language training, the executive could learn several skills concurrently and increase his negotiating power.

If he wishes to combine both skills and pursue this approach, two methods from foreign language pedagogy seem to be potentially valuable. The first is Charles Curran's Counseling-Learning (C-L). C-L, from a Japanese perspective, involves our first principle, *amae*, or active dependency which fosters shared feelings of group support when learning the foreign language. Negotiating could be practiced in the C-L group guided by the stylistics of Eastern cooperation rather than Western adversity, since C-L develops cooperation within the group as a basis for the entire methodology.

The second methodology, one of the newest methods of teaching a foreign language, is Strategic Interaction, a foreign language/foreign culture teaching-learning method developed by Robert J. Di Pietro. In the case of negotiations, it seems to be the only method that promotes the teaching of the cultural aspects of language, so crucial to negotiating skillfully. Furthermore, Di Pietro's notion of "dynamic tension" is closely related to the Japanese concept of situational "hot" *haragei*. The open-ended scenarios developed to implement this methodology already contain problems of negotiation—only the situational vocabulary need be changed to make it directly applicable to Japanese-American negotiations. This specific use of Strategic Interaction to strengthen the experienced executive's skills and enlighten trainees would provide needed strategies and counterstrategies in all three dimensions: interactional, transactional, and linguistic.

CONCLUSION

A fundamental concept, *amae,* or "active interdependency" has been identified as an underlying bicultural psychological/sociological phenomenon that can influence the nature of negotiations between Japanese and Americans. Mutual understanding, appropriate revision of expectations, and, most of all, patience can mitigate most of the potentially negative impact. *Amae* should be discussed and understood by each negotiator before any negotiating begins.

Haragei is a communicative strategy shared by both sides, but is openly named and acknowledged by the Japanese. As a strategy containing vagueness of language, ambiguity, and culturally determined paralinguistic phenomena, it is potentially confusing. But at the same time, it is potentially advantageous, that is, the negotiator may get more than he needs because misinterpretation in his favor may occur. But, as a strategy of brinkmanship, it is dangerously dooming and can doom the company. In the example of Prime Minister Sato's *haragei* with President Nixon, it doomed an entire industrial culture—in that case, textiles. Brinkmanship in crucial situations, however, can also lead to a "win," as in the sample using rhetorical questions as an unspoken threat. *Haragei,* as a technique to be studied beforehand and perhaps practiced in dry-run negotiations, could be beneficial to both sides if the negotiators are experienced. For trainees, an experienced teacher can inform in a superficial way, but *haragei* requires "gut instincts," savvy, mind-reading abilities, and a knowledge of both languages. It is not recommended as a technique for every negotiating session, certainly not for the less experienced negotiator. In brinkmanship, or "hot" situations, *haragei* is a last resort due to potential miscommunication. In "cool" situations, it should be avoided if possible, but experienced executives may start using it naturally or unthinkingly without realizing all of the cross-cultural complications.

The various linguistic difficulties presented here are concerned with the expressions of agreement and disagreement. "Yes" is a potential problem that can be explained and understood before negotiations begin by all. "No" is more complex, requiring time and judgment on the part of the American negotiator, and understanding patience on the part of the Japanese negotiator.

Other difficulties regarding the interpretation, formal and colloquial levels of language, and bilingual ability in a negotiating team may be remedied by more time for preparation, more money, a commitment to learning the other language, patience, and the will to persevere.

REFERENCES

Barnlund, Dean. 1975. Public and private self in Japan and the U. S. Tokyo: Simul Press.

Blaker, Michael. 1977. Japanese international negotiating style. New York: Columbia University Press.

Blanchfield, Robert A. 1983. To Japan? Your first (good) trip. Wilmington: Du Pont, Inc.

Christopher, Robert C. 1983. The Japanese mind. New York: Linden Press/Simon & Schuster.

Cleaver, Charles G. 1976. Japanese and Americans: Cultural parallels and paradoxes. Minneapolis: University of Minnesota Press.

Coffin, Royce. 1973. The Negotiator: A manual for winners. New York: Amacom.

Cullison, A. E. 1983. U. S. asks Japan to review its industrial standards. The Journal of Commerce. March 9, 1983. Vol 355. p. 23B.

Curran, Charles A. 1976. Counseling learning in second languages. Apple River, Ill. Apple River Press.

Di Pietro, Robert J. 1981. Discourse and real-life roles in the ESL classroom. TESOL Quarterly 15(1) 27–33.

_____ 1982. The open-ended scenario: A new approach to conversation. TESOL Quarterly 16(1) 15–20.

Doi, Takeo. 1971. The anatomy of dependence. Tokyo: Kodansha.

Fast, Julius. 1970. Body language. New York: Lippincott.

Glazer, Herbert. 1968. The international businessman in Japan. Tokyo: Sophia University Press.

Goffman, Erving. 1969. Strategic interaction. Philadelphia: University of Pennsylvania Press.

_____ 1981. Forms of talk. Philadelphia: University of Pennsylvania Press.

Graham, John L. 1983. Brazilian, Japanese, and American business negotiations. Journal of International Business Studies 14(1) 47–61.

Greenwald, John. 1983. The negotiation waltz. Time No. 31. August 1, 1983. 41–2.

Grice, Paul H. 1975. Logic and conversation. Syntax and semantics 3, ed. by P. Cole and J. Morgan, 41–58. New York: Academic Press.

Halloran, Richard. 1969. Japan: Images and realities. Tokyo: Tuttle.

Imai, Masaaki. 1975. Never take yes for an answer. Tokyo: Simul Press.

Karass, Chester. 1970. The negotiating game. New York: World Pub.

Lebra, Takie Sugiyama. 1976. Japanese patterns of behavior. Honolulu: The University Press of Hawaii.

Masatsugu, Mitsuyuki. 1982. The modern samurai society. New York: Amacom.

Matsumoto, Michihiro. 1975. Haragei no ronri. (The logic of Haragei) Tokyo: Asahi Press.

_____ . 1978. Haragei (a 10-article series in the weekly Culture section). Asahi Evening News, January 24–March 28th.

McCreary, Don R. 1984. Communicative strategies in Japanese-American negotiations. Unpublished doctoral dissertation. Ann Arbor, MI: University Microfilms International.

Mitchell, T. F. 1975. The language of buying and selling in Cyrenaica: A situational statement. T. F. Mitchell, ed., Principles of Firthian linguistics, 167–200. London: Longman.

Miyoshi, Masaya. 1982 (October 28). An expanding international role. Address before The Royal Institute of International Affairs. London.

Nakane, Chie. 1970. Japanese society. Berkeley: University of California Press.

Pascale, Richard T. and Anthony G. Athos. 1981. The art of Japanese management. New York: Simon and Schuster.

Richardson, Bradley M., & Taizo Ueda (Eds.). 1981. Business and society in Japan: Fundamentals for businessmen. New York: Praeger Press.

Sacks H., Schegloff, E., & Jefferson, G. 1974. A simplest systematics for the organization of turn-taking in conversation. Language 50(4) 696–735.

Schegloff, E. A., & Sacks, H. 1973. Opening up closings. Semiotica 8(4) 289–327.

Tsurumi, Yoshi. 1981. Social relations and Japanese business practices. Business and society in Japan: Fundamentals for businessmen, 304–322. New York: Praeger Press.

Ueda, Keiko. 1974. Sixteen ways to avoid saying "no" in Japan. Intercultural encounters with Japan, ed. by John C. Condon and Mitsuko Saito, 185–192. Tokyo: Simul Press.

Van Zandt, Howard F. 1970. How to negotiate in Japan. Harvard Business Review, November–December 1970, 45–56.

Yoshimoto, Y. 1983. Written interviews and correspondence with Don R. McCreary in March 1983 and September 1983.

PART V

BRIDGING THE LANGUAGE GAP: INTERPRETATION AND TRANSLATION

THIRTEEN

Translation Policy in Brazil*

Leland E. McCleary

University of California, Los Angeles, and Associação Alumni, São Paulo, Brazil

INTRODUCTION

Translation Policy

Translation is an ancient activity which has played a key role in political, cultural, and economic history wherever linguistically diverse groups have come into contact. Nevertheless, it has been largely an invisible, unheralded activity taking place behind the scenes and never acquiring, until very recently, the potential for social significance which would bring it to public attention. Why this has been true is a fascinating inquiry unfortunately beyond the scope of this paper: why translation, a practice at least as old as medicine, did not begin to forge a professional consciousness in the form of codes of behavior and guilds until well into this century. Whatever the reasons, the fact is that the practice of translation had neither melded its practitioners into associations of common cause, nor been considered of sufficient social importance to merit the attention of public policy.

Events of the postwar era, however, have begun to require that more attention be paid to translation as a profession: by its practitioners, by its consumers, and by government planners. Among these events are the establishment of the United Nations and regional multinational bureaucracies such as the European Economic Community; the rapid growth of science and advances in communications technology; and the accelerated movement for sovereignty and economic development in the Third World—all events which have intensified interlingual contact and have raised the stakes of international communication. Still, the conception of translation as an activity that merits or requires regulation, either internal or external, is a very new one, and "translation policy" has begun to take shape only recently.

In its strictest sense, *translation policy* is any measure taken by a government with the aim of affecting the practice of translation. ("Translation" is used here for convenience as a cover term for the production of both written and oral text, the latter being referred to professionally as "interpretation.") Translation policy,

---

*My thanks to Ângela Levy, Björn Jernudd, Carlos Gohn, and Clifford Prator for their advice and comments on an earlier version of this paper; and to Etilvia Arjona and Regina Elias Alfarano for their generous contributions.

where it exists at all, will most commonly be found in disperse and fragmented guises rather than as a comprehensive plan: it may result from an education policy that mandates the use of vernaculars for which there are no texts; it may be part of a political policy aimed at translating propaganda or literary works for foreign or domestic consumption; or it may be narrowly focused on the supply and regulation of certain classes of translators for specific purposes, such as for diplomacy or the domestic courts.

In whatever form, translation policy is best viewed as a single element in response to a general problem: how to overcome language barriers where they block desired political, economic, or social goals. Language barriers may exact considerable cost in lost political, economic, and social opportunities, but the bilingualism which is required to overcome them has its own cost, and that cost must be apportioned among alternatives. When Sputnik forced the English-speaking world to take Soviet technology seriously, there was a concerted effort, in both the United States and Great Britain, to overcome a serious language barrier in the scientific community. Subsidies were made available for both the training of teachers of Russian and for the translation of Russian scientific journals. Some of those journals have been able to survive in the market without subsidies, but there is a limit to how much journal translation can be tolerated without great expenditure of public money.

The form that translation policy takes will therefore depend on many factors, among them:

1. Linguistic history and demography
2. Literacy and educational levels
3. Population
4. Level of development
5. Nature of the political and economic systems
6. National goals

Measures and attitudes affecting the practice of translation can also be taken outside government, by practitioners of translation themselves and by their clients. These measures constitute translation policy in the broadest sense. Policy within the private sector may affect—and shape—public policy, and vice versa, and these together will condition the status of translation within a country.

In what follows, the current state of translation policy in Brazil will be put into the perspective of the various forms policy has taken in other parts of the world. First, a brief sketch of Brazil's social, political, economic, and linguistic reality will be presented as the context within which translation policy is being debated. Then the recent growth of the translation profession—its associations and training institutions—will be traced, both internationally and in Brazil. This will be followed by a close look at several types of translation, each having a particular mix of involvement and interest from both the public and private sectors. In each case the situation in Brazil will be compared with what is happening elsewhere.

The Brazilian Context

Brazil is a nation of roughly 125,000,000 people, some 97% of them native speakers of Portuguese. That puts Portuguese in seventh place among the languages of the world, on a par with German, Japanese, and Arabic (Fromkin and Rodman 1978). There are important minorities, however, including German, Italian, and Japanese colonies of close to 1,000,000 each, and some 13 other European and Middle Eastern colonies of between 10,000 and 200,000 each, especially in the south of Brazil. Although these colonies often maintain schools of their own, the Brazilian government mandates compulsory education in Portuguese, and most parents are eager for their children to learn Portuguese. Brazil has traditionally been tolerant of racial diversity, such that minority groups have not tended to become polarized. The indigenous peoples, speaking almost 200 different languages, constitute less than 0.1% of the population. The result is that Brazil, for all its great size and population, is by and large linguistically unified.

Since 1964 Brazil has had a military-backed government committed to capitalism and to rapid industrial growth. Foreign investment has been attracted to develop an industrial sector which in 1981 produced 58% of export earnings, concentrated in machinery, construction materials, rubber, sugar and wood processing, chemicals, textiles, arms, and vehicles. Brazil has thus depended upon a heavy influx of foreign technology (including nuclear technology from the Federal Republic of Germany, the second largest investor after the United States, Japan being third) (Europa Year Book 1983:1677, 1784). At the same time, Brazil has sought markets for the export of engineering technology as well as for raw and manufactured products in Africa, Latin America, and the Middle East. All of these activities have increased interlingual contacts and created a demand for both language teaching—principally English—and translation.

Emphasis on modern-sector development has brought with it growth in higher education, producing a total of close to 200,000 university graduates and over 10,000 postgraduate degrees (UNESCO Statistical Yearbook 1982). At the same time, however, adult illiteracy still stands at about 24% nationwide, and as high as 44% in the northeast (Europa Year Book 1983:1678). This contrast in educational levels is reflected in income levels. In the mid-1970s, the top 5% of the population earned nearly 40% of the income, with an equal share being earned by the bottom 80% of the population (Adelman 1979). One of the implications of these facts is that the affluent reading public, which constitutes the market for published material, is relatively small, adversely affecting the economics of publishing and thereby the practice of translation.

Politically, Brazil is a federal republic. While political parties are permitted and congress and state legislatures do function, much of the business of government is controlled directly by the executive and its ministries at both the federal and state levels. This control is felt in the private sector, in part, in the imposing presence of semiautonomous state enterprises which consume 50% of tax revenue (Europa Year

Book 1983:1977), and in the indexing of salaries, rents, interest, and prices; in education in the form of state and federal control of curriculum; and in labor relations in
the narrow sanctions exercised over labor unions (*sindicatos*).

THE GROWTH AND CURRENT STATUS OF THE TRANSLATION PROFESSION

The contemporary history of translation began with World War II and the political,
economic, and technological changes which ensued. To monitor this politically
changed world, the United Nations was founded and, with it, its many international
agencies of cooperation. This for the first time created a permanent international
multilingual forum and hundreds of task forces and permanent committees, all of
which required the services of trained translators and interpreters. From this new
perspective, the United Nations saw clearly that there was no profession organized
to meet the translation needs of the future, and that governments were largely obliv-
ious to the problem. In 1953 the Fédération Internationale des Traducteurs (FIT)
was founded under the auspices of UNESCO in order to

> group professional translators throughout the world, to make them and the general
> public aware of the importance of their profession, and to render the profession a fac-
> tor in the establishment of friendly relations between peoples of all nations. (Congrat-
> Butler 1979:10)

Progress toward these goals has not been easy, but some advances have been
made. Today there are some 34 member translators' associations in 29 countries,
many of which have modeled their guidelines after the FIT code. FIT publishes a
bulletin, *Babel,* which has conducted extensive surveys of the translation profession
worldwide[1] (Caillé 1974:130–141; Hendrickx 1975:101–106; Schwarz 1977b:
145–151), and has made recommendations for the protection of translators' rights.

Translators' Associations

The members of FIT are associations, not individuals. A few of them predate FIT
by as many as 20 years, but 50% have appeared since 1970. Congrat-Butler's 1979
directory of translation and translators lists 80 associations, chapters, or centers in
34 countries. The associations formulate professional standards; organize conferences, symposiums, receptions, prizes, subsidies, and scholarships; publish journals, reports, glossaries, and directories of members; conduct surveys and other research; prepare and lobby for favorable legislation; and mediate professional
disputes. In 1976 UNESCO approved the recommendations of FIT on "The Legal

---

[1] The surveys are necessarily spotty. They can do no better than assemble the information available to
member national associations, many of which are small and do not have the resources to conduct adequate surveys of their own. Nevertheless, they give an overview of the chaotic state of translation policy
and practice.

Protection of Translators and Translations and the Practical Means to Improve the Status of Translators'' (UNESCO House 1976:4–18; Schwarz 1977a:49–51; Library of Congress 1980:33–36). This is a concise and complete statement of the goals proposed for translation policy which provides national translators' associations with an authoritative guide on which to base their own petitions. Some governments have taken steps to act on the recommendations, but no recent survey of action is available.

With few exceptions the associations are private voluntary organizations with no official sanction, although some have developed a working relationship with their governments in an advisory capacity. Because translation is almost universally *not* legally recognized as a profession,[2] the associations almost universally have no legal authority to regulate or to certify translators or interpreters.[3] Two notable exceptions are the Registry of Interpreters for the Deaf (RID) in the United States and the National Translation Institute of Science and Technology (NATIST) in Japan (see below). In the absence of other demonstrations of competence, in many cases diplomas or certificates awarded by college translation programs have come to fill this gap.

In Brazil an association to promote the interests of translators was founded in Rio in 1974: the Associação Brasileira de Tradutores (ABRATES), a member of FIT. In 1982 it had a membership of some 800, with branches in São Paulo, Minas Gerais, and Brasília. ABRATES publishes a bimonthly newsletter and a journal, *Tradução & Communicação: Revista Brasileira de Tradutores* and organizes national colloquia on the problems of the profession. Specialized associations also exist for interpreters, public translators, and theatrical translators. As is the norm, none of these associations exercises any accrediting authority (for the special case of public translators, see below).

Professional Training for Translators

Accompanying the postwar increase in the demand for translation and the growth of professional associations has been the appearance of programs for the training of translators and interpreters. Virtually unknown before the 1950s, certificate and degree programs have multiplied as fast as the associatons themselves in the last 30 years in a wide variety of guises ranging from undergraduate options within language or comparative literature programs to full-scale Bachelor's, Master's, and

---

[2] The situation in Canada, described by Peter Gawn, Director of Departmental Translation Services, Translation Bureau, Secretary of State, Canada, is typical: "There is in fact no legislation governing the translation profession in Canada and translators do not have any particular legal status. Translation in the private sector is unregulated, and none of the professional associations has so far been able to convince the appropriate level of government to recognize the profession of translation" (Personal communication, March 5, 1982).

[3] In 1972, the American Translators Association began an Accreditation Program, on its own authority, which establishes minimum standards and administers tests. By 1978, about half of its members had taken the exams and about 300 had received certificates.

Ph.D. programs in translation. Based on a sample of such programs worldwide for which information is available (Congrat-Butler 1979:31–41), 56% were established after 1970. A 1982 American Translators Association (ATA) guide lists 74 colleges in the United States that offer courses in translation and interpretation, including 31 that offer some kind of certificate or degree (Arjona 1982). Some schools offer no more than one course in the theory of translation or a translation workshop; others accept annotated translations as theses or dissertations.

Translation courses or programs in Brazil first appeared in 1972 at Associação Alumni, São Paulo; Faculdade Ibero-Americana, São Paulo; and Pontifícia Universidade Católica (PUC), Rio. By 1982 there were 12 institutions offering a variety of courses, options, B.A.s or specialization certificates in translation.[4]

The degree and certificate programs in translation are being created to provide training for which there is clearly a market, but they are forming professionals for which there is no legally recognized profession: no generally sanctioned means of accreditation, no universally accepted codes of practice, and no guarantees of due compensation nor legal means of bargaining. Nevertheless, the schools themselves and their students become a new force with a vested interest in pressuring governments to establish an infrastructure for their profession.

TYPES OF TRANSLATION AND TRANSLATION POLICY

Thus far we have been looking at the profession of translation chiefly from the point of view of the practitioners themselves, primarily as an index to the growth of the profession. In what follows we will discuss specific problems and policies as they derive from specialized translation activities. These policies will in many cases be shaped by the goals of government or the requirements of business and industry, as well as by the grievances of the translators themselves. The diversity of translation and interpretation activity is much greater than is generally thought, each speciality with its peculiarities of social and legal status. This fact contributes to the difficulty with which the public views translation as a profession, to the difficulty which translators themselves have in organizing their profession, and to the complexity of translation policy.

Literary and Book Translation

The prototypical translators, perhaps, are the literary translators. These are the ones who become known for their craft if anyone does. The best of them have literary talents in their own right, coupled with profound knowledge of other languages. In Russia, where literary expression is limited by the government, many literary artists

---

[4] They are: Universidade Federal, Rio Grande do Sul; PUC, Porto Alegre; Universidade de São Paulo; PUC, São Paulo; Faculdade Metropolitanas Unidas, São Paulo; Manuel da Nóbrega, São Paulo; Universidade Estadual, Rio Preto, São Paulo; Universidade Estadual de Caxias do Sul, Rio Grande do Sul; and Universidade de Brasília.

turn to translation as a creative outlet (Ginsberg 1970:357); in the West, too, practice in translation has often been a source of training and inspiration for writers. Just
as these are the translators who are most in the public eye, they are the ones for
whom subsidies and prizes are created (Congrat-Butler 1979:19–30). This should
not be interpreted to mean that they are the most highly respected and highly compensated translators, however; on the contrary, as a class they are among the lowest
paid (Hendrickx 1975:104). Two of their primary grievances are (a) acknowledg-
ment and (b) royalties. Surprisingly, it is not yet universally the practice to list the
name of the translator on the title page of books, and it is even more common that
critics and book reviewers will neglect to reveal the name of the translator, much
less to comment on the quality of the translation (Gross 1970:156; Astley
1970:310–11).

Theoretically, royalties for translators of literary works are protected under international copyright convention. Literary translations are considered adaptations of
original intellectual work, and, as such, the translator who has received permission
from the original copyright holder thereby may hold the copyright on the adaptation
and exercise the same rights and privileges as an author (Library of Congress
1980:33–34). That is the theory. In fact, however, in only a few countries is the
payment of royalties the standard practice.[5] In most countries, translations are considered commissioned works and therefore not subject to the payment of royalties.
Translators are paid a flat fee, usually on a per-word or per-page basis, and they are
obliged to sign a waiver of any further rights to the work (Congrat-Butler 1979:43).
As an example of the inequities of this system, the Yugoslav translator of *One Hundred Years of Solitude*, who is permitted to profit from the success of his translation,
has earned $30,000 for his work, and will continue to earn money as long as the
book is reprinted. The Brazilian translator, on the other hand, for the same labor,
earned a flat fee of $300 (Portinho 1981).

Without strong translators' associations to exert collective pressure, or without
government intervention, there is no reason for this situation to change, and the
quality of literary translation will suffer as a result. This will be especially true in a
country whose reading public does not yet demand quality translations.

If conditions are unfavorable for literary translation, they are even more so for
other types of book translation, for which the literary skill of the translator is not at a
premium: translation of popular fiction, nonfiction, textbooks, and encyclopedias.
Very few book translators are employed full time by publishers. The vast majority
work on a free-lance basis in their own homes and get paid on a piece-work basis.
Many of them specialize in technical areas, sometimes areas in which they have
worked or are working professionally.

---

[5] In socialist countries the state publishing houses pay royalties; in Federal Germany royalties and
lump sum payment coexist; in Sweden the translator may choose; in France royalties are compulsory; in
Canada, Italy, and the United States, lump sum is the rule, although royalties are not unknown (Caillé
1974:131).

Literary Translation as a Political Tool.   As is to be expected, the countries which have taken translation most seriously as an object of national policy are the communist countries in which availability of information and the formation of public opinion are considered prerogatives of the state. In postrevolutionary China, the government concerned itself both with what was to be translated and with translation technique (Bauer 1964:6). The Party and the government attempted to organize translation and publishing so that duplication of effort could be avoided and resources could be applied efficiently to the translation of important foreign books. Of first priority, of course, was a vast communist literature from Russia, followed by other Western ideological classics. In line with the philosophy of the government, group translation and criticism were encouraged. Nevertheless, some of the same complaints are heard in China as are common in the West: "Today the great majority of our translators are part-time translators; some are administration cadres, some school teachers, some still students; only very few are professional translators" (Mao Tun, quoted in Bauer 1964:8).

Also in Russia, the statistics on books published in translation reveal a preponderance of doctrinaire works. But that is not the whole story. In Russia the role of translation is profound; the Soviet Union is a multinational state comprised of between 100 and 200 ethnic groups, some of which have extensive written literatures, others of which have rich oral traditions but no written language. Writing and literacy became major goals of the communist government as a means of eradicating traditional beliefs and promoting orthodox collectives. Major unwritten languages were reduced to writing and massive translation was undertaken, not only of minority literatures into Russian, but also of Russian into minority languages, and even from one minority language into another: "The Soviet Literary Encyclopedia boasts that more translations are published in the Soviet Union than in any other country in the world. Translation in Russia is done from and into more than one hundred languages, and more than half of the books published in Russia are translations" (Ginsberg 1970:358). There are two notable aspects of this translation effort. One is that the vast majority (over 90%) of all translation is fiction. The other is that, since Stalin's death, translations from Asian and African literatures have not been limited to countries within the Soviet sphere. Works from India, the Arab countries, Iran, Afghanistan, and Indonesia have been translated into as many as 28 languages. What could be the motivation behind a policy which would have Indonesian literature translated into Adyg, a Caucasian language spoken by about 90,000 people— "comparable . . . in relative importance on the overall Soviet scene to the language of a group like the Navahos in the United States" (Winter 1961:175)? Remember that these are neither educational nor ideological works, but works of literature. One interpretation, that of Werner Winter, is that

> to take works of the literature of a nation and to make them available to members of another culture, is to take that nation's literature, that nation's culture, and that nation itself seriously. Such an effort, however ulterior its motives, is bound to impress the cultured strata of that country much more deeply than any attempt from an outside

country to export its own literature. For the attitude of the taker will be interpreted as one of interest and respect, that of the giver as superiority and contempt. (1961:174-5)

The Soviet policy seems to focus translation efforts on writers from geographical areas of interest to them politically. The contrast with United States policy is striking. Not only is the total percentage volume of translation published in the United States minimal (2.9%, compared with Russia's 50%; Caillé 1974:139), but most of what is published in the United States are the canonized "classics" of world literature. Ironically, the operation of the free market in this case limits the availability of translated works to the already-familiar, and perpetrates its own type of provincialism, a provincialism that may have serious consequences (Gross 1970). Throughout the entire American involvement in Indochina, very few Americans had read any literature from the area; only a handful of scholars could name a single Vietnamese author (although a greater number of dissidents were reading Ho Chi Minh in translation). A similar indifference exists toward all literatures of the developing world, most inexcusably toward the rich and varied literatures of Latin America, despite the efforts of such organizations as the Center for Inter-American Relations. The image of Latin America as an extension of a Mexican border town fading off into the jungle is still only a sight exaggeration for many U. S. citizens, and it is unlikely that American policy toward the region will greatly improve in effectiveness until citizens and lawmakers cultivate a more sophisticated understanding of the political and cultural realities of the separate Latin American countries. This is an area where concentrated translation efforts could pay dividends in the form of more rational and favorable political policies.

In this regard, part of a comprehensive translation policy for a Latin American country like Brazil might well include incentives for the dissemination of the national literature in English in the form of translation subsidies or prizes and bilateral agreements with American and European publishers in an effort to make a more intimate view of Brazilian reality available abroad (Caillé 1974:139).

Translation for Theater and Film

Translation for the theater and film presents a pattern of its own. In Brazil, translators for the stage are among the best paid. Competition is such that the quality of translation is maintained at a consistently high standard, and the translator is compensated by receiving a percentage of the box-office sales. In contrast, translation of film scripts for the purpose of dubbing and subtitling—work which reaches a much wider though less sophisticated audience—is not so generously rewarded and is considered to be of very low quality. An issue of concern among Brazilian translators is that much of this translation is out of their control. The lion's share of imported films comes from the United States, and of these, the vast majority enter Brazil already translated. A very recent development in Brazil has resulted from videocassette technology, which is currently generating a sizeable market for translation in São Paulo. Here, the communications industry recognizes the importance of quality translations, and is attempting to establish its own professional standards.

Government Translation

In many countries the greatest consumer of translation is the government. Government translators and interpreters are employed in all areas of defense, security, diplomacy, international trade, and international law. They perform tasks as diverse as monitoring foreign language broadcasts and newspapers, interpreting for official visitors and for international meetings, translating policy statements and treaties, and translating propaganda to be broadcast or distributed in foreign countries. In an officially bilingual or multilingual country, the volume of translation is even greater, as internal documents must be translated into the languages required by law. It is not surprising, then, to find that governments sometimes have an internal mechanism for insuring the quality of translation for at least the most critical of these functions. In the United States, both the Defense Department and the State Department train and certify language specialists. Although as a group, government translators may have a greater sense of cohesion than other types of translators—in the United States the first professional association of translators was the Society of Federal Linguists, founded in 1920 to represent government-employed translators—it should not be assumed that the level of translation in government is consistently high nor that government translators are a privileged class. Here also is prevalent the idea that anyone who can speak another language can translate or interpret. As a result, it often happens that subordinate government officials are called upon to translate or interpret, or that haphazard criteria are used in hiring translators. Inequities and inefficiencies recognized within the Federal Government of the United States led to the introduction of legislation in the House of Representatives in June 1978 for the creation of a Federal Translation Coordinating Council, with the primary purpose of studying ways in which to improve translation services within the Federal Government. The Translation Coordinating Council would be charged with conducting surveys of: the community of practicing translators; the institutions of higher education in the United States providing training in translation; the translation needs of the Federal Government; and translation policies and practices in foreign countries. The bill died in Committee without as much as a hearing. In Brazil, it was the chaotic application of hiring standards in government that led translators in public service to first petition for a legally regulated profession in 1974. Only in January 1979 was a presidential decree published dealing with the inequities among translators within the government. That decree required all future candidates for the job of translator to have a college degree in translation.

Certified Public Translation

Another distinct group of translators in many countries are the sworn public translators. These translators are licensed to translate documents that must be used for legal purposes. In Brazil and in other Latin American countries, these are the only translators who enjoy the official recognition of their profession and who must follow strict guidelines established by the government. Control of the profession in Brazil is exercised by the Ministry of Justice, through the State Secretariates of Justice.[6] Certified public translators have their own professional association, but no union with legal bargaining powers. By contrast, in the United States no such category of translators exists, it being sufficient in most cases for a translator of a legal document to sign an affidavit that the translation is faithful to the original.[7]

Translation and the Courts

The civil rights concern with accurate translation and interpretation in the courts has sometimes been the stimulus for legal action regulating translation. Legislation regulating court interpreters and/or translators exists in Argentina, the Federal Republic of Germany, Holland, Poland, Austria and, now, in the United States (Schwarz 1977b:147). In the United States, the Court Interpreters Act of October 28, 1978, was an attempt to guarantee the rights of the Fifth and Sixth Amendments for the deaf and other non-English-speakers in courts of law. It charges the federal court system with the responsibility of "establishing and certifying the qualifications of persons who will serve as interpreters in Federal Courts in bilingual proceedings, including the hearing or speech impaired [and for] maintaining a current master list, as well as a schedule of fees for services rendered by interpreters" (U.S. House Committee on the Judiciary 1978:2). This legislation potentially affects over 25,000,000 Americans, including 15,000,000 deaf Americans. No such legislation regulating court interpreting exists in Brazil, nor is there any association of court interpreters.

Commercial and Technical Translation

A large and diverse group of translators are those who work in business, in science, and in industry, handling the mass of ephemeral daily communication that is the lifeblood of those sectors of society: the letters, invoices, reports, news releases, brochures, advertisements, operating instructions, manuals, parts lists, abstracts, technical articles, patents, contracts, and so on. This is by far the fastest-growing area of translation activity, and it is to some extent upon the effectiveness of this type of translation that modern-sector growth in many countries depends. Individuals within an English-speaking environment may have difficulty appreciating the ubiquitous demand for translation in minority-language countries which are importers of technology or exporters of goods. English has become the most widely used language of technology and trade, such that only English permits access to the bulk

---

[6] The State agency directly responsible for supervising the profession is the *Junta Comerical*. It establishes the rates for various types of documents and the formats which may be used to type up the translations, copies of which must then be kept in bound volumes. When the market requires it, it organizes public competitions to fill a predetermined number of positions. The competitions require no formal training as a prerequisite.

[7] The acceptability of this practice varies from state to state.

of technical literature (McCleary 1982; Baldauf and Jernudd 1983). Faced with this dilemma, minority-language countries must allocate resources not only to the teaching of English (or other language of wider communication) to their scientists, doctors, engineers, and executives, but also to the training of translators. Neither of these activities alone is sufficient; it is not reasonable to expect that the teaching of English could be generally enough available and sufficiently successful to obviate the need for translation. Translators possess an adjunct skill that makes them as indispensible to business and industry as are accountants, statisticians, machinists, and computer programmers.

Once again, the greatest barrier to viewing translation in this light is the widespread belief that translation involves little more than a combination of reading a foreign language and typing, and that it can therefore be done by anyone possessing these two skills. This is a blatantly irrational attitude for business and industry, which depend heavily on such communications specialists as advertisers and technical writers.

The problem is compounded in science and technology by the fact that translation normally is being done from a language lexically developed in the area of speciality into another language lexically deficient, often requiring that terms be created in the recipient language. The translator, therefore, needs to be not only literate in two languages in the speciality he is translating, he needs also to be aware of the problems involved in the standardization of terminology. The standardization of terminology is a mammoth task of immediate concern to industry. In São Paulo, Volkswagen do Brasil has embarked on a long-term project with translation students of the Faculdade Ibero-Americana to standardize the technical and administrative terms used internally in five languages: Portuguese, German, French, English, and Spanish. In Europe, standardization of technical terminology has reached highly sophisticated levels using computerized data banks. Much of this work is coordinated by the International Information Centre for Terminology (INFOTERM) under the UNESCO program UNISIST (Arjona 1983). In Brazil, the Brazilian Academy of Letters by 1982 had not yet captured the major funding required for the computerization of its project to codify the Portuguese language (Murphy 1981).

Perhaps because technical translation has only recently become a major enterprise, there are only a few schools specialized in the training of technical translators. In the United States, the Technical Translation Program, Rose-Hulman Institute of Technology, and the Soviet and East European Center, University of Texas at Arlington, are the only institutions offering Certificates in Technical Translation (Arjona 1982).

Also, a few professional associations have been formed specifically to assist the scientific and technical translator and to set standards for the profession. Unique among these is the National Translation Institute of Science and Technology (NATIST) of Tokyo, which is authorized by the Japanese government to examine and certify technical translators. The Indian Scientific Translators Association (ISTA) of New Delhi conducts surveys on the translation needs of the country, translates selected scientific journals, research papers, and textbooks, trains translators, conducts terminological research, compiles bilingual and multilingual dictionaries, and maintains terminology banks. Its members include major participating national universities and research institutes (Congrat-Butler 1979). No such organization exists in Brazil, but recently in São Paulo attempts have been made to found an association of translators and interpreters whose primary focus will be technical translation.

The immediate economic consequences of faulty translation in business and industry have caused many firms to take an active interest in the training of translators and the regulation of the translating profession, and have made them more effective allies of translators than publishing houses have tended to be.

Conference Interpreting

One of the most demanding and specialized of language services to business, science, and government is conference interpreting, both consecutive and simultaneous. Partly because of the difficulty of this craft and the special talents required, conference interpreters are some of the best organized professionally, though still not legally recognized in most places and except for certain functions, such as courtroom interpretation. Simultaneous interpretation got its start after World War II during the Nuremberg trials, made possible by advances in electronic technology. Today it is a widely popular means of conducting international meetings of all kinds. Because of the acute post-WW II demand for conference interpreting, coupled with its inherent difficulty, schools to train interpreters were among the first to appear and are among the oldest and most prestigious training institutions for translators and interpreters.[8] Associations of conference interpreters are also among the most effective in regulating and providing cohesion for their profession. The international umbrella organization, which sets the pattern for the national member associations, is the Association Internationale des Interprètes de Conférence (AIIC), founded in 1953. AIIC and member associations require strict adherence to their codes of professional conduct. In Brazil, the daughter organization, Associação de Profissionais de Intérprete de Conferência (APIC), was founded in 1972 by a small group of interpreters all of whom had studied in Geneva. Since they were the only trained interpreters in the market at the time, they were able to impose the same rigorous standards used internationally. Not all practicing interpreters in Brazil today are members of APIC, but the established prestige of this organization (and the corresponding associations in other countries) exerts a strong formative influence on the profession. Conference organizers come to expect the level of professionalism upheld by the associations.

---

[8] Ecole de Traduction et d'Interprétation, Geneva; l'Institut Supérieur de l'Etat de Traducteurs et d'Interprètes, Brussels (1958); Ecole Supérieure d'Interprètes et de Traducteurs, Université de la Sorbonne (1957); Georgetown University, Washington; and Monterey Institute of Foreign Studies, Monterey (1955).

Still, the fact that in most places, except for court interpreters, there is no official recognition of the profession puts a hardship on those who practice it, and conference interpreters have joined translators in pressuring for professional recognition.[9]

CONCLUSION

The Current Status of the Profession in Brazil

The situation for translation and translators in Brazil is typical of what is found in most other parts of the world: the profession is unrecognized and unregulated except for a small class of Sworn Public Translators; only theatrical translators and conference interpreters enjoy slight bargaining advantages; most translators are free-lance, work at home, supply their own materials, and get paid on a piece-work basis at rates incommensurate with the complexity of their task;[10] they do not receive royalties and are often not cited on title pages or in reviews; there are associations for translators (ABRATES) and interpreters (APIC), but they have no accrediting authority; little is known about the numbers or training of translators working in the different sectors, for lack of the means to carry out the necessary research; there are a growing number of schools which offer degrees and specialization in translation and interpretation, but except for their validity as a prerequisite for government civil service translation exams, they do not yet carry a great deal of weight in the market because of the widespread competition from laypersons and the absence of minimum rates; technical translators working in industry tend to be better paid and have more job security than other categories; and finally, recent efforts to improve the status of translators have resulted in a stalemate.

In 1977 ABRATES was asked to make suggestions on proposed legislation. The resulting bill established the name of the profession ("Tradutor de Textos") and criteria for the exercise of the profession, limiting it to holders of a Bachelor's degree in translation or any Bachelor's degree with a one-year translation complement, either a Brazilian diploma or a foreign diploma revalidated in Brazil; or to those who had been practicing the profession up to the date on which the law took effect. A modification was later suggested in 1979 by the colleges of translation in São Paulo and endorsed by ABRATES, to require the complementary translation courses to be of at least two years duration; also to make allowances for translators of languages not covered in translation programs.

---

[9] They would like sanctions for such contractual requirements as two interpreters per booth to enable the interpreters to rest every twenty minutes, paid study time, the availability of written documents before the conference, and other conditions necessary to efficient and accurate interpretation.

[10] "If we earn on the average only Cr$150.00 per page (about $1.50 at the time) to do a translation, we must remember that a typist charges Cr$50 just to type the page. This means that ⅓ of what we earn for the translation really corresponds to the work we do typing it" (Mario Galvao, quoted in Magaldi 1981:5).

That legislation was not signed into law, although it had received approval from the competent ministries and departments. Instead, as mentioned above, in 1979 the government acted only to establish minimum criteria for those applying for government employment. That year the government changed, and the legislation to establish similar criteria for nongovernment translators was faced with the possibility of gaining a new set of ministry approvals. It never did. Instead, the new minister of justice, in September 1979, announced that the legislation would be shelved because "the supply of translators is greater than the demand" (Matos 1980:3). This amazing statement misinterprets the intent of the proposed legislation to be simply that of increasing the supply of people who translate. In fact, the intent was to establish a minimum level of competence. Whether the proposed legislation was the means by which to achieve the desired goal is open to debate. The effect of the bill would be essentially to "close" the profession to anyone but students of translation schools (except for those already practicing). This is a thorny issue. On the one hand, it might be questioned whether the college programs in translation are prepared to supply the needed professionals with an adequate level of training in the near future; on the other hand it can be argued that, without the stimulus of a "closed" profession, the schools will not acquire adequate prestige and strength. A second doubt that arises is whether the schools, which have a vested interest in graduating numbers of students, are the best judges of whether their trainees have attained the target minimal competence level at which the profession aims. The legislation as proposed does not provide for access to the profession apart from the diploma.

A third and potentially more serious problem involves the great variety of translation activity within the profession, as discussed at length above, and the variety of skills it requires. This is especially true of technical and business translation. There can be no hard-and-fast demarcation between translators and technical specialists. Good technical translators must be expert in their technical fields; therefore, specialists who have the talent and disposition should not be barred from producing translations. Nor can firms be expected to hire only persons with degrees in translation to perform the myriad translation services now handled by bilingual secretaries.

As of October 1983, no progress had been made toward legally constituting the profession, nor had a separate attempt to gain author's royalties for book translators met with success.

The Formation of a Translation Policy

It is entirely appropriate that translator associations have begun to give a growing number of translators a means of acting collectively to formulate norms for their profession and of lobbying the authorities as well as their clients for improved conditions of work. It is a movement that is perfectly consistent with the increasing volume and importance of translation in contemporary life.

The arguments which these translators' groups have proposed to justify their grievances are drawn primarily in terms of the correction of social inequities, the avoidance of social costs, and the positive social good that would result from an improvement in the status of the profession:

1.   Correction of inequities: lack of translation or faulty translation may deprive individuals of civil rights; translators are not compensated commensurate with their training, the difficulty of the task, or the social and economic value of their work.

2.   Avoidance of social costs: faulty translation or unavailability of translation can have direct economic consequences and more far-ranging costs in lost political, economic, or cultural advantage.

3.   Positive good: accurate translations can enrich the cultural life of a nation and can help to ensure and accelerate the participation of government, business, and individuals in major world developments.

The first set of justifications—the correction of inequities—is by far the easiest to document, and it is not surprising that much existing translation policy deals with the accuracy of legal documents and courtroom proceedings. The issues of translator compensation and working conditions are less clear because of the powerful rebuttal of the marketplace. Market inequities alone (e.g., low pay for proficient translators due to competition from untrained individuals) are not sufficient cause to invoke a policy which has the effect of distorting market prices (e.g., limiting access to the profession). Normally they must be accompanied by other goals, such as the avoidance of social cost: it is demonstrably in the interest of public safety and the public welfare to license medical practitioners, legal and tax practitioners, architects and engineers, teachers, and so on. The arguments justifying interference in the market on behalf of translators are not so easily supported. The internal policies of many business and technical firms which have upgraded the status of translators and given them enhanced job security are the result of a sensitive assessment of the economic value of accurate translation. No universally accepted apparatus exists to assess the value of other types of social goods, such as the cultural value of quality literary translations. The result is that support for these social goods is difficult to sustain in a market economy and in the absence of an overriding political doctrine pursued at public cost. The economics of publishing, especially in a country and in a language with a limited and undemanding market, will limit the latitude for improvement that the translator can reasonably expect to achieve.

Translation is an activity which, for whatever reasons, did not acquire throughout its long history, until very recently, sufficient symbolic value to become singled out as a profession, that is, to attract the attention either of its own practitioners as a class (as manifested in associations, codes of ethics, theory, and so on) or of the public power (as expressed in regulatory policy). Clearly, events of recent decades reveal that the environment which has sustained that state of limbo for so long is now changing rapidly: the last ten years have seen a doubling in the number of associations and training institutions; the European Economic Community now employs one translator or interpreter for every three technocrats; multinational corporations are becoming concerned with the supply of professional technical translators; and at least one study of 1972 concluded that by the end of this century the demand for translation will be three times as large as it is today. Moreover, translation will rank third in the list of 'goulots d'étranglement', or bottlenecks, which means that the lack of translations—at the right time and place—will be one of the three main obstacles to the progress of science and technology, the other two being the lack of raw materials and the shortage of specialized labour. (Hendrickx 1975:104)

However accurate this specific prophecy proves to be, translation is now beginning to be felt to have a potential for social impact on a scale that was unimagined 40 years ago. In this new environment it is inevitable that a profession will take shape. The shape that it ultimately takes, internationally, in Brazil, or in any other country, will depend upon the interplay of international and local forces: private and public goals, market conditions, and demography. Translation policy will both reflect and fashion these developments.

REFERENCES

Adelman, Irma. 1979. Growth, income distribution and equity-oriented development strategies. The political economy of development and underdevelopment, ed. by Charles K. Wilber, 312–23. New York: Random House.

Arjona, Etilvia. 1982. Colleges that offer courses in translation and interpretation in the U.S.A. Ossining, N.Y.: American Translators Association.

————. 1983. Terminology research focuses on training and resources. Channels 2(3).1–2.

Astley, George. 1970. The problem as seen from England. The world of translation. Papers delivered at the Conference on Literary Translation, P.E.N. American Center, New York, 307–311.

Baldauf, Richard B., & Bjorn H. Jernudd. 1983. Language of publications as a variable in scientific communication. Australian Review of Applied Linguistics 6.97–108.

Bauer, Wolfgang. 1964. Western literature and translation work in communist China. Frankfurt/Main: Metzner.

Braga, Ney. 1976. General study: Copyright protection in Brazil. Copyright Bulletin 10.21–23.

Caillé, Pierre-François. 1974. Translators and translation: 1975 survey. BABEL: Revue Internationale de la Traduction 20.130–41.

Congrat-Butler, Stefan. 1979. Translation and translators: An international directory and guide. New York: R. R. Bowker Co.

Doron, Marcia Nita, & Marilyn Gaddis Rose. 1981. The economics and politics of translation. Translation spectrum: Essays in theory and practice, ed. by Marilyn Gaddis Rose, 160–67. Albany: State University of New York (SUNY).

Europa Year Book. 1983. A world survey. Vol. 1. London: Europa Publication, Limited.

Fromkin, Victoria, & Robert Rodman. 1978. An introduction to language. New York: Holt, Rinehart & Winston.

Ginsberg, Mirra. 1970. Translation in Russia: The politics of translation. The world of translation. Papers delivered at the Conference on Literary Translation, P.E.N. American Center, New York City, 356–60.

Gross, Gerald. 1970. On publishers and translators. The world of translation. Papers delivered at the Conference on Literary Translation, P.E.N. American Center, New York City, 153–60.

Hendrickx, Paul V. 1975. Should we teach translation? BABEL: Revue Internationale de la Traduction 21.101–106.

Library of Congress, Copyright Office. 1980. Request for comments on the status of translators. Translation Review 5.33–36.

Magaldi, Sabato. 1981. Os tradutores: das amargas odisseias aos pequenos triunfos. Jornal da Tarde, Caderno de Programas e Leitruas (March 3), 4–5.

Matos, Marco Aurelio. 1980. Regulamentacao da profissao de tradutor e de interprete. ABRATES 5(3).3.

McCleary, Leland. 1982. The dissemination of scientific knowledge across language barriers. Unpublished seminar paper, UCLA.

Murphy, Tom. (Dec. 27, 1981). Linguist forsees 10–12 dominant languages. The Houston Post.

Portinho, Waldivia Marcchiori. 1981. A valorização do tradutor como profissional. Paper delivered at I Encontro de Tradutores e Intérpretes sobre a Classe Profissional em São Paulo, Associação Alumni, São Paulo, Nov. 25–27, 1981.

República Federativa Do Brasil. 1979. Decreto no. 82.990 de 05 de janeiro de 1979. Diário Oficial (January 8).

Schwarz, Hans. 1977a. The UNESCO recommendations on translators' rights. Lebende Sprachen 22.49–51.

_____ . 1977b. The legal and social status of the translator. Lebende Sprachen 22.145–51.

UNESCO House. 1976. Special intergovernmental committee of technical and legal experts to prepare a draft international recommendation for the protection of translators. Copyright Bulletin 10(3).4–18.

UNESCO Statistical Yearbook. 1982. Paris: UNESCO.

U.S. House Committee on the Judiciary, Subcommittee on Civil and Constitutional Rights. 1978. Court Interpreters Act: Hearings, July 19–August 9.

Winter, Werner. 1961. Translation as political action. The craft and context of translation, ed. by William Arrowsmith and Roger Shattuck, 172–76. Austin: University of Texas Press.

FOURTEEN

The Constitution of Japan and Its English Translation

Kyoko Inoue
University of Illinois at Chicago

INTRODUCTION

The present Constitution of Japan is a product of unprecedented political circumstances in the history of Japan. It is a democratic constitution that was initially drafted in one week by the staff of General MacArthur's Occupation Army and was given to the Japanese in February 1946. After eight months of intense bilingual and bicultural negotiations between the Japanese and American authorities, it was finally promulgated on May 3, 1947.

Since the mid-1950s, after the peace treaty was signed and Japan regained its sovereignty, the Japanese people have repeatedly debated both the legitimacy of the constitution because of its foreign origin and the adequacy of some of its key concepts. Yet despite the controversies, this constitution has survived for more than 35 years without a single amendment. Moreover, it has played a vital role in radical social and political changes of postwar Japan.

Two years ago, I began to ask myself how it happened that this constitution, given by foreigners and embodying ideas and ideals that were new to ordinary Japanese citizens, has not only survived, but has also become such an integral part of contemporary Japanese society. It is commonly believed that alien concepts can take root in a society only if they conform to its traditional values. So I wondered what made it possible for the Japanese people to accept this constitution. To answer such a question adequately, one would need to examine carefully Japanese history and various political and sociological factors that might have contributed. I am not qualified to undertake such a task. But I came to realize that language, as well as political and social factors, must have played an important role. The language of the constitution must have been understandable enough, or familiar enough, for them to accept it. So I began to compare the text of the Japanese Constitution with its English translation, for I thought that the differences of phraseology and diction between the two texts, which are inevitable in any translation, might provide some clues to why the Japanese text was so acceptable to the Japanese people.

In this paper, I will compare and contrast the Japanese and English texts of Chapter III, "The Rights and Duties of the People." I will also refer to four other documents; the initial draft, prepared by the Americans, now known as the MacArthur Constitution; the draft prepared by the Japanese and now called the March 2nd version; the Meiji Constitution; and the American Bill of Rights. They all influenced the Constitution as we find it today. I will focus my discussion on three key factors that distinguish the Japanese text from the English, namely, different sentence patterns, some key expressions found in the verb phrases, and the semantics of the key noun phrases.

I suggest that these linguistic changes, while very subtle, have not only helped reduce the translation flavor of the Japanese text as a whole but, more importantly, made the alien concepts more acceptable to the Japanese people. Of course, I cannot demonstrate conclusively their rhetorical impact on the millions of Japanese who have read this document in the past 35 years. But it is legitimate for a linguist not only to investigate the linguistic characteristics of a document such as this one, but also to speculate on their rhetorical impact on important social and political changes.

I will begin with a summary of the process of drafting the Constitution of Japan, followed by a section on the nature of the language used in this document. Finally, the heart of this paper is a detailed grammatical and rhetorical analysis of the text.

THE DRAFTING OF THE PRESENT CONSTITUTION[1]

Japan has had two written constitutions since the mid-nineteenth century. The first, known as the Meiji Constitution, was promulgated on February 11, 1889, after more than ten years of careful studies of various European systems of government, by the leaders of the Meiji Government. It was an imperial constitution, modeled after the Prussian Constitution of 1850. The second is the democratic constitution promulgated on May 3, 1947 in the Occupied Japan of post–World War II.

When the Pacific War finally ended on August 14, 1945, with Japan's unconditional surrender, President Truman quickly appointed General Douglas MacArthur the Supreme Commander for the Allied Powers. On August 30th, MacArthur arrived in Japan and began the seven-year American Occupation of Japan. The objective of the occupation was to help Japan reconstruct itself as a peaceful democracy. The United States, as well as other Allies, thought that one of the measures of democratization should be a constitutional reform.

In the beginning of October 1945, MacArthur suggested to the Japanese government that they consider a constitutional reform. Given the policy of indirect military occupation, the Americans wanted the reform to be initiated and undertaken by the Japanese themselves. The Japanese officials, who were anxious to retain as much of the old order as possible, were not eager for any drastic constitutional reform. But the Cabinet deferred to MacArthur and appointed a committee, the Constitutional Problem Investigation Committee, headed by Joji Matsumoto, the Minister of State and a legal scholar, to study the possible revision.

---

[1] This is an abridged version of the discussion found in Inoue (1982).

Four months later, on February 1, 1946, one of the leading Japanese newspapers printed what it called a near final version being prepared by the committee. The document was conservative, retaining nearly half of the Meiji Constitution, including Japan's status as a monarchy. MacArthur, who had not been happy with the Japanese government's lack of enthusiasm and slowness, was very displeased.

On February 3rd, he ordered the staff of the Government Section of General Headquarters to draft a Japanese constitution. A week later, they had prepared a draft and sent it to MacArthur for approval. On February 13, 1946, they delivered this document, now known as the MacArthur Constitution, to the Japanese government for acceptance as its own. The Japanese were stunned.

Nine days later, on February 22nd, realizing it was futile to try to block the new constitution, the Japanese officials met with the American authorities to discuss the content of the document. They did their best to impress upon the Americans that translating the MacArthur Constitution into Japanese involved a great deal more than putting the English words and phraseology into Japanese. It required translation into classical Japanese, an ancient form of the language used by the Emperor and in all legal documents. But MacArthur was in the midst of a power struggle with the Western Allies, and was determined to push his version through as soon as possible. So the Japanese went to work.

At 10:00 A.M., March 4th, they delivered their version, known as the March 2nd version, still in Japanese, to GHQ (General Headquarters). For the next 30 hours, the Americans and Japanese intensely negotiated the two documents until they completed a final version, in both English and Japanese. MacArthur approved the English version of this document. At 5:00 P.M., March 6th, the Japanese government made public what they called the "outline" of the new Japanese Constitution in Japanese, and it was printed in the morning papers of the following day for all Japan to read.

From June to October, the new constitution was debated at the two Houses of the 90th (and last) Session of the Imperial Diet. On November 3, 1946, the entire text of the new constitution, revised and approved by the Diet, was officially made public. On May 3, 1947, it went into effect.

THE LANGUAGE OF THE CONSTITUTION

The new constitution was written in a very different language than the first Japanese Constitution. This change not only enhanced its democratic character, but also contributed greatly to language change in postwar Japan.

As I mentioned earlier, the Meiji Constitution was the result of 10 years of careful study. Its language reflected the care that was taken in drafting it. The main text was written in *bungo-tai*, a highly stylized classical Japanese. The Preamble was written in a still more formal style, the Imperial language, for the Constitution was a proclamation by the Emperor of Japan to his subjects. It also used many difficult Chinese characters, along with *Katakana*, the syllabary employed in formal writings of the period. Finally, the entire text was unpunctuated. The archaic language and the formal orthographic conventions made this text difficult for the ordinary citizen to read.

In contrast, the present constitution employs *koogo-tai*, the written version of colloquial Japanese. It also uses *Hiragana*, the syllabary that has become commonly used in the postwar era, and standard punctuation marks. It is thus readable by any contemporary Japanese citizen. Both the language and the standard orthographic conventions contribute to this constitution's democratic character.

Initially, however, this had not been the intention of the drafters. Joji Matsumoto, the head of the Constitution Problem Investigation Committee, who, in effect, was responsible for drafting the entire text, had the enormously difficult task of rephrasing and putting into natural Japanese a large number of phrases and expressions that were originally in the MacArthur Constitution. He then had to translate them into the classical Japanese he thought appropriate for the nation's highest legal document. Time pressure compounded his difficulties.

In the midst of his struggle, on March 26, 1946, an organization of concerned writers and scholars called *Kokumin-no Kokugo Undoo Renmei* (Association for the People's National Language Movement) submitted a series of linguistic recommendations to the Japanese government. They argued that a new democratic constitution should be written in a language readable by any citizen of Japan, and recommended that: (a) the constitution be written in colloquial Japanese; (b) difficult phraseology be avoided; (c) difficult Chinese characters be avoided; (d) the number of Chinese characters be restricted; (e) *Hiragana* syllabary be used; and (f) punctuation marks and other standard orthographic devices be used.

One member of this group has written that when they first approached Joji Matsumoto and other government officials with the recommendations and a sample text, they were met with vehement opposition (Yokota 1981:265–272). But Matsumoto says that he later decided to accept their recommendations and change the language of the constitution because he felt there was no way that he could erase the translation flavor and put the document into proper classical Japanese so quickly. Since the Japanese government had to maintain the facade that it had drafted this constitution, Matsumoto thought that using colloquial Japanese would make it easier to conceal that the major portion had been translated from English to Japanese (Shimizu 1962: vol. 4, pp. 132–133).

Thus this change in constitutional language was undertaken for a purely pragmatic reason peculiar to the political circumstances under which it was written. I might add that when the Japanese requested GHQ's permission for this linguistic change, the Americans were at first hesitant to grant it. They were afraid it was a ploy on the Japanese side to weaken the democratic principles expressed in the constitution (Sato 1955: no. 173, p. 26). But these fears were wholly misplaced.

The shift in the constitutional language has had a profound effect on postwar Japanese. Immediately after the drafting of the constitution, the Japanese government directed government agencies to use the colloquial language in their documents (Hayashi 1981:242–250). All government documents, including laws, are now written in the same colloquial Japanese found in the constitution. The use of classical Japanese prose has virtually disappeared from contemporary Japanese. The use of *Katakana* as the primary syllabary has been discontinued; it is now primarily used for loan words, serving a function similar to italics in English. The Imperial language, too, has been completely eliminated. Today, the Emperor uses the same colloquial Japanese as everyone else. The result has been to democratize the political process in Japan by making all legal and governmental documents accessible to the educated public.

TEXTUAL ANALYSIS OF CHAPTER III

One of the most striking innovations of this new constitution was Chapter III, ''The Rights and Duties of the People.'' On March 4th and 5th, 1946, when the Americans and the Japanese negotiated over the MacArthur Constitution and the March 2nd version, the Americans insisted that their version be adopted as the basis for this chapter (Sato 1955: no. 170, p. 15). As a result, it resembles the American Declaration of Independence and the Bill of Rights, and contains many concepts that were new to ordinary Japanese. The chapter contains 31 of the 103 articles of the entire text. It sets forth, for the most part, the rights of the people. In comparison, Chapter II of the Meiji Constitution, ''Rights and Duties of Subjects,'' contained only 15 of the 76 articles of the entire document. Moreover, that chapter stressed the duties of the people rather than their rights. Chapter III of the new constitution is the heart of the document, and it has contributed greatly to changes in the way of life in postwar Japan.

In my analysis, I do not use the standard linguistic method of relating form and meaning in a systematic and hierarchical manner. Instead, I will discuss three particular features that differentiate the Japanese and English texts because they help explain why the new constitution embodying foreign concepts was acceptable to the Japanese. These three features are the different sentence patterns, the key verbal expressions, and the noun phrases.

Sentence Patterns Affecting Familiarity of Concepts

By far the most outstanding difference between the Japanese and English texts lies in the sentence patterns used. While the majority of the sentences in the Japanese text are in what is known as the topic-comment construction, those found in the English version are in the agentless passive construction. I suggest that this grammatical change has contributed in a subtle way to the acceptance of the new concepts and ideas by the Japanese people. Before discussing examples, however, I will briefly explain the characteristics of the subject-predicate and topic-comment constructions in Japanese.[2] In English, a sentence such as ''John is standing in front of the station'' can be used in at least two different contexts. In the first, the speaker

---

[2] The original claims regarding the subject-predicate vs. topic-comment construction in Japanese were made by Kuroda 1965 and Kuno 1973.

simply notices and informs the addressee that John is standing in front of the station. The description of such a scene has no relation to the topic of the conversation between the two. The second context will be one where the two are talking about John. The speaker notices that John, about whom they have been talking, is standing in front of the station and says so. In the first case, the entire sentence provides new information, and, in the second, it is only the predicate that is new to the addressee. In English, the distinction between the two is made, typically, by two different intonation patterns. In the first case, the entire sentence receives a sustained high pitch, but, in the second, "John" is given a low pitch, and the intonation rises in the rest of the sentence.

In Japanese, this distinction is typically made not by intonation but by two postpositional particles, -ga and -wa, suffixed to "John." Compare the two Japanese counterparts given below: (1a) is the sentence uttered in the first context, and (1b) in the second.

(1) a. *John -ga*   *eki*   *-no*   *mae -ni*   *tat*   *-te*   *i*   *-ru.*
       -Subj.   station   's   front   at   stand   -Gerund   be   -Nonpast
   b. *John -wa*
       -Topic

-Ga, which is called the subject marker, is also the marker of new information, while *-wa,* which is called the topic marker, is the marker of old information, or shared information between the speaker and addressee. It is important to note also that because the speaker can talk about anything he chooses, the topic marker *-wa* can be suffixed not only to the subject, but also to any other element in the sentence. Also, the topicalized element is often fronted. A typical instance is the following. In response to someone saying, "Who bought this book?", one would say,

(2) *sono*   *hon*   *-wa*   *watashi*   *-ga kat*   *-ta.*
    that   book   -Topic   I   -Subj. buy   -Past
    "That book, I bought (it.)"

A word of caution is necessary at this point. While the distinction in use between *-ga* and *-wa* in this case is quite clear, and the distinction between old vs. new information is viable, other uses of these forms in natural discourse are not so clearly discernible. In the various uses of *-wa,* native speakers clearly sense a feeling of familiarity and sharedness, but to my knowledge, no one has been able to define either precisely what is meant by shared or old information, or the rules determining exactly when to use *-wa* and when not to.

To return to the constitution, there is an important difference between the topic-comment sentences found in the Meiji Constitution and the present Japanese Constitution. In the Meiji Constitution, all sentences specifying the rights and duties of the Japanese subjects begin with the topicalized subject noun phrase *Nihon shinmin-wa* "Japanese subject(s)-Topic." The comment consists of the predicate specifying the duty or right. Thus a familiar subject is coupled with a predicate containing "new" information. And in fact much of this information *was* new, because it referred to rights and duties that had not previously been specifically stated. Below are two examples with the official translations.

(3) *dai nijuu-ichi -joo.*   *Nihon shinmin -wa*   *hooritsu-no*   *sadamur*   *-u*
    twenty first article   Japan subject-Topic   law   's   determine   -Nonpast
    tokoro-ni shitagai   *noozei -no*   *gimu -o*   *yuu-su*
    according to   pay tax   's duty-Obj.   have
    "Article XXI. Japanese subjects are amenable to the duty of paying taxes, according to the provisions of law."

(4) *dai nijuu -ni -joo.*   *Nihon shinmin -wa*   *hooritsu-no*   *hani-nai-ni*
    twenty second article   Japan subject-Topic   law   's   within
    oi-te   *kyojuu*   *oyobi*   *iten -no*   *jiyuu -o*   *yuu-su*
    at   abode   and   change 's   liberty-Obj.   have
    "Article XXII. Japanese subjects all have the liberty of abode and of changing the same within the limits of the law."

In contrast, in the present Constitution, we find two types of sentences, namely the ones with the topicalized subject-noun phrase representing "the people," and those with the topicalized object-noun phrase representing a right or duty. Consider these examples (translations by the author):

(5) *dai nijuu-shichi -joo.*   *subete*   *kokumin*   *-wa,*   *kinroo-no*   *kenri -o*
    twenty seventh article   all   national   -Topic   work   's   right-Obj.
    yuu-shi,   *gimu*   *-o*   *ow*   *-u.*
    have-do   obligation   -Obj.   have   -Nonpast
    "Article 27. All nationals have the right and the obligation to work."

(6) *dai juu-sen -joo.*   *subete*   *kokumin*   *-wa,*   *kojin*   *-to*   *shi-te*
    thirteenth article   all   national   -Topic   individual   as
    sonchoo s   *-are*   *-ru.*
    respect do   -Pass. -Nonpast
    "Article 13. All nationals are respected as individuals."

(7) *dai juu-kyuu -joo.*   *shisoo*   *oyobi*   *ryooshin -no*   *jiyuu*   *-wa,*
    nineteenth article   thought   and   conscience 's   freedom   -Topic
    kore -o   *okashi-te-wa*   *nar*   *-ana*   *-i.*
    this-Obj.   violate   become-Pass.   -Nonpast
    "Article 19. As for freedom of thought and conscience, (one) must not violate this."

Article 27 given in (5) begins with the topic/subject, *subete kokumin-wa* "All nationals," followed by a comment/predicate in the active voice, *kinroo-no kenri-o yuu-shi, gimu-o ow-u* "have the right and the obligation to work." Article 13 given in (6) begins with the same topic/subject, *subete kokumin-wa,* but it is followed by a comment/predicate in the passive voice, *kojin-to shi-te sonchoo s-are-ru* "are respected as individuals." Finally, Article 19 given in (7) begins with the topicalized object, *shisoo oyobi ryooshin-no jiyuu-wa* "As for freedom of thought and conscience." This is followed by a comment that takes the form of an active sentence with the deleted subject, *kore-o okashi-te-wa nar-ana-i* "(one) must not violate this." The use of *kore-o,* standing for "freedom of thought and conscience," implies emphasis.

Let us now look at the English text, which was the basis for the Japanese text. As I mentioned earlier, the primary sentence pattern used in this text is the agentless passive, e.g.

(8) Article 18.   No person shall be held in bondage of any kind.

(9) Article 20.   Freedom of religion is guaranteed to all.

What is important is the systematic approach that the drafters adopted in translating the English sentences into Japanese. To begin with, all the English sentences with the surface subject noun phrases representing "the people" were translated into the topic-comment sentences in Japanese retaining the same topic/subject as in the Meiji Constitution (the details regarding the phrase "the people" are discussed in the final section). The active sentences with the subject representing "the people" and the agentless passive sentences with the surface subject representing the same were translated into the respective topic-comment counterparts in Japanese. For instance, the English version of Article 27 is:

(10) Article 27.   All people shall have the right and the obligation to work.

The Japanese translation of Article 27 is given in (5).

Similarly, Article 13 in English states:

(11) Article 13.   All of the people shall be respected as individuals.

The Japanese translation of Article 13 is provided in (6).

But in a most significant contrast, the agentless passives in English representing rights and duties in their surface subjects are all translated into active sentences with the topicalized and fronted object in Japanese. An example is Article 19. The official English version is:

(12) Article 19.   Freedom of thought and conscience shall not be violated.

The Japanese version is found in (7).

Similarly, Article 20, quoted in (9) above, which reads:

(9) Article 20.   Freedom of religion is guaranteed to all.

is rendered in Japanese as:

(13) *dai nijuu -joo.*   *shinkyoo -no*   *jiyuu -wa,*   *nanibito*
     twentieth article   religion 's   freedom -Topic   anyone
     -ni   *taishi-te-mo*   *kore -o*   *hoshoo*   *su -ru.*
     to   this-Obj.   guarantee   do -Nonpast

"Article 20. As for freedom of religion, (one) must guarantee this to anyone."

There are 18 such sentences in the active voice out of a total of 64 sentences of the Japanese text in this chapter. Moreover, each one of these laws expresses a substantive right of the people.

These changes in the sentence patterns between the English and Japanese texts have two important rhetorical consequences. On the stylistic level, changing sentences from passive to active has significantly reduced the translation flavor of the Japanese text as a whole. The pure or ordinary passive in Japanese is a relatively new device that has developed under the influence of English, and it has a much more restricted use in Japanese than in English. But the second change is far more important for my purposes. The topic-comment construction with the fronted object representing a right implies the familiarity with the idea of rights. I suggest that this has contributed to impressing upon the Japanese people that the rights expressed in the constitution are not alien to them. The significance of this point becomes clear when we look at the Meiji Constitution. All the rights and duties in the latter are specified in the comment/predicate, indicating that they are being created. In the new constitution, on the other hand, they are treated as familiar concepts. Since many of those sentences express substantive rights that were, in fact, new to the ordinary Japanese, I believe the grammatical change is particularly significant. I suggest that this change made these new ideas more acceptable.

Verbal Expressions Affecting the Types of Speech Act

An issue immediately related to sentence types is the kinds of verbal expressions that are used which influence the type of speech act being performed by the sentences. For example, the American Bill of Rights is a command issued by the people of the United States to the government to protect their rights. This is indicated in the use of the modal "shall" in all but one amendment, the tenth. Moreover, they appear in the negative, for example, "the right of the people to . . . shall not be violated," indicating that it is by not infringing upon the rights of the people that the government is to protect them.

In the English text of the Japanese Constitution as well, the modal "shall" is used in all but 15 of the sentences. Out of those 15, nine are simple assertive sentences with "be," and the rest take "may," "have" and "must." Examples of "shall" and "be"-sentences are:

(14) Article 13.   All of the people shall be respected as individuals.

(15) Article 19.   Freedom of thought and conscience shall not be violated.

(16) Article 23.   Academic freedom is guaranteed.

However, there is an important difference between the American Bill of Rights and the Japanese Constitution. As in Chapter II of the Meiji Constitution, Chapter III of this constitution expresses the duties, as well as the rights, of the people. Therefore, several of the instances of "shall" involve commands to the Japanese people, and not by the people. Articles 12 and 24 are good examples.

(17) Article 12.　The freedoms and rights guaranteed to the people by this Constitution shall be maintained by the constant endeavor of the people, who shall refrain from any abuse of these freedoms and rights and shall always be responsible for utilizing them for the public welfare.

(18) Article 24.　Marriage shall be based only on the mutual consent of both sexes and it shall be maintained through mutual cooperation with the equal rights of husband and wife as a basis.

Who is the commander of the duties? It would appear that it is the Government of Japan that is commanding them to fulfill their duties, but the commanding agent is only implied. Looking back on the circumstances in which the document was drafted, it was in fact the American drafters who were commanding the Japanese people, and the government as well, to establish a democratic society.

Even more interesting is the Japanese text. It turns out that there are only 14 sentences out of 64 that use the expression of command which is comparable to "shall" in English. The expression is -nak-er-e-ba nar-ana-i, which literally means something like "if one does not, then it does not become" and which is usually translated into "must" in English, and its negative form, -te-wa nar-ana-i "must not."[3] The remaining sentences take the form of simple assertions. In other words, the ratio of command vs. assertion in the Japanese text is almost exactly the opposite of what it is in the English text.

Let us look at an example where the Japanese and English sentences differ:

(19)　*dai juu-ichi -joo. kokumin-wa,　subete-no　kihon-teki　jinken*
　　　eleventh　article national-Topic　all　's　fundamental　human right
　　　-no　kyooyuu　-o　samatage-rare -nai.
　　　's　enjoyment　-Obj.　prevent -Pass.-not

The literal translation would be something like:

"Article 11.　The nationals are not/will not be prevented from enjoying all of the fundamental human rights."

But the official translation says:

---

[3] Japanese has -nak-er-e-ba nar-ana-i and -nak-er-e-ba ike-na-i that somewhat parallel "must" and "should" in English. But because the precise semantic distinction between the two Japanese terms and the way they compare with the English terms are not crucial to this discussion, I have simply chosen to use "must" to stand for -nak-er-e-ba nar-ani-i.

"Article 11.   The people shall not be prevented from enjoying any of the fundamental human rights."

These two sentences represent two different kinds of speech act. The Japanese sentence simply asserts that the people have the right not to be prevented from enjoying the fundamental human rights. Presumably it is the Government of Japan that assumes the responsibility to guarantee such a right. In contrast, the English sentence implies that the government is being commanded not to invade the individual rights of the people who grant it authority.

The tenor of the Japanese text as a whole is thus significantly different from that of the English text because of the choice of verbal expressions. The Japanese version suggests that the Japanese government asserts itself—its authority and responsibility—much more strongly than the American government. In the English text, the government is commanded to act on behalf of the people. This difference in tone, I believe, reflects the difference in the tradition of the two societies.

It is also interesting that all but one of the instances of "must" and "must not" in the Japanese text, which express both the obligation of the government to protect individual rights and the people's obligation to abide by the democratic principles, are in the first half of the document where the substantive rights are stated. Possibly because the writers of the Japanese version were familiar with laws expressing procedural rights, they simply followed the traditional diction. But in writing laws expressing substantive rights that were new to them, they took extra care in accurately translating English to Japanese. In so doing, they deviated—perhaps inadvertently—from traditional Japanese diction.

The Meaning of the Word "People"

A final important difference between the Japanese and English texts of the constitution concerns the words for "people." The English version uses two terms, "people" and "person(s)." Both terms appear with various modifiers, for example, "all of the people," "all people," and "every person," "all persons." But there is a fairly clear distinction in the use of these terms. In the first half of the chapter, where the substantive rights are expresed, both "people" and "person(s)" are used. In contrast, in the second half, which concerns procedural rights, only "person(s)" is used. The reason for this distinction is straightforward. The term "people" refers to human beings both as individuals and as a collective entity, while the term "person(s)" generally signifies human beings as individuals. The provisions concerning human rights apply to people both as individuals and as a collective entity, so the term "people" is proper. Procedural rights, on the other hand, are the rules that specify how individuals are protected, particularly when accused of a violation of the law, and therefore the term "person" is appropriate. It also turns out that the laws in the first half of the section which use "person" are the ones that apply to people as individuals.

The Japanese text also uses two terms for "people," but the distinction between them is quite different. The first term is *kokumin,* consisting of *koku* "nation" and *min* "people/person(s)," meaning "national(s)." The other word is *nanibito,* a combination of *nani* "what" and *bito*[4] "person(s)," meaning "anyone" or "no one" depending on the context in which it is used. It also turns out that *kokumin* is used in all of the instances where "people" appears in the English text, while *nanibito* is used in all of the instances of "person(s)."

Whether to use both Japanese terms, however, created a controversy between the Americans and Japanese. After the outline of the constitution was made public on March 7, 1946, in the process of drafting the final text, the Japanese officials decided that all of the instances of *nanibito* "anyone" should be changed to *kokumin* "national(s)." They requested permission from GHQ to make this change, arguing that the title of the chapter, *Kokumin-no Kenri-to Gimu* "The Rights and Duties of the Nationals," indicated that the constitution was for Japanese citizens. The Americans refused, saying that the two English terms serve different functions, so they had to be differentiated in the Japanese text. In the end, the Japanese gave in and used both terms (Irie 1976: 284–285).

From the documents available to me, it is not clear whether the Americans explained the two English terms to the Japanese. But the choice of the term *kokumin* "national(s)" to stand for "the people" has an important practical consequence. From a purely linguistic point of view, the term "the people" used in the American Constitution is open to at least two interpretations, "We the citizens of the United States," and "We the people who reside in the United States." And, in fact, most constitutional rights belong to residents as well as citizens. The term *kokumin* in Japanese has no such ambiguity. It refers only to the people who hold Japanese citizenship, most of whom are native-born Japanese. Therefore, the Japanese Constitution seems to guarantee substantive rights only to Japanese nationals, but procedural rights to both citizens and noncitizens. As one might suspect, this issue was brought up at the 90th Session of the Imperial Diet in 1946 before the passing of the constitution, and it has been a controversial issue among the lawmakers and legal scholars since then (Shimizu 1962: vol. 2, pp. 194–198). But no change has been made.

But could the Japanese have honored the important semantic distinction between the "people" and "person(s)" in English by choosing a different set of terms? Interestingly enough, the answer seems to be "no." To begin with, the term *nanibito* is primarily a negative polarity term, most often used to mean "no one." Thus it lacks the important sense of collectivity. Japanese has an informal term, *hitobito*, which can be translated as "persons/people" and is often used in a compound, *Nihon-no hitobito*, that is, the literal translation of "the people of Japan." However, when the Japanese use this term, they always mean "Japanese nationals residing in Japan," in contrast to "those residing overseas." They do not mean "anyone who resides in Japan."

Finally, there is a formal term, *jinmin* that is translated as "people." This term, however, is used either in reference to the people of other nations, such as the Peo-

---

[4] *bito* is the voiced variant of *hito* that appears in compounds.

ple's Republic of China; or in compounds conveying foreign concept, for example, *jinmin sensen* "people's front" used in socialist literature. It is interesting that the original translation of Chapter III of the MacArthur Constitution was entitled *Jinmin-no Kenri oyobi Gimu* "The Rights and Duties of the People." There was no way that the Japanese government could have used such a title and still have claimed that it was a document originally drafted by them.

In short, from a strictly linguistic viewpoint, the Japanese officials did not have a choice in the matter of selecting the Japanese term that precisely stands for "the people." From this evidence, some people might immediately infer that lack of such a term indicates that the Japanese people have such a strong sense of Japanese identity that they are prejudiced towards foreigners. I believe, though, that the relationships between language, culture, and national character are too complex to allow such an easy inference. Nevertheless, there is no denying that the choice of language made by the translators contributed significantly to changing the character of the constitution from that originally intended by the American drafters. And it probably also contributed to the Japanese people's acceptance of the document as their own.

SUMMARY

The present Constitution of Japan was initially drafted by the staff of MacArthur's Occupation Army and then given to the Japanese for them to adopt as their own in 1946. Despite controversies over its foreign origin and the appropriateness of its democratic character, this constitution has survived without a single amendment, and has greatly influenced Japan's social and political development for more than 35 years.

In this paper, I have discussed three grammatical features of the Japanese text which distinguish it from the English version and which, I suggest, have contributed to the Japanese people's acceptance of this constitution as their own. The first is the topic-comment construction, particularly the one with the topicalized and fronted object representing a right, which is used to translate the agentless passives in English. This construction not only decreases the translation flavor of the Japanese text as a whole, but also implies that those rights were familiar to the Japanese people. The second is the choice of the verbal expressions. The Japanese text uses simple assertive sentences to state the rights and duties of the Japanese, while the English version uses the modal "shall." The English text implies that the Japanese government is being commanded by the people to protect their rights and duties, but the Japanese document indicates that the government is asserting its authority and responsibility to do so. This reflects an important difference in the role of the government in the two societies.

Finally, two words, "people" and "person(s)" used in the English text have been translated into *kokumin* "national(s)" and *nanibito* "any one/no one," respectively. The two sets of terms represent quite different semantic distinctions. The English terms allow a distinction between people as individuals and as a collective entity. The Japanese terms, on the other hand, create a distinction between citizens and noncitizens. I suggested that because Japanese has no formal word exactly comparable to the "people" in English, the translators had no choice but to use *kokumin*. But this usage has made Chapter III of this constitution in Japanese very different from what the Americans had originally intended. It is also likely that this has contributed to the Japanese people's acceptance of this constitution as their own.

REFERENCES

Hayashi, Ooki. 1981. Hooritsu-to Bunpoo-ya (Law and a grammarian). Hoo-to Nihongo, ed. by Ooki Hayashi and Junichi Aomi, 241–250. Tokyo: Yuhikaku.

Hayashi, Ooki, & Junichi Aomi (Ed.). 1981. Hoo-to Nihongo (Law and the Japanese language). Tokyo: Yuhikaku.

Inoue, Kyoko. 1982. The making of a Japanese constitution - A linguist's perspective. Language Problems and Language Planning 6(3). 271–285.

Irie, Toshio. 1976. Kenpoo Seiritsu-no Keii-to Kenpoo-joo-no Shomondai (The process of the making of the constitution and some constitutional problems). Tokyo: Daiichi Hoki.

Kuno, Susumu. 1973. The structure of the Japanese language. Cambridge, Mass.: MIT Press.

Kuroda, S.-Y. 1965. Generative grammatical studies in the Japanese language. Unpublished Ph. D. dissertation, MIT.

Sato, Tatsuo. 1955. Nihonkoku Kenpoo Tanjoo-ki (The birth of a Japanese constitution), nos. 1–17. Toki-no Hoorei, nos. 169–175; 177–180; 182–187.

Shimizu, Shin (Ed.). 1962. Chikujoo Nihonkoku Kenpoo Shingi-roku (A record of the debate at the National Diet). 4 vols. Tokyo: Yuhikaku.

Yokota, Kisaburo. 1981. Kenpoo-no Hirakana Koogo (Hirakana colloquial of the constitution). Hoo-to Nihongo, ed. by Ooki Hayashi and Junichi Aomi, 265–272. Tokyo: Yuhikaku.

FIFTEEN

Sign Language Interpretation And Public Policy In The United States

Robert M. Ingram
American Sign Language Associates

For much of our nation's history many cultural and ethnic minorities have found themselves excluded from the benefits and privileges of full membership in our society. For many of these people who speak a language other than English the key to their experience of separation has been a virtually insurmountable inability to communicate with either individuals outside of their own culture or the institutions of our system of government. (Tobriner 1978:189)

Deaf people—approximately 400,000 of them in the United States—constitute a cultural and linguistic minority (Alcorn and Kanda n.d.; Baker and Battison 1980; Baker and Cokely 1980; Benderly 1980; Boese 1964; Gannon 1981; Higgins 1980; Lieth 1977; Meadow 1972; Padden and Markowicz 1976; Reich and Reich 1974; Schein 1968; Schlesinger and Meadow 1972; Vernon and Makowsky 1969). Like other minorities, they interact with one another through a common language, American Sign Language (ASL), but they often encounter difficulty in attempting to interact with members of the majority. They have frequently been denied access to such public services as courts, health care, welfare, employment, education, and government proceedings. In the 1970s, the federal government began to redress this discrimination with three laws: the Rehabilitation Act of 1973 (PL 93–112), the Education for All Handicapped Children Act (PL 94–142), and the Court Interpreters Act (PL 95–539). The history of this legislation reveals not only the struggle for equal rights for deaf people but also changing attitudes toward sign languages and the interpretation of sign languages.

Until the mid-1960s, interpretation for deaf people was an eleemosynary service provided by religious workers, family members, teachers of the deaf and, more recently, rehabilitation counselors. (See Figure 15.1.) These "interpreters" had little, if any, formal training in sign language let alone interpretation, and the quality of their services varied greatly. They called themselves "interpreters for the deaf," because they did not view hearing people as consumers of their services. The need for their services, as they saw it, arose from the inability of certain people to hear, not from the absence of a common language between two interactants. This clinical, or sociopathological, view of interpretation, derived from the medical model in human services, predominated through the 1960s and 1970s and persists, though less

| Religious Work | Family Relations | Education | Rehabilitation | Communication |

Figure 15.1.   Trends in Interpretation.

forcefully, even today (cf. Domingue and Ingram 1978; Ingram 1977, 1978, 1982).

These early "interpreters for the deaf" also did not recognize that their function was interlingual; that is, they did not recognize that they were dealing with two distinct languages: English and American Sign Language (ASL). To them, as well as to the general public and even the academic community, ASL was "broken English," and deaf people who used it were "low verbal." William Stokoe exposed these myths in his monograph on *Sign Language Structure* in 1960. Stokoe (1960) showed that ASL is not a form of English at all but a completely distinct language with its own grammatical structure. Subsequent investigations (e.g., Klima and Bellugi 1979; Lane and Grosjean 1980; Wilbur 1979; Woodward 1973) have substantiated Stokoe's basic claims. These studies have also verified the existence of a pidgin, now commonly referred to as Pidgin Sign English (PSE), resulting from the application of ASL signs to simplified English syntax. During this period, some educators (Anthony 1966, 1971; Gustason, Pfetzing and Zawolkow 1972; Wampler 1971, 1972) attempted to manufacture manual systems to represent English at the morphological level (with far less than ideal success). Most of these developments, however, did not impact heavily on the majority of practicing interpreters until the mid-1970s.

Lacking an awareness of ASL as a linguistic system, the early "interpreters for the deaf" conceived of and defined interpretation and translation in terms that seem unorthodox or even bizarre today. The following quotation is typical.

> In translating, the thoughts and words of the speaker are presented verbatim. In interpreting, the interpreter may depart from the exact words of the speaker to paraphrase, define, and explain what the speaker is saying. Interpreting requires adjustment of the presentation to the intellectual level of the audience and their ability to understand English.
>
> When translating, the interpreter is recognizing that the deaf person is a highly literate indivdual who prefers to have his thoughts and those of hearing persons expressed verbatim. Translating is not commonly used as highly literate deaf people frequently do not need the services of an interpreter unless they are in situations where misunderstanding might arise which could result in financial or personal loss. For deaf people who have been well educated but have difficulty with the common idioms of the English language, it may be necessary to do some explaining in the interpreting process. For many deaf people, it is necessary to paraphrase, define, and explain a speaker's words in terms and concepts which they can understand. This is interpreting. The lower the verbal ability, the greater is the need for simplification of the presentation. (Youngs 1965:1)

This quotation is taken from a U.S. government publication, and it reflects the view not only of interpreters in the mid-1960s but of the federal government as well. The

Vocational Rehabilitation Administration (as it was then called) sponsored the publication of *Interpreting for Deaf People* and three conferences that preceded it, beginning in 1964. At the first of these conferences, known as the Ball State Conference, the Registry of Interpreters for the Deaf (RID) was born. In 1965 Congress passed the Vocational Rehabilitation Amendments, which, for the first time, authorized interpretation as a case service for deaf clients. The 1965 Amendments also marked the first time any branch of the federal government had recognized interpretation for deaf persons as a "professional" service. The Vocational Rehabilitation Administration continued to play a major role in the development of the profession through grants to the RID from 1968-1972 and the National Interpreter Training Consortium (NITC) from 1974–1979.

The clinical model of interpretation fostered by the government through the Rehabilitation Services Administration was not challenged in print until 1972. Fant (1972), borrowing from Stokoe's pioneering linguistic research, called for a redefinition of interpretation and translation. Interpretation and translation, argued Fant, are interlingual processes, translation dealing with written texts and interpretation with spoken discourse. Recognizing ASL (or "Ameslan", as he called it) as a language, Fant reasoned that the reproduction of messages from ASL to English and vice versa should be called interpretation. On the other hand, PSE and the various forms of Manually Coded English (MCE) are not distinct languages but manual glosses of English. Consequently, Fant suggested the term "transliteration" for the reproduction of messages between PSE or MCE and (spoken) English. Fant's terminology is now generally accepted in the field, though the term "interpreting" is frequently used as a generic term to refer to both interpretation and transliteration.

Fant also challenged the use of the term "reverse interpreting," widely used at the time to refer to the process of interpreting from ASL to English. According to the RID and the Vocational Rehabilitation Administration, one interprets from English to ASL but reverse interprets, or reverses, from ASL to English (Youngs 1965). As Fant and others (Ingram 1974, 1977, 1978, 1979a, 1979b; Fritsch-Rudser 1979) have pointed out, the term "reverse interpreting" disregards the linguistic legitimacy of ASL and implies that it is "normal" to speak in English but not in ASL.

Fant's brief article is significant not only for its redefinition of important terms but for creating a break from the clinical view of interpretation so predominant at the time. Fant showed that interpretation is not a rehabilitation process but a cross-linguistic, cross-cultural communication process.

Another shift in the government's policy toward deaf people and, by implication, toward sign language and sign language interpretation began with the passage of the Rehabilitation Act of 1973. Title V of this act contains four sections that greatly expand the guarantee of equal access for disabled persons. Section 504 has been described as "historic in its scope, the single most important civil rights provision ever enacted on behalf of disabled citizens in this country" (Bowe 1978:205). Patterned after the Civil Rights Act of 1964, Section 504 reads simply, "No otherwise qualified handicapped individual in the United States . . . shall, solely by reason of his handicap, be excluded from participation in, be denied the benefits of, or be subjected to discrimination under any program or activity receiving Federal financial assistance.''

Like other civil rights legislation, Section 504 was not won without a fight. President Nixon twice vetoed the bill, largely because of the perceived impact of Section 504, before Congress passed a revised Rehabilitation Act by a wide margin. Though he signed the bill into law on Sept. 26, 1973, Nixon delayed the issuance of guidelines and regulations implementing 504 for the remainder of his term in office. On April 28, 1976, President Ford issued Executive Order 11914 authorizing the former Department of Health, Education and Welfare (HEW) to be the lead agency in drafting 504 regulations. Despite pressure from consumer groups, courts, and even the Congress, delays persisted through the end of President Ford's term and into the term of President Carter. As a candidate, Carter had campaigned in support of 504. In a press release dated Sept. 22, 1976, Carter said,

> I oppose discrimination in any form, and when my administration moves against discrimination it will vigorously seek out and redress discrimination against the handicapped . . . As President, I will take all necessary action, through specific legislation and the appropriate exercise of executive powers, to insure our handicapped citizens equal protection under the law, equal opportunity for education, employment, and other services, and equal access to public accommodations and facilities . . . . No administration that really cared about disabled citizens would spend three years trying to avoid enforcing Section 504. (quoted in Bowe 1978:208)

But Carter's HEW Secretary, Joseph Califano, actually tried to rewrite and weaken the regulations before issuing them. Incensed by this action, consumer groups issued an ultimatum. If the regulations were not signed by April 4, 1977, they would take political action. When, on April 5, the regulations had still not been signed, over 5000 disabled people and their supporters staged sit-ins at 10 federal buildings around the country. In San Francisco, the sit-in—supported by the Gray Panthers, the Black Panthers, church groups, and civic leaders—lasted 25 days. During this time, a massive letter-writing, telephone, and telegram campaign was waged, two vigils were held in front of the White House, and disabled leaders called on top White House officials, members of Congress, and leading civil rights organizations. Finally, Secretary Califano gave in to the pressure and signed the regulations into effect on April 28, 1977-nearly four years after the bill had been signed into law. The Reagan Administration, through the Bush Task Force on Deregulation, has attempted to weaken the 504 Regulations, but has been thwarted in its attempts by heavy pressure from consumer groups and Congress.

The HEW Regulations are only one set of 504 Regulations; each federal cabinet department and agency—33 of them—must issue its own regulations, though about half of them have still not done so; but the HEW Regulations are significant, because they serve as a model for all other federal agencies.

The HEW 504 Regulations contain seven subparts: (A) General Provisions, (B) Employment Practices, (C) Program Accessibility, (D) Preschool, Elementary and Secondary Education, (E) Postsecondary Education, (F) Health, Welfare and Social Services, and (G) Procedures. Three of these subparts, (B), (E), and (F), contain specific references to interpreters.

Section 84.12 under Subpart B introduces the notion of reasonable accommodation in employment. It reads in part,

> (a) A recipient (of federal financial assistance) shall make reasonable accommodation to the known physical or mental limitations of an otherwise qualified handicapped applicant or employee unless the recipient can demonstrate that the accommodation would impose an undue hardship on the operation of its program.
>
> (b) Reasonable accommodation may include: (1) making facilities used by employees readily accessible to and usable by handicapped persons, and (2) job restructuring, part-time or modified work schedules, acquisition or modification of equipment or devices, the provision of readers or interpreters, and other similar actions. (HEW 1977b:22680–22681)

In other words, any agency, institution, or program receiving federal financial assistance cannot discriminate against deaf people in employment solely on the basis of their deafness and may have to employ or contract with interpreters for the preemployment interview and even to assist the deaf employee on the job.

Likewise, postsecondary educational institutions may be required to provide interpreters for deaf students. Under Subpart E, Section 84.44(d) says:

> (1) A recipient . . . shall take such steps as are necessary to ensure that no handicapped student is denied the benefits of, excluded from participation in, or otherwise subjected to discrimination under the education program or activity operated by the recipient because of the absence of educational auxiliary aids for students with impaired sensory, manual, or speaking skills.
>
> (2) Auxiliary aids may include . . . interpreters or other effective methods of making orally delivered materials available to students with hearing impairments . . . ''
> (HEW 1977b:22684)

As the number of deaf students attending colleges and universities has risen appreciably in the past decade, so too has the number of sign language interpreters working in these domains.

Section 84.52(c) requires hospitals and other health care providers to provide interpreters or other means of communication access to deaf patients and to deaf parents of hearing patients who are under the age of consent. Seeking to clarify this section, the Office for Civil Rights under the Department of Health, Education and Welfare issued a policy interpretation on April 21, 1980. It says, in part:

> that recipient health care providers (must) be prepared to draw upon a full range of communication options (auxiliary aids) in order to insure that hearing impaired persons are provided effective access to health care services. This range of options, which must be provided at no cost to the hearing impaired patient, must include formal arrangements with interpreters who can accurately and fluently express and receive in sign language, supplemental hearing devices, written communication, flash cards and staff training in basic sign language expressions relevant to emergency treatment. The names, addresses, phone numbers and hours of availability of interpreters must be readily available to the recipient's employees. Family members may be used only if they are specifically requested by the hearing impaired person. (HEW 1980:1)

The choice among the communication options, the policy interpretation goes on to say, belongs to the deaf patient: "The patient's judgment regarding what means of communication is necessary to insure effective communication must be accorded great weight. In the event of disagreements between the health care provider and the hearing impaired patient, there will be a presumption favoring the hearing impaired patient's self-assessed need" (HEW 1980:2). Presumably, this stipulation means that the deaf patient may not only choose among the various modes of communication (signed, written, oral) but may also select the specific type of sign language (ASL, PSE, MCE) he or she prefers.

Some of the provisions of 504 have been challenged in the courts, but the case law remains somewhat unclear at this time. In *University of Texas v. Camenisch*, the Fifth Circuit Court of Appeals upheld the right of Camenisch, a deaf graduate student, to have interpreters provided at the university's expense for his classes, but, on appeal, the U.S. Supreme Court returned the matter to the lower courts on a technicality without actually ruling on the substance of the appeal.

In any event, 504 represents a significant change in the attitude and policy of the federal government toward disabled people in general and toward deaf people, sign language, and sign language interpretation in particular. Though it is contained in a piece of rehabilitation legislation, it is really a civil rights law which establishes disabled citizens as a protected class. In terms of interpretation, it marks a small but not insignificant shift away from the old-school clinical philosophy toward a cross-cultural, cross-linguistic philosophy.

Two years after enactment of the Rehabilitation Act of 1973, Congress passed the Education for All Handicapped Children Act (PL 94–142). This law mandates a "free appropriate public education" in the "least restrictive environment" for all disabled children between the ages of three and 21. Because it opened the way for hundreds, perhaps thousands, of disabled school children to escape from residential institutions and enter local community schools where they are educated alongside nondisabled students, PL 94–142 is often referred to incorrectly as the "mainstreaming law." However, the word "mainstreaming" is not used anywhere in the law, and the law does not say that all disabled children shall be educated alongside nondisabled children. Many deaf children, for example, prefer to attend residential schools for the deaf where they are assured access to a community of peers and role models who share their language and culture.

PL 94–142 stipulates that disabled children shall be educated in their native language, which is defined pursuant to Section 703 (a) (2) of the Bilingual Education Act. PL 94–142, however, contains the additional provision that "if a person is deaf or blind, or has no written language, the mode of communication would be that normally used by the person (such as sign language, braille, or oral communication)" (HEW 1977a:42479).

Though interpretation is not mentioned per se in the law or the accompanying regulations, it is generally assumed to be included in the law as a "related service," and, in fact, hundreds of sign language interpreters have been hired to interpret in the public schools as a direct result of PL 94–142. This trend suffered a major set-back in the case of *Rowley v. Board of Education of Hendrick Hudson (NY) Central School District*. In this case, the U.S. Supreme Court ruled by a vote of six to three that the school district was not obligated to provide sign language interpreters for Amy Rowley, a young deaf student, because she was already making above-average grades without the service. Apparently, the court did not consider the possi-bility that Amy might be an exceptional student and might perform even better with the aid of interpreters.

PL 94–142 has other deficiencies with regard to interpretation services which will be discussed later in this paper.

A more substantial indication of the federal government's shift away from a clin-ical to a communicational view of interpretation is the Court Interpreters Act (PL 95–539), enacted in 1978. This act provides for the use of interpreters in federal courts. Specifically, it stipulates that the Director of the Administrative Office of the U.S. Courts

(1) shall establish a program to facilitate the use of interpreters in the courts of the U.S.; (2) shall prescribe, determine, and certify the qualifications of persons who may serve as certified interpreters . . . ; (3) shall maintain a current master list of all inter-preters certified by the Director; (4) shall report annually on the frequency of requests for, and the use and effectiveness of, interpreters; and (5) shall pay the salaries, fees, expenses and costs . . . from sums appropriated to the Federal judiciary.'' (quoted in Arjona 1983:2)

Like the Rehabilitation Act of 1973, the Court Interpreters Act has a long and scarred history, described by Arjona (1983:1):

Representatives of the speech and hearing impaired community had already brought these complex issues of due process, fair trial, and language handicap before the courts for resolution by 1925. In the early 1960s, the 'foreign' language speaking community joined them in demanding that the rights of the language-handicapped person in the courtroom be addressed. In the early 1970s, a study by the U.S. Commission on Civil Rights and one by the Institute for Court Management summarized these concerns and described the highly ineffective system of interpretation services used in the courts.

What eventually emerged as the Court Interpreters Act is the result of eight House bills and four Senate bills dating back to 1973.

The Court Interpreters Act is significant in terms of the philosophical issue I have been addressing throughout this paper—i.e., the clinical versus communicational view—because it marks the first time that the federal government has officially compared sign language interpretation to the interpretation of spoken languages. In other words, it recognizes that interpretation is a process—a process that is essen-tially the same whether the languages involved are spoken or signed.

Important as it is, the Court Interpreters Act is not without its shortcomings. ''One serious shortcoming in the Act,'' notes Arjona (1983:4), ''is that it totally ignores the issues of training. No provisions are made, for example, for the in-service training of practitioners nor for the appropriate funding of such programs.'' Such training could be used, she argues, to address the demand for interpreters of uncommon languages.

Another area neglected by the Act is working conditions. Arjona notes that the Act makes no provisions for ''the unusual demands and the extraordinary stress that accompany interpretation practice . . . '' (Arjona 1983:4).

The Court Interpreters Act also fails to provide for the use of simultaneous interpretation booths and of recording equipment.

Though a program of evaluation and certification has been implemented for Spanish/English interpreters, certification is lacking for the other 34 languages that have been used in district and bankruptcy courts. Rather than institute its own system of evaluating sign language interpreters, the Administrative Office of the U.S. Courts has chosen to adopt the evaluation and certification system administered by the RID. The problem with this decision is that the RID system has been shown to be an invalid measure of interpreter proficiency (Culton 1982). In fact, the RID has suspended evaluations for the legal specialist certification for more than two years.

As if certification were not already a problem, the Act allows judges to use noncertified interpreters at their discretion.

Furthermore, there exists no mechanism or funding for validation and/or evaluation studies of the certification process that does exist.

Some of the shortcomings of the Court Interpreters Act cited here also apply to Section 504 of the Rehabilitation Act of 1973 and PL 94–142. PL 94–142 does provide funds for the training of interpreters at the discretion of local school districts, but 504 contains no funding provisions at all. Neither 504 nor 94–142 mandates the use of certified interpreters and, in fact, the overwhelming majority of persons hired to interpret in the public schools possess no certification at all. Many are hired right out of sign language classes with little or no formal training in interpretation, and most function as bilingual teacher aides rather than exclusively as interpreters. Salaries for these workers are extremely low, as one might expect.

Recently, the Office for Handicapped Information and Research awarded a grant to the University of California at San Francisco to conduct research on sign language interpretation, or, more precisely, on interpreting ''for the deaf,'' but the funds were part of a larger package, and the proportion allotted for research on interpretation is very small. None of the three laws discussed here contains specific provisions for research.

Enforcement of the laws, as always, varies from one administration to another. The current administration in Washington has shown very little interest in enforcing 504, 94–142, and the Court Interpreters Act.

None of these laws addresses the question of professional privilege either. Everything that an interpreter interprets should be regarded as privileged communication, but interpreters have been subpoenaed to testify about interpreted communications, and there is currently no federal legislation to protect them should they refuse.

While the federal government has begun to recognize interpretation of sign languages, it has not yet recognized ASL. ASL is not mentioned by name in any of the three laws. These laws do represent important advancements for sign language interpreters—especially with regard to the trend toward a cross-linguistic, cross-cultural philosophy. This trend will not be complete, however, until the government officially recognizes ASL as a language.

REFERENCES

Alcorn, B., & Kanda, J. n.d. Deaf culture. Videotape. Overland Park, Kans.: Johnson County Community College.

Anthony, D. 1966. Seeing essential English. Unpublished manuscript. Ypsilanti: Eastern Michigan University.

_____. 1971. Seeing essential English. Vols. 1 and 2. Anaheim, Calif.: Educational Services Division, Anaheim Union School District.

Arjona, E. 1983. Language planning in the judicial system: A look at the implementation of the U.S. Court Interpreters Act. Language Planning Newsletter 9. 1–6.

Baker, C., & Battison, R. 1980. Sign language and the deaf community: Essays in honor of William C. Stokoe. Silver Spring, Md.: National Association of the Deaf.

Baker, C., & Cokely, D. 1980. American sign language: A teacher's resource text on grammar and culture. Silver Spring, Md.: National Association of the Deaf.

Benderly, B. L. 1980. Dancing without music: Deafness in America. Garden City, N.Y.: Anchor Press/Doubleday.

Boese, R. J. 1964. Differentiations in the deaf community. Unpublished manuscript. Vancouver: University of British Columbia.

Bowe, F. 1978. Handicapping America: Barriers to disabled people. New York: Harper and Row.

Culton, P. 1982. A study of the validity and reliability of the Comprehensive Skills Certificate evaluation for sign language interpreters: A report to the profession. RID Interpreting Journal 1(2).16–37.

Domingue, R., & Ingram, B. 1978. Sign language interpretation: The state of the art. Language interpretation and communication, ed. by D. Gerver and H. W. Sinaiko, 81–86. New York: Plenum Press.

Fant, L. 1972. The CSUN approach to the training of sign language interpreters. The Deaf American 24.56–57.

Fritsch-Rudser, S. 1979. Interpreting: Difficulties in present terminology. Interprenews 5(3).1–2.

Gannon, J. R. 1981. Deaf heritage; A narrative history of deaf America. Silver Spring, Md.: National Association of the Deaf.

Gustason, G., Pfetzing, D. & Zawolkow, E. 1972. Signing exact English. Rossmoor, Calif: Modern Science Press.

HEW. 1977a. Federal Register. Vol. 42, No. 163. 1977. Education of handicapped children. Washington, D.C.: Office of Education.

HEW. 1977b. Federal Register. Vol. 42. No. 86. 1977. Nondiscrimination on basis of handicap. Washington, D.C.: Office of Education.

HEW. 1980. OCR's position on the provision of auxiliary aids for hearing impaired patients in inpatient, outpatient and emergency treatment settings. Memorandum: Office of the Secretary, April 21, 1980. Washington, D.C.: Department of Health, Education, and Welfare.

Higgins, P. C. 1980. Outsiders in a hearing world.: A sociology of deafness. Beverly Hills: Sage Publications.

Ingram, R. 1974. A communication model of the interpreting process. Journal of Rehabilitation of the Deaf 7(3). 3–9.

_____ . 1977. Teaching deaf students how to purchase and use interpretation services. The Deaf American 29(9). 3–7.

_____ . 1978. Sign language interpretation and general theories of language interpretation and communication. Language interpretation and communication, ed. by D. Gerver and H. W. Sinaiko, 109–118. New York: Plenum Press.

_____ . 1979a. Reverse interpreting. Proceedings of the First National Conference of Interpreter Trainers. Mimeo.

_____ . 1979b. Terminology. Unpublished manuscript.

_____ . 1982. Focus. Interpreterviews 7(4). 3.

Klima, E. S., & Bellugi, U. 1979. The signs of language. Cambridge: Harvard University Press.

Lane, H., & Grosjean, F. (Eds.). 1980. Recent perspectives on American sign language. Hillsdale: Lawrence Erlbaum Associates.

Lieth, L. 1977. Døv i Dag 3. København: Danske Døves Landsforbund.

Meadow, K. 1972. Sociolinguistics, sign language and the deaf sub-culture. Psycholinguistics and total communication: The state of the art., ed. by T. O'Rourke, 19–34. Washington, D.C.: American Annals of the Deaf.

Padden, C., & Markowicz, H. 1976. Cultural conflicts between hearing and deaf communities. Proceedings of the VIIth World Congress of the World Federation of the Deaf, ed. by F. B. Crammatte and A. B. Crammatte, 407–413. Washington, D.C.: National Association of the Deaf.

Reich, P., & Reich, C. 1974. A follow-up study of the deaf. Toronto: Research Service, Board of Education, No. 120.

Schein, J. D. 1968. The deaf community: Studies in the social psychology of deafness. Washington, D. C.: Gallaudet College Press.

Schlesinger, H., & Meadow, K. 1972. Sound and sign: Childhood deafness and mental health. Berkeley: University of California Press.

Stokoe, W. C. 1960. Sign language structure: An outline of the visual communication systems of the American deaf. Buffalo: University of Buffalo.

Tobriner, J. 1978. Dissenting opinion. Jara v. Municipal Court, 21 Cal. 3d 181, 189.

Vernon, M., & Makowsky, B. 1969. Deafness and minority group dynamics. The Deaf American 21. 3–6.

Wampler, D. 1971. Linguistics of visual English. Santa Rosa, Calif.: Early Childhood Education Department.

_____ . 1972. Linguistics of visual English. 2322 Maher Dr. 35, Santa Rosa, Calif.

Wilbur, R. B. 1979. American sign language and sign systems. Baltimore: University Park Press.

Woodward, J. C. 1972. Implications for sociolinguistic research among the deaf. Sign Language Studies 1. 1–7.

_____ . 1973. Implicational lects on the deaf diglossic continuum. Unpublished dissertation, Georgetown University.

Youngs, J. P. 1965. Introduction. Interpreting for deaf people, ed. by S. P. Quigley, Washington, D. C.: U.S. Department of Health, Education, and Welfare, Vocational Rehabilitation Administration.

SIXTEEN

Foreign Language Use In International Trade And Commerce: Trends In The Southeastern United States—Part I: International Business in the Southeastern United States and its Foreign Language Needs

Anne E. Harland

Harland Translation/Interpretation Atlanta, GA

INTERNATIONAL BUSINESS IN THE SOUTHEASTERN UNITED STATES

This paper illustrates the influx of international trade and commerce from German-, French-, Japanese-, and Spanish-speaking countries to the Southeastern United States. For the purpose of this paper, the Southeast is defined as the states of Alabama, Florida, Georgia, North Carolina, South Carolina, and Tennessee. The time frame under consideration is 1978 to 1983. The paper addresses the implications of this economic growth with regard to language requirements in these four major foreign languages in business and industry in the Southeast.

While foreign languages have been a familiar aspect of life in large metropolitan areas on the East and West coast, it has only been in this past decade that the South has been confronted with foreign languages in industry and business, as it has emerged as the choice of relocation of multinational U.S. companies traditionally located in the North, as well as the preferred location of foreign businesses attempting to establish themselves in the U.S. market.

Up until the mid-1970s, most foreign investors were attracted by those states that already had large concentrations of industry.[1] This was especially true if they wished to enter the market through acquisition. Regional preferences have begun to change since, however, in that an increasing number of large-, medium-, and small-sized foreign businesses are being attracted to the Sunbelt. The trend in this past decade is characterized by slower growth rates in the Northeast, and an increase in growth in the Southeast and Southwest. There has been a trend toward decentraliza-

---

[1] Mainly in the large metropolitan areas of the East coast.

tion of jobs and movement of population away from the established, large metropolitan areas of the Northeast toward the South. Most new manufacturing plants are now built in the Southeastern United States.

Motives for Investment and Relocation
The motivation for foreign companies considering entrance into the U. S. market is complex, but pragmatic. Basic considerations for involvement in the U. S. market include the following.

The Political Situation at Home.   A grave political concern in those European states bordering on the Iron Curtain is the ever-present shadow of the Russian tanks. Afghanistan, Poland, and even the recent Korean jetliner incident have nurtured these fears. In addition, the political developments in the individual European countries in the past five years, for example, in France and Germany, have contributed to entrepreneurs' and investors' view of the United States as the last safe bastion of capitalism, and in pursuing a philosophy of "dual investment,"[2] they move a portion of their investment capital across the Atlantic.

The Market Situation.   Many industries and businesses overseas have reached the limits of their domestic markets and are looking for ways to expand. As they reach out to find larger markets and less congestion as well as room for expansion, the Southeast seems to be a logical choice. Alabama, Florida, Georgia, North Carolina, South Carolina, and Tennessee, for instance, cover an area almost as large as that of all West European states combined. The Southeast has a population of 31 million. The region contains approximately 13 million nonfarm workers and profits from almost $121 billion in retail sales and almost $200 billion in effective buying income annually. The growth of the Southeast region has far surpassed the national rate of economic growth in recent years. Between 1970 and 1979, while the nation's retail sales increased almost 126%, the Southeast's retail sales increased almost 164%. While the nation's buying income increased 112%, the Southeast's buying income grew 137%. The growth record of the Southeast illustrates that the region is a viable U. S. market whose economy is growing faster than that of the nation as a whole, and whose share of the total U. S. market is steadily increasing (Atlanta Chamber of Commerce 1982:4). (See Figure 16.1.) The Sunbelt's population gain in the seventies was 12 million persons. Immigration from other parts of the country, notably the Northeast and the West, accounted for most of the growth. Overall, the Sunbelt's population gain from immigration during the seventies was 49.8% of the total population increase (Watters 1982:54).

---

[2] This term can be defined as limiting the entrepreneurial risk by investing at home and abroad.

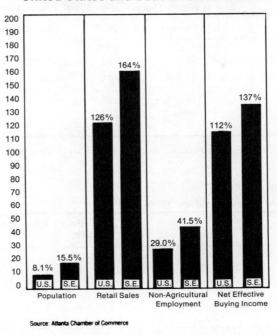

Figure 16.1   Source: Atlanta Chamber of Commerce: *Atlanta Facts Book*, p. 3.

The Labor Situation.   Another factor which made foreign businesses decide to come to the United States was the dramatic increase in labor costs in the seventies. A comparison of the labor costs of foreign countries in the period between 1970 and 1977 shows, for instance, that France, Germany, Japan, the Netherlands, and Switzerland had dramatic increases in labor costs as compared to the United States (see Table 16.1). While the hourly compensation of U.S. workers almost doubled between 1970 and 1978, it increased by a factor of 4 in France and in Germany, a factor of more than 5 in Japan, and a factor of almost 5 in the Netherlands (see Table 16.2). A look at the fringe benefits in foreign countries (Table 16.3) shows that the outlays for leave time pay, social security, bonuses, and so on (e.g., the add-on to earnings of workers) in France and the Netherlands are twice as high as in the United States; in Germany, the add-on is almost twice as high. To quote an example: If a Dutch worker gets sick, the government must pay 80% of his salary. Luckier German workers get 100% of net earnings delivered to them. German employers, for instance, are further burdened by codetermination laws and stipulations severely restricting the firing of employees.

Table 16.1. Unit Labor Costs for Other Countries 1970–1977

Country	Rise in Hourly Compensation		Rise in Unit Labor Costs	
	Local Currency	US $	Local Currency	US $
Canada	110%	106%	68%	65%
France	162	194	85	108
Germany	117	241	48	133
Japan	193	291	107	178
Netherlands	159	282	69	149
Switzerland	80	224	37	147
United States	75	75	44	44

Source: Walter B. Wriston, *Investment Guide to the United States* (New York, 1980), p. 13.

Table 16.2. Labor Cost Increases 1970–1978

	Hourly Compensation in U.S. $	
	1970	Mid-1978
United States	$4.19	$8.26
Canada	3.46	7.54
France	1.74	6.90
Germany	2.35	9.18
Japan	0.99	5.65
Netherlands	2.14	9.62

Source: Walter B. Wriston, *Investment Guide to the United States* (New York, 1980), p. 13.

**Table 16.3. Fringe Benefits for Workers
in Other Countries (In % of average hourly earnings)**

	Pay for leave time	Bonuses	Add-on to earnings
Canada	9.3	0.2	20.4
France	13.7	4.8	62.3
Germany	16.6	5.1	48.0
Japan	*	*	13.2
Netherlands	20.0	6.9	60.2
United States	8.8	0.6	30.0

*Bonuses and leave-time pay in Japan included under hourly earnings.
Source: Walter B. Wriston, *Investment Guide to the United States* (New York, 1980), p. 13.

The Tax Situation. Another consideration prompting overseas investors to look beyond their borders is the tax situation at home, once they have exhausted all possibilities of reducing taxes in their home countries. Double-taxation agreements favorable for the investors aid them in deciding to establish an operation overseas.

FOREIGN TRADE

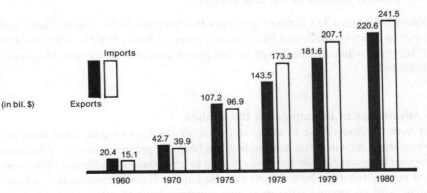

Figure 16.2 Source: U.S. Department of Commerce from the German American Chamber of Congress, Inc. *Economic Survey*, 1982:218.

Exporting. Due to the limitations of the relatively small markets of European countries, exports are encouraged. Figure 16.2 shows the enormous extent of exports to the United States by Canada, Japan, Mexico, and Germany, for instance. In the course of this exporting activity, the companies realize the enormous market potential of the United States, causing them to look into the possibility of establishing presence in this market.

Exporting to Third Countries. For the manufacturing industry that buys products from overseas to incorporate into their products, the increasing costs of imports due to exchange rate fluctuations is also an important aspect in deciding to move abroad. The U.S. location could, in many cases, also serve to facilitate exports to third countries. Many foreign companies that have manufacturing plants in the U.S. export their products to countries in Central and South America.

Overcoming Export Barriers. In this respect, foreign operations also serve to overcome trade and export barriers. Those overseas companies who are suppliers of U.S. companies gain proximity to their customers. In this world of high technology, an important consideration is the proximity to the technical know-how that might be among the decisive factors for overseas companies to locate in the United States. Thus, technology transfer is much facilitated.

In summarizing, the major motives for overseas businesses to establish themselves in the United States are:

1. To extend business activities to new markets
2. To secure and control sales in the new market
3. To secure and extend the existing markets

4. To create an export basis for a product of the parent company
5. The political stability of the host country.

Between 68 and 102 German companies that invested in the United States and took part in a survey conducted by a research group in Bonn, F.R.G.—60% to 90% of all surveyed—attached very high to high importance to these motives (Kayser et al. 1980:267).

The Advantages of Investment in the Sunbelt

What does the South have to offer, and what are the reasons that, apart from the above-average growth rates, the Sunbelt has been the preferred choice of location for foreign investors? While this country used to be the land of unlimited opportunities, it is now regarded by foreigners as the land of limited opportunities which, however, still go beyond what their own countries have to offer.

Taking a look at the infrastructure of the Sunbelt, we find that within a radius of 300 miles of Georgia, for instance, one has access to a population of 23 million with an annual disposable income of $133 billion (Harrold and Otto 1980). In other words, infrastructure is the Sunbelt's strong point: The network of highways, rails, and trucking facilities is exemplary (see Figures 16.3 and 16.4), complemented by a large number of seaports along the Southeastern coast that lend themselves as efficient links between the investor's country of origin and his new U.S. location.

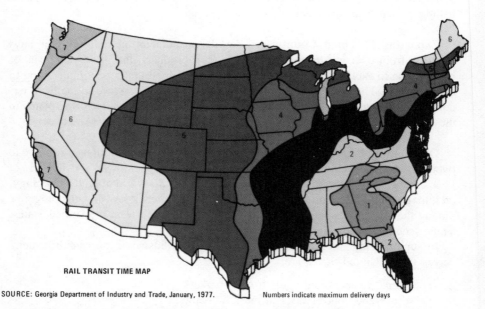

RAIL TRANSIT TIME MAP

SOURCE: Georgia Department of Industry and Trade, January, 1977.   Numbers indicate maximum delivery days

Figure 16.3 Source: Georgia Department of Industry and Trade, January, 1977 (*Industrial Survey of Georgia* 1982:14–18).

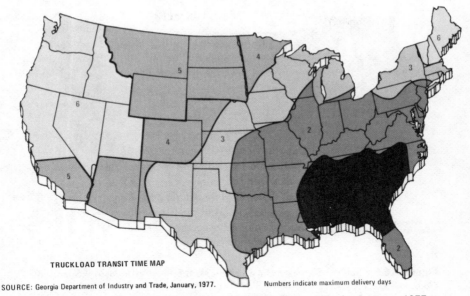

TRUCKLOAD TRANSIT TIME MAP

SOURCE: Georgia Department of Industry and Trade, January, 1977.   Numbers indicate maximum delivery days

Figure 16.4   Source: Georgia Department of Industry and Trade, January, 1977 (*Industrial Survey of Georgia* 1982:14–18).

One may ask, what came first—the chicken or the egg? Our claim is that foreign investment in the Sunbelt would not have happened if overseas air transportation services had not been instituted when they were. In the wake of this expansion of air service, Atlanta became the number five Europe gateway in 1982, followed by Miami. Ranking before Atlanta are New York, Boston, Chicago, and Los Angeles. The large number of direct overseas flights that have been instituted in the past five years have certainly been among the decisive contributing factors in the development of foreign investment in the Sunbelt. One U. S. carrier and four European carriers now connect the Southeast with Europe on a daily basis. Load factors have been in the 70% range, which is considered very satisfactory. This is to show that the bulk of air service was not instituted until 1978, 1979, and 1980. We can see that the international influx to the Sunbelt is of a very recent nature ("Atlanta to Europe flights pass another milestone," June 8, 1983). Once the investors are here, they also have efficient domestic air service at their disposal. It provides the ability to reach 79% of the nation's population within two flight hours from Atlanta. Hartsfield International enplanes nearly 18 million passengers annually and is the hub of flight operations for the Southeast (Georgia Department of Industry and Trade 1982).

Other factors in favor of locating industries in the Sunbelt are:

1.   The availability of energy and resources at prices that are far below those of the Northeastern states.

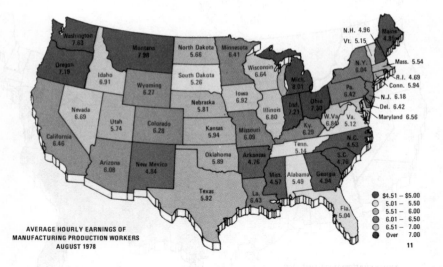

AVERAGE HOURLY EARNINGS OF
MANUFACTURING PRODUCTION WORKERS
AUGUST 1978

Figure 16.5 Source: *Employment & Earnings*, reprinted in *Industrial Survey of Georgia* 1982:11.

2.   Lower property costs in the Sunbelt have been another aspect in attracting investors to the Southeast.

3.   The same applies to lower wages. Figure 16.5 clearly shows that the average hourly earnings of manufacturing production workers in the Sunbelt are among the lowest in the nation. It is cheaper to build and operate a plant in the Southeast. Having reached a ceiling as far as the return on investment (ROI) in their home country is concerned, many foreign entrepreneurs are looking for a better ROI, which they hope to realize in the most capitalist of all countries.

4.   The South also has fewer labor problems. It shows a lower degree of unionization than other areas of this country based on the "Right-to-Work" laws which most of the Southeastern states have adopted. This makes for a favorable social climate as far as employers are concerned.

5.   Last but not least, President Carter, who was the first president from Georgia, was instrumental in focusing attention on the South, thus making this area of the United States better known to foreign investors.

The Sunbelt states have made an effort on their part to attract foreign businesses and to facilitate U.S. establishments overseas. Georgia, for instance, has trade promotion offices in Belgium, Japan, and Canada, and a part-time office in Brazil. North Carolina has an office in Dusseldorf, Germany. Alabama has an office in Bern, Switzerland, and Florida is represented in Stuttgart, Germany. South Carolina's trade promotion office is located in Brussels. The State of Tennessee is the only one not represented overseas. Most of the Southeastern states offer foreign investors incentives such as free location studies, free site selection services, industrial revenue bond financing—which is available for plants and warehouses and offers very favorable financing terms with interest rates far below average rates—one-step environmental permits, industrial and government research labs, and college and university facilities.

The Southeast has, in the wake of incoming foreign investment, developed the required support services, such as international banks, for example. There are now 19 foreign banks represented in Atlanta, versus nine in 1978. Foreign trade zones have been instituted. These are free trade zones where firms can delay, reduce, and sometimes completely eliminate customs duties on important items. Abundant freight forwarding services are available. The Southeast has outstanding convention facilities. Atlanta, for instance, the convention capital of the Sunbelt, features the largest single-level exhibit hall in the United States (350,000 square feet), including facilities for simultaneous interpretation in six languages. The convention industry is the biggest industry in the Atlanta area, employing 81,000 persons in 6,000 convention-related businesses. Even in 1982, a recession year, Atlanta hosted 1,100 conventions and trade meetings, attracting 1.2 million convention delegates, among them an increasing number of international representatives. The State of Georgia, for instance, also offers joint venture and other assistance to foreign investors.

Foreign Investment by States

A survey of the directories published by each of the Southeastern states listing the foreign companies operating in the Southeast (except private investors) showed the following results. (All states have heavy British activity, but due to the nature of this study, which concentrates on foreign languages, these British companies are not reflected in this paper.)

The directory supplied by the State of Alabama lists all manufacturing investments (Table 16.4). While six foreign-owned companies had located in Alabama in 1971, there were 64 foreign-owned companies in Alabama in 1983. Of those, 16 (25%) were established between 1978 and 1983. Alabama also has a strong German-speaking contingent of investors, represented by 13 German operations and three Swiss operations. Canada has eight operations, France has five, Japan has two, and Alabama has one Spanish-speaking foreign operation. Japan, which seems to concentrate on sales activities in the United States, has only two manufacturing investments in Alabama. French presence in Alabama is relatively strong. The major products of foreign investors are chemicals, metal products, wood, paper, and electricals.

Table 16.4.   State of Alabama (as of March, 1983)

	Corporations	Operations
Japan	2	2
Fed. Rep. of Germany	13	13
(Switzerland/Austria)	(3/-)	(3/-)
Canada	8	8
The Netherlands	2	2
France	5	5
Spanish-speaking countries	1	1

Table 16.5.   State of Florida (as of June, 1983)

	Corporations	Operations
Japan	12	14
Fed. Rep. of Germany	36	42
(Switzerland/Austria)	(5/1)	(6/1)
Canada	19	36
The Netherlands	8	11
France	16	19
Spanish-speaking countries	3	3

Table 16.6.   State of Georgia (as of January, 1983)

	Corpora-tions	Opera-tions	Headquartered in Southeast	Manufac-turing
Japan	94	101	9	18
Fed. Rep. of Germany	92	99	28	28
(Switzerland/Austria)	(20/1)	(23/1)	(2/-)	(4/1)
Canada	85	99	17	38
The Netherlands	41	55	14	8
France	44	44	8	15
Spanish-speaking countries	3	3	–	–

Germany is the leading investor in Florida (Table 16.5) in terms of the number of foreign operations, with 42 operations, plus six Swiss and one Austrian operation, followed by Canada, France, Japan, the Netherlands, and Spanish-speaking countries. It is apparent that Japan is not as well represented in Florida as it is in other states; French representation in Florida is very strong. The only Spanish-speaking operations listed are two large newspapers and one flower importer. The spectrum includes an immense variety of products, with no overriding industry.

Japan has the largest number of operations in Georgia (Table 16.6), followed closely by Germany—including Switzerland and Austria—Canada, the Netherlands, and France. Surprisingly few Spanish-speaking countries are represented. Of the 99 German operations in Georgia, more than one-fourth are headquartered here in the Southeast. Another 28 are in manufacturing. Of the 99 Canadian operations active in Georgia, 17 are headquartered in the Southeast, and 38 are in manufacturing. The Japanese companies seem to operate differently. We find 101 Japanese operations in Georgia, but most of these are sales offices; only nine of them are headquarters, and 18 of them are manufacturing plants. Investment-dollar wise, the Netherlands are leading in investment in Georgia, with $600 million invested as of October 1982 (including private investment). Second to the Dutch are the Canadians, with $450 million. The United Kingdom is third with $400 million. As of October 1982, two-thirds of the foreign firms in Georgia were involved in real estate. Another one-third of foreign investment in the State of

Table 16.7.   State of North Carolina (as of October, 1982)

	Corpora-tions	Opera-tions	Headquartered in Southeast	Manufac-turing
Japan	21	24	–	11
Fed. Rep. of Germany	73	105	3	60
(Switzerland/Austria)	(22/3)	(22/3)	(–)	(8/1)
Canada	32	34	1	18
The Netherlands	23	24	4	11
France	14	18	–	9
Spanish-speaking countries	1	1	–	1

Georgia is in manufacturing, and Georgia ranks second in the Southeast in attracting foreign investment in manufacturing, after North Carolina. The main products of investors in Georgia are metals, automobiles, chemicals, pharmaceuticals, paper, telecommunications, engineering, agriculture, parts, and tools. In the service industry, foreign investors are mainly active in real estate management, consulting, banking, insurance, freight, and trading.

A comparison of the latest statistics on international facilities in Georgia shows an increase in the manufacturing investment from $1.3 billion in 1978 to $2.4 billion in 1982.[3]

As reflected by Table 16.7, the vast majority of investors in North Carolina come from German-speaking countries, with 105 German operations, 22 Swiss operations, and three Austrian operations. Canada ranks behind Germany, followed by the Netherlands, Japan, and France. The Spanish-speaking countries have only one operation in North Carolina. In contrast to Georgia, few firms are headquartered in North Carolina; the overwhelming majority are engaged in manufacturing. The main products here are wood, paper, furniture, veneers, textiles, electronics, electricals, chemicals, trucks, automotive industry, and tobacco.

South Carolina (Table 16.8) supplied a breakdown and listing by country and investment dollars. There are 65 German operations active in South Carolina, plus 28 Swiss and two Austrian operations. Germany, then, is by far the most important investor in South Carolina, followed by the Netherlands with 16 operations, France with 14 operations, Japan with nine and Canada with eight operations. No Spanish-speaking investors were listed. According to the nature of the listing, a comparison of the investment volume by country before 1980 and in 1982 can be made. Before 1980, Germany had $884 million invested in South Carolina, followed by France, with $562.9 million, and Japan with $258.4 million. The Netherlands investment accounted for $186.6 million before 1980. In 1982, the German investment totaled $1.22 billion. Swiss investment was $356 million; Austrian investment, $0.5 million. Again, France was second highest in investment dollars, totaling $593.4 million, followed by the Netherlands, with $232.7 million. Germany is by far the

---

[3] Statistics supplied by the Georgia Department of Industry and Trade, Atlanta, Georgia.

Table 16.8.   State of South Carolina (as of December, 1982)

	Corpora-tions	Opera-tions	Dollar Investment Volume	
			Before 1980	Total in 1982
Japan	8	9	258.4 mil.	421.6 mil.
Fed. Rep. of Germany	38	65	884.0 mil.	1.2 bil.
(Switzerland/Austria)	(25/2)	(28/2)	(180.4/0.5 mil.)	(356/0.5 mil.)
Canada	8	8	59.8 mil.	71.6 mil.
The Netherlands	11	16	186.6 mil.	232.7 mil.
France	10	14	562.9 mil.	593.4 mil.
Spanish-speaking countries			N O L I S T I N G	

Table 16.9.   State of Tennessee (as of January, 1983)

	Corpora-tions	Opera-tions	Headquartered in Southeast	Manufac-turing
Japan	19	19	–	11
Fed. Rep. of Germany	21	25	–	22
(Switzerland/Austria)	(7/1)	(10/1)	–	(7/1)
Canada	31	31	(not listed)	15
The Netherlands	8	8	1	7
France	2	2		1
Spanish-speaking countries			(N O T L I S T E D)	

leader, with 30.5% of the total foreign investment. France is very strong, with 14.8% of total foreign investment in South Carolina, and Japanese investment accounts for 10.5% of the total foreign investment. The major products in South Carolina are textile-related products (e.g., yarn, fibers, bobbins, dyes and chemicals) and textile machinery.

As we can see in Table 16.9, Canada is the leader in Tennessee, with 31 operations, followed by Germany with 25 operations plus 10 Swiss and one Austrian operation, followed by Japan with 19 operations, the Netherlands with 8, France with 2, and according to the listing, no Spanish-speaking foreign operations. It is obvious from the data that Tennessee is viewed as a manufacturing location by foreign investors. In the case of Germany, for instance, 22 out of the 25 operations are manufacturing plants. Of the 19 Japanese operations, 11 are manufacturing; out of the 31 Canadian operations, 15 are in manufacturing; and seven of the eight Dutch operations are involved in manufacturing. Japan's total capital and planned investment come to $800 million. Of this, $13 million was invested after 1978. The main products are wire, sheet metal, fibers, chemicals, textiles, electricals, tools, pharmaceuticals, parts, and devices.

Germany and Japan: The Predominant Investors in the Southeast

As may be seen from the numbers reflected in the directories supplied by the six Southeastern states, the Southeast has undergone a considerable degree of internationalization with regard to its industrial structure. The figures also reflect that the Federal Republic of Germany and Japan have emerged as the predominant and most visible investors in the Sunbelt.

German Investment in the Southeast.   While the overall German investment in the United States amounted to $5.3 billion (Figure 16.6) (German American Chamber of Commerce 1982) in 1980, German investment in the Southeast amounted to $1.8 billion ("Foreign investment is helping turn Atlanta into next great world city," October 17, 1982), i.e., approximately one-third of the overall German investment in the United States is located in the Sunbelt.

A reputable German business magazine states that in the first six months of 1982 alone, an additional $1.4 million German marks were invested in the U. S. (Walbroel 1983). Germany is the leader in foreign investment, before Belgium, Luxembourg, France, and Switzerland. The annual growth rate of investments until 1981 was approximately 24%. The trends discerned in the types of businesses that invest in this country are as follows.

In the early 1970s, the first group of investors comprised mainly chemical groups. The second group of investors were mainly family businesses, banks, and insurance companies. At the present time, the country is experiencing a third group of German investors, medium- and small-sized companies, looking for market niches for foreign products that may be larger than the entire domestic market for these items (Walbroel 1983:31).

While the Southern region of the United States is the most dynamic growth area for German investment capital, Florida is missing out because of an antiquated marketing approach, according to the Consul General of the Federal Republic of Germany in Atlanta ("German investors bypass state," July 1983). According to

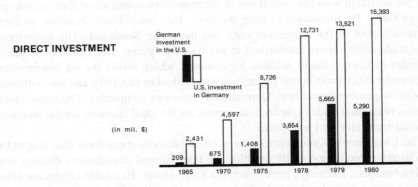

Figure 16.6 Source: U.S. Department of Commerce from the German American Chamber of Commerce, Inc. *Economic Survey,* 1982:220.

his statement, Florida is not sharing this growth in investment because it concentrated too long on just advocating tourism. It is exactly this image that Florida has cultivated in European countries.

Japanese Investment in the Southeast.   The Southeast has been fortunate in its economic relationship with Japan. After California, it is the second fastest growing area for Japanese investment in the United States, according to statistics from the Consulate of Japan for the Southeast. The six Southeastern states host 179 Japanese enterprises, including 46 manufacturing plants employing 10,100 persons ("Japan bullish on Georgia," June 5, 1983).

American Companies Active in the International Marketplace
However, foreign investors are not the only ones that create a market for foreign language skills. Just as important are U. S. companies expanding their market overseas due to the recession in recent years, and the opening of the world market in general. High tech from the United States is welcomed on overseas markets. While large U. S. corporations established themselves overseas decades ago, small- and medium-sized American companies have successfully entered foreign markets in the more recent past.

FOREIGN LANGUAGE NEEDS IN THE INTERNATIONAL BUSINESS COMMUNITY

The Service Industries

Trade Offices and Chambers of Commerce.   In the wake of the influx of foreign investors, trade offices of foreign countries have sprung up. They require bilingual staff to conduct the day-to-day affairs with their home countries. Many times they are affiliated with the consulates of the respective countries or form an integral part of them. By the nature of their business, they are actively involved in every business aspect of the respective state and the entire Southeast. The majority of these trade offices were established in the past five years. The German American Chamber of Commerce in Atlanta, for instance, which serves the six Southeastern states under discussion in this paper, was established in late 1978 and has witnessed a boom in membership of both German and American companies. The membership of these binational trade organizations represents the ideal clientele for the business-oriented translator and interpreter.

The Chambers of Commerce of the six Southeastern states have also adapted to the changing requirements by establishing international departments dealing with foreign business. Language proficiency is a prerequisite. Extensive efforts are being made to attract more foreign industry by means of trade offices located overseas, as mentioned earlier. Trade missions manned by distinguished representatives of the business world are sent overseas to sell the Southeastern states. Comprehensive investment support services are offered to foreign investors, once they have chosen the Sunbelt as the site of their new U. S. operations. These activities have made an abundance of promotional and informational material in foreign languages necessary.

Fairs and Conventions.   Metropolitan areas of the Sunbelt like Atlanta, Charlotte, or Miami are the sites of international fairs, exhibitions, conventions, and international conferences. Fairs like the International Carpet and Rug Market in Atlanta, the Bobbin Show and International Agricultural Show attract an increasing number of international exhibitors and buyers. The hub of the Southeast is the site of numerous international meetings, but only in the past five years have the sponsors and organizers of these events realized that international participation brings with it a need for effective communication, that is, translators and interpreters. The assumption that this aspect has often been overlooked in organizing fairs, conventions, and conferences, is corroborated by the nonavailability of concrete data of international participation from convention sponsors and organizers.

The Hospitality Industry.   Another area of the service industry that is of great importance to the translator and interpreter is the hotel and restaurant business, which has had to adapt to the needs of foreign businessmen and -women. Five years ago, foreign language material in this industry did not exist. In the meantime, hotels and restaurants in the Southeast have come to realize the immense buying power of their international clientele and have responded by providing leaflets, brochures, and menus in several foreign languages. A survey conducted by the Georgia Hospitality and Travel Association shows that in 1982, five out of eight hotels and restaurants in the Atlanta area had foreign language material. In 1983, six out of eight provided such material. While at present only the larger establishments are providing this service, others will have to follow suit in the years to come. Major department stores have reacted as well by providing multilingual personnel to assist shoppers from abroad in meeting their needs.

The Travel Industry.   Another industry catering to foreign businessmen and women and visitors is the travel industry. There is a great need for efficient foreign language tour guides and for good translations of sightseeing brochures. In 1982, three out of 12 sights in the Atlanta area had foreign language material; in 1983, five did. The increase in international ties between the Sunbelt and foreign countries is also reflected by the number of professional visits. The Southeast has become the destination for representatives of foreign governments, unions, newspaper publishers, journalists, foreign professionals, political commissions on fact-finding missions, and parliamentary groups. The majority of the overseas visitors are familiar with the Northeast, Midwest, and the West of the United States and have only recently discovered the South, following the trend of industry.

The Professional Services

Lawyers. Foreign languages have become very important in the legal field as well. Almost any step that a foreign investor takes in establishing a subsidiary in this country requires the involvement of a lawyer, whether it be purchases, sales, contracts, government applications, or joint ventures. All major law firms in Atlanta—the legal center of the South—have in the past three years established international departments and hired lawyers who are either natives of foreign countries with a law degree obtained in the United States, or individuals with law degrees from both countries.

The author's experience is that there is an extreme shortage of translators and interpreters trained in legal translation and interpretation. The increasing presence of overseas companies also results in claims, actions, liability suits—mainly in the area of product liability—and depositions and court work, necessitating thoroughly trained language professionals.

While the Federal Examination for Court Interpreters has been instrumental in establishing a nationwide standard in legal interpretation, this examination is available only in Spanish at this time. Training courses in preparation for this demanding examination would find a ready market in the Sunbelt.

Certified Public Accountants. It is easy to deduce that the immense number of foreign operations in the Sunbelt results in an immense number of tax questions. CPAs with language skills have become a desirable and valuable asset to all major CPA firms in the Sunbelt in the past five years. For the translator and interpreter the field of accounting can be one of the most difficult ones to master. The task of translating annual reports, balance sheets, and profit and loss accounts requires specialized training in both languages and in the accounting systems of both countries. In view of the complex tax matters with which foreign companies are confronted, this field offers great opportunities for competent translators and interpreters.

Banks. Banks, too, are geared toward the needs of the international investors. Respective assignments for the language professional include contracts, credit documents, annual reports, and other documents. Knowledge in the field of banking is compulsory to complete translation and interpretation assignments to the customer's satisfaction.

Realty Companies. Large realty companies, as major law firms and CPA firms, nowadays employ professionals possessing language skills in order to more effectively deal with their overseas clientele or with foreign investors that have relocated to the Sunbelt. As the practices involved in the sale or purchase of real property may vary immensely from those applicable overseas, the language specialist assisting a realtor client must have a thorough knowledge of the cultural and business differences involved.

Typesetting and Printing.   Last, but by no means least, is the typesetting and printing industry that has been confronted with printing and typesetting projects in foreign languages in recent years, necessitating the involvement of experienced translators and the employment of in-house personnel familar with the languages required. In order for a U. S. company to be successful overseas, for instance, it requires company profiles, brochures, sales material, and technical specifications in the foreign language. Numerous American companies enter overseas markets through participation in trade shows in the respective countries. In order to compete successfully, they have to provide potential customers with foreign language PR material and therefore rely on the language professional at home to do printing-quality work. It has been the experience of the author that, unfortunately, the translator often has to function as the typesetter's assistant in order to secure the quality of the translation assignment.

CONCLUSION

There is no doubt, on the basis of the statistics available, that the need for foreign language professionals in the Sunbelt is on the rise. In the past five years foreign investment has increased dramatically. Although experts project that this increase will somewhat level off in future years, *qualified* language professionals, bilingual secretaries, translators, and interpreters will be in strong demand. Specialization in the fields of engineering, law, real estate, and finance will be more necessary than ever to meet the requirements of the clientele comprising private foreign investors, foreign companies, multinationals, U. S. companies, and the professions serving all of these. The material presented shows that vast numbers of German- and Japanese-speaking investors operate in the Southeast. This raises the question whether colleges and universities in the Southeast have adequately responded to the existing situation. What are the reasons for the acute shortage of well-trained and highly specialized translators and interpreters in these languages in the Southeast? Why are even high-level U. S. executives at times unaware of the cultural differences between two countries that threaten to avert a business deal? How can we improve the training of translators and interpreters and at the same time create an awareness of this profession among its potential clientele? Part II of this paper will address the universities' approach to this issue.

REFERENCES

Atlanta Chamber of Commerce, Atlanta, Georgia. 9-1982. Atlanta Facts Book.
Atlanta to Europe flights pass another milestone. June 8, 1983. Atlanta Constitution.
Foreign investment is helping turn Atlanta into next great world city. October 17, 1982. Atlanta Constitution.
Georgia Department of Industry and Trade, Atlanta, Georgia. 1982. Industrial Survey of Georgia. 1982.
German American Chamber of Commerce, Inc. 1982. Economic Survey 1982.

German investors bypass state. July 1983. Jacksonville Seafarer.

Harrold Jr., T., Otto, H-H. 1980. Der amerikanische Suedosten oder Dornroeschen ist erwacht. Unpublished article.

Japan bullish on Georgia. June 5, 1983. Atlanta Constitution.

Kayser, G., Kitterer, B. H., Naujoks, W., Schwarting, U., Ullrich, K. 1980. Erfahrungen deutscher Auslandsinvestoren in ausgewaehlten Industrielaendern. Göttingen: Verlag Otto Schwartz.

Walbroel, Werner. 1983. USA — Entwicklung des deutschen Engagements. Welthandel 3-1983.

Watters, Pat. 1982. Southern growth. Atlanta Magazine, 3.54-58.

Wriston, Walter B. 1980. Investment Guide to the United States. New York: Citibank.

SEVENTEEN

Foreign Language Use in International Trade and Commerce: Trends in the Southeastern United States—Part II: The Universities' Response

Bettina F. Cothran
Georgia State University

THE IMPORTANCE OF FOREIGN LANGUAGES FOR INTERNATIONAL BUSINESS

The figures just discussed show a phenomenal increase of international involvement in the Southeastern United States. Business dealings with our trade partners abroad highlight the increasing role of foreign languages in the business world. English has been the language for international trade, but this may change over the next 20 years. Until now, Americans have relied on the ability of their foreign trade partners to speak English. Traditionally, Europeans and Japanese have had the "advantage" of being forced to learn foreign languages to sell their products on the European markets and worldwide. Knowledge of foreign cultures, lifestyles, and business habits gives them a decisive edge when it comes to marketing their products over-seas. Americans are competing against European products on the domestic and world market. If they are unfamiliar with the language, culture, history, and tech-nical know-how of their trade partners, they cannot effectively compete as peers with other nations. The increasing competitiveness of the world market, and indeed the large trade deficit of the United States, has started a rethinking process on the issue of foreign language skills for the American business executive.

Numerous studies have pointed out the necessity of foreign language skills for the American executive. The *Report of the President's Commission on Foreign Language and International Studies* (Strength Through Wisdom 1979:70) came to the following conclusion:

> We must be able to provide our international business concerns with people who pos-sess the linguistic and cultural skills that enable them to operate effectively abroad. Failure to do so will mean that we will not be able to meet the growing challenge of foreign competition and the need to penetrate foreign markets to sell our goods and services.

Many multinational corporations have instituted their own language programs for their executives. To quote key advice given by Edward T. Hall, an internationally known business consultant, to all those working in a foreign country: "Three things are essential: learn the language, learn the language, learn the language!" (Hall and Hall 1983:87).

The question is then: Where do we learn the foreign language? When do we learn it? And which language do we chose?

RESPONSE OF THE UNIVERSITIES

Past Situation in Foreign Language Departments
In light of the conclusion about the importance of foreign languages for the business executive, it may come as a surprise that many programs at universities training future businessmen have no foreign language graduation requirement, not even all programs entitled "International Business." A nationwide survey conducted in 1983 shows that of International Business Programs on the Bachelor's level, 51% require a foreign language, on the Master's level only 21% do, and on the Doctoral level merely 26% do. The proficiency level reached in the majority of these programs is defined as "limited working," or level 2 on the Foreign Service Institute scale (Bowley 1983:67).[1]

Most students acquire their foreign language skills during their undergraduate studies. The question must therefore be: have foreign language departments provided adequate courses for those students who are interested in practical language skills? Have we responded? Or do we hide in our proverbial ivory towers and behind a secure tenure system which permits us to ignore the postulate of the marketplace? As everywhere in a free economy, clients vote with their feet; in the university, enrollment figures speak a clear language. In departments of languages and literature, declining enrollment has been the order of the day. Whereas beginning classes may be filled with science, music, or psychology majors needing a foreign language for graduation, advanced classes are usually underenrolled. Students can no longer afford to major in subjects which have no practical application. A competitive marketplace within the university gives the "useful" new priority.

University professors, however, are not always so "otherworldly" as their reputation may have it. Sometimes nolens-volens, sometimes with enthusiasm, language departments do respond with innovative courses. Language courses stressing practical application are added to curricula. The most promising of this "new crop" are courses on "commercial language." Other innovative courses include courses

---

[1] I wish to call special attention to the Bowley study, which contains an extensive bibliography. This dissertation came to the author's attention when work on the present paper was already well underway. Dr. Bowley's conclusions and my own reinforce each other in all major points. I would like to express my gratitude to Dr. Bowley who has been extremely kind and generous in providing me with a copy of her dissertation and even extracting figures for me from her survey pertaining to the universities in the Southeast.

for the medical and legal professions, the hotel industry, and the traveler. New certificates provide a tool for universities and the business community to measure language skills in the new areas. Another growing field is that of translation and interpretation. A few colleges are adding courses or even a certificate program in this area.

So universities are responding. There is a new excitement, a fresh wind blowing in the hallowed halls formerly entirely devoted to the study of literature and to literary research. As figures prove, this new trend in course offerings may have saved many foreign language departments from drastic cutbacks. It may also have helped to update the image foreign language departments have generally in the eyes of businessmen who claim that the university does not adquately prepare its students for practical application of their language skills. In the opinion of a majority of business executives, the university is the best place for students to develop such language skills (Bowley 1983:82).

New Courses

We want to look now at the various programs offered at universities in the six Southeastern states. The figures are based on a survey of the foreign language departments of 76 educational institutions, adequately representing the states: Alabama: 11; Florida: 14; Georgia: 12; North Carolina: 17; South Carolina: 11; Tennessee: 11. The questions asked tried to establish the exact nature of the courses, how long they have been in existence, how many students are typically enrolled, and whether the foreign language department cooperates with any other department of the university. Futhermore, queries on the nature of the program, the problem areas, and trends for the future were solicited.

Courses in Commerce and Language

Of the universities surveyed, 57% (or 44 of a total of 76) presently offer courses in the commercial track. Of those, 90% offer just one course with the title "Business Language" or "Commercial Language"; 10% offer two courses. Generally, these are courses on the junior/senior level. Approximately 20% of these universities offer their students a major in the commercial track. Fifty-five percent of these courses have been instituted within the last two to five years; 15% have been in existence for more than five years, and 20% have been added to the curriculum more recently. Ten percent have no commercial course at all. Only 12% of the foreign language departments in question have a working agreement with their business department and/or offer a double major. The most popular languages—and this comes as no surprise—are Spanish, French, and German, listed in descending order of popularity. Spanish is offered by 77%, French by 61%, and German by 48%. Twelve institutions, or 16%, offer commercial courses in all three languages.

When these figures are combined with those of proposed programs in commercial language, the case for this new trend becomes even more convincing. Thirteen institutions have tangible plans to add such courses to their curricula, bringing the total number to 57, or 75% of all universities surveyed. In addition, seven institutions, or almost 10%, have plans for expanding, usually including one of the popular languages not offered heretofore.

In general, one can say that on the undergraduate level, a majority of universities have found it profitable and feasible to include commercial courses as a regular part of their course offerings. Student numbers appear to hold steady at an acceptable level and most courses have been firmly established for several years. For medium-sized universities, the optimal program is a major in commercial language. This includes two courses with a specific "commercial" tag, a course in "contemporary issues," "mass media," "techniques of translation" (using predominantly business texts), a culture course, and sometimes an internship with a local company doing business abroad. Obviously, urban settings and areas with foreign business concentration prove a more successful environment than the small college in the remote countryside.

Programs which offer a combined degree with the business department or a double major are the most successful ones. The program at Auburn University in Alabama entitled "Foreign Language and International Trade" or "FLIT" for short, is one of the "showcase" programs in the Southeast. In only six years it has grown to 80 majors.

The possibility of combining foreign languages with a business program on the Master's level is even more promising, for the following reasons: (a) A Master's in Business aims at preparation on the executive level. This allows the language material to be selected accordingly. (b) The length of the period involved (two years in addition to the four undergraduate years) allows the student to perfect his/her language skills, thus making achievement of the "professional or working proficiency" level a feasible goal. This is defined as level 3 on the scale of the Foreign Service Institute. This skill level has been identified as the most desirable one in an ideal Master's program (Bowley 1983:100). (c) A Master's program often affords the opportunity to complete an internship in the foreign country, thus adding first-hand cultural experience to on-the-job training.

The outstanding program of this kind in the Southeast is the Master's of International Business at the University of South Carolina (or MIBS for short). The degree involves a two-year program for students in French, German, Spanish, and Portuguese. Prior successful completion of the language program is a prerequisite for continuation in the business part. A six-month internship with a multinational corporation abroad equips the student with a language competence of at least working proficiency. Since 1982, Arabic and Japanese have been added as language options. As there are still fewer students in those nontraditional courses, MIBS students attend the established language programs at Cornell for Arabic and Johns Hopkins and Georgetown for Japanese. In addition, they complete one year of study at the universities of Cairo and Keio respectively, before starting their internships. The total enrollment of the MIBS program is expected to level off at approximately 300 students, of which 25% may be foreign students. (Presently, there are approximately 250 students in the program.) Job prospects for graduates from this program have been excellent. Average starting salaries are around the $26,000 mark.

One Master's program presently in the advanced planning stage is the Master's of Science with a major in International Business at Georgia State University in Atlanta. As an urban university in a large metropolitan area, Georgia State has always placed top priority on programs responding to the needs of the business community. Realizing the job potential in an area heavily sought after by international investors, this new program also aims at the utilization of all resources within the university. The Foreign Language Department has had language courses with a business component for about 10 years and offers the option of a major in commercial language for Spanish, French, and German. Under the new Master's program, successful completion of a commercial language course on the junior level is a prerequisite for graduation.

Courses in Translation and Interpretation

For international business executives who did not profit from this new and enlightened direction in higher education, a translator or interpreter becomes the means to solving the communication problem. This is not to say, of course, that foreign language competence obviates in all cases the need for such a mediating professional. Few executives, if they have only conversational command of the language, would jeopardize the outcome of their negotiations by not availing themselves of the expertise of a professional translator/interpreter.

In response to a growing need for such professionals in the Southeast, several universities have added courses in translation and/or interpretation. This study only comprises those educational institutions which went beyond the traditional "techniques of translation" course. Such a course, however useful, only introduces students to the basics of linguistic structure of the language at hand and illustrates the difference between the grammatical and semantic structure of source and target language.

On the undergraduate level, Florida International University offers a minor in General Translation Studies for Spanish only. Due to the large number of Spanish-speaking people, enough students with fluency in Spanish are available. A two-year program offers two courses each in translation and interpretation. In addition, students are required to take three courses of immediate relevance from other departments, like political science, economics, international relations, sociology, anthropology or computer science. Students are prepared for the Federal Courts Examination in Spanish, given in major cities all over the United States. The program has been in existence for three years and is quite successful.

Another program at the undergraduate level existing for three years is the "Certificate Program in Translation" at the University of North Carolina at Charlotte. Courses are offered in all three major foreign languages. However, as students are predominantly Americans, only translation into English is stressed. In the fall quarter all students are grouped together for the theoretical introductory course, where topics like nonverbal communication, the development of the language, translation theory and history, English stylistics, and professional aspects are discussed (For a detailed discussion on the program at the University of North Carolina at Charlotte, see Parks 1982.). Students are encouraged to take courses in other departments as well and to develop a speciality. Residency abroad is also strongly recommended.

The most extensive program in translation and interpretation in the Southeast is the Certificate Program at Georgia State University in Atlanta. A two-year program in French, German, Spanish, and Italian leads to a certificate in translation and/or interpretation. Students are selected on the basis of their language proficiency and academic qualifications. Many students are foreign nationals living in the United States. The strongest languages are French and Spanish, with enrollment for translation being appreciatively higher than enrollment for interpretation. Of 49 certificate recipients, 33 were certified in tranlation, seven in interpretation, and nine in both fields. The certificate is awarded after successful completion of an exit exam. Most of the students who are graduated from this program also take professional examinations offered by other associations, such as the American Translators Association, or the Federal Court Interpreters examination, with excellent success.

Other Innovative Courses

The universities' willingness to respond to the language needs of the community has been proven further by the implementation of other courses. The presence of Spanish-speaking people has resulted in numerous courses specifically geared to professionals coming into contact with this language group. Five foreign language departments are presently offering courses like "Intensive Spanish for Health Professionals" or "Medical Spanish"; these courses are often requirements for majors in other disciplines. Six universities have plans to add courses combining Spanish with education, social sciences, or law. Courses combining Spanish with other disciplines are not confined to Florida—as one may think—but also exist in North Carolina, Georgia, Alabama, and Tennessee. One of the novel approaches is the development of textbooks which utilize specialized vocabulary from the very beginning. Business students will find it more interesting to learn about dative and accusative cases within the context of commercial vocabulary than with the traditional "tourist" setting. Also, their extensive knowledge of the subject matter will probably increase their overall progress (For a discussion of a program using business vocabulary and specialized teaching methods geared to the business student see Armaleo-Popper 1982:46-52). Special textbooks and specialized teaching methods have been successfully used. Textbooks for beginning language courses using business vocabulary exist so far only in Spanish; however, they are being developed for other languages as well.

Certificates

Testing is an essential part of each teaching program. In the case of standardized tests, this does not only provide a check for the student and the instructor to see if the material has indeed been absorbed, but it also defines a goal and sets a target helpful in determining teaching materials and methods.[2]

The examinations given by the Chambers of Commerce of Paris and Madrid in the area of language and commerce are not tied to any particular university and indeed are applicable to anyone qualified. Those exams are successfully used at universities in this country to establish competency of their graduates in International Business Programs or other programs combining Spanish or French with business. For German, the development of an "Advanced Diploma in Business German" is almost complete. The Diploma represents a combined effort of a standing committee of American university professors, and from the German side, the Goethe Institute, the Carl-Duisberg Society, and the German American Chamber of Commerce. By virtue of this "binational" input, the validity of the Diploma in the United States and Europe has been assured.

In the area of translation and interpretation, a variety of accreditations from outside agencies and associations supplement the accreditations awarded by the universities. On the national level, the best-known accreditation for translators is the one by the American Translators Association, given annually in the larger cities in several language combinations.

Interpreters can be accredited by the Department of State in Washington as escort, seminar, or conference interpreters. An examination given by the Federal Courts accredits court interpreters for Spanish only. Professional associations on the national or regional level often provide accreditations or ratings also.

Problems and Issues
Changes in the traditional curriculum place new challenges on the faculty. New courses often demand reevaluation of teaching methods and materials as well as possible retraining of staff.

Three problem areas can be identified:

1. Reluctance of foreign language departments to accept the new courses
2. Lack of competent staff
3. Unwillingness between departments to cooperate

"Provincial thinking" is a frequent complaint. Reorientation of departments is necessarily a slow process, given the existing tenure system. The problem appears to be twofold. First, tenured faculty educated in the literary field find themselves not only ill-prepared but somewhat unwilling to take on courses which in their eyes may be more of a "vocational" nature. These are probably the same professors deciding on tenure and promotion, thus being in a position to "penalize" faculty interested in

---

[2] Michael Roeder, director of the language division in the Goethe Institute, Atlanta, made the statement in an interview that the Diploma of Business German currently being developed will serve as a guide in this way for future courses taught by the Goethe Institute.

this direction. Conversely, faculty members able and willing to teach language courses with a practical application are reluctant to pursue a direction where their efforts are not rewarded.

Qualified staff is an even greater problem in the area of translation and interpretation. Whereas business vocabulary and knowledge about the commercial structure of a foreign country can be acquired relatively quickly, most professors cannot become experienced translators or interpreters overnight. For such programs, the hiring of specialists seems a necessity. It is therefore not surprising that only a few universities have branched out in this direction.

One of the most difficult hurdles to overcome is the unwillingness of departments to cooperate on an interdisciplinary level. Business departments especially, glutted with students as it is, show little inclination to listen to proposals from their colleagues in foreign languages.

One very important issue deserving our attention is the choice of foreign languages. Several studies have addressed the issue of ranking the foreign languages. Studies on the national level identify the following as most useful for business: Spanish, French, German, Portuguese, Italian, Japanese (Arnett 1975 quoted in Bowley 1983:42). On the regional level, the order varies. A 1975 study of South Carolina firms reveals the most frequently used languages as German, French, and Spanish. At the same time, the greatest current unmet needs are identified as German, Spanish, Japanese, and Portuguese (Morgenroth, Parks, and Morgenroth 1975).

Japanese is the most interesting case. Our economic survey revealed Japan as one of our major trade partners. Japanese, however, is currently ranked fourth, fifth and seventh as the accepted foreign language for international business programs on the Bachelor's, Master's and Doctoral levels respectively (Bowley 1983:74). In ranking foreign languages on an ideal Master's program scale, educators put Spanish first, French second, and Japanese third.

We can only hope that this shift in perception, reflecting the economic situation, will cause the addition of more Japanese courses to undergraduate curricula. As our survey has revealed, no foreign language department in the Southeast presently offers a course in "Japanese for Business." The single program in international business in our region having the option of Japanese is the MIBS at the University of South Carolina. The only other department planning to add "Japanese for Business" as an undergraduate course in the foreign language department is North Carolina State University at Raleigh.

Why is Japanese so underrepresented? Interviews with the public relations officer at the Japanese Consulate General in Atlanta, with Japanese professors at universities in the Southeast, and with free-lance translators/interpreters corroborate the commonly held view that Japanese is a language so difficult to learn for Westerners that few people put forth the effort.

However, in light of the expanding trade with Japan, this attitude must be reevaluated. For Americans to effectively counter Japanese competition worldwide, Japanese must figure more prominently among the foreign languages taught in our educational institutions, and Japanese must be mastered by our business executives.

TRENDS FOR THE FUTURE

The Universities' Side
The developments over the last five years show a definite change within the university. The survey of foreign language departments in the Southeast proves that the vast majority have added courses with practical language application. The new courses are very successful and contribute to rising enrollment numbers in foreign language courses. Course contents and teaching methods are more specialized and are tailored to professional needs in an increasingly international community. Courses emphasizing the commercial aspect are the most successful ones. Other novel courses address the medical and legal sector, the hotel industry, and the traveler. Translation and interpretation courses train specialists for a profession in growing demand in an increasingly international region.

Cooperation between departments is seen as a key in the new trend. As foreign languages pervade so many areas of "real life," universities have realized that the answer must be integration of foreign languages with other disciplines. Since these programs must be funded, grants given by federal and local agencies reflect a phenomenal growth of interdisciplinary programs. The Fund for the Improvement of Postsecondary Education in the U. S. Department of Education, for instance, received 125 proposals for the year 1981, chiefly concerned "with an infusion of international perspectives into curricula, . . . and instruction in foreign language" (Groennings 1983:48).

The Business Executive's Side
Foreign language skills are essential for the American business executive of today. A foreign language is not just a tool for conducting business negotiations more effectively. Understanding of the foreign culture, the differences of lifestyles, and attitudes of other nations are most important. You are ruining your chances when in meeting your German trade partner, you greet him with your biggest smile and the friendly introduction: "My name is Fred; what's yours?" Even if you can say that sentence in German, you are missing the fact that a German just isn't on a first name basis with his business partner. At this point, you can only hope for the German's understanding of the American way of life.

In learning another language, we become aware of the differences between nations and we learn to see things from their point of view. As is pointed out in the President's Report, we need the linguistic *and* cultural skills to operate effectively in international trade. And besides this, a foreign language gives us the means to reach out on a personal level and make a friend. Language skills should be acquired as early as possible. Foreign language departments at the universities provide the programs which stress practical language application.

It may have taken Americans a long time to emerge from their isolationist view; but whoever laughs last, laughs best. I predict a great future for the bilingual and trilingual American.

250   BRIDGING THE LANGUAGE GAP

REFERENCES

Armaleo-Popper, Lore. 1982. Der Einstieg ins Deutsche über Fachsprachen: Business German. Die
    Unterrichtspraxis 15.46–52.
Arnett, M. R. 1975. Languages for the world of work: Executive summary. Lake City, Utah: Olympus
    Research Corporation.
Bowley, Barbara A. 1983. Foreign language policies and practices of international business programs in
    U. S. higher education. Doctoral dissertation, Miami University.
Groennings, Sven. 1983. Beachheads in international education. Educational Record, 48–52.
Hall, Edward T., & Hall, Mildred Reed. 1983. Hidden differences. Studies in international communica-
    tion. Hamburg, W. Germany: Stern Verlag.
Morgenroth, R. L., Parks, L. H., & Morgenroth, W. M. 1975. Progress report on the South Carolina
    market for foreign languages study. Eric Document Reproduction Service No. Ed. 119471.
Parks, William. 1982. Translation at UNCC: A viable career option. Die Unterrichtspraxis. 15.53-59.
Strength through wisdom: A critique of U. S. capability—A report to the president from the president's
    commission on foreign languages and international studies. 1979. Washington, D. C.: U. S.
    Government Printing Office.

UNIVERSITIES SURVEYED

Alabama
Alabama State University, Montgomery
Auburn University, Auburn*
Birmingham Southern University, Birmingham
Jacksonville State University, Jacksonville*
Samford University, Birmingham
Troy State University, Troy
University of Alabama, Birmingham*
University of Alabama, Huntsville
University of Alabama, University*
University of Montevallo
University of Southern Alabama, Mobile

Florida
Eckerd College, St. Petersburg
Flagler College, St. Augustine
Florida Atlantic University, Boca Raton
Florida International University, Miami
Florida Southern College, Lakeland
Florida State University, Tallahassee*
Jacksonville University, Jacksonville
Stetson University, De Land
University of Central Florida, Orlando*

---

* The asterisk indicates universities with enrollment above 5000.

University of Florida, Gainesville
University of Miami, Coral Gables*
University of South Florida, Tampa*
University of Tampa
University of West Florida

Georgia
Armstrong State College, Savannah
Brenau College, Gainesville
Columbus College, Columbus
Emory University, Atlanta
Georgia Institute of Technology, Atlanta*
Georgia Southern College, Statesboro*
Georgia State University, Atlanta*
Kennesaw Junior College, Marietta
North Georgia College, Dahlonega
University of Georgia, Athens*
Valdosta State College, Valdosta
West Georgia College, Carrollton

North Carolina
Duke University, Durham*
East Carolina University, Greenville*
Guilford College, Greensboro
High Point College, High Point
Johnson C. Smith University, Charlotte
North Carolina Agricultural & Technical State University, Greensboro*
North Carolina Central University, Durham
North Carolina State University, Raleigh*
Queens College, Charlotte
Salem College, Winston Salem
University of North Carolina, Asheville
University of North Carolina, Chapel Hill*
University of North Carolina, Charlotte*
University of North Carolina, Greensboro*
University of North Carolina, Wilmington
Wake Forest, Winston Salem
Western Carolina University, Cullowhee

South Carolina
Citadel, Charleston
Clemson, Clemson*
College of Charleston, Charleston
Columbia College, Columbia

South Carolina (*continued*)

Converse College, Spartanburg
Furman University, Greenville
Presbyterian College, Clinton
South Carolina State College, Orangeburg
University of South Carolina, Columbia*
Winthrop College, Rock Hill
Wofford College, Spartanburg

Tennessee

Austin Peay State University, Clarksville
Christian Brothers College, Memphis
East Tennessee State University, Johnson City*
Memphis State University, Memphis*
Middle Tennessee State University, Murfreesboro
Tennessee State University, Nashville
Tennessee Technical University, Cookeville
University of Tennessee, Chattanooga
University of Tennessee, Knoxville*
University of Tennessee, Martin
Vanderbilt University, Nashville*

PART VI

LANGUAGE PLANNING IN EDUCATION

EIGHTEEN

Guerrero: A Pilot Study for the Decision-Making Process on Language Policy in Mexico

Georganne Weller
Centro de Investigación para la Integración Social
Mexico City

INTRODUCTION

Setting

To situate oneself in the Montaña de Guerrero is not an easy task for most Mexicans, and much less so for foreigners. Figure 18.1 which shows the geographical distribution of the Mexican States, with the Montaña de Guerrero darkened in, serves as an aid in understanding the physical placement of the area under study; however, geographical considerations represent only one small aspect of the many social, psychological, political, and economic factors which come into play when studying language policy decisions in a predominantly Indian area. Figure 18.2, which represents the distribution of the many different language groups present in Mexico, gives us a better idea of the linguistic surroundings of the Indian tongues (Nahuatl, Tlapanec, and Mixtec) of the Montaña, as well as of Mexico's rich plurilingual and pluricultural heritage. Lastly, Figure 18.3 is a close-up of the municipalities which conform the Montaña and an indication of which ethnic groups inhabit these geographic areas.

It is important at this initial point of the paper to mention that the Montaña constitutes one of the most backward zones in the Mexican Republic with respect to per capita income, schooling, health, life expectancy, and other socioeconomic indicators. Politically the State of Guerrero and its State University have been characterized as being extremely leftist, with irregular but constant strikes, rioting, and guerrilla activities.

In the next two sections of the Introduction several of the most outstanding and pertinent policies of the past two political regimes regarding language policy on a national level will be described. Hopefully these overall policies will shed light on why certain research projects were carried out in the Montaña de Guerrero on a pilot basis.

255

Figure 18.1

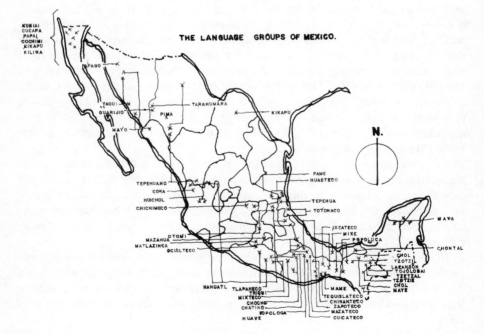

Figure 18.2

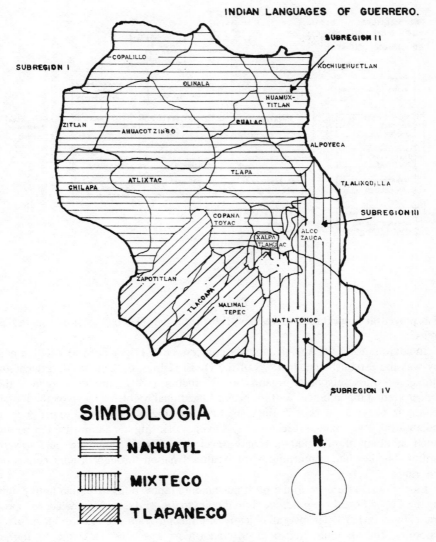

Figure 18.3

The José López Portillo Administration (1976–1982)

Aware of the disadvantaged situation of the Montaña de Guerrero, ex-President López Portillo decided to include this region in the program known as COPLAMAR (Coordinación General del Plan Nacional de Zonas Deprimidas y Grupos Marginados), established in 1977 to oversee the policies of the various agencies that worked directly or indirectly with marginal populations, such as the INI (Instituto Nacional Indigenista), el Patrimonio Indígena del Valle del Mezquital, Productores Forestales de la Tarahumara, Fideicomiso de la Palma, and others. COPLAMAR

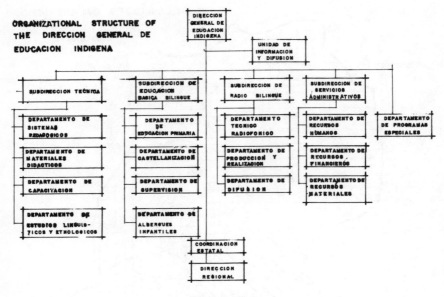

Figure 18.4

also played an important role in the "Educación para Todos" program in Indian areas.

In addition to COPLAMAR, another cornerstone of López Portillo's Indian policy was the establishment in 1978 of the DGEI (Dirección General de Educación Indígena), whose elaborate organizational structure (see Figure 18.4) reflects the concern felt at that moment for the special educational problems faced by the Indian groups in Mexico. A very distinguished anthropologist with broad experience in Indian affairs was named director of this agency. During his administration he did much in favor of bilingual materials development in 22 languages and toward turning Mexico into a plurilingual-pluricultural nation through official education programs.

Lastly, with reference to the most outstanding innovations of Indian policy during the López Portillo regime, we should point to the "Educación para Todos" program begun in 1978. The overall objectives of this program were to provide primary schooling for all children, to teach Spanish as a second language to Indian preschoolers without detriment to their Indian tongues, and to support literacy and basic education for illiterate adults.

As can be seen from this brief description, and as will be seen in the following section in greater detail, the López Portillo administration was instrumental in providing a more solid institutional framework for social development and educational programs in the Montaña de Guerrero and Mexico in general.

The Miguel de la Madrid Hurtado Administration (1982–1988)

What has happened during the first 10 months of the new political regime with respect to Indian matters in general and to the Montaña de Guerrero in particular?

First of all, on December 20, 1982, a presidential decree eliminated COPLAMAR, claiming that it was an organization whose functions overlapped not only those of certain government agencies but those of the Ministries of State as well (Politi and Godau 1982b:30).

The DGEI, following the same general lines as before, is now headed by a trilingual and academically prepared leader of Indian descent. The previous director was appointed director of the INI, thus allowing for an unusually high degree of continuity in Indian programs, particularly with respect to the new bilingual-bicultural programs in the first grade of primary school.

Another interesting development to follow is the growing importance of Indian associations in support of their own cause. The two most prominent examples are the CNPI (Consejo Nacional de Pueblos Indígenas) and ANPIBAC (Alianza Nacional de Profesionales Indígenas Bilingües, A. C.). In September, 1983 the Mexican chapter of CLALI (Consejo Latinoamericano en Apoyo de las Luchas Indígenas) was born. This organization is open to both Indians and non-Indians interested in active support of Indian concerns in Latin America.

Lastly, in December of 1982, President de la Madrid—only a few days after taking office—announced the decentralization of public education programs in Mexico in an attempt to more justly distribute funds and the decision-making process. It is hoped that this policy will be beneficial to Indian areas such as the Montaña de Guerrero which has very specific regional problems due to the varied ethnic make-up of its communities.

INTEGRAL DEVELOPMENT PLAN FOR THE MONTAÑA DE GUERRERO

This plan was designed as one of the components of the COPLAMAR program in 1978 and was aimed at fostering a better balanced system of integration in some of the most critical zones of the country, among which the Montaña de Guerrero stands out. Due to its integrative nature, this plan covered the agricultural, commercial, and industrial sectors, as well as the establishment of health and educational services.

The sector of greatest interest to us in this paper is public education, for which a more specific plan was drawn up. Known as the Programa de Desarrollo Educativo de la Montaña, it was officially inaugurated in April of 1978. The Programa was charged with the responsibility of implementing a new modus vivendi for education in the rural areas of Mexico (Sub-Delegación General de la Montaña de Guerrero 1978). Among the specific goals of the plan are the following:

1. To create a sufficient supply of educators to be able to cover 100% of the demand at the preschool level in the 20 municipalities that make up the Montaña de Guerrero.
2. To reduce the index of monolingualism by 50% at the end of the sexennium.
3. To lower the index of illiteracy by 50% at the end of the sexennium (Secretaría de Educación Pública 1979:11).

In order to achieve these goals four specific projects were formulated (SEP, DGEI, INI, CONAFE 1980:40), among which the Proyecto Prescolar de Castellanización was entrusted to my research institution (Centro de Investigación para la Integración Social). The main objective was for all the Indian communities with monolingual or bilingual populations to have teachers who would teach Spanish as a second language at a preschool level living in the communities to remedy the fact that to date there were some 80,886 non-Spanish-speakers in the area, of which approximately 9,640 were preschoolers. During the 1977–78 school year only 2,943 preschoolers were provided with this service, leaving 7000 unattended (Sub-Delegación General de la Montaña de Guerrero 1978).

In an effort to change the existing situation a program of specific measures was drawn up to attack these problems on three different levels: first, at the level of supervisors, who would receive special training courses to oversee the work of the promoters who, in turn, would do the actual teaching of Spanish to the Indian preschoolers, who constituted the third level of the pyramid as the immediate beneficiaries of the program.

The Centro de Investigación para la Integración Social has collaborated over the years at all three levels, be it through the design and development of the teaching materials, through specialized training seminars for the supervisors and promoters, through the planning and supervision of the whole teaching-learning process, and—during the past four years—in the evaluation of the overall program, for which it was necessary to carry out extensive fieldwork to apply proficiency tests and socioanthropological questionnaires as part of the evaluative procedures.

This paper contemplates three phases of the evaluative aspects of the educational program in the Montaña de Guerrero, precisely those related to the following projects: (a) the Selection Process of the Bilingual Bicultural Promoters (1978); (b) the Placement Test for Indian Preschoolers (1979); and (c) the Achievement-Proficiency Test for Indian Second Graders. In the next section these specific projects are outlined and, subsequently, the main results are discussed.

AN OUTLINE OF THREE PILOT EVALUATIVE RESEARCH PROJECTS IN THE MONTAÑA

In the previous section we mentioned that three specific lines of research constitute the major contribution of the Centro de Investigación para la Integración Social within the educational sector plan for development in the Montaña de Guerrero. In the following paragraphs these studies will be outlined with a brief description of the main objectives of each study, the type of instrument employed, the time span, and so on. Major results are reported in a later section of this paper.

Battery of Tests for the Selection of the Promoters

This battery of tests was administered in Chilapa, Guerrero in November, 1978, to 441 candidates; it was aimed at selecting in the most objective way possible the best people for teaching Spanish to Indian preschoolers. To this end we designed a battery of tests that included four separate parts: a socioanthropological questionnaire

with some 200 questions on the community the candidate was from, his school record, linguistic and cultural attitudes, ethnicity and other sociodemographic characteristics; a written test in Spanish to cover grammar and reading comprehension; an
oral test in Spanish and the native language consisting of the description of a market
scene; and the Raven psychological test to see how they would react to an exercise
designed to measure their powers of abstraction, originally formulated for a Western urban society.

Placement Test for Indian Preschoolers

This test was given in September 1979 to some 2,241 children of Nahuatl,
Tlapanec, and Mixtec orign by the bilingual promoters selected by the battery of
tests described above. The main purpose of applying this test was to determine if the
Indian children had any knowledge at all of Spanish before formal schooling and, if
so, how much. It also allowed them to be placed in a beginners or more advanced
preschool class. This test was composed of four sections: comprehension in Spanish, repetition in Spanish, vocabulary in Spanish and the Indian tongue, and production in Spanish. This test is very colorful and sturdy. It comes enclosed in a wooden
box with a long shoulder strap for easy carrying during the long journeys into the
mountains where the villages are found. It includes, among other stimuli, a collapsi-
ble horse with put-ons such as a sarape, fruit, and so on.

Achievement-Proficiency Test for Second Graders

In February 1982, this test was given to 332 Indian children of the 2,241 who originally took the placement test, as well as to 38 monolinguals in Spanish from the
major towns of Olinalá, Chilapa, Tlapa, and Zapotitlán Tablas who served as a control group for the command of Spanish typical of this particular age group in the
Montaña. The test consisted of 65 items that included questions, sentence comple-
tions, and multiple choice in a notebook with colorful illustrations. This exercise
was complemented by a picture of a rural school patio which they were asked to
describe in their own words.

This test had originally been conceived as an achievement test to be given at the
end of the year of preschool Spanish, but, due to a series of political and administrative problems, it was not possible to apply the expanded version to include
proficiency until the children were in second grade, which meant that they had been
exposed to a year of preschool Spanish and approximately a year and a half of Spanish in rural public schools where the language of instruction is the official one.

In the next section we will report on the major findings of these three series of
tests.

MAIN RESULTS OF THESE INVESTIGATIONS

In this section we will outline some of the most noteworthy results stemming from
these three research projects. With the limited scope of this paper and the broad
nature of the work, it will be necessary for the reader who wishes to have first-hand
information to consult the original documents.

Battery of Tests for the Selection of the Promoters

Of the 441 candidates from the three ethnic groups, 190 were selected as teachers based on their performance on this battery of tests. Of particular interest to us at a research level were the results of the linguistic sections and the socioanthropological questionnaire. Figure 18.5 (Godau and Politi 1981:72) illustrates the point system for the language sections, which were the only ones graded as such. The Raven Test was used as a screening process, and the questionnaire was used to determine social variables that have their impact on the level of proficiency of the candidates in Spanish.

Figure 18.5. Point System For Language Sections

Diagnóstico lingüístico (100)	Parte escrita (100)	– Estructura gramatical del español (80)	
		– Comprensión de lecturas (20)	– primer cuento (10) – segundo cuento (10)
	Parte oral (90)	– Componente fonológico (30)	– fonología (10) – inteligibilidad (10) – ritmo (10)
		– Componente morfo-sintáctico (30)	– concordancia (10) – orden sintáctico (10) – subordinación (10)
		– Componente cognitivo/semántico (30)	– elaboración (10) – léxico (10) – comprensión (10)

Lucia Politi and Rainer Godau. "Realidad social y panorama lingüístico de la Montaña de Guerrero." Mexico City: CIIS, 1982 (manuscript), p. 72.

Written Language Test. The average obtained by the subjects under study was 74 points. The average of the 25 lowest grades fluctuated between 25 and 62 points, while the 25 highest grades fluctuated between 86 and 99 points. Some 90% of those who took the test answered more than half of the questions correctly, which leads us to the conclusion that this part of the language test was not difficult for them (Godau and Politi 1981:31).

An in-depth analysis revealed that the candidates managed the grammatical part better than the reading comprehension section. When looking at the overall averages (see Figure 18.6) we see that the Nahuatls had the highest average, followed by the Tlapanecs, and the Mixtecs in last place (Godau and Politi 1981:35).

Oral Language Test. In this section of the language diagnosis the candidates obtained an average of 61.3 points out of 90, or 68.1 out of 100. Compared to the written section, this average is somewhat lower. The grades of the lowest 25% wavered between 7 and 52 points, and the highest 25% between 70 and 89 points, showing more dispersion than on the written part and apparently indicating a more difficult task (Godau and Politi 1981:36–37).

Figure 18.6. Means of the Written Language Test

PRUEBA LINGUISTICA ESCRITA
$\bar{X} = 74.039$
S.D. = 16.085
N = 438

GRUPO X	GRUPO Y	GRUPO Z
$\bar{X} = 81.099$	$\bar{X} = 68.337$	$\bar{X} = 71.876$
S.D. = 12.322	S.D. = 16.737	S.D. = 16.150
N = 171	N = 178	N = 89

F = 32.5724   P. < .01   Eta^2 = .1303
Grupo X = Nahuatls
Grupo Y = Mixtecs
Grupo Z = Tlapanecs
Source: Godau and Politi 1981:35.

Figure 18.7. Means of the Oral Language Test

PRUEBA LINGUISTICA ORAL
$\bar{X} = 61.290$
S.D. = 13.454
N = 438

GRUPO X	GRUPO Y	GRUPO Z
$\bar{X} = 63.509$	$\bar{X} = 57.567$	$\bar{X} = 64.472$
S.D. = 12.920	S.D. = 14.357	S.D. = 10.679
N = 171	N = 178	N = 89

F = 12.2249   P. < .01   Eta^2 = .0532
Grupo X = Nahuatls
Grupo Y = Mixtecs
Grupo Z = Tlapanecs
Source: Godau and Politi 1981:39.

In Figure 18.7 we have the overall results of the oral language section by native tongue (Godau and Politi 1981:39). In this particular case the Tlapanecs proved to be more proficient than the other two groups, although the difference with the Na-huatls was slight. It is obvious that these results are important since it is through the oral expression of the teacher that the Indian children are exposed to Spanish more than through any other medium or personal contact.

Socioanthropological Questionnaire. The analysis of this questionnaire led to the development of a causal model to explain the relationships that exist between language proficiency in Spanish and certain socioeconomic variables. To fully understand this model it is necessary to read Chapter III of Godau and Politi (1981). Very briefly, they found that the variables that had the greatest effect on language proficiency in this study at an individual level were experience at skilled labor, schooling, and an appreciation of under what circumstances the native language can be used. At the family level, family expectations were the most important variable, and at the level of the community, how modern the town was seemed to have the most impact (Godau and Politi 1981:62).

Placement Test for Indian Preschoolers

In the four sections of this test the main results were the following.

In the comprehension section our data indicate that the mean attained by the children was 2.85 points of 5 possible points. Table 18.1 indicates the results on the comprehension section according to ethnic group. The Nahuatl group was superior in this exercise (Politi and Godau 1982:28).

With respect to the repetition exercise, the group average was 3.06 out of 5, a slight improvement over the comprehension exercise. If we examine Table 18.2, we can see that once again the Nahuatl children came out on top (Politi and Godau 1982:31).

The vocabulary section, which was administered by showing pictures of objects from their environment, was carried out both in Spanish and in the Indian tongue. In addition to being interested in whether or not they could name the objects in Spanish, we also wanted to know if they were familiar with the object and could name it in their mother tongue. The mean of the group as a whole in the mother tongue was 9.74 as compared to 9.35 in Spanish (Politi and Godau 1982:37). It is not surprising that they have a better command of their native tongue in general; what is very interesting is that the Nahuatl group showed inverse results and this finding is lost if we only look at group averages. This and other findings will be discussed at the end of the paper. The specifics can be found in Table 18.3.

In the last section—production—the mean for the group was 10.36 only out of a possible 25 points. Table 18.4 shows the differences that exist between the different ethnic groups on this section (Politi and Godau 1982:42).

Lastly, if we look at the overall results in Table 18.5, we can see that the average number of points obtained out of 50 was 25.52, with the Nahuatl group in first place, the Tlapanecs in second, and the Mixtecs in third (Politi and Godau 1982:44).

Table 18.1. Results in Comprehension by Ethnic Group

Ethnic Group	Number	X̄	Stand. Dev.
Group as a whole	2237	2.85	1.98
Nahuatls	1034	3.34	1.87
Tlapanecs	618	2.49	1.98
Mixtecs	585	2.34	1.96

Source: Politi and Godau 1982:28.

Table 18.2. Results in Repetition by Ethnic Group

Ethnic Group	Number	$\bar{X}$	Stand. Dev.
Group as a whole	2237	10.36	7.36
Nahuatls	1034	12.39	7.23
Tlapanecs	618	8.77	7.19
Mixtecs	585	8.45	7.19

Source: Politi and Godau 1982:31.

Table 18.3. Results in Vocabulary by Ethnic Group

Ethnic Group	Number	Mother Tongue		Spanish	
		$\bar{X}$	Stand. Dev.	$\bar{X}$	Stand. Dev.
Group as a whole	2237	9.74	5.38	9.35	4.24
Nahuatls	1034	8.54	5.54	10.28	4.12
Tlapanecs	618	10.60	5.03	8.73	4.01
Mixtecs	585	10.97	5.00	7.99	4.27

Source: Politi and Godau 1982:37.

Table 18.4. Results in Production by Ethnic Group

Ethnic Group	Number	$\bar{X}$	Stand. Dev.
Group as a whole	2237	10.36	7.36
Nahuatls	1034	12.39	7.23
Tlapanecs	618	8.77	7.19
Mixtecs	585	8.45	7.19

Source: Politi and Godau 1982:42.

Table 18.5. Overall Results by Ethnic Group

Ethnic Group	Number	$\bar{X}$	Stand. Dev.
Group as a whole	2237	25.52	12.48
Nahuatls	1034	29.16	12.06
Tlapanecs	618	23.10	11.77
Mixtecs	585	21.59	12.13

Source: Politi and Godau 1982:44.

Achievement-Proficiency Test for Second Graders

Due to budget restrictions, only 52 of the 332 tests could be graded. All 38 of the control group have been evaluated. As was explained in the previous section, it was not possible to administer the original achievement test at the proper time, so open-ended questions and the description of a picture were added to measure proficiency. It should be mentioned that in spite of the fact that all the children should have been in second grade, it turned out that this was the case of only half of our sample. Numerous children had failed a grade, had dropped out of school for various reasons, or simply were not to be found in their community. To be able to have enough children for valid results once the sample was selected, we had to resort to including the next largest grouping after those who were "clean" in second grade—those who for diverse reasons had been kept back a grade but who had been in school and exposed to Spanish as a language of instruction for two years.

Achievement Test.   The average points attained on this section was 152.45 out of a possible total of 328. The average of the children in second grade was slightly better than that of those in first grade (157.56 versus 147.35). Even though the control group did not take the year of preschool Spanish since they are native speakers of the language, we applied the test to them also since it was bound in the same notebook. Their average was 237.07 out of 328 (Finegold, López Chávez, and Weller 1983:60). Many of the questions they "missed" were not necessarily mistakes; as a matter of fact, they often had more natural answers than those sought, but due to the fact that this section was graded according to the structures and mechanisms taught (audiolingual method), the native speakers often lost points. This particular case points to the dangers of using discrete-point systems when seeking to determine language proficiency.

Proficiency Test.   The same general tendency we saw for the achievement test was true also for the proficiency test. The overall average for the group under study was 144.65 points out of a total of 260 points for the notebook. Once again, the second graders did better than the first graders (155.23 versus 134.08), while the control group attained an average of 198.51 on the notebook section. With regard to the picture, which was graded for grammar and lexical readiness, the following averages were in order: 5.48 for the bilingual group, with the second graders superior to the first graders (5.87 versus 5.25), but inferior to the control group (8.34) out of a perfect score of 10 for the grammatical score. Lexical readiness, which was graded according to a complicated statistical system (Finegold, López Chávez, and Weller 1983:63), is an index and not a grade; however, the same pattern holds as we can glean from the following data: 1.620 was the bilingual group's average index, with the second graders attaining an index of 1.656 and the first graders an average of 1.602. Once again, the control group showed its lexical superiority by reaching an index of 2.538 (Finegold, López Chávez, and Weller 1983:86).

Further data are available on the achievement and proficiency tests in Table 18.6. In addition to these data on relative levels, it is of special interest to applied and sociolinguists to note the regional differences that exist as well. In Table 18.7 we can observe the means for both tests for the bilingual and control groups on a regional basis. For the bilingual group the means include all the children sampled and graded (52) regardless of grade level who, in turn, have been grouped geographically according to the closest main town where the monolingual Spanish speakers were sampled (Finegold, López Chávez, and Weller 1983:86). More will be said about the interpretation of these data in the discussion section.

It is evident that the municipality of Olinalá for the bilingual group was superior in all evaluations except for lexical availability or readiness, where it ran a close second. For the monolingual control group in Spanish, Chilapa was more consistently in first place, with Olinalá second in almost all cases. Tlapa was always in last place for the bilingual group. For the control group Tlapa also consistently had one of the lowest averages. Zapotitlán Tablas constantly held third place out of four with the Indian bilinguals but wavered between second, third, and fourth place for the native Spanish speakers. More will be said about these discrepancies in the discussion section.

Table 18.6. Means of Achievement and Proficiency Tests

Test	Mean	S.D.	Var	N
ACHIEVEMENT (max. 328)				
first grade	147.35	75.60	5496.30	26
second grade	157.56	76.10	5569.20	26
general for bilingual group	152.45	75.28	5558.81	52
control group	237.07	33.96	1122.77	38
PROFICIENCY (max. 260) *cuaderno*				
first grade	134.08	45.55	1995.30	26
second grade	155.23	42.80	1761.41	26
general for bilingual group	144.65	45.05	1990.23	52
control group	198.51	15.74	241.09	38
grammar				
first grade	5.25	1.81	3.16	26
second grade	5.87	1.76	2.90	26
general for bilingual group	5.48	1.82	3.25	52
control group	8.34	1.48	2.13	38
(index) *lexicon*				
first grade	1.602	0.73	0.52	26
second grade	1.656	0.66	0.40	26
general for bilingual group	1.620	0.73	0.52	52
control group	2.538	1.021	1.015	38

Table 18.7.   Means of Achievement and Proficiency Tests On A Regional
Basis

	BILINGUALS			MONOLINGUALS		
	Mean	S.D.	N	Mean	S.D.	N
ACHIEVEMENT (max. 328)						
Chilapa	169.30	61.30	10	257.05	24.63	10
Olinalá	211.81	35.39	8	230.75	39.12	10
Tlapa	125.05	83.80	13	218.22	37.94	9
Zapotitlán Tablas	136.52	79.60	21	240.72	22.93	9
PROFICIENCY (max. 260) *cuaderno*						
Chilapa	153.30	27.68	10	193.25	9.60	10
Olinalá	185.37	33.13	8	211.14	9.00	10
Tlapa	129.38	50.09	13	194.44	17.37	9
Zapotitlán Tablas	134.48	44.49	21	193.61	19.11	9
(Index) *lexicon*						
Chilapa	1.64	.40	10	3.05	1.17	10
Olinalá	1.58	.66	8	2.67	.69	10
Tlapa	1.10	.97	13	2.33	1.18	9
Zapotitlán Tablas	1.39	.97	21	2.02	.80	9
grammar						
Chilapa	4.60	1.83	10	9.19	.93	10
Olinalá	5.46	1.76	8	9.01	1.63	10
Tlapa	4.08	3.10	13	7.92	1.35	9
Zapotitlán Tablas	4.48	2.94	21	7.08	.94	9

Sociolinguistic Variables.   Some of the major sociolinguistic variables included in this analysis are a) the native languages the children speak; b) the geographical area they are from; and c) the use of Spanish or the Indian tongue by
teachers at school and by relatives at home. While the pilot study does not allow one
to draw definitive conclusions, it can be gleaned from the preceding section that the
area the children were from did have a strong impact. As has occurred on the other
tests, the Nahuatl children had the highest averages after the native Spanish speakers. The Tlapanecs and Mixtecs were very close in grade averages, with the Mixtecs
slightly ahead. If we go back to Figure 18.3, we will see on the map that Nahuatl
speakers are concentrated precisely in the municipalities of Chilapa and Olinalá, the
regions that demonstrated the highest level of proficiency. With respect to the use of
Spanish and/or the Indian tongue in the classroom, we found that the highest level
of proficiency correlated well with the exclusive use of Spanish, followed by the use
of both languages, while the lowest scores were achieved by those whose teacher
spoke mostly in the vernacular. These results are not surprising. We found the same
to be true with regard to proficiency in Spanish when the parents and siblings had a
good command of the official language, and when both languages were used at
home. These findings deserve further comment later on in the paper.

DISCUSSION

Although the preceding pages only scratch the surface of three large-scale research projects in which many, many children, teachers, and researchers from different disciplines have participated, we think this paper does provide the reader with a solid idea of the kind of applied and sociolinguistic research that is presently being carried out in Mexico related to Indian studies.

In this section we are going to reconsider some of the more salient results and other facts or implications which might not have emerged during such a cursory examination as the one that has appeared in the previous sections.

An important result which cannot be gleaned from the tables is that in all three tests, the Nahuatl subjects showed less dispersion in their grades than did the other groups, tending to cluster around their group mean, while the Tlapanec and Mixtec grades in general were quite scattered. Seemingly this would allow us to think of the Nahuatls as having a more homogeneous group language proficiency than the others, where individual performance is more varied. There are obvious testing implications that stem from this observation, as well as the need for follow-up studies and classroom observation to verify what impact these individual differences are having on the learners.

On the promoter selection test it is interesting to note that the grades on the oral section were lower than those on the written section and that the three groups were considerably closer in their means: $\bar{X}$ written 81.099, 68.337, and 71.876 for the Nahuatls, Mixtecs, and Tlapanecs versus $\bar{X}$ oral 63.509, 57.567, and 64.472 respectively. Perhaps this reflects the schooling process where tests are typically like those included in the written part, while oral, open-ended exercises are highly unusual. The written section was discrete point, while the oral part was pragmatic, global, and evaluated against native proficiency, which led us to put more faith in this section as a reflection of their proficiency in Spanish.

Similar results, although not comparable in the strict sense due to different techniques, age, and so on, were obtained by the preschoolers on the placement test—the lowest average was precisely on the oral production part, where they were asked to carry out the same type of task as the promoters, that is, describe what was happening in a picture.

Another fact that caught our eye is that on the first language oral production section in the promoter selection test, those selected from all three ethnic groups (18 year olds) had a satisfactory to excellent level of proficiency in their mother tongue, but on the socioanthropological questionnaire only 68% of the Nahuatls reported that the language is generally spoken well in their communities, versus 92% for the Mixtecs and 90% for the Tlapanecs (Godau and Politi 1981:42). On the placement test for the five to seven range age group, we see that on the only section (vocabulary) that requires use of the mother tongue the Nahuatl children had a higher average in Spanish than in Nahuatl (10.28 versus 8.54), while for the Tlapanec and Mixtec groups the opposite was true. With such limited information it would be risky at this stage to venture any more than an educated guess, but there are indications from these studies that Nahuatl is in the process of displacement by Spanish in the

Montaña de Guerrero. This is not surprising since similar results have been reported for Nahuatl in the Sierra de Puebla (Hill and Hill 1977; Knab 1980) and other parts of Mexico, as well as for the Indian tongues in general.

In the achievement-proficiency test for second graders we witnessed a chronic problem which has plagued other research projects in Indian areas: a high attrition rate in the number of subjects participating in a given study, thereby making efforts to do longitudinal studies very difficult. As was mentioned previously, the analysis of this study is incomplete. It will be particularly useful to match the results of the socioeconomic questionnaires with those of the socioanthropological questionnaires of the promoters surveyed some four years before, especially in light of the fact that they were these childrens' Spanish teachers. The results of the achievement-proficiency test indicate that there is formal learning of Spanish going on in the classroom (second grade averages are considerably higher than first grade averages), but at the same time they also indicate a distinct gap between those who learn Spanish as a second language and native speakers from the same geographical areas and socioeconomic class. Whether this gap will be closed as the Indian children are exposed increasingly on both a formal and informal basis to Spanish is one of the major questions we hope to find the answer to in the coming years.

One last comment, and perhaps the most important across-the-board finding from these three research projects, is that the Nahuatls are the most consistently proficient group in nearly all cases, whether their proficiency in Spanish be measured directly through testing procedures, or indirectly based on regional results. A vital research question is why is this the case? Is it due to the fact that basically the Nahautls live in communities that are geographically more accessible to mainstream market centers, that their language is structurally closer to Spanish and therefore easier to learn, that they see a greater need to learn Spanish and as a result have a more positive attitude toward the language, or what?

These and many other valid questions have caught our attention over the years. Hopefully during this sexennium the answers to some of these intriguing questions will be found.

CONCLUSIONS

What conclusions can be drawn from such broad yet specific investigations? First of all, one must remember two important facts: the pilot nature of these projects and the fact that many people, often with different conceptualizations of project objectives, have participated at individual, community, administrative, research, and political levels. It would be presumptuous for one researcher to take the responsibility for arriving at definitive conclusions, but at the same time a few final words are in order.

In this spirit, it must be pointed out that there have been several high-level policy changes that affect the practical applications of the research projects we have described. Spanish as a second language will no longer be taught at a preschool level in Indian areas where bilingual-bicultural primary school education is in effect since the children will first become literate in their native language and Spanish will be introduced as a second language in second grade. This decision makes the pilot research projects of the selection process for bilingual promoters at a preschool level and a preschool placement test seem superfluous, as would be the case for an achievement test if Spanish is just going to be introduced in the second grade; however, in addition to "putting out fires" and "mending fences," one has to recognize the long-term benefits or potential benefits of having first-hand information on the Spanish language proficiency (as opposed to self-reported data or second-hand census data) of different ethnic groups and of various age ranges within these groups. How is it possible to design good programs and materials in Spanish as a second language at the level of full-scale bilingual-bicultural education when you do not have basic data on student and teacher language skills? These research projects have pointed to a definite gap in the command of Spanish between Indian children and native Spanish speakers from similar geographic and socioeconomic backgrounds. There is an imperative need to do language assessment in all Indian-dominant areas of Mexico and not just in the Montaña de Guerrero. Fortunately, progress is being made in this sense in Oaxaca and the Valle del Mezquital.

As was mentioned in the discussion section, one cannot help but notice the superiority of the Nahuatl group with respect to language proficiency in Spanish. An explanation for this phenomenon and similar phenomena in other areas must be found, not as an academic exercise, but in an effort to understand what ingredients lead to a better command of Spanish, since this is a declared goal of the Mexican government. These results are also of interest to the Indian groups who have affirmed their desire not to become a part of the Mexican mainstream. Going beyond specific cases, the general tendency toward increased proficiency in Spanish or the desire to attain this status, points to language shift in Mexico, a problem which cannot be ignored at an ethnic, professional, and governmental level.

Though it may not be overtly mentioned in the text, there is a clear need for classroom observation. It is one thing to test, to analyze, to predict on a theoretical level; it is quite another to verify the subjects in action. In the case of the teachers, is their proficiency reflected in teaching ability? Do they have communicative competence in Spanish and are they capable of transmitting this to their students? What type of ongoing training courses do they need to recognize and improve their shortcomings in Spanish? Or, on the other hand, if the goal of Mexico is to have a plurilingual/pluricultural nation and the hypothesis that a better command of Spanish is equal to a loss in the command of the native tongue is borne out, should second language learning in the classroom be sacrificed or relegated to a lower level of priority in an effort to concede more prestige to the Indian tongues?

Longitudinal studies and the difficulty of achieving them is another keypoint that has to be taken up. There is a very high attrition rate at all levels of schooling in Mexico. This has been proved in other studies by the CIIS and governmental agencies within public education. A one-shot attempt at proficiency or attitudes does not provide a clear picture. These features need to be followed up, evaluated with great care, and complemented by ongoing socioeconomic data, which in turn leads to the next conclusion.

This conclusion is the imperative need that exists for solid socioeconomic and attitudinal data to be collected at the time of the language survey. It is our feeling at this time that teacher and economic variables have the greatest impact, but more information is needed before we can draw definitive conclusions.

Lastly, we have also seen the importance of including control groups when feasible, at least for the language measurements. In part, this would complement data which exist to a certain extent in a linguistic atlas which is presently being processed in the Colegio de México and, even more importantly, would provide us with a more valid yardstick by which to measure language proficiency than if we use the native speaker judgments of researchers from Mexico City whose socioeconomic and educational backgrounds are very, very different.

This has been a long paper, yet justice has not been done to all the efforts expended on these projects. Hopefully they have set some standards to be followed in other research projects in Mexico and at the same time their shortcomings can be improved upon by future attempts. Undoubtedly these research efforts will find echo in other Third World countries with similar problems in the realm of language planning and policy. As researchers we have the responsibility of sharing our experiences in the hope that our particular situation might be of use to others and their ongoing efforts.

REFERENCES

Aguirre Beltran, Gonzalo. 1973. Teoría y práctica de la educación indígena. Mexico City: Sría de Educación Pública, Colección SEP-Setentas.
————. 1982. Lenguas vernáculas. Su uso y desuso en la enseñanza: La experiencia de México, 3 vol. Mexico City: CIESAS, Cuadernos de la Casa Chata 68.
Alonso, Ma. Teresa, Gonzalez, Judith, & Velazquez, Elizabeth. 1978. Manual de organización para las actividades preescolares. Mexico City: CIIS.
ANPIBAC. 1979. Conclusiones del Primer Seminario Nacional de Educación Bilingüe y Bicultural. Mexico City. Mimeographed.
ANPIBAC-SEP. 1981. Instrumentación de la educación bilingüe y bicultural. Oaxaca City. Mimeographed.
Bravo Ahuja, Gloria. 1976. La enseñanza del español a los indígenas mexicanos. Mexico City: El Colegio de México.
Brice Heath, Shirley. 1972. La política del lenguaje en México. Mexico City: SEP/INI 13.
Calvo, Beatriz, & Donnadieu, Laura. 1982. El difícil camino de la escolaridad (el maestro indígena y su proceso de formación). Mexico City: CIESAS, Cuadernos de la Casa Chata 55.
————. 1983. Un magisterio bilingüe y bicultural: el caso de la capacitación diferencial de los maestros indígenas del Estado de Mexico. Mexico City: CIESAS, Cuadernos de la Casa Chata 73.
Caso, Alfonso et al. 1973. La política indigenista en México, 2 vol. Mexico City: SEP/INI 20–21.
Celorio, Eduardo, & Bravo Ahuja, Gloria. 1978. Guía para el promotor bilingüe bicultural. Mexico City: CIIS.
CIIS. 1978, 1979, 1980. Método integral de español, Unidades 1 y II. Mexico City: CIIS.
Coronado De Caballero, Gabriela, Muñoz Cruz, Héctor, and Franco Pellotier, Victor Manuel. 1981. Bilingüismo y educación en el Valle del Mezquital. Mexico City: CIESAS, Cuadernos de la Casa Chata 42.
Diaz Gutierrez, Marinao, & Reyes Sales, Nohemí. 1978. Fundamentos didácticos para la educación preescolar en el medio indígena. Mexico City: CIIS.

Diaz Polanco, Héctor et al. 1979. Indigenismo, modernización y marginalidad, una revisión crítica. Mexico City: CIIS/Juan Pablos Ed.

Duran Aguilar, Lucila Elba. 1983. El proceso de selección del maestro mazahua. Mexico City: CIESAS, Cuadernos de la Casa Chata 81.

Ferre D'Amare, Ricardo, & Baez-Jorge, Félix. 1978. Lineamientos para la reorientación de la educación bilingüe y bicultural en México. América Indígena. 290–298 Mexico City: INI.

Finegold, Lynda. 1982. El lenguaje y la sociedad: un estudio exploratorio del programa de castellanización en la Montaña de Guerrero. Master's Thesis. Mexico City: CIIS. Mimeographed.

Finegold, Lynda, López Chávez, Juan, & Weller, Georganne. 1983. Proficiencia oral en español de niños indígenas en la Montaña de Guerrero. Mexico City: CIIS. Manuscript.

Godau, Rainer, & Politi, Lucia. 1981. Marginalidad y bilingüismo: El caso de la Montaña de Guerrero. Mexico City: Cuadernos del CIIS 5.

Hamel, Rainer, & Muñoz, Héctor, 1982. El conflicto lingüístico en la zona bilingüe de México. Mexico City: CIESAS, Cuadernos de la Casa Chata 65.

Hernandez López, Ramón. 1976. Acción educativa en las áreas indígenas. Mexico City: Sría. de Educación Pública, DGEI.

Hill, J. H., & Hill, K. C. 1977. Language death and relexification in Tlaxcalan Nahuatl. Linguistics 191. 55–69.

Knab, Tim. 1980. La muerte del lenguaje. Ciencia 31. 141–154.

Martinez Ruiz, Jesús. 1977. Densidad territorial de los monolingües y bilingües de México en 1960–1970. Mexico City: UNAM. Instituto de Investigaciones Sociales.

Modiano, Nancy. 1974. La educación indígena en los Altos de Chiapas. Mexico City: INI.

Parodi, Claudia. 1981. La investigación lingüística en México (1970–80). Mexico City: UNAM, Instituto de Investigaciones Filológicas.

Pozas, Ricardo, & de Pozas, Isabel H. 1982. Los indios en las clases sociales de México. Mexico City: Siglo XXI.

Politi, Lucia, & Godau, Rainer. 1982a. Realidad social y panorama lingüístico de la Montaña de Guerrero. Mexico City: CIIS. Manuscript.

_____ . 1982b. Desaparecido COPLAMAR, los marginados reciben más promesas. Proceso, December 1982.30

Rios Morales, Manuel. 1982. Los mixtecos, tlapanecos y nahuas en las relaciones sociales de producción capitalista. Master's Thesis. Mexico City: CIIS. Mimeographed.

Ros Romero, Consuelo. 1981. Bilingüismo y educación. Un estudio de caso en Michoacán. Mexico City: INI.

Scanlon, Arlene, & Lezama, Juan. 1982. México pluricultural: de la castellanización a la educación indígena bilingüe y bicultural. Mexico City: Porrúa Ed.

Secretaría de Educación Pública (SEP). 1979. Educación para todos. Mexico City: Dirección General de Publicaciones y Bibliotecas de la SEP.

SEP, DGEI, INI, CONAFE. 1980. Informe anual de labores 1979–80, Programa de educación preescolar y castellanización, primaria bilingüe-bicultural para todos los niños indígenas. Mexico City: Editora Colorprint.

Sitton, Nahmad et al. 1977. Siete ensayos sobre indigenismo. Mexico City: INI, Serie Cuadernos de Trabajo 6.

Sub-Delegación General De La Montaña De Guerrero. 1978. Programa de desarrollo educativo de la Montaña de Guerrero. Mexico City: Presidencia de la República. Manuscript.

Swadesh, Mauricio. 1979. Juegos para aprender español. Mexico City: SEP.

Troike, Rudolph, & Modiano, Nancy. 1975. Proceedings of the first inter-American conference on bilingual education. Washington, D. C.: Center for Applied Linguistics.

_____ . 1982. Creó la SEP 5 mil 796 plazas para atender a 600 mil niños indígenas. Uno más Uno, August 13, p. 2.

NINETEEN

Re-training of French Teachers in the United States in French as a Business Language: An Example of Franco–American Cooperation*

Robert Crane

Lyon Graduate School of Business Administration, France

Why learn a foreign language? This question may appear to be a very easy one, especially when one thinks of a schoolboy seated on his bench (whose opinion on the subject has, perhaps, not been sought) repeating "I am, you are, he is . . . ." Of course, no one criticizes this young student who, thanks to his perseverance, may even learn the language.

It is important to consider the parents' thinking when choosing a language. Sometimes, they argue that "German (or Latin) forms the mind" or "The best students take Russian" or, perhaps less often, "Our child will be able to become acquainted with Italian literature or civilization." Finally, another more realistic parental attitue is "English is the international language" or "the language of international trade" or again "English will open doors for him/her in many fields."

It is this last "practical" or "applied" argument which interests us. We refer here to a university context rather than that of an elementary school and to the United States rather than Europe. Multilingual and multicultural Europe enjoys a certain unity thanks to the European Economic Community. As a result, contact with foreign languages is much more frequent in Europe than in a basically monolingual country like the United States. In like manner, the importance of foreign languages in business is much more evident on a continent where business partners who live only a short distance away may speak different languages. Consequently, there is a long tradition of teaching foreign languages with a business orientation in Europe, whether it is in French business schools, in Great Britain's Polytechnics, or in the German *Hochschules*.

On the other hand, interest in the commercial application of foreign languages is a rather recent phenomenon in the United States. Due to the efforts of some hard-working pioneers at the beginning of the 1970s, the idea of Business French (to cite only one example) has been accepted on a handful of American campuses. Even

---

* Translated from the French by Nancy Schweda-Nicholson.

though this new type of course was often viewed by university administrators with a certain amount of skepticism at the outset, the experience has proven itself to be worthwhile because it fulfills a need perceived by the students themselves. Thus, very "avant-garde" courses such as those started by Mrs. Claude Legoff at Rutgers University in New Jersey in the mid-1970s enjoy ever-increasing success. To reiterate, this success stems from student interest.

Since then, Business French courses have become more widespread and their popularity continues to grow. There are two main reasons for this growth. On one hand, as we have already indicated, students are interested in such courses from a practical point of view. Language competence with a business orientation increases their job possibilities, especially with international companies. It also enhances students' marketability if, in addition to a language, they have acquired an understanding of a particular country's market and the mentality of its commercial practices. Briefly stated, French Business courses often open the door to an interesting career in international trade.

A current trend in the United States is teaching foreign languages as an integral part of an international studies program. This plan was endorsed by the Perkins Commission, established under the Carter Administration to evaluate American foreign language needs and to make recommendations on how to respond to these needs. In its report, "Strength Through Wisdom" (1979), the Commission was forced to recognize the catastrophic situation of foreign language teaching in the United States. The number of students enrolled in foreign language courses has been declining since the late 1960s. In order to solve this serious problem, the Commission emphasized (among other things) the importance of international studies, of which Business French is a part.

Later, the colloquium, "Toward Education With a Global Perspective," organized by the National Assembly on Foreign Language and International Studies in 1980, dealt with the same theme. The colloquium's final report included a list of practical suggestions, the first of which was the encouragement of international studies. In this connection, the report noted that, in order to implement such courses of study, schools (generally, universities) should consider additional training for some of the faculty and offer credits for such a retraining program. The final report emphasized the importance of increasing the role of foreign languages in the framework of existing university structures, and especially in "business and professional schools" ("Toward education with a global perspective: AAC assembly recommendations" 1981:43–45).

Thus, in the general context of a partial reorientation of language studies in the United States toward international studies (accomplished through cooperation among different university departments), students expressed a desire for foreign language courses with a business emphasis. These two tendencies seemed to coincide. The colloquium, "Toward Education With a Global Perspective," indicated that what was often lacking was training of French teachers in the field of commerce. Training of French teachers in the United States has traditionally been literary, which, with the possible exceptions of *The Counterfeiters* or *The Miser*, does not at all prepare them to teach economic material. Fortunately, there is an organization in France, the Paris Chamber of Commerce and Industry (CCIP), which is providing the necessary training.

The CCIP has been expecting this idea to come of age for a long time, ever since it was given the responsibility of promoting Business French some 20 years ago. Since that time, the CCIP's Administrative Board has conceived and implemented a series of carefully coordinated actions to accomplish this objective. One facet of the CCIP's work is to offer summer seminars in Paris for foreign French teachers. In addition to these training seminars for teachers, the CCIP also organizes courses for students. Here also, there are two kinds of training: on one hand, there is an introductory seminar on business life in France that is not followed by an exam and, on the other hand, there is a training course which leads to taking one of the Business French exams for foreigners, which are given in various provinces. It is important to note that these internationally known examinations are extremely useful for Business French teachers since the two most common levels (Practical Certificate in Economic and Commercial French, and Advanced Diploma in Business French), representing two different degrees of knowledge, can serve as objective goals for a Business French course.

In addition to seminars for teachers and students, CCIP also organizes Business French courses for a third target group: businessmen. This last type of training is rather personalized and can be geared either toward linguistic goals or toward acquiring specific knowledge.

With regard to seminars offered to French teachers, the CCIP has four. The first, entitled "French Socio-Economic Reality," is very short (five days). The seminar's theme is the French economic and political situation. The coursework includes an analysis of French political institutions as well as an evaluation of the status of the French economy and its different sectors. There are plans to visit the Paris Stock Market and a business establishment during future seminars.

The second seminar, "Instructional Training," is, as its name indicates, for teachers who wish to start a French Business course or prepare their students for the CCIP examinations. The seminar concentrates on specialized business language, on background material in the field, and on methodological approaches in addition to the CCIP examinations for foreigners. This seminar lasts two weeks.

International relations are emphasized in a third training session entitled "1984 European Overview." This two-week seminar examines diverse aspects of Europe, from the construction of a common European defense to a possible independent industrial policy. Other subjects of discussion include agricultural Europe, unemployment, the North–South dialog, and the hypothetical existence of a European culture.

The fourth and final CCIP seminar, entitled "Enterprise and French Businesses in Their Economic Environment," takes the form of assisted self-instruction. Even though the training session is organized around three areas of interest—namely, economic and political issues, socio-professional issues, and sociocultural issues—and is highlighted by visits to diverse institutions and organizations, what makes this seminar stand out in comparison to the other CCIP courses is the three days spent in a business establishment. During these three days, trainees in groups of two study the company's structures, objectives, and development so that they can fully participate in the day-long working session that follows their business experience. This seminar lasts four weeks.

So, for the first time, thanks to its wide variety of training courses, to the background material it has assembled, and also to its free newsletter *Business French* (which provides for a fruitful exchange of ideas among teachers from different countries), the Paris Chamber of Commerce and Industry has been able to respond to the demand for additional training in the business field for French teachers in the United States. But, "Paris is not France" or, as some people say, "France is not Paris." Whatever the case may be, a new demand has arisen since the beginning of the 1980s for a seminar in the provinces on what one can call "Grass-roots France." In response to this demand, two new Business French courses were established in July of 1983: one in Vichy and another in Lyon. The Vichy seminar is organized by a very well-respected institution in the field of French as a foreign language, the Modern Languages Audio-Visual Center (CAVILAM). As concerns its summer courses in Business French for American teachers, the overall orientation is pedagogical with three areas of concentration: first, improvement of general language skills; second, language development in the field of economics and business; and third, group work on classroom strategies for the teaching of Business French. More specifically, the 1983 CAVILAM program included the study of oral and written documents such as the "Revue de Presse" on France Inter every morning and suggestions for in-class use of the documents. Furthermore, CAVILAM organized meetings with business and industrial leaders as well as with local and regional officials. Finally, case studies were performed, in-class exposés given, and lectures and debates organized.

The Lyon training course is organized by the Lyon Graduate School of Business Administration, one of the outstanding business schools in France. Given the orientation of this institution, it is completely natural for its Business French training to emphasize the day-to-day functions of a business in France, e.g., appropriate terminology and the difficulties which arise from the context. Almost all of the topics presented in the classroom are the object of a visit to a business establishment, a procedure which allows the trainees to become acquainted with the commercial and industrial reality of the second economic region of France and to ask people about their professional problems "on the job." Among the companies visited are the Carrefour supermarket chain, the B.S.N. food and glass group, the Imagine audio-visual studios, the Part-Dieu commercial center, and such non-business institutions as Documentation Française. The seminar is highlighted by a business game whose dual purpose is to allow the students to assimilate the knowledge acquired during their training and to assess the possibilites of adapting the game to their needs. Finally, despite the very intensive nature of the course, the cultural component is in no way forgotten. In this connection, visits are offered to Cluny and to other Romanesque churches in Burgundy, to the Roman city of Vienne, and, of course, there is the possibility of an evening at a restaurant so the students can enjoy the famous "nouvelle cuisine." For 1984, the topic, "Introduction to the French Business Enterprise," has been retained with its practical focus on business life and professional and cultural visits, including an optional trip to the Beaujolais area to taste the local wine while studying the wine-growing side of French agriculture. In sum, the goal of the Lyon Business School's seminar is not only to acquaint the students with the various aspects of day-to-day life of a business in France, but also to make the most of its own region (Rhône-Alpes) with its numerous commercial, industrial, technological, cultural, and gastronomical advantages and opportunities.

In conclusion, we can observe that France and the United States have established a cooperative effort in the area of Business French. On the American side, part of foreign language teaching's evolution has taken an "applied" direction. In other respects, groups like the Perkins Commission and the colloquium, "Toward Education With a Global Perspective," have recommended university studies with an international orientation in which languages play a role. In this context, American students on several campuses have expressed the desire to be able to take language courses with business applications, a desire that posed problems with respect to business preparation on the part of French teachers. Now, thanks to the Paris Chamber of Commerce and Industry, CAVILAM in Vichy, and the Lyon Graduate School of Business Administration, training courses of this kind have been established, helping French educators teach what are essentially the commercial aspects of French civilization.

Obviously, the possibilities for the application of languages are numerous. One is tempted to say, "Thank heavens, there are still so many left!" Among these, the study of French as a Business Language seems to be on the right track.

REFERENCES

Strength through wisdom. 1979. Report of the Perkins Commission.
Toward education with a global perspective: AAC Assembly Recommendations. 1981. Profession 81. New York: Modern Language Association.

TWENTY

Language Policy For Education In Niger

John P. Hutchison
Boston University

INTRODUCTION

Postindependence Africa has produced a plethora of movements, programs, and policies designed to free African countries from the bonds of their colonial past, in all senses of the words. Finding that the token achievement of political independence was not sufficient to free them from this heritage, postindependence African countries have embarked in diverse directions in an effort to achieve economic, social, cultural, and linguistic independence to solidify their political independence. To city only a few of the many efforts in this direction, we have observed Guinée's isolationism, Zaire's authenticity, Chad's imitation of Zaire's authenticity, Somalia's more recent revolutionary imposition of the Somali language, and Tanzania's ongoing development of the Swahili language and Bantu culture. In the areas of public and adult education, many countries have also implemented language policies for education involving the development of their own national languages as a step in the same direction. The motivations for these movements and policies have varied greatly historically, ranging from the vain attempts of narrowminded politicians or dictators to secure their power, to the more noble and, in some cases, successful efforts to completely break the remnant ties of colonial, often, bondage, through linguistic and cultural measures.

The recent history of the Republic of Niger has been characterized by events and developments which may come to constitute a new and workable model for achieving true independence in the cultural and linguistic sense. From the time of its accession to power in 1974, the military regime of General Seyni Kountche has taken steps toward the complete reorganization and reorientation of the social, political, and administrative structures within the country. Kountche's government has coined the label "Société du Développement" or Development Society (DS) as the rubric to refer collectively to all of their past, present, and especially future programs designed to effect this change of direction for Niger.

The orientation of their efforts is admirable in the sense that they are driven by no readily apparent selfish or political motive, and that their tenure in power has yet to show signs of the excesses and abuses of power that have characterized so many African leaders and their regimes, whether military or elected. They avoid using popular terminology to describe their philosophy and their politics, and also avoid alignment with powers outside of the country which might be entailed by the adoption of a given ideology. Their model for the future development of Niger is one that has grown out of their own beliefs and convictions concerning how their country can survive, given the harsh realities of Niger's economic plight, geographical setting, and ecological situation. Recognizing that transplanted development models have failed to alleviate Niger's problems, the Government of Niger (GON) now welcomes outside help and support only when it is provided according to their own terms, and in keeping with the plans and priorities of the DS. They stress development and change that are uniquely suited to their country, involving and affecting all of the people of Niger, at all levels of the society. They want Niger's future to be in the hands of Nigeriens, and not determined by exterior political and economic forces. The DS entails a nationwide network of cooperative organizations designed to encourage local participation and which will eventually assume many of the local functions and responsibilities previously assigned to agencies of the government.

Given these priorities and the comprehensive nature of their plans, it goes without saying that achieving the goals of the DS will require a complete transformation of the systems of education and training throughout the country. Also important to the government of Niger at this time is the implementation of research which will lead to the discovery and development of appropriate technology uniquely adapted to the Nigerien context and in keeping with the DS.

During 1982, more than 250 Nigeriens from all levels within the education system participated in a national conference/debate on educational reform, held in Zinder. That national conference/debate, the proceedings of which were widely publicized throughout the country, resulted in the Zinder Declaration, which is a lengthy document outlining proposed reforms, changes, and, in short, the complete reorganization and reorientation of the educational system so as to complement the philosophy and goals of the DS. It will be the purpose of the present paper to discuss the historical role that languages have played in Nigerien educational policy, and to contrast that historical model with the one that is inherent in the goals of the DS as expressed in the Zinder Declaration. The unique way in which the government is planning to develop the numerous national languages, and to establish a unifying language other than French, will also be described in detail. Clearly only time can judge the efforts being made by Niger. However, presently available information indicates, in my opinion, that this new Nigerien model for development represents an admirable departure from those that have plagued West African countries since time immemorial. It is a model that may finally solve some of the endemic problems—especially of Sahelian countries—rather than only create more problems.

THE GEOGRAPHIC, ETHNIC, AND LINGUISTIC SETTING

Niger is a vast landlocked country which stretches across the Sahel region in West Africa. The surface area covered is 458,995 square miles, the equivalent of the States of Texas and California combined. It is bounded to the west by Mali and

Upper Volta, to the east by Chad, to the south by Benin and Nigeria, and to the north by Algeria and Libya.

As is characteristic of the map and its borders throughout Africa, Niger was clearly a victim of the lines of the ruler's edge wielded by colonial cartographers. The effect of the map, and also of the colonial treatment of ethnic groups and their languages, on the peoples of Africa is well summarized in the following passage written by a Nigerien:

> Because of the arbitrary division of Africa between the imperialist powers . . . which preceded colonial conquest and domination, the territories colonized by these different powers do not correspond to any linguistic unities. This situation was aggravated still further in many cases by later divisions effected by each imperialist power to satisfy the needs of political domination and economic exploitation. As a result, the nations in contemporary black Africa created on this basis have linguistic problems heightened by the policy of "divide and rule" and the systematic suppression of African languages. (Moumouni 1968:278–9)

In 1969, the official population of Niger was 3,775,000. Today it is estimated that there are nearly 6,000,000 Nigeriens, with the major ethnic groups being represented in Table 20.1.

No two of Niger's languages are mutually intelligible, and they represent a heterogeneous mix of people. Niger has languages from diverse branches of three of the four major language families of Africa. Hausa is a Chadic language of the Afroasiatic family, Songhai-Zerma is a Saharan language of the Nilo-Saharan family, Fulfulde is a West Atlantic language of the Niger-Congo branch of Niger-Kordofanian, Tamasheq is a Semitic language of the Afroasiatic family, and Kanuri and Tubu are members of the same branch of Saharan in the Nilo-Saharan family. Perhaps through sheer strength in numbers, Hausa and Zarma (or Djerma) have emerged as the two most important ethnic groups, and thus their languages have become the most important in the country. Historically speaking, since independence, struggles for power and political influence have centered for the most part on the Hausa-Zarma axis, with the Zarmas traditionally feeling somewhat intimidated and embittered over the numerical strength of the Hausas, and the consequent position of importance which has been ceded to the Hausa language over time.

Though no government of Niger has specifically imposed Hausa for either governmental or educational purposes, the language has become extremely important

Table 20.1. Major Nigerien Ethnic Groups

Group	Approximate %
Hausa	51%
Songhai-Zarma	21%
Fulfulde	12%
Tamasheq	10%
Kanuri	4%
Tubu	1%

Source: Laya 1977:285.

not only throughout Niger, but throughout West Africa as a whole. To a certain extent the status of Hausa in Niger can, of course, be related to its very powerful position in neighboring Nigeria. Laya underlines the importance of Hausa by stating that "nearly 85% of Nigeriens understand Hausa; and in fact, one can make oneself understood throughout the country if one speaks Hausa and Zarma" (Laya 1977:285). Though it has yet to be announced which of Niger's languages will replace the official language (French) and become the "langue unitaire" of Niger (as suggested in the Zinder Declaration discussed above), it is safe to say that the only serious single candidate for this role is Hausa.

Because of the way that the map was drawn, Niger's borders are thus artificial and unfaithful, in the historical sense, to the peoples they enclose and the nation that they attempt to define. Each of the ethnic groups is essentially estranged from a significant portion of its own number by these borders: with a majority of the Hausa in Nigeria, probably half of the Songhai-Zarma in Mali, Fulfulde everywhere, a significant population of Tuaregs (Tamasheq) in Mali, and with a majority of the Kanuris and Tubus in Chad and Nigeria. The composite picture can therefore hardly be called homogeneous, since each group (or portion of a group) is the modern-day successor and remnant of a major historical empire which once encompassed a vast and unified portion of West Africa. With regard to religion, however, Niger's population can be said to be homogeneous since more than 85% of Nigeriens are Moslem.

THE HISTORY OF LANGUAGE POLICY FOR EDUCATION IN NIGER

An important figure in the history of Nigerien education has been Dr. Abdou Moumouni. Originally a physicist by training, he later became Rector of the University of Niamey. In *Education in Africa,* he treats the history of education in francophone Africa. His prescriptions for the future needs of African education have clearly an influence on the modern educational policies of a number of African countries, and have also inspired some of the changes currently being initiated and implemented in Niger. There—as in the rhetoric of the Kountche regime—the criticism of French colonial policy with regard to education is a predominant theme, and deservedly so. Throughout the colonial period, and ever since independence as well, there has been a controlled resistance in Niger against French colonial policy in the area of education. Much of francophone Africa remains burdened with the remnants of that policy up until today.

France's policy espousing the assimilation of Africans to a higher "civilization" of course required that general education must be carried out in French, and at the same time discouraged the use of local African languages as media of communication and subjects of instruction in the school system (Spencer 1971; Gorman 1974; Bokamba and Tlou 1977). France's linguistic policy was regulated by a number of ordinances and decrees. The first ordinance was the Metropolitan Ordinance of Villers-Coxteret of 1539 which forbade the use of languages other than French in all official functions within the territories of France. The second was the Ordinance of February 14, 1922, which regulated private education and religious teaching in overseas territories (Bokamba and Tlou 1977; Spencer 1971). Moumouni quotes the text of a later decree, that of May 10, 1924, which reorganized education in French West Africa. Here are selected excerpts:

> Article 2. The essential goal of elementary education is to bring the greatest number of indigenous people closer to us, to familiarize them with our language, our institutions and our methods, to lead them gradually towards economic and social progress by the careful evolution of their own civilization.
> Article 64. French will be the sole language in the schools. Teachers are forbidden to use local language with their students. (Moumouni 1968:44)

Moumouni adds—perhaps from his own experience—that "the students themselves were threatened with disciplinary action when they expressed themselves in their native tongues in the school area" (Moumouni 1968:45). Later he elaborates that "one of the cornerstones of the 'depersonalization' of educated Africans was the relegation of African languages to the back seat and their more or less complete elimination from the educational process" (Moumouni 1968:55).

In evaluating and examining the history of education in Niger, and in attempting to determine the degree to which true "independence" has been achieved in this area, it is important to separate educational policy into two different branches: that of public education, and that of adult education. From the time of independence to the present, these two branches have taken rather different courses, as will be shown. It is only today under the Kountche regime that their histories begin to merge and to complement one another within the structure of the DS.

Language Policy Trends in Public Education

It is estimated that in 1960, at the time of independence, less than 10% of Niger's school-age children were in school. As evidenced in Table 20.2, Niger's enrollment statistics for the 1961–62 school year show that an extremely small percentage of Niger's population was in school at that time.

Access to primary education has increased dramatically since independence in 1960, when the 26,609 school children represented between 5% and 10% of their age group. By 1970 there were 84,000, 187,000 in 1979, and 250,000 by 1980, the latter figure representing 18% of school-age children. By the beginning of the 1982-83 school year the pupils enrolled represented 21% of their age group.

For all Nigerien school children, in keeping with the colonial tradition, French was the only medium of instruction throughout the country, at least until the advent of the Kountche regime in 1974. The primary school curriculum that is presently in use in Niger has undergone few noteworthy changes since independence, and re-

Table 20.2. 1961-62 Enrollment Statistics

Grade Level/School	Number of Students
Primary	26,609
Secondary	1,359
Technical	61
Higher	47

mains essentially the preindependence curriculum established by the French in 1949. The only changes have involved subject matter and exam content, mostly in the social studies area. Subjects and materials relating to France and Europe have been replaced by those relating to Niger and Africa. In keeping with this kind of change, more appropriate textbooks have been adopted whenever possible. Texts based in the francophone Africa milieu have now replaced those developed for use in France. The subjects currently being taught in the traditional francophone school in Niger are the following: French, reading, writing, transcription, arithmetic, art, music, physical education, civics, science, history, geography, and directed activities. French is the medium of instruction of nearly all of these subjects, and the subject 'French' takes up an average of 20% of the classroom hours in each of the six years of primary school.

Though there has been a long-felt need to implement major changes in the linguistic, cultural, and academic orientation of this curriculum in Niger, and though national languages were being implemented in the adult education curriculum, it was not until 1974 that certain cautious and preliminary steps were taken in the direction of change. It was during that year that a special branch of the Ministry of National Education was established. Labeled INDRAP (National Institute for Pedagogical Documentation, Research and Animation), it was commissioned by the Kountche government to take on the task of implementing educational reform (see p. 287).

Language and Educational Policy for Adult Education

From the time of independence on, adult education began to develop not only in French, but also in national languages. Its history is thus distinct from that of public education up until the time of the accession to power of the present government, the beginning of educational reform (see p. 287), and the establishment of the experimental school with maternal languages as the medium of instruction. Much of the expertise and experience that now comes to play in the implementation of Niger's new language and cultural policy for public education is the result of the many years during which the five major languages have been used in education for adult literacy.

In the area of adult education, Niger has a long and varied experience. Because of the total estrangement of adults from the educational process during the colonial period, the literacy campaign confronted a reputed 95% illiteracy rate in Niger at the time of independence in 1960. It is readily apparent that up until that time, Niger's educational system had very little to do with Nigeriens. From the time of its inception shortly after 1960, the goal of adult education has been to integrate it with rural development. The campaign was fully launched in 1963, with the backing of UNESCO, in the five major languages.

Regional Literacy Service offices were created in the principal administrative headquarters of the country staffed by Nigerien school teachers reassigned to do literacy work and by Peace Corps volunteers. These staff, with the help of local support committees, set up literacy centers in several dozen villages of each geographic area, the choice largely dictated by the availability of local school teachers to assume the function of literacy instructor and by the willingness and interest of the population. Courses were held several nights a week throughout the dry season in crude shelters built by the villages and were open to anyone over 15 years of age. The regional offices provided instructional materials produced by the Literacy Service in Niamey, trained instructors, and periodically inspected the centers.[1] At that time eight adult literacy newspapers were begun, six of them in Hausa, one bilingual in Hausa/Zarma, and one in Tamasheq.

The first literacy campaign was a success in the sense that considerable experience was gained and a support network was established across the country. Little dent, however, was made in the illiteracy rate due to the lack of experience and training of Nigerien literacy agents, uncertainties of material supply, and the fact that Nigerien villagers for the most part saw little reason to invest effort in becoming literate in their own language when reading materials were nearly unavailable and local conditions offered few opportunities to put literacy to use.

In 1967–68, various regional literacy programs began to experiment with forms of literacy more closely related to ongoing rural development activities. "Alphabétisation" became more "fonctionelle," in keeping with the skill-oriented training methods which had been strongly recommended by a 1965 UNESCO literacy conference in Teheran. A literacy component became an integral part of the program of the Nigerien Cooperative Union (UNCC), and nationally-sponsored pilot projects were set up in the major agricultural regions of the country as well as in rural health campaigns. The results of this campaign were more successful than the first, but the aforementioned USAID project descriptions cited the following obstacles:

1. Their continuance and expansion required a degree of operational integration among rural development services which proved impossible without strong government support. 2. The initial projects were organized in large part by foreign technical assistance and Nigeriens were insufficiently involved in their conception, partially because of a dearth of national staff with the requisite planning abilities. 3. The Sahelian drought soon intervened, drastically reducing all rural development activities.

After the drought, the literacy campaign continued. However, in the rural area development programs which ensued, less emphasis was placed on functional literacy due to the urgency placed on the priority of food production and distribution.

Under Kountche, the importance of cooperative organization again became a priority, and he placed renewed emphasis on widespread literacy. In the three-year plan for 1976–78, a campaign of massive literacy was called for to make 30% of Niger's population literate. The Service of Literacy and Permanent Education (for adults) was to heighten its campaigns to teach adults reading and writing in maternal languages. In 1977, the government of Niger, with aid from Switzerland and the

---

[1] From United States Agency for International Development (USAID) project descriptions. Undated, untitled. Niamey, Niger.

World Council of Churches, established the CFCA (Centre de Formation des Cadres de l'Alphabétisation), a national training center for literacy agents. It is through this organization that improvements and reforms are being made in the literacy service throughout the country. The CFCA is also a crucial element in the implementation of the educational reforms of the DS.

Different Orthographies in Different Countries. The year 1966 saw a UNESCO conference in Bamako at which standardized orthographies for five of the languages were proposed and accepted. Though this conference represented an important step in the development of the languages for education and in establishing public awareness of the ongoing work, the report was not as explicit for certain of the languages as might be desired. Instead of the needed orthography rules, only the letters of the alphabet of certain languages were listed. In the case of Hausa— Niger's most important language (and also one of the three most important languages of Nigeria)—colonial heritage once again raised its ugly head, resulting in the division of the Hausa-speaking peoples of Niger and Nigeria over the issue of how to write their language. Niger wrote Hausa with long vowels doubled, some tone-marking, and certain idiosyncratic spellings which could only have been the result of French orthographic principles. Nigeria on the other hand had its own way of writing Hausa, and for years there was little hope of agreement or compromise. It was not until 1980 at a regional meeting organized in Niamey by CELHTO (Centre pour les Etudes Linguistiques et Historiques par la Tradition Orale) that Niger and Nigeria finally agreed to adopt the same Hausa orthography.

As described by Moumouni for all of Africa, this is a manifestation of the suppressive measures of the colonial powers. He states:

> Attempts were made to assimilate Africans completely, to isolate and crystalize the linguistic groups in a single colony, and to create a multitude of different systems of written characters used for administrative rather than cultural purposes. At times the suppression of languages resulted from an outrageous obscurantism masked by a supposed respect for African customs. Furthermore, the diversity of methods used to 'treat' cultural problems by the different imperialist powers has added additional elements of complexity: unequal development of the same language depending on the colonial power which controlled the region where it is spoken, and the problem posed by the language of the former home country. (Moumouni 1968:279)

This was indeed the case with the Hausa language. British colonial policy in Nigeria actually favored the use and development of Hausa, while at the same time suppressed the development and use of other northern Nigerian languages (see Paden 1968). French policy in Niger, however, left the Hausa language at a disadvantage in terms of its stage of development for use in the educational system and as a medium for literacy. Partly because of the orthographical differences, Hausa materials from Nigeria could not be used for education in Niger up until 1980.

LANGUAGE POLICY AND EDUCATIONAL REFORM

The government turned fully to the question of educational reform in 1975 when, in a national seminar on educational reform, it was decided to make the educational system more responsive to the basic needs of Nigeriens, and less imitative of the French system. In the following year, 1976, a national commission met on instructional reform and revision of the school system. During its two meetings, resolutions were adopted to reflect the national policy of using maternal languages. The primary school system was to introduce maternal languages in the first three grades, and eventually give instruction in the French language during later years of primary schooling. From that time on, INDRAP (as indicated in USAID project descriptions) has had as its mandate to develop and proliferate primary school texts for the full three years in all five of the major maternal languages of the country.

In gearing up for the implementation of maternal languages and for general reform of all education and training throughout the system, Niger has received some support, largely financial, from USAID in order to make possible the development of the teaching materials necessary in the five languages. The second year of that funding is now complete, and the project is in its third year at the time of this writing. Teams of researchers from INDRAP were equipped with tape recorders, batteries, and cassettes and sent out to all parts of the country to collect oral literary material, traditional knowledge, oral histories from older people, and other culturally-oriented texts. The teams were sent to all of the language areas, in proportion to the population density of each of the five major ethnic groups. The collected materials were all returned to INDRAP in Niamey, where they have been transcribed and now typed into handbook form. It is from these materials that crucial elements of the new maternal languages curriculum are being gleaned. The texts for grades one through three are now near completion. INDRAP is now printing national language readers in the five languages, one for each of the first three years in each language. The books are illustrated anthologies of traditional literature, including stories, poems, riddles, and tales. They are graded and include texts which the teacher can read to the pupils, as well as those that a pupil can read. The texts represent the culmination of years of work on orthography development and standardization, and two years of collection and development by INDRAP. The texts, however, include neither the teaching of writing nor the pedagogical devices needed to facilitate the prereading stage. Further development of texts and teachers' guides is necessary, as is the development of other appropriate texts in math, science, agriculture, and other subject areas in the national languages.

The National Debate on Educational Reform and the Declaration of Zinder

In a speech which he delivered during a trip to Diffa, shortly before the opening of the Zinder conference/debate, Kountche underlined the reasons for the debate on educational reform as follows:

(The need for reform) . . . is due to the incompatability of the Nigerien school with the nation's social fabric, and due to the cost of this school, and further it is due to our wish that the Nigerien school be the affair of all Nigeriens, and not simply of the State. That is why all Nigeriens or their representatives must be present in Zinder, whatever time it may take, in order to produce something that will be the bible on which the State will rely for putting into practice the education program. (Sahel Newspaper, Government of Niger) (translated from the French by John P. Hutchison)

The GON sees the area of educational reform as one which will be crucial to the future development of the country. The great conference/debate of Zinder was given widespread publicity, and the proceedings and results were produced in all journalistic and media forms. Presiding over the great debate in Zinder was the Commandant Moumouni Djermakoye Adamou, Minister of Public Health and Social Affars, and also President of the National Commission for the Implementation of the DS. Also present were: Chef d'Escadron Youssoufa Maiga, Minister of Education; Garba Sidikou, Minister of Higher Education and Research; Ari Toubo Ibrahim, Minister of Rural Development; Issoufou Mayaki, Minister of the Public Function and Works; Modieli Amadou, Secretary of State for National Education; and Commandant Amadou Seyni Maiga, Prefect of Zinder, among many others. It is clear from this cast of characters that the government was prepared to propose educational reform touching all sectors of Nigerien society, and in which all elements of the society would have a voice. It is important to note that the proposals that resulted from this conference/debate represent the educational mirror, designed to complement the structures, goals, and priorities of the Development Society. The overriding goal is clearly to integrate the educational system back into the society, and to make it relevant to the development of the country and to the entire population.

The Declaration of Zinder was published in full in the *Sahel* newspaper of Saturday-Sunday, April 3–4, 1982, at the close of the conference/debate. It is a lengthy document, covering several full pages of the newspaper, of which only a summary is presented here.

The document was divided into three sections dealing with the orientation and development of the school, training and "encadrement," and financing and planning, respectively. The first section calls for a revalidation of Niger's culture, including social, moral, cultural, and authentic value systems. The conference judged it urgent and indispensable to let national languages play their natural role in the system of education and training. The ZD called specifically for the use of national languages as a medium of instruction for the first two years of primary education, after which, the one of them chosen as the language of teaching at the national level would be used as the medium of instruction. The remaining four languages would remain as subjects contained within the curriculum. The language of teaching at the national level is very likely the same as the *langue unitaire*—"unifying language"—which the ZD also referred to. The conference proposed that the GON should adopt a unifying language for education, and so on. With regard to the content of education, more than a general theoretical education is called for in the ZD. The need for a functional liaison between theory and practice is emphasized.

The structure and time schedule for the educational system is to be rearranged. Many of the examinations inherited from the French are to be abolished in an effort to keep people in the system rather than to discourage them. The school year was also reorganized into three trimesters. The school day is to be from 7:30 to 12:30, with afternoons given to the organization of a training cycle for the retraining of teachers, productive activitites, cultural and athletic activities, and literacy education for adults and adolescents.

It was further proposed that many of the existing educational institutions in the country be readapted with an orientation more in keeping with the development goals of the country. The university would have its mission reoriented toward the area of training and employment, with priority given to technical and scientific branches. They called for a reduction of the number of students in letters, law, and the economic sciences.

The conference called for a reevaluation of the function of the teacher and the institutionalization of a national civil service for training, the regular retraining of teachers, and the keeping of valuable people in the system even after retirement. Many of the liberal arts-type programs of the various educational institutions would be altered for the training of all levels of manpower relating to development goals. They underlined the need for the training of middle-level manpower for the productive sector, for rural development, mines and industry, and for small- and middle-sized businesses. They called for the training of Nigeriens at higher level technical positions in order to free Niger from her dependence on foreign technicians.

With regard to the financing of education, the conference proposed many reforms which would reduce the cost of education to the government. They called for the progressive elimination of dormitories and cafeterias in the sedentary parts of the country, the creation of gardens and educational cooperatives for funding education, village communities and territorial collectivities to locally take on part of the cost of education, parents to contribute to the cost of education and training, local materials and traditional architectural methods to be used in construction to keep costs down, and the creation of a national fund to support general, technical, and professional education. It is this area of the financing of education that has become quite controversial during the last year or two. The proposals contained in this section may constitute one important reason for the government's not having adopted all of the proposals of the ZD at once.

Experimental Schools and the Primary Curriculum

''Reform'' in relation to Niger's educational system has taken on a compendium of meanings over the last 10 years, and has thus become somewhat ambiguous in current parlance. Generically, it implies the betterment of Nigerien education more in keeping with the country's cultural, linguistic, and economic realities. Specific reference to reform may refer to the sweeping ensemble of statements making up the Zinder Declaration, or sometimes, only to the implementation of national language curricula in primary education. This latter definition, currently the most widely espoused, is embodied in the experimental school program.

It was during the 1973–74 school year that controlled experimental schools were begun, using maternal languages as the medium of instruction. One such school was begun in a Zarma-speaking area west of Niamey, and one in the Hausa-speaking town of Zinder. Since then, similar experimental schools have been set up in Kanuri-, Tamasheq-, and Fulfulde-speaking areas. In the beginning, no autonomous structures were established to assist these schools or to guarantee quality of instruction, curriculum development and standardization, and so on. In 1980, the Permanent Secretariat for Reform was created to supervise these schools in collaboration with the Ministry of Education and INDRAP.

In the preliminary efforts one observes the first stage of development and implementation of Niger's language and cultural policy for education. Since that time Niger has broadened its field of experimentation and proceeded to develop the necessary textual materials to support the reforms. Efforts in the area of personnel training have also begun in preparation for the implementation of the new educational policy of the DS.

By the beginning of the 1982–83 school year there were 20 experimental schools. Table 20.3 indicates the distribution by language.

Table 20.3 Language Class in 1982-83

Languages	Schools	Classes
Hausa	9	19
Djerma	4	8
Kanuri	3	5
Fulfulde	3	3
Tamajaq	1	3
Total	20	37

In total, 92 teachers have been given initial training for work in these schools. Placement of all of the trained teachers in experimental schools is behind schedule because of arrears in the school construction program.

The planning, development, and elaboration of a new curriculum for implementation in the reformed experimental schools is in its beginning stages at INDRAP and has yet to be forwarded to the Ministry of Education for approval. In the proceedings of the seminar/workshop on the development and evaluation of curricula, the following content percentages were suggested for grades 1 through 3, the primary years for which the new national language curricula are being developed. See Table 20.4.

The curriculum content and teaching methodology proposed encourage increased participation of the pupil in his/her own education, and mutual teaching among pupils. The maternal language content is designed not only to teach reading and writing, but also cultural orientation, making use of a wide range of traditional oral literary forms. Similarly, in math and science, the skills taught are made relevant to the child and his/her environment. Scientific education includes the *étude de milieu*

Table 20.4 Content Percentages by Subject Matter

Subject	1st grade	2nd grade	3rd grade
maternal language education	40%	40%	25%
scientific education	0	0	0
mathematics education	30%	30%	30%
practical activities	15%	15%	15%
sociocultural and sports activities	15%	15%	5%

and encompasses basic applied physics and biology, local history, and geography. Practical and productive activities are oriented toward the development of relevant manual skills, a production cooperative, school gardens, and cooking. The use of traditional games is encouraged in the sociocultural and sports element. It should be noted that the teaching of a second national language or French during the third grade is not included in the above proposal, but will very likely become a part of the language component once a unifying language is selected and established.

Due to the current economic crisis which affects Niger and a number of other West African countries, the GON did not develop a comprehensive five-year plan to follow up on their 1979–83 five-year plan. Instead, an interim three-year plan for consolidation has been proposed. This modest plan is designed to proceed cautiously forward with long-range plans, until the time when economic conditions are better. Thus it is economically impossible at this time for the GON on its own to finance the general implementation of the maternal language experiment throughout the primary school system. Nevertheless, in the interim plan it is proposed that by the end of the three-year period a new primary school curriculum will be in effect. This curriculum is to be based in the national languages and to contain a comprehensive program of practical and technological activities that are development-oriented. It is clear that these plans are based on certain of the proposals of the ZD. In the same plan it is also proposed that the Permanent Secretariat for Reform should be strengthened with more expertise, personnel, and office facilities. The fact that all of these elements are included in a cautious consolidation plan demonstrates the GON's degree of commitment to the reform of education in Niger.

Niger's policy stands in marked contrast to that of its southern neighbor, Nigeria. Niger has proceeded cautiously and methodically. Nigeria, on the other hand, implemented its Universal Free Primary Education Policy, supposedly in the 12 major regional languages of the country, in 1976, without adequate groundwork and preparation. In many parts of Nigeria all that has been done to prepare for the implementation of this radical change in educational policy was to put up school houses, without consideration for problems of supplies, teaching materials, teacher retraining, and in some cases, even the assigning of teachers to the new schools. As a result, parts of the population developed a fear of the educational system, since no efforts were made to make it relevant to, for example, rural populations (see Hutchison 1981).

NIGER'S EDUCATIONAL POLICY IN THE AFRICAN CONTEXT

Moumouni's approach to the history of education in French West Africa represents a clear, no-nonsense approach providing hard facts and describing harsh realities in an unemotional and extremely effective way. He provides us with a new objectivity and fresh perspective on the effects of colonialism. In his prescriptions for the future he states:

> Due for the most part to the stagnation of African languages under the colonial regime and the limitations imposed on them, the difficulties cannot be eliminated by continuing to provide education in a foreign language. In truth, how and why will the weapon that so effectively served colonialism in its obscurantist policy be transformed into an instrument of progress simply because Africans now have political power in their hands? Unless one is afraid of the truth, facts must be seen for what they are: it is clearly a question of suicide. The only way to avoid it is to reject the weapon, in other words, to give definite priority to African languages in teaching. (Moumouni, 1968:127)

Moumouni was clearly ahead of his time in terms of postindependence francophone Africa, and also in relation to Niger. He wrote his book in the early 1960s on a subject that was not to reach the level of political implementation in many francophone countries for more than a decade from the time of his writing. The tenets of his observations, however, might have been the crucial elements of the achievement of a true independence, had they been heeded at the time he wrote.

Many of Niger's efforts at breaking from the heritage of French colonial educational policy which were carried out during the postindependence period are certainly admirable. When boiled down, however, it is apparent that their total impact, seen over the period from 1960 to the mid-1970s or later, never, in fact, made any significant inroads into reducing the primacy of the role played by the French language in Niger. The same can be said about the efforts of any number of other francophone African countries. Generally speaking, their efforts never benefited from the kind of philosophical reorientation in education and training that Kountche's government is preparing to embark on today. They were perpetually constrained and hindered by the administrative and political structures within which they were implemented, that is, a Western and clearly non-African model. Writing as recently as 1981, Mahamane Inoua warned of the danger of patting oneself on the back for efforts of the kind under consideration here. He observed that Niger's National Broadcasting Corporation translates nearly all of its programs into the five major Nigerien languages, and then went on to warn:

> Though commendable in certain respects, this attempt to rehabilitate our national languages is not a real step towards genuinely promoting them. After all, French remains the sole medium for social advancement and the sole working instrument in our local government. It should however be recognized that these steps nonetheless represent a major transitional preparatory stage, and one which we realize is necessary for true cultural independence. (Inoua 1981:150)

As monolingual creatures of Western comfort, it is difficult for us to conceive of how gargantuan a task it might be to replace a colonial language through the development and promotion of one's own languages. Recent history has shown, however, that half-baked plans for the implementation of one or more local languages in only certain sectors of society may never lead to the desired severance from the colonial language and all of its accoutrements. It is perhaps only in making the complete break suggested by people like Moumouni that true freedom from the colonial heritage can be achieved, and that the colonial language can subsequently be reincorporated into the society and its educational system in a newfound and more realistic position in relation to the African society. Perhaps only in this way can the proper perspective be achieved. This is indeed what Niger is now attempting to do.

The case of Somalia represents one of the few African countries where the policy of complete severance from colonial languages and influences has been implemented and pursued.

> On the third anniversary of the (Somali) revolution, President Maxamaed Siyaad Barre announced the introduction of a national orthography using Latin characters and established it as the sole official language of the state, the bureaucracy, and (in different stages) the school system. Civil servants were given three months (later extended to six) to learn the new script and to become proficient in reading and writing Somali. The script was promoted nation-wide through mass literacy campaigns in 1973–74 and 1974–75 when 15,000 teachers, students, army and police officers, and civil servants spread systematically through the cities and countryside teaching the new alphabet. Somalis generally found the new orthography easy to learn and by 1977, 60% of the population had passed literacy tests. (Adam and Geshekter 1980:vii)

Efforts in Tanzania to develop Swahili in a similar way have proven successful, though not as dramatic as in the Somalia case since they have been implemented over a longer period of time, and less dogmatically.

Perhaps in the francophone Africa context, the present effort that is underway in Niger is comparable to the "revolutionary development" of the Somali language. As described in the ZD, and in this paper, Niger's goal is to equip the entire population for effective participation in the development effort, and it is this goal which explains the work of the Development Society in the area of educational reform. The design that they have adopted for their development cannot be implemented without the kind of educational reform that resulted from the National Conference/ Debate on Educational Reform. Time alone will reveal whether or not the Republic of Niger can accomplish this formidable task.

REFERENCES

Adam, Hussein M., & Geshekter, Charles L. 1980. The revolutionary development of the Somali language. Occasional Paper No. 20, UCLA African Studies Center.

Bokamba, E. G., & Tlou, J. S. 1977. The consequences of the language policies of African states vis-a-vis education. Language and linguistic problems in Africa, edited by P. Kotey and H. Der-Houssikian, Columbia: Hornbeam Press.

Bokamba, E. G., & Tlou, J. S. 1977. The consequences of the language policies of African states vis-a-vis education. Language and linguistic problems in Africa, edited by P. Kotey and H. Der-Houssikian, Columbia: Hornbeam Press.

Declaration of Zinder. April 3-4 1982. Sahel. Niamey: Government of Niger.

Gorman, T. P. 1974. The development of language policy in Kenya with particular reference to the educational system. Education and language in Kenya, edited by W. Whitely. Nairobi: Oxford University Press.

Heine, Bernd. 1970. Status and use of African lingua francas. Munich: Weltforum Verlag.

Hutchison, John P. 1981. Languages and language policy in Nigeria. Boston University: Walter Rodney Seminar Series.

Inne, Marcel. 1981. The role and importance of the languages of Niger in educational broadcasting. African languages: Proceedings of the meeting of experts on the transcription and harmonization of African languages, Niamey, Niger, July 17-21, 1978. p. 147–48. Paris: UNESCO.

Inoua, Mahamane. 1981. The importance of the languages of Niger in associating the people with the development effort. African languages: Proceedings of the meeting of experts on the transcription and harmonization of African languages, Niamey, Niger, July 17–21, 1978. p. 149-50. Paris: UNESCO.

Laya, Dioulde. 1977. Niger. Langues et politiques de langues en Afrique noire, edited by Alfa Ibrahim Sow. p. 285–97. Nubia: UNESCO.

Legum, Colin. (ed.) 1980-81. Niger: Stability and growing prosperity. Africa Contemporary Record 13. B557-B565. New York: Africana Publishing Company.

Madougou, Salissou. 1981. Experiment in literacy training and adult education. African languages: Proceedings of the meeting of experts on the transcription and harmonization of African languages, Niamey, Niger, July 17–21, 1978. p. 184–91. Paris: UNESCO.

Moumouni, Abdou. 1968. Education in Africa. New York: Frederick A. Praeger.

Oumarou, Mamane. 1974. L'Intégration de la population au processus du développement au Niger. Series F:No. 10. Ottawa: Institute for International Co-operation.

Paden, John N. 1968. Language problems of national integration in Nigeria: The special position of Hausa. Language problems of developing nations, edited by Joshua Fishman, Charles A. Ferguson, and Jyotirindra Das Gupta. 199–213. New York: John Wiley and Sons.

République du Niger. April 15, 1975. Sahel Hebdo: special commemorative edition. Niamey: Government of Niger.

République du Niger, INDRAP. 1982. Programmes et instructions officielles de 1949 applicables dans les écoles primaires. Document No. 154. Niamey.

————. 1983. Séminaire/atelier sur le développement et évaluation des programmes. Document No. 167. Niamey.

Sère de Rivières, Edmond. 1965. Histoire du Niger. Paris: Editions Berger-Levrault.

Sow, Alfa Ibrahim, ed. 1977. Langues et politiques de langues en Afrique noire. Nubia: UNESCO.

Spencer, J. 1971. Colonial language policies and their legacies. Current trends in linguistics, volume 7: Linguistics in Sub-Saharan Africa, edited by T. Sebeok. The Hague: Mouton.

UNESCO. 1981a. African languages: Proceedings of the meeting of experts on the transcription and harmonization of African languages, Niamey, Niger, July 17–21, 1978. Paris.

————. 1981b. African languages: Proceedings of the meeting of experts on the use of the regional or subregional African languages as media of culture and communication within the continent. Bamako, Mali, June 18–22, 1979. Paris.

Weinstein, Brian. 1980. Language planning in francophone Africa. Language Problems and Language Planning 4 (1). Austin: University of Texas Press.

Author Index

Subject Index